Violence and Justice in Bologna

Violence and Justice in Bologna

1250–1700

Edited by Sarah Rubin Blanshei

LEXINGTON BOOKS
Lanham • Boulder • New York • London

Published by Lexington Books
An imprint of The Rowman & Littlefield Publishing Group, Inc.
4501 Forbes Boulevard, Suite 200, Lanham, Maryland 20706
www.rowman.com

Unit A, Whitacre Mews, 26-34 Stannary Street, London SE11 4AB

British Library Cataloguing in Publication Information Available

Library of Congress Cataloging-in-Publication Data Available

ISBN 978-1-4985-4633-1 (cloth : alk. paper)
ISBN 978-1-4985-4634-8 (electronic)

∞™ The paper used in this publication meets the minimum requirements of American National Standard for Information Sciences Permanence of Paper for Printed Library Materials, ANSI/NISO Z39.48-1992.

Printed in the United States of America

Contents

Acknowledgments

The idea for this book was the fruit of a stimulating conversation I had with Brian Hill, acquisitions editor for Lexington Books, at the 130th annual meeting of the American Historical Association in January 2014. At the time I was debating the nature of my next project and it was that encounter that steered me in the direction of editing an anthology that would bring a multi-vocal perspective to a topic too vast for any one author—the continuities and changes in violence and criminal justice during five centuries of Bolognese history, from the late medieval to the early modern era. I knew that an unusually large number of scholars were currently at work on various aspects of that topic and to my surprise and delight all from whom I requested an essay responded enthusiastically and positively to my invitation. I am deeply appreciative of their willingness, despite their many other commitments, to join this project and to work together so cooperatively and cheerfully to meet demanding deadlines. I also thank Nicholas Terpstra for his kind help in identifying and obtaining the cover illustration and Brian Hill, Eric Kuntzman, and Laura Chappell of Lexington Books for their exemplary courtesy, patience, and encouragement in shepherding this project from inception through production.

On behalf of the contributors to this volume, I wish to express our gratitude to the director, Elisabetta Arioti, and the archivists and custodians of the Archivio di Stato di Bologna who have given indispensable guidance to all of us over the years and have made the Bolognese Archives one of the most accessible and agreeable centers of scholarly endeavor in Italy—special thanks to Francesca Boris, Giancarlo Busati, Massimo Giansante, Giorgio Marcon, Rossella Rinaldi, and Diana Tura.

My own efforts have been fortified for years by the warm encouragement and hospitality of wonderful *amici*—Francesca Bocchi, Rita Ventura, Andrea

Gardi, Rita de Tata, Gloria Fabbri, and Azzo Gamberini. Above all I owe a tremendous debt to Sara Cucini, friend and colleague, who assisted me at every stage of this project and sustained me through many a crisis—*grazie tante*.

Theresa Federici translated the essay by Margaux Buyck and Sarah Rubin Blanshei translated the essay by Massimo Vallerani.

Introduction

The vibrant field of Italian criminal justice and criminality in the late Middle Ages and early modern period has attracted major attention from historians since the 1970s and has gained even greater attention in more recent years, stimulated by the search for the "lost peoples" of the past and a renewed interest in state formation and conflict resolution.[1] *Violence and Civil Disorder in Italian Cities 1200–1500*, edited by Lauro Martines and published in 1972, was an avatar of the burgeoning subfield and the prominence of premodern Italy in that scholarship.[2] It reflects the deep concerns over the fierce civil upheavals that marked the era and focused on what Martines called "the more obvious forms of violence: crime, civil disorder, and war." The collection was framed from the viewpoint of government and its efforts to achieve stability, moving chronologically from a period around 1500, in which the authors saw a "more fully evolved" state, backwards to the thirteenth century, pictured as a period of hatred, civil conflict, and political passion. That portrayal was consonant with the traditional and pathological view of medieval man as enslaved by his emotions, exemplified in Johann Huizinga's famous opening chapter in *The Waning of the Middle Ages*—the "Violent Tenor of Life."[3] That medieval violence was endemic and unrestrainedly brutal remained (and remains) an axion of historical study, despite the cogent criticism of Trevor Dean and Kate Lowe, who pointed out that the very nature of medieval judicial records, which presented the bare criminal act and ignored previous relations between perpetrator and victim, made violence seem impulsive.[4] The Huizinga-esque portrait of the age received further powerful support in the "discovery" by historians of the sociologist Norbert Elias's theory of the "civilizing process," published in German in three volumes in 1939, but largely ignored for decades and not translated into English until 1978–1982.[5] In brief, Elias postulated that lengthening chains of socioeconomic interdependency and subsequently increased internalized self-control and changed manners and behavior resulted in a dramatic and progressive decline of medieval violence, beginning in the French courts of the sixteenth and seventeenth centuries and lasting until the mid-twentieth century. Moreover, by explicitly linking Ted Gurr's statistical findings on the decline of homicide rates from the "unrestrained brutality" of the Middle Ages to Elias's theory, Eric Johnson and Erick Monkkonen and the essays in their 1996 anthology established a new conceptual framework for the study of criminal justice that quickly gained primacy among historians.[6] The "civilizing process" continues today to command the field and a popular version of the theory, Steven Pinker's *Better Angels of Our Nature*, has achieved considerable attention and acclaim.[7] But Elias's theory has also drawn harsh criticism.[8] The theory's teleological, progressive, and statist underpinnings and its "hydraulic" view of human nature as instinctively violent has been challenged by historians' general rejection of the Grand Narrative of Modernity, new insights of anthropologists into pre-statist societies, and the new research of neurobiology. Many historians of interpersonal violence now emphasize that expressive or spontaneous violence does not signify merely a lack of self-control, but is a learned, cultural response to provocation.[9] The abundance of scholarship on premodern violence is expanding exponentially today, but it also is ever more controversial.

Italian criminal justice and criminality have been central to the scholarship on premodern violence since the 1972 publication of Martines's *Violence and Disorder*, but it is also a highly atomized area of study, both geographically (reflecting the political divisions of premodern Italy), and chronologically, as scholars, faced with an over-abundance of archival sources, albeit only for certain cities, have been forced to confine themselves to case studies within limited time frames. Trevor Dean in his overview of *Crime and Justice in Late Medieval Italy* (2007) sought to overcome the "enduring localism of Italian historiography" by organizing his study on the distinctive nature of various sources (narrative, court records, treatises, legal opinions), and by building overlapping "pictures" of criminal court procedure and what contemporaries labeled as deviant behavior.[10] That approach successfully opens windows onto the typologies of crime as extracted from diverse sources, but it does not lend itself to situating criminal justice and criminality within their socioeconomic and political contexts or analyzing change over time. Various anthologies have also sought to provide overviews of the field, but from necessity feature works from different cities and periods. As valuable as such collections are, they also are unable to draw conclusions concerning change over time since typically the chronological framework for each essay and the historical context for each city vary significantly. For example, one cannot extract a pattern of development in the prosecution of crime by obtaining results from thirteenth-century Siena and comparing them to data from fifteenth-century Ferrara, and then deduce the causes behind that development, given the divergent political configurations of republican Siena and signorial Ferrara. Only a few Italian cities, despite the abundance of their archival sources, have collections that permit analysis of developments in violence, conflict, and justice over the *longue durée* of the late medieval and early modern era.

One of those exceptional cities is Bologna, the largest city of what is today the region of Emilia-Romagna in central Italy and the focus of the essays in this anthology. The criminal court records and normative materials (statutes and legislation) extant in the Bolognese archives from circa 1250–1700 constitute an extraordinary treasure trove, one that surpasses the documentation available for nearly any other Italian city. Moreover, its riches have attracted a large cohort of researchers over the past forty years and has put Bolognese scholarship at the forefront of studies on Italian medieval and early modern criminal justice and criminality. This conjuncture of sources and scholars provides a unique opportunity to view violence, conflict, and justice from a long-range diachronic viewpoint, tracing continuities and change over nearly five centuries of development. Moreover, as a "multivocal case study," it also offers a variety of scholarly approaches and methodologies with which to understand that development.

A PROFILE OF LATE MEDIEVAL AND EARLY MODERN BOLOGNA

The city of Bologna itself offers a fruitful setting for contextualizing crime and conflict. Until recently, Bologna was relatively neglected by the multitude of Italian and international scholars investigating the histories of Italian cities in the medieval and early modern periods, with the great mercantile-banking cities of Venice, Florence, Genoa, Siena, and papal Rome dominating the field. But that situation has changed dramatically in recent decades and has led to a keener appreciation of Bologna's strategic importance as a hinge of intercity military alliances, as a network city of international and regional economic exchange, and especially as a cultural crossroads, with its *studium*, the oldest in Europe, making it a cosmopolitan center of study in law, medicine, and the arts, enhanced by the study of theology in the Dominican *studium generale*. Moreover, Bologna offers a "laboratory of innovation" in its socioeconomic configurations and developments. In the twelfth and thirteenth centuries, the economy's engine was the *studium*, augmented by interregional trade and the bankers, shopkeepers, and craftsmen (wool, cotton, book production) who served the students and masters. In the fourteenth century the city suffered demographic losses and a stalled economy even before the devastation of the Black Death of 1348. Its population shrank from approximately 50,000 inhabitants in the city (and another 50,000 in the *contado*), which had put it on par with cities such as Paris, Venice, Milan, and Genoa, down to 23,000 after the Black Death of 1348. Its agricultural base was severely ravaged and its fiscal resources drained by warfare (especially a major war with the Marchese d'Este of Ferrara at the end of the thirteenth century and continuous military engagements in the first half of the fourteenth century). But during that same century the foundations were laid for an economic recovery based on technological innovation that made Bologna a leader in the Italian silk industry, and a corresponding demographic recovery that surpassed its late medieval apex (72,000 in 1587) and lasted until the end of the seventeenth century.[11]

In its political structures Bologna was exceptional: the level of participation in political life and decision-making in the thirteenth century was extremely high, despite the Guelf/Geremei/*popolo*-dominated government's exclusionary policies against magnates, the (Ghibelline) Lambertazzi faction, persons of *contadino* ancestry, and those engaged in occupations forbidden to organize in guilds (e.g., vegetable vendors, stationers). However, from the turn of the thirteenth century the major development in sociopolitical life was the strengthening of the oligarchical class, a process that ultimately resulted in the final formation of a hereditary civic nobility in 1490. Political participation by the end of the sixteenth century was limited to fifty families, in contrast to the exercise of political rights by over one-third of the urban population in the late thirteenth century.[12] Bologna experienced long periods of extreme political volatility and civil strife over those centuries—most notably civil war and mass expulsions of political opponents in 1274–76 and 1306, and ten revolts and regime changes between 1376 and 1403. Beginning with the submission of the commune to the lordship of Cardinal Bertrand du Pouget in 1327, control of the government alternated between different signorial and republican regimes, punctuated by periods of foreign domination, until relative stability was achieved by the Concordat of 1447 with Pope Nicholas V, which established a *governo misto* of papal overlordship and local autonomy. From that point until 1506 when they were expelled from the city by Pope Julius II, the Bentivoglio family held a para-*signoria* over the city. After that the papacy gained direct control of the city under a papal legate or governor, with a narrow class of *bolognesi* participating as hereditary members of the Senate. This intense volatility makes Bologna a valuable resource not only for the study of interpersonal violence but also for the study of political conflict.[13]

HISTORIOGRAPHY: PERSPECTIVES ON BOLOGNESE CRIMINAL JUSTICE AND VIOLENCE

Bolognese scholarship in crime and criminal justice has a venerable tradition of international dimension that precedes the explosion of studies in recent decades. Nineteenth-century historians were mainly interested in combing the court records for the "romantic" crimes of nobles, picaresque instances of student violence, and horrific capital and corporal penalties, but in 1908 Hermann Kantorowicz published the first volume of his magisterial edition and study of Albertus Gandinus's handbook on criminal procedure, and compared Gandinus's theoretical axioms with actual court practices in Bologna, Perugia, and Lucca, where he served as a judge in the late thirteenth century.[14] For the next fifty years, however (not surprisingly, given the horrific traumas of depression and two world wars), the criminal records were left relatively untouched and continued to lack even a rudimentary inventory. Exceptional were two *tesi di laurea*, which focused on quantitative analysis of court records viewed as directly documenting actual criminal behavior, in line with the dominance of the positivist approach of those decades.[15] Scholarship was moving away from positivism, however, and in a series of articles in the late 1970s and early 1980s Sarah Blanshei emphasized use of the Bolognese court records as reflections of governmental policies and prosecution patterns, rather than of actual levels of violence.[16] But her work at that time remained anchored in statist assumptions that were simultaneously being challenged by dramatic transformations in historical studies and by the development in criminal justice of two new approaches, the microhistorical and the processual, both strongly influenced by the new anthropology of the mid-twentieth century.

Although it had parallels and proponents elsewhere, microhistory was born in northern Italy, especially in Bologna, as exemplified in the work of Carlo Ginzburg and Carlo Poni. They defined their approach as "the intensive historical investigation of a relatively well defined smaller object, most often a single event, or 'a village community, a group of families, even an individual person." In part it was a reaction against the then-dominant focus on quantitative social science and "deep structural continuities"; an "escape" from an institutional and legal history encased in statism. It sought to find the individuals hidden in the abstract categories of quantitative analysis and to elucidate their social interactions and episodic life experiences.[17] Incorporating this approach, Carol Lansing since 1997 has plumbed the late thirteenth-century Bolognese criminal court records for her recreations of non-elite women's lives.[18] Over the same period Trevor Dean has used micro-stories in many of his studies of Bolognese criminality and criminal justice and Craig Monson has devoted an entire volume to the "tale" of two murdered nuns in seventeenth-century Bologna.[19] The microhistorical approach of these historians is distinguished from the sensationalism of nineteenth-century historians by Edoardo Grendi's concept of the "normal exception," that is, by linking the story of a particular person or event to mainstream historical developments.[20]

The scholarship of anthropologists such as Sally Falk Moore and Simon Roberts in the 1970s also has had a great impact on criminal justice historians. By demonstrating that conflict resolution was possible in "stateless" societies, the new anthropology highlighted the importance of understanding the relationship between institutional procedures and the behaviors labeled as criminal, and of doing so within political, social, and cultural contexts.[21] The processual approach is exemplified in Massimo Vallerani's path-breaking studies, beginning in 1997 on criminal justice in late medieval Bologna. In this methodology the trial is treated "not as an entity unto itself but as part of a process that begins in relationships between the parties before the trial and may have consequences between the parties before and after the trial."[22] Rather than viewing the tremendous growth of the criminal courts in the second half of the thirteenth century as a product of the growth of the state and repressive government policies, Vallerani demonstrates how the courts attracted and served litigants and that reconciliation, not revenge, was the primary goal of criminal justice.[23] The processual approach, for example as structured by Daniel Lord Smail, has its critics (including Vallerani himself), especially from advocates of "legalism," who favor what John Jordan describes as a "rule-centered paradigm [which] focuses on the rules that govern and inform social life and behaviour, while the processual concentrates on how people follow, use and sidestep those rules." As Jordan points out, what is needed is greater "exchange and engagement between legally and processually minded historians," which is what several of the contributors to this volume in fact seek to achieve.[24]

Recent scholarship has focused on the political context of criminal justice and on the use of criminological and sociological theory in interpreting court records. Giuliano Milani in a major work has brilliantly documented how Bolognese factional strife in the late thirteenth and early fourteenth centuries resulted in the criminalization of political opposition, using the massive lists of the politically excluded and the hitherto largely neglected records of the court of the *capitano del popolo*.[25] Blanshei's monograph shows that in the same period politics and justice were not separate, albeit related spheres, as they are customarily viewed today, but fully integrated expressions of public action and the socioeconomic shape of communal life. Using closure theory, she analyzes institutional structures (governmental and socioeconomic) prosopographically, demonstrating how political life was based on the exclusion of certain sociopolitical categories while simultaneously functioning on Bologna's remarkably broad basis of participation, and how in the early decades of the fourteenth century the governing classes narrowed under the pressure of war and economic change and protected themselves by juridical privileges and immunities and new court practices.[26] In a recent essay she also explores the applicability of new scholarship in evolutionary psychology, biology, and macro-sociology that suggests the existence of an indirect but significant relationship between politics and interpersonal violence.[27] The premises of that theory, as found in works by Randolph Roth, Gary LaFree, and Mark Cooney, are that governmental policies of repression can only lower rates of violence and homicide to a limited degree and that societies tend to be more violent or more cooperative in their social relationships according to the attitudes of people toward their governments.[28] She proposes that confidence in criminal justice as a mode of dispute settlement could not thrive in late medieval Bologna, especially in the fourteenth and early fifteenth centuries, in a situation where rapidly changing regimes overthrew the judicial decrees of their predecessors, and where executive officials and legislative bodies, in both republican and signorial governments, intervened regularly in court proceedings; that the goal of reconciliation of the thirteenth century was largely replaced by mistrust and the instrumentalist use of the courts for revenge.

Trevor Dean has utilized the theories of criminologists such as C. Gabrielle Salfati, Kirk Williams, and Robert Flewelling to directly challenge the "fury and fenzy," "butchery," and "unrestrained brutality" view of medieval interpersonal violence, fundamental to Elias's "civilizing process" and to the work of his leading proponent today, Pieter Spierenburg.[29] He contrasts the description of furious killings (political enmity, revenge, and passion) in Bolognese narrative sources of the fifteenth century with the significantly scant appearance of such types of homicide in the criminal court records. In a similar vein, Scott Jenkins, in his dissertation comparing student violence in Oxford and Bologna, maintains that the dominant image of medieval student life as "anarchic, deviant and destructive" stems from the literary tropes of the "true" and "false" scholar and does not correlate with the quantitative evidence of the Bolognese criminal court records. Using social identity theory as formulated by the psychologists Henri Tajfel and John C. Turner (1979), he finds that the key to student violence lies in the strong bonds of their attachment to their community and their efforts to increase their self-image by enhancing the status of the group with which they identified.[30]

A third perspective on criminal justice and conflict emphasizes *iurisdictio* (in its original sense as the power to pronounce law) and its relationship to the legitimatization of political conflicts. The concept of rebellion is central to this approach, with a departure from the assumption that political conflicts represent a "disruptive, even pathological, force," as, for example, in the organizational schema of Martines's anthology, discussed above, with its fundamental contrast between "order" and "disorder." As Patrick Lantschner notes, today many historians no longer view "[c]ollective action, disputes, *vendetta*, violence, and warfare [. . .] as pathological phenomena, but as integral parts of cultural, social, and political interaction." His thesis revolves around the pluralism of the organizational structures in late medieval cities, with their multiple political centers, co-existing kinds of law, authorities whose power varied greatly, and the instability of institutional configurations. In the case of Bologna, Lantschner shows the importance of *iurisdictio* in uprisings, such as the revolt in Bologna in March 1376 against papal overlordship by a coalition of Bologna's guilds, *studium*, and its two main political factions, which successfully invoked the concept of jurisdictional liberty, named itself the *stato popolare e di libertà*, and emphasized its continuity and restoration of earlier jurisdictions. The city negotiated a treaty with the pope in July 1377, by which a *governo misto* of shared jurisdiction was established, but this did not end contestation between city and papacy and revolts followed in 1393, 1399, 1401, and 1403, finally culminating in the Concordat of 1447. According to Lantschner, the law represented a contested set of values, not mere rhetoric, and he shows how significant it was that regimes when canceling exile sentences (bans) were careful to follow judicial and jurisdictional parameters. The turbulence of political strife in Bologna, in this view, becomes not mindless conflict nor class warfare but is embedded "in the unfolding dynamics of political processes."[31]

Sara Cucini's 2014 two-volume dissertation in part shares Lantschner's approach and perspective. He treats the late fourteenth and early fifteenth century; she the middle and second half of the fifteenth century. Cucini delves deeply not only into the issue of executive control of the judiciary—the use of *iurisdictio* in factional conflicts and in the struggle over authority between papacy and city—but also analyzes the development of court procedure and the typologies of crime prosecuted in that period. It is a monumental work, including an edition of the criminal rubrics from the 1454 statutes and a quantitative analysis of court records—in sum a work that combines many of the approaches and methodologies described above.[32]

In the sixteenth century the court of the *Tribunale del Torrone* gradually replaced the communal courts of the podestà after the papacy gained direct control of Bologna. The sheer quantity of documentation from the *Torrone* is overwhelming (approximately 11,000 registers survive from the early modern era, more than twice as many as are extant from the medieval period), and presents a daunting obstacle to historical research, but one which Giancarlo Angelozzi and Cesarina Casanova, working in tandem, have successfully overcome. Their approach is institutional criminal justice history at its best: an invaluable and detailed review of the functioning of the *Torrone* court—reforms, practices, procedures, penalties, pardons, use of torture, execution rates—based on data extrapolated from normative, legislative, and trial sources. One of the most important topics in their work is the phenomenon of noble violence, at first tolerated but then ultimately confronted and successfully overcome by the papal government at the end of the seventeenth century through the development of a new ethos, the social disciplinary code of the *scienza cavallaresca.*[33]

Colin Rose, in his recent dissertation (2016) has also tackled the voluminous *Torrone* records, analyzing quantitatively ten-year samples of homicide cases from 1600–1700. He ties the pattern of homicidal violence to the centralizing efforts of the *Torrone* court and emphasizes how that prosecutory policy led initially to increased violence by sectors of the nobility which, however, was ultimately overcome to a great degree. Moreover, he also explores homicidal violence qualitatively, seeking to understand its motivation by distinguishing between immediate and proximate causes, for example, whether personal relationships existed between killers and victims, and more structural and material causes, such as the great plague of 1630 and, turning as did Blanshei, to Randolph Roth's theory—to a decline of trust in political and social institutions as an explanatory tool. In doing so he shows that the pattern of violence in Bologna differed significantly from Elias's "civilizing process" as interpreted by Pieter Spierenburg, whose research indicated steep declines in homicide rates in northern Europe during the seventeenth century. Rose finds the reverse pattern occurred in Bologna, where homicidal violence increased from the middle of that century when socioeconomic crisis and a recalcitrant nobility undermined the earlier state-building achievements of the late-sixteenth-century papacy in Bologna. Only by dismantling the feudal jurisdictions in the *contado* and exiling rebellious nobles did the papacy finally advance its goals. Rose's conclusions also modify Angelozzi and Casanova's emphasis on the nobility's self-adaptation to a new social ethos as a vital part of their transformation to a relatively pacified class. Rose's homicide-rate calculations follow a curve from lows in the city and *contado* in the mid-1620s, dropping even lower in in the following decades, but then rising sharply in 1660 to sixty per 100,000 inhabitants (the urban rate is a spectacular 105.9; the rural rate is "only" 41.7), then dropping again in the rest of the century to the level held in 1600.[34] He recognizes that these data, like almost all such premodern calculations, are very fragile at best, but they do relate to mid-century political tensions. Moreover, they may be suggestive of an overall pattern for these centuries when compared to data collected by Trevor Dean and Sarah Blanshei in separate studies. Blanshei found a high rate of eighty per 100,000 inhabitants in the 1350s and a lower rate of thirty earlier and later in the century; Dean postulated urban rates of approximately thirty per 100,000 in his sample from the 1340s and 1440s, which as he noted would be at the lower end of estimates for late medieval Italy and Europe.[35] As Dean and Lowe recently concluded, "[m]urder was normal in Renaissance Italy."[36]

A fourth major perspective in Bolognese criminal justice studies reflects the impact of scholarship over the past thirty years on gender history. Carol

Lansing and Trevor Dean (the former for the thirteenth century, the latter for the mid-fourteenth to the mid-fifteenth century) have highlighted the appearance of women in the court records "not only as victims, particularly of domestic abuse, but as litigators in property disputes, as perpetrators of violent crimes, and as key figures in marital, inter-class and political conflicts."[37]

Angelozzi and Casanova in 2014 published an overview of female violence in Bologna, with particular attention to the so-called "gender gap," that is, the difference between men and women in their propensity to commit crime and as victims of violence. They tested the images of women and crime in European-wide literature of the early modern era with data from the *Tribunale del Torrone* and analyzed quantitatively the presence of women in the court records in sample years from 1583 to 1779 and found a higher proportion of the cases were against women in the city than in the *contado*, which they attributed to underreporting by the local officials of the rural communes. They also extracted the typologies of female crime according to the *Torrone* records—verbal violence (29.5 percent), assaults (42.3 percent), and property crimes (20.6 percent)—and showed that the so-called stereotypical "female" crimes of infanticide, abortion, adultery, procuring, and contraventions of moral and public order norms comprised only 7.6 percent of the sample. Their data also confirm the traditional concept of the low propensity of women to homicide (less than 5 percent of their sample). Moreover, in only one-quarter of the seventy cases did they find that the death (or serious injury) of the victim was the result of premeditation.[38]

Sara Cucini found that a similar and serious imbalance between women and men in criminal court records, particularly those for the *contado*, may in part be explained by underreporting of female crime and the nature of their criminal acts in the fifteenth-century courts—female violence was generally of a minor nature, as were most reported crimes, but unlike comparable acts by men, those by women were largely ignored by the courts. Female acts were reported only when they fit the stereotypes of female violence—poisoning, infanticide, and servant-killers of their masters' children.[39]

A fifth and final perspective focuses on penalties, rituals of corporal and capital punishment, and issues of brutality and judicial violence. Nicholas Terpstra includes Bologna as well as Florence in his study on the rituals of "mutilation and exhibition" inflicted on the criminal body and the efforts of lay comforting confraternities to gain salvation for the condemned by transforming them from criminals into converts or even martyrs. The act of comforting was a distinctive characteristic of the "theater of execution" in Italy. Cities with comforting confraternities and their concern for the soul of the condemned performed mutilating executions, but usually only after the actual execution and not in stages on the living prisoner as was done elsewhere in Europe.[40] Terpstra also traces "a distinct politicization of justice" in fifteenth- and sixteenth-century Bologna and a shift from exiling to executing (or even murdering) political opponents, as occurred after the Malvezzi conspiracy of 1488, and the "blood bath" after the overthrow and expulsion of the Bentivoglio in 1506, when executions were moved from the Piazza del Mercato inside the city walls to the city center—the Piazza Maggiore—and were carried out by defenestration from the windows of the Palazzo del Podestà. The level of executions in general in the sixteenth century peaked in 1540, a year of famine and epidemic. Terpstra's data and his interpretation of those data closely link the level of executions to partisan politics, with execution rates rising and the number of thefts, murders, and factional violence spiking during the 1540s, but subsiding with increased pacification in the 1470s.[41]

Blanshei has categorized certain capital and corporal penalties in the thirteenth and early fourteenth century as being "ordinary" or "standard" in the eyes of contemporaries: decapitation for homicide, hanging (which was considered a more shameful death) for recidivists and highway robbers, and immolation for arson, sodomy, sorcery, bestiality, and incest. For other crimes, such as forgery or false testimony, the penalties were amputation of a limb or cutting out of the tongue, and for lesser theft the penalties were blinding, branding, or whipping the culprit through the streets. Hired assassins were mandated by statute to be hanged after being dragged by the tail of an ass through the city streets. In general, those who could not pay their fines suffered bodily punishment. The second category consists of extraordinary and exemplary penalties—flaying alive, implantation (burying the culprit alive, head first), castration, and quartering—that were never mentioned in the statutes, were rarely inflicted, and were reserved for crimes perceived as especially heinous.[42] Trevor Dean (and Andrea Zorzi for Florence) maintains that in Bologna in general there was a shift beginning in the late fourteenth century from capital and corporal punishment to fines and imprisonment, but in the case of theft and sex crimes, penalties became more severe later in that century.[43] The shift was not, however, a linear or smooth one. In the case of sodomy, for example, Dean found that the courts stopped executing sodomites in the early fifteenth century, instead marking and isolating them though corporal punishments and imprisonment. However, by the mid-sixteenth century it was executing them again.[44]

Horrific penalties remained rare, but even the usual practice of quartering the corpse only after execution of the criminal, described above, was suspended in particular cases, as in the quartering while they were alive of three men who in 1540 had killed a prominent citizen and former member of the *anziani* magistracy.[45] Periods of leniency or repression varied by political regime: Blanshei found that poverty pleas and peace accords were frequently used to mitigate penalties in the late fourteenth century, but the especially tumultuous political decades at the turn of the century saw a renewal of judicial repression—the execution rate increased, especially after a rebellion in 1411; the death penalty was implemented for any murmur of verbal dissent; and the mitigation of penalties diminished radically in frequency.[46]

The most infamous and dominant feature in the historiography of medieval and early modern judicial violence is the use of torture. This view, however, has been significantly qualified by Massimo Vallerani for the late medieval period and Giancarlo Angelozzi and Cesarina Casanova for the early modern era. The Bolognese statutes of 1250 limit torture to major crimes such as multiple theft, highway robbery, and homicide. The scope of eligible crimes was broadened considerably in the 1288 statutes, yet such crimes comprised a very small minority of the courts' total caseloads. As Vallerani has shown, judges were required in theory and practice to have strong circumstantial evidence (*indicia*) before they could proceed to the torture of even notorious thieves, and Blanshei found that in such cases they carefully, if much more speedily, interrogated witnesses before proceeding to torture.[47] In a sample of over 1,000 trials by inquisition procedure from 1285–1326 she found only sixty-nine instances of torture, and in that sample she found that status was the key factor in determining the use of torture—the majority of those tortured were persons of ill-repute, foreigners, and *contadini*.[48] The enfranchised classes of the *popolo* (which consisted of all members of the guilds and arms societies, approximately 12,000 men in a city of 50,000 inhabitants), rarely were subjected to torture and indeed had built special protection from torture for themselves into the judicial system.[49]

Over the course of the fourteenth century, however, protection for *popolani* eroded and by 1454 the special protective provisions no longer appear in the statutes redacted that year. Indeed, a provision from 1380 that had loosened the controls against torture by permitting the judges to apply torture a second time without new *indicia* in cases of "urgency," and also against "*personas viles*," was incorporated into the 1454 statutes.[50] But again the process was not linear: in contrast to the repression of the courts under Cossa in the early fourteenth century and despite the harshness of policies under Bonaccorso Bonaccorsi in the 1670s, Angelozzi and Casanova have deconstructed the traditional picture of the *Torrone* tribunal's notoriety for violent practices, finding that the infliction of torture was rare and almost always applied scrupulously according to the norms regulating its use.[51] A parallel revisionism is prominent in the recent work of literary historians. Larissa Tracy describes torture and exemplary punishments in late medieval literary texts as not being mimetic of judicial practice, but as works of dissent and satire, and critiques what she calls the "dominant mythology" of the arbitrary use of "sadistic torment" in late medieval law courts.[52]

CHANGE AND CONTINUITIES IN BOLOGNESE VIOLENCE AND JUSTICE

What does this anthology aim to contribute to the rich literature discussed above? One of our goals is not only to set forth new research that clarifies and nuances some of the key issues, but also to present works that explore new facets of Bolognese criminal justice and contemporary perceptions of violence, in some cases using sources that have been neglected or never used. The authors of these chapters comprise a transgenerational group of scholars, some senior, some mid-career, and some presenting very recent doctoral research. Almost every chapter includes new research and/or presents scholarship hitherto unavailable in English, and each chapter focuses on a different micro-variant of Bolognese criminal justice and criminality. The chapters are divided into two distinctive but closely related sections—criminal court procedures and practices in the first, and the conceptualization and treatment of particular crimes over time in the second. To be sure, the barrier between the two categories is highly permeable and certain issues and concerns are common to both, but the essays in the first section (Roberts, Vallerani, Blanshei, Dean, Rose) have as their starting point institutions and how they functioned—policing, court procedures, and modes of interrogation in the late medieval podestarial courts and increased "professionalism" in the early modern *Tribunale del Torrone*, whereas the second group (Cucini, Buyck, Lansing, Vise, Carlsmith) focuses on certain typologies of crime—rebellion, poisoning, blasphemy, rape, student violence—and how treatment of those crimes by the court changed over time.

Gregory Roberts in his chapter challenges the currently predominant view that vendetta, the notorious *leit-motif* of medieval violence, was tolerated, even sanctioned, by medieval communal law and governments. He draws his evidence from an archival source that has rarely been utilized—a collection virtually unique to the Bolognese Archives, the *Corone ed Armi* (Crowns and Arms) series, which contains, in addition to contraventions of the sumptuary laws, the police-patrol records of those found in violation of curfew, gambling, and weapons-carrying laws, and the ensuing trials. In contrast to the trial records in the *Accusationes*, *Libri Inquisitionum et Testium*, and *Sententiae* archival series, these trials had the culprit in custody and resulted in a high conviction rate. Roberts shows how impersonal the policing and enforcement of these laws was (including conviction of nobles and elite members of the governing *popolo*), and how the prevention of violations and vendetta violence were policing goals. Furthermore, police power increased and the government became more coercive in the enforcement of weapon-possession laws over the course of the thirteenth and into the early decades of the fourteenth century—the government not only sought to control interpersonal violence through peace accords and reconciliation, as currently emphasized by scholars, but also sought to suppress it by police power. Roberts is careful to distinguish this increase in government authority from Max Weber's famous theory of state formation as the government's efforts to gain a monopoly of violence, nor does he view it as a "public" policy against "private warfare." Rather, the growth in police power stemmed from the willingness of the *popolo* to be policed and to suppress violence, and was not a movement toward a police state.[53]

One of the most controversial aspects of the role of criminal justice in state formation is the relationship between *accusatio* and *inquisitio* trial procedures. Traditionally, the growth of *inquisitio* trials, initiated by the court on the basis of denunciations from officials or *publica fama*, is contrasted to the older procedure of *accusatio*, a trial initiated by a charge (*libellus*) from private persons who would be responsible for proving the charge and paying for trial expenses if the charge was not proven, and was interpreted as evidence of the growth of the state. In his essay, Massimo Vallerani confounds the statist and teleological biases of that historiography, showing that in the late thirteenth century a flood-tide of litigants were attracted to the courts, using *accusatio* procedure to pursue dispute resolution, but that the importance of criminal court procedures in communal life lies paradoxically in how communal justice was nevertheless an instrument of the commune for governing the population and regulating conflicts. Criminal justice played a vital role in the growth of the state, but that growth depended not on repressive measures but on the capacity of the courts' procedures to serve litigants and the broad scope of persons involved in those procedures. He traces the origins and development of the *ordines* and practices of criminal court procedure from the twelfth century, their relationship to the notarial *artes* and the *studium*, and the growing complexity of the trial in the thirteenth century in the form of increased participation by *curatores*, *fideiussores*, and *procuratores*. He challenges current views, especially those of Daniel Smail, that reduce the activities of *accusatio*-based trials to a vindictive and ultimately futile play of accusations and counter-accusations by investigating in detail what actually happened during a trial, and concludes that the trial's significance lay in its clarification of social identities. He further emphasizes the material basis of the violent encounters brought to the courts (disputes that originated over contested possessions) and in so doing, undercuts the assumption of the "civilizing process" (although he makes no reference to Elias's theory) that violent encounters stemmed from irrational outbursts of uncontrolled anger. Vallerani also traces the origin and development of *inquisitio*, but for him the important issue is not its relationship to *accusatio* procedure, but the multiple functions and flexibility of *inquisitio*: first, elimination from society of certain persons, undesirable and dangerous *ipso facto* by their lifestyles; second, the self-expulsion by contumacy of those who could not sustain a trial; and third, the granting of a trial with due process to those who could post sureties and prove their good *fama*. Finally, Vallerani treats the political dimensions of the trial, especially the role of local jurists who gave legal opinions (*consilia*) to which the foreign judges of the court usually adhered and which often served to preserve the property rights of citizens.

Sarah Blanshei in her chapter also treats criminal trial procedures, but focuses her investigation on the fourteenth and fifteenth centuries. Her data provide quantitative evidence of the shift in procedure over those centuries from *accusatio* to *inquisitio*, and her inquiry evaluates possible explanations for that shift and its significance—the expenses of an *accusatio*-initiated trial, the effects of war, the expansion of legal privileges and immunities granted to thousands of members of the *popolo*'s guilds and arms societies, the use of petitions (the *querela* to the *consiglio del popolo*, and petitions and pardons to and from *signori*, the exclusion of the use of the *consilium sapientis* by litigants). She concludes that the dominance of *inquisitio* procedure after the crises of the mid-fourteenth century stemmed in great part from a growth of state power in criminal justice under both republican and signorial regimes as the executive branch of government expanded its control over the judiciary and broadened the *arbitrium* of criminal court judges. *Inquisitio* trials became less complex and briefer by the use of new techniques (*licentia*, *requisitio*, *circumdatio*). But at the same time she finds that increased control was accompanied by new policies of clemency—the poverty plea and increased use of the peace accord (*pax*)—that became regular court practices. The state did increase its capacity to take the initiative in law and order, but that development did not occur in a linear fashion. Rather it depended on the vacillating strength and weakness of shifting regimes, whether republican or signorial, and became a system more geared to protection of governmental hegemony than to preservation of due process.

Trevor Dean applies a less sweeping and more concentrated perspective to court procedure in his investigation of the court's interrogation techniques in the fifteenth century. He utilizes a seldom-used source, the *bastardelli* or *vacchetini*—the journals kept by the podestà's criminal court notaries—that from the mid-fifteenth century recorded the day-by-day hearings of the court, including many facets that were not later copied into the court registers of the *Accusationes* and *Inquisitiones*, such as the use of torture during interrogation. Of the twenty-two cases of homicide that he found, he investigates five in detail, using analytical approaches from modern forensic linguistics and medieval jurisprudence. It was the judge who carried out the investigation of a murder and the search to identify the killer, going in person to the scene of the crime and structuring his actions with the *indicia* (circumstantial evidence) discussed in juristic treatises in mind. As Dean notes, this thorough process contrasts with the simplified and accelerated process of the mid-fourteenth century (described in Blanshei's chapter), indicating again that the development of late medieval criminal justice was not a smooth or linear process.

Colin Rose's chapter includes evidence that the interrogation techniques of the podestarial courts did not change in the early modern period with the establishment of the *Tribunale del Torrone*, but that other transformations indeed took place in court procedure. The transition from the medieval podestarial courts occurred only gradually after Pope Julius II took direct control of Bologna's government in 1506, with the new court appearing in the records by 1525. The court faced two major challenges—an apparent decline in the control of the *contado* by the podestarial courts of the fifteenth century and the acquisition of jurisdictional enclaves by nobles who acquired fiefs in the city's territory. The resulting inefficiencies of the system pushed plaintiffs, lawyers, and jurists to respond positively to the efforts of the papal legates to centralize and professionalize the *Tribunale del Torrone*. Here we have a governmental effort to gain a monopoly over criminal justice in the Weberian tradition, and indeed Rose maintains that the papacy was more successful in Bologna than similar efforts of the era in Florence and Rome itself. But the consolidation of the *Torrone*'s authority took almost a century and a half to accomplish and in exploring why that process was so arduous Rose emphasizes that the court functioned, as did its medieval predecessor, even though all trials followed *inquisitio* procedure, not only as an instrument for the prosecution and punishment of malefactors, but as a forum for conflict resolution, with frequent use of the peace accord and subsequent pardons. The ultimate success of the court lay in its capacity to offer a system that was more attractive and professional than that offered by the courts of the feudal nobility. He thus portrays the development of the court not only in Weberian "top-down" but also in Durkheimian "bottom-up" terms. Moreover, although certain aspects of the podestarial courts, such as the use of torture, continued (it was used at least into the 1630s), the use of capital punishment declined (917 executions between 1540 and 1600; 556 between 1600–1700), and were replaced in part with sentences of exile or the papal galleys, although as Rose notes, the latter was in fact "a functional death sentence." Rose also points out that the vast majority of trials were conducted without the presence of lawyers, a significant development to be contrasted with Vallerani's emphasis in his essay on the important presence in the podestarial courts of the late thirteenth and early fourteenth centuries of *curatores, procuratores*, and *fideiussores*.

The chapters in Part II concentrate on specific crimes, but like those of Part I, are situated in their political and cultural contexts. Sara Cucini studies the fifteenth-century *signoria* of the Bentivoglio and the judicial responses of the regime to conspiracies that challenged its authority—the Canetoli plot of 1445 and its aftermath in the following years, the Fantuzzi and Pepoli insurgency of 1449–50, the Malvezzi conspiracy of 1488, and the Marescotti plot of 1501, showing how the Bentivoglio turned these conflicts into "political crimes." Her chapter demonstrates how essential was the connection between the maintenance of political power and at least the appearance of judicial integrity. She analyzes a provision of 1447 that defined the judicial process for treating crimes as "rebellion." Management of this crime was placed in the hands of the executive council—the *Sedici Riformatori dello stato di libertà*, the Bolognese arm of the *governo misto* that was based on shared power between Bologna and its overlord, the pope. This provision marked a significant change in the management of political crimes, shifting authority from earlier officials and their courts (all from outside Bologna)—the *capitano del popolo* in the thirteenth century and the *executor iustitie* (later called the *conservator iustitie*) earlier in the fifteenth century. According to Cucini, this transformation signified a shift to direct local competency over political crime (the pope had gained the right to appoint foreign officials). It also meant the executive body of the *Sedici* increased its control over common crime by labeling certain criminals as rebels. Cucini also delineates the various ways in which the *Sedici* enhanced their power in response to political conflicts, but had to do so with finesse in order to maintain their delicate relationship with the papacy. That sensitivity was shattered in response to the Marescotti conspiracy. Four of the conspirators were imprisoned in the palazzo comunale, without official authorization from the *Sedici* or judicial recording of that act, although the *Sedici* had the necessary prerogatives to do so. Four days later, all four were, according to the narrative sources, "cut into pieces like dogs" by the *signore*'s son with the help of the sons of some members of the *Sedici*. They were never punished. The resolution of political conflict had already become situated (after the Malvezzi conspiracy) not only outside the courts, but outside the normative system developed by the *Sedici* under Bentivoglio domination, by which the *Sedici* acted as an extraordinary court when faced with situations that endangered the regime. After the Marescotti conspiracy the Bentivoglio abandoned the mask of judicial process and opened a pathway for the papacy to gain direct control of Bologna.

Margaux Buyck in her chapter on poisoning also connects judicial treatment of a crime to political tensions. She shows how the second-century Roman *lex Cornelia de sicariis et veneficis*, which defined poisoning as an act more heinous than homicide by the sword, was transmitted to late medieval jurisprudence in the *Digest* and how the crime became recognized in the statutes and legislation of late medieval Bologna and other cities of what is today Emilia-Romagna as a crime of greater gravity than "mere" homicide.[54] She also treats the ambiguities in the statutes over time (from the late thirteenth century to the beginning of the seventeenth century)—variations and vacillations in the punishment (whether a capital penalty or a fine) of poisoning, if committed with malice aforethought (*dolus*), and if the victim died. She concludes that there was in general a progressive evolution in the prevention and punishment of poisoning in Bologna's norms as *dolus* became the key element for imposing severe penalties against poisoners, including those who did not succeed in their attempts. In order to test the application of these changing norms in judicial practice, Buyck compiled a sample from the entire period of ninety-seven cases from the Bolognese judicial archives and found that only rarely was the death penalty applied for attempted poisoning. The severity for this crime in the early modern normative system was not carried out in practice. However, she does find that the penalties followed a pattern other scholars have postulated for crime in general: in the sixteenth and seventeenth centuries hanging was preferred over decapitation and the latter punishment was reserved for the nobility. Although considered an especially atrocious act, as with other crimes, only when a case of poisoning was considered extraordinarily outrageous were exemplary punishments meted out—in the seventeenth century Buyck found two cases of quartering after hanging. For attempted poisoning the punishment most frequently inflicted was exile, often accompanied by fines that rarely corresponded to those in the statutes but were rather tied to the culprits' social status. Despite the declared atrocity of the crime, peace accords were permitted and negotiated. Moreover, Buyck concludes that although legislative norms seem to indicate that the penology of poisoning became more repressive in the early modern period, its evolution from the thirteenth to the seventeenth century varied and depended primarily on political circumstances and the level of tensions, and that social status above all shaped the penalty, not the perceived enormity of the crime itself.[55]

Poisoning was a rarely committed crime and so was blasphemy, the subject of Melissa Vise's essay. But blasphemy came to be viewed in the secular sphere as a crime that endangered the entire community. Vise seeks to understand the cultural context of blasphemy by studying in tandem cases prosecuted both in the court of the podestà as well as those tried by the Dominican inquisitor. Blasphemy is seldom studied by scholars of civic crime and criminality, but Vise emphasizes that the barrier between the two jurisdictions was porous and how in both the civic and the ecclesiastical spheres the gravity of the offense received greater recognition between the late thirteenth and the late fourteenth and early fifteenth centuries. In the Bolognese court of the office of the inquisition, blasphemous words came to be viewed as comprising a sin so potent that it warranted prosecution as if it were a heresy—*verba heretica*. A manual for heresy inquisition, anonymous but written in Bologna circa 1321 does not treat blasphemy per se, but blasphemy is predominant in the register of Fra Johannes de san Domenico, Dominican inquisitor from 1392–95. His is the only extant inquisitorial register from Bologna from that century and in it he did not record a single case of heresy; remarkably almost all his prosecutions were against men and women who had blasphemed God and/or the saints. The penances meted out by the inquisitor, however, were mild, intent on rehabilitation of the sinner, not punishment. In the podestà's court, in contrast, blasphemous words, even if not accompanied by a physical assault, were punishable by fines and humiliation if the fines were not paid. Gradually, the breadth of geographical locations shielded by the law increased in scope until the entire city was protected. The fines became increasingly high, and if the fines could not be paid, the penalty incurred was whipping or bodily mutilation and banishment from the city. Vise maintains, however, that beneath these diverse judicial responses to blasphemy lay the perception shared by both civic and ecclesiastical authorities that blasphemy was a form of violence. The civic and ecclesiastical authorities differed on what was the best judicial response—punishment or rehabilitation—but they concurred that it was violence. What Vise does not do in this chapter, which is largely methodological in its contribution, but what she is pursuing in her current research, is explore why blasphemy came to be viewed with increasing concern in both spheres. David Nash in his discussion of early modern blasphemy recognizes how early it became a part of social disciplining, and he notes that it predates Elias's "civilizing process." Nash also maintains that blasphemy "clearly constituted a species of violence, which society countered to preserve the coherence of the community."[56] A question for future research is whether the political divisions that wracked the cohesion of late medieval and early modern Bologna related to the deepening perceived need to protect the community from God's wrath and what other factors may have contributed to that changing perception.

Low-status women constituted a huge number of the "lost peoples" of the past, and the crime of rape is one of the most difficult to study because of its underreporting, but Carol Lansing has found documentation from the 1280s that enables her to bring new insights to both topics. A major trope in current scholarship is that non-elite women and their families were often reluctant to bring charges of rape to court. Indeed, as evidenced in the chapters by Dean and Vallerani in this volume, social identity and reputation were crucial aspects of plaintiffs' and defendants' strategies. The risk of lodging a rape charge was presumably too high unless accusers were seeking settlement by marriage with the rapist. By focusing on the social status of victims, however, Lansing offers an important revision of this issue—in more than half of the accusation cases, the victims were unmarried, without parents, or with few resources, suggesting that vulnerable women of the lower classes comprised the majority of rape accusers; women of the more elite classes with family and their concerns for honor received more protection *ipso facto* from their status. Further, by detailed analysis of an *inquisitio* for rape against a member of an elite family, she illuminates the existence of prior relations between the alleged rapist and his victim, the importance of differences in their status, and the impact on the trial outcome of community values. Lansing also asks why there was evidently a sharp decline in accusations of rape between the late thirteenth and late fourteenth centuries, and hypothesizes a possible link between that development and the decline of accusations discussed in Blanshei's chapter in this volume.

The most notorious rape and abduction case in medieval and early modern Bologna was committed by a student from Valencia who in 1321 kidnapped the niece of one of Bologna's most prominent jurists, Giovanni d'Andrea. The court responded quickly and harshly, capturing and executing the culprit. The response of the outraged students was also rapid—the majority left Bologna for Imola and later Siena, and major concessions had to be made in order to persuade them to return. But as Christopher Carlsmith shows in his chapter in this volume, this crime does not fit the profile of most student violence in the thirteenth and early fourteenth centuries, when court cases against students were similar to those against the rest of the population and indeed many students were victims and were given special legal protections. The attitude of the government had changed by the sixteenth century, however, when Archbishop Gabriele Paleotti described them as becoming "more licentious and more insolent" every day, carrying weapons and attacking each other during classes. Carlsmith focuses on the later period and asks what was unique to student violence and what were its causes. He finds a key answer in the proliferation in Bologna in the sixteenth and seventeenth centuries of student colleges—usually structured on "national" lines and each with its own statutes, buildings, and academic regalia—a structure that led to students having a strong sense of identity with their colleges and to rivalries among these residential colleges that revolved around issues of hierarchical status and "precedence." Brawls ensued when groups of students met on the streets and fought over who had *precedenza*—the right of way that recognized the college's greater prestige. Moreover, these conflicts became more intensive in the sixteenth and seventeenth centuries as international rivalries sharpened and the colleges became more numerous. Like much of the general interpersonal violence in the Duecento and early Trecento (Vallerani), this increase in student violence was purposeful, but had a unique institutional context.

What conclusions or hypotheses concerning changes and continuities between the thirteenth and seventeenth centuries in Bolognese criminal justice history can we derive from recent Bolognese historiography and the essays in this collection? Most obvious perhaps is the non-linear shape of change: for example, although *inquisitio* ultimately totally replaced *accusatio* procedure, it did not do so in a continuous decline and more importantly that development did not diminish the podestarial and *Torrone* courts' concern for the reconciliation as well as the repression of interpersonal violence and dispute resolution (Rose). Student violence increased in the sixteenth and seventeenth centuries in contrast to levels of violence in the population in general (Blanshei, Rose). The peace accord was as key a feature of the seventeenth-century court as it was in the thirteenth century, and interrogation techniques were similar in both eras (Dean and Rose). Moreover, the Weberian thesis that state formation stemmed from governmental efforts to gain a monopoly over violence needs to be modified in the Bolognese context. Communal government did not "tolerate" vendetta, but it did seek to limit legitimate violence to "collective entities" (Roberts). However, the fifteenth-century Bentivoglio *signoria* ultimately employed extrajudicial violence to quell political opposition (Cucini), and it was only gradually in the seventeenth century that the government and its *Torrone* court embarked on policies and reforms designated to rival and subdue competing feudal jurisdictions in the *contado* that had risen in the fourteenth and fifteenth centuries (Rose). Yet the effort to control the violence of nobles, both in the city and *contado*, was mixed and even retrogressive at times. Although the *popolo* government sought to confront and control the violence of nobles (Roberts), their resistance was strong and effective both in the last decade of the thirteenth century (Blanshei) and during the Bentivoglio regime which countenanced the flaunting of the law by its adherents (not only of nobles but also their partisan allies of lower status), and surged again in the seventeenth century and was not relatively subdued until the end of that century by the papacy (Rose).

What of the traditional image of premodern violence as largely spontaneous, mindless, and brutal? None of the chapters in this volume support the Eliasian view. To be sure, poisoning, although by its very nature a premeditated crime, rarely occurred (Buyck). However, even the interpersonal violence that constitutes the bulk of court cases indicates not senseless anger but *purposeful* conflicts over material resources, and the court procedures for those cases show the centrality of social relations in those disputes that provoked physical violence (Vallerani). Student violence also correlated with status concerns—that of the group and rivalries over group precedence—and followed a choreographed pattern of predictable, self-conscious insult that led to violence of a performative nature (Carlsmith). Rape cases, like much of interpersonal violence, seem often to have been part of "broader conflicts" rather than spontaneous, opportunistic attacks by strangers (Lansing). Blasphemy was largely associated with gambling and taverns and impulsive violence, but most of the few cases prosecuted were verbal and not accompanied by physical assault (Vise).

Where we do find brutality is not so much in everyday social relations but in judicial practice—in the use of torture in interrogation and the meting out of mutilation and corporal punishments and ritualized executions, but this repressive treatment constituted only a subset of the judicial system and its harshness varied by regime and by the status of the culprits. Interpersonal violence was not "endemic," but it indeed was widespread with high levels of homicide that spiked in time of crisis, indicating its causes were not so much immediate (uncontrollable neurological responses to provocation) as they were largely proximate and ultimate, stemming from socioeconomic and political structures and events. In sum, recent historiography and the chapters in this volume on Bolognese criminal justice and violence challenge the still frequent portrayal of the late medieval and early modern centuries as an era in which "[e]verybody was violent"; "the brutality of human relations was a universal social language, considered normal and necessary"[57] and "[v]iolence was less a problem to be solved than an almost accepted aspect of interpersonal discourse."[58] The sensationalist presentations in chronicles and literature are not confirmed in the judicial records.[59] It is all too easy to forget the thousands of *popolani* of the republican commune—a great majority of the population—who enacted and adhered to a law and order regime and also attempted to curb the violence of magnates and recalcitrant elite *popolani*, or the fact that the rebellious nobles of the seventeenth century who were ultimately defeated and exiled by the papacy formed only a minority of their socioeconomic class. To be sure, late medieval and early modern interpersonal violence was often viewed as a negotiable and reconcilable event by government and society unless it concerned infamous recidivists and marginals, but brutality was not a "normal" or "necessary" feature of social relations. Violence could take the shape, as it did in the majority of court cases, of a minor assault, but it too often was a harsh response, a tragic choice that many people and certain regimes made in an environment of cataclysmic demographic and economic crises such as the great plague of 1630, ravaging warfare, and the fear, distrust, and hatred unleashed by a volatile, faction-based system of governance.

NOTES

1. Muir and Ruggiero, *Microhistory & the Lost Peoples*; Gamberini and Lazzarini, *The Italian Renaissance State*.
2. Martines, *Violence and Civil Disorder in Italian Cities, 1200–1500*.
3. Huizinga, *The Waning of the Middle Ages*. The well-known chapter title is from the 1924 English translation.
4. Dean and Lowe, *Crime, Society, and the Law*, 5–6. For introductory overviews of the concept of violence in the historical scholarship on the period, see Carroll, *Cultures of Violence*, 1–43; Broomhall and Finn, *Violence and Emotions*, 1–18. On definitions of medieval violence, see Brown, *Violence in Medieval Europe,* 1–30. All demonstrate the difficulty of discussing "violence" outside the parameters of particular societies and eras. Brown explicitly recognizes the problem of concentrating on the quantity and not the quality of an era's violence.
5. Elias, *The Civilizing Process*.
6. Johnson and Monkkonen, *The Civilization of Crime*. The statistics were compiled by Ted Gurr, "Historical Trends in Violent Crime" in 1981, and amplified by Manuel Eisner, "Long-Term Historical Trends" in 2001.
7. Pinker, *The Better Angels of Our Nature*. The leading proponent of Elias's theory today is Pieter Spierenburg, whose most recent among numerous works is *A History of Murder*.
8. See Stuart Carroll's online lecture, "Stuart Carroll on Homicide and the Civilizing Process" (accessed 8 October, 2017). The essays in Katherine Watson's *Assaulting the Past*

revolve around modifying, nuancing, or rejecting Elias's theory. Randolph Roth's various articles and his important study of American homicide not only demonstrates that the evidence does not fit the thesis of the "civilizing process" but also offers a new theoretical explanatory framework. Roth, *American Homicide*.

9. Stollberg-Rilinger, "The Impact of Communication Theory"; Riches, "The Phenomenon of Violence"; Roth, "Biology and the Deep History of Homicide"; Carter Wood, "The Limits of Culture?" and Idem, "Conceptualizing Cultures of Violence and Cultural Change."

10. Dean, *Crime and Justice*.

11. Giusberti and Roversi Monaco, "Economy and Demography."

12. Gardi, "The Making of an Oligarchy." For oligarchy at the turn of the thirteenth century in Bologna, see Blanshei, *Politics and Justice* and Eadem, "Postfazione." The growth of oligarchy in the early modern period was paralleled by a trend to aristocratization in other Bolognese institutions, e.g., in the lay confraternities. Terpstra, "Confraternities and Civil Religion."

13. Tamba, "Civic Institutions" and Duranti, "*Libertas*, Oligarchy, Papacy."

14. Mazzoni Toselli, *Racconti storici*; Idem, *Cenno sull'antica storia*; Zaccagnini, *Storia dello Studio*; Frati, *La vita privata*; Kantorowicz, *Albertus Gandinus*.

15. Cagali, "La criminalità a Bologna," and Quadrini, "Primi sondaggi."

16. Blanshei, "Crime and Law Enforcement"; Eadem, "Criminal Law and Politics," and Eadem, "Criminal Justice in Medieval Perugia."

17. Muir and Ruggiero, *Microhistory & the Lost Peoples*, vii–ix. Also quoted in Magnusson and Szijarto, *What is Microhistory?*, 4.

18. Lansing, "Poisoned Relations"; Eadem, "Concubines, Lovers, Prostitutes"; Eadem "Donna con Donna?"

19. Dean, "Marriage and Mutilation"; Idem, "Domestic violence"; Idem, "Fornicating with nuns"; Idem "Gender and insult"; Idem, "Theft and Gender"; Monson, *Habitual Offenders*.

20. Grendi, "Micro-analisi e storia sociale."

21. Falk Moore, *Law as Process*; Roberts, *Order and Dispute*.

22. Blanshei, "Foreword to the English Edition," ix.

23. Vallerani, *Medieval Public Justice*. See Cummins and Kounine, "Introduction: Confronting Conflict," 2, for the "consumer-led state formation process" with reference to the works on reconciliation of Daniel Smail, "Telling Tales" and Idem, *The Consumption of Justice*; Sbriccoli, "Legislation, Justice, and Political Power"; and Cummins and Kounine, "Introduction: Confronting Conflict," 6, on the importance of peacemaking in Italian historiography in contrast to other national traditions. On Bolognese peace contracts, see Wray, *Communities and Crisis*.

24. Jordan, "Rethinking Disputes and Settlements," 25, 33–34.

25. Milani, *L'esclusione dal comune*.

26. Blanshei, *Politics and Justice* and Eadem, "Postfazione." See McCormick, *Machiavellian Democracy* and Winters, *Oligarchy*, for the typologies of oligarchy.

27. Blanshei, "Homicide in a Culture of Hatred."

28. Roth, "Biology and the Deep History of Homicide"; LaFree, *Losing Legitimacy*; Cooney, *Warriors and Peacemakers*; Gould, *Collision of Wills*. Also see Roth, *American Homicide*, 455 and his approach to the violence of the 1960s as tied to the state's losing its legitimacy in comparison to Martines's "Introduction" in *Violence and Civic Disorders*, discussed above.

29. Dean, "Eight Varieties of Homicide"; Salfati, "The nature of expressiveness and instrumentality in homicide"; Williams and Fleweling, "The Social Production of Criminal Homicide"; Spierenburg, *A History of Murder*.

30. Jenkins, "Medieval Student Violence." See Dean, *Crime in Medieval Europe*, 113–14, who earlier reached the same conclusion.

31. Lantschner, *The Logic of Political Conflict*, 5–7, 90, 95–130; Idem, "Justice Contested and Affirmed," 85; Idem, "'The Nourisher of Seditions.'"

32. Cucini, "Législation statutaire."

33. Angelozzi and Casanova, *La nobiltà disciplinata*; Idem, *La giustizia criminale in una città di antico regime*.

34. Rose, "Homicide in North Italy," 189–93.

35. Blanshei, "Homicide in a Culture of Hatred," 113; Dean, "Eight Typologies of Homicide," 85. Dean ties the high rates of the mid-fourteenth century to the increased presence of mercenaries in the city.

36. Dean and Lowe, "Introducing Renaissance Killers," 9.

37. Blanshei and Cucini, "Criminal Justice and Conflict Resolution," 352.

38. Angelozzi and Casanova, *Donne criminali*, 73–85.

39. Blanshei and Cucini, "Criminal Justice and Conflict Resolution," 352–53; Cucini, "Violenza 'femminile' e violenza 'maschile.'"

40. Terpstra, "Body Politics." For mutilations before execution, see Angelozzi and Casanova, *La giustizia criminale in una città di antico regime*, 415–24.

41. Terpstra, "Theory into Practice," 119, 121, 143.

42. Blanshei, "Gruesome Penalties."

43. Dean, "Criminal justice in mid-fifteenth century Bologna," 27; Idem, "Fathers and daughters," 87–89; Idem, "Gender and insult," 229; Idem, *Crime and Justice*, 41. Zorzi describes a similar trend to leniency and "monetization" of penalties in Florence, Zorzi, "Le esecuzioni delle condanne," 152–53. His data have been criticized by Cohn, "Repression of Popular Revolt," 118. Cohn concludes that brutal repression increased with the growth of the state in the fifteenth, sixteenth, and seventeenth centuries, Cohn, "Repression of Popular Revolt," 120. The leniency view, however, is currently dominant; see for example, Geltner, *Flogging Others*, 63.

44. Dean, "Sodomy in Renaissance Bologna," 442.

45. Terpstra, "Theory into Practice," 118.

46. Blanshei, "Gruesome Penalties"; Terpstra, "Body Politics," 48n11; Idem, "Theory into Practice," 121. On repression during the regime of Baldassare De Cossa (1403–15), see Dondarini, "The Bentivoglio and Agreements with the Church," 131.

47. Vallerani, *Medieval Public Justice*, 31, 157–59; Blanshei, "Cambiamenti e continuità nella procedura penale."

48. Blanshei, *Politics and Justice*, 328–29.

49. Blanshei, *Politics and Justice*, 371–73, 601–39.

50. Milani, *L'esclusione dal comune* and Idem, "Banditi, *malesardi* e ribelli" on the extension of torture to those charged with conspiracy; Blanshei, "Gruesome Penalties."

51. Angelozzi and Casanova, *La giustizia criminale in una città di antico regime*, 343–65, 535–51.

52. Tracy, *Torture and Brutality*. On the role of torture and violence in medieval dramatists, see Enders, *The Medieval Theater of Cruelty*.

53. Coincidentally but significantly, Joanna Carraway Vitiello in a forthcoming article, "Vengeance, Vendetta, and Justice in Late Medieval Italy," has come to a similar conclusion in her treatment of vendetta in Reggio Emilia. Both Vitiello and Roberts specifically support Trevor Dean's earlier interpretation of vendetta, in contrast to that of Andrea Zorzi and other historians. Dean, "Violence, Vendetta, and Peacemaking"; Idem, *Crime and Justice*, 126–31; Idem, "Marriage and Mutilation," 7–9.

54. Alessandro Pastore in a recent article notes how the Bolognese jurist Ippolito Marsili (1450–1529) in his commentary on that law, attributed its enormity not only to betrayal but to the inability of its victims to defend themselves as was possible when weapons were used. Pastore, "Poison and Poisoning in Renaissance Italy," 229.

55. However, the mix of rarity, atrocity, malice, and perpetrators of noble status in certain cases of poisoning could garner great attention and notoriety, as in the case of Ippolita Passarotti and Lodovico Landinelli, decapitated in 1587 in Bologna for the murder of her father by poison because he opposed their marriage. The case is noted in Pastore, "Poison and Poisoning," 236 and in Terpstra, "Body Politics."

56. Nash, "Blasphemy and the Anti-Civilizing Process," 61.

57. Muchembled, *A History of Violence*, 14 and 8, also quoted in Broomhall and Finn, *Violence and Emotions*, 3.

58. Ruff, *Violence in Early Modern Europe*, 117, again also quoted in Broomhall and Finn, *Violence and Emotions*, 3.

59. For a revisionist interpretation of violence in literature, see Tracy, *Torture and Brutality*.

Abbreviations

Archives and Libraries

ASB	Archivio di Stato di Bologna
ASF	Archivio di Stato di Firenze
ASL	Archivio di Stato di Lucca
ASP	Archivio di Stato di Perugia
BCA	Biblioteca Comunale dell'Archiginnasio di Bologna
BUB	Biblioteca Universitaria di Bologna

Archival Sources

ASB, Accusationes
ASB, Comune-Governo, Curia del Podestà, Giudici ad Maleficia, Accusationes.
ASB, Bandi e Stampe
ASB, Assunteria del Torrone, 3a, Constitutiones Turroni, Bandi e Stampe.
ASB, Carte di Corredo
ASB, Comune-Governo, Curia del Podestà, Giudici ad Maleficia, Carte di Corredo.
ASB, Constitutioni e Bolle del Torrone
ASB, Assunteria del Torrone, 3c, Constitutioni e bolle del Torrone.
ASB, Constitutiones Turroni Bononiae
ASB, Assunteria del Torrone, Bandi e Stampe, Constitutiones Turroni Bononiae.
ASB, Corone ed Armi
ASB, Comune-Governo, Curia del Podestà, Corone ed Armi.
ASB, Demaniale
ASB, Archivio Demaniale
ASB, Giudici
ASB, Comune, Capitano del Popolo, Esecutore e Conservatore di Giustizia, Giudici del Capitano del Popolo
ASB, Inquisitiones

ASB, Comune-Governo, Curia del Podestà, Giudici ad Maleficia, Libri Inquisitionum et Testium
ASB, Liber Fantini
ASB, Comune-Governo, Signoria Viscontea, Ecclesiastica e Bentivolesca, Liber Fantini 308.
ASB, Liber Novarum Provisionum
ASB, Comune-Governo, Signoria Viscontea, Ecclesiastica e Bentivolesca, Liber Novarum Provisionum 306.
ASB, Liber Novissimarum Provisionum
ASB, Comune-Governo, Signoria Viscontea, Ecclesiastica e Bentivolesca, Liber Novissimarum Provisionum 307.
ASB, Libri Mandatorum
ASB, Comune-Governo, Riformatori dello Stato di Libertà, Libri Mandatorum
ASB, Libri Partitorum
ASB, Comune-Governo, Riformatori dello Stato di Libertà, Libri Partitorum
ASB, Libri Provisionum
ASB, Comune-Governo, Signoria Viscontea, Ecclesiastica e Bentivolesca, Libri Provisionum.
ASB, Notai Forensi
ASB, Curia del Podestà, Notai Forensi.
ASB, Provvigioni
ASB, Comune-Governo, Provvigioni dei consigli minori
ASB, Registro Cavalcate
ASB, Assunteria del Torrone, Registro Cavalcate
ASB, Riformagioni
ASB, Comune-Governo, Riformagioni del Consiglio del Popolo e della Massa
ASB, Riformagioni e Provvigioni Serie Cartacea
ASB, Comune-Governo, Riformagioni e Provvigioni Serie Cartacea
ASB, Sententiae
ASB, Comune-Governo, Curia del Podestà, Giudici ad Maleficia, Sententiae
ASB, Sindacato
ASB, Comune-Governo, Curia del Podestà, Sindacato, Ufficio del Giudice al Sindacato
ASB, Statuti
ASB, Comune-Governo, Statuti
ASB, Vacchetini
ASB, Comune-Governo, Curia del Podestà, Giudici ad Maleficia, Vacchettini e Bastardelli
ASB, Atti e Processi
ASB, Tribunale del Torrone, Atti e Processi

A Note About the Editor

Violence and Justice in Bologna: 1250–1700 is, first and foremost, the result of a great deal of hard work by Sarah Rubin Blanshei, who conceived of the idea, brought together the contributors, gently cajoled chapters from each of us, edited them all assiduously, and organized them into a coherent approach to the complex judicial history of a city whose significance for broader Italian developments is now quite clear.

Those who have spent any time in the *Archivio di Stato di Bologna* will likely have met Sarah, and having met her, will know that the good cheer, generosity and spirit with which she has organized this volume are part and parcel of her approach to scholarship and to maintaining the community of scholars of which she is a dear member.

I first met Sarah when I was a graduate student, at the 2011 conference *Bologna: Cultural Crossroads*, organized through a grant from the *Fondazione Carisbo* to promote collaboration between Italian and Anglo-American scholars of Bologna. When I entered the church-cum-library of *San Giorgio in Poggiale*, there was Sarah standing at the door, greeting in person every attendee at the conference. When I returned to Bologna for the bulk of my doctoral research in 2012-2013, I was pleasantly surprised when Sarah approached me in the ASB and asked if *I* remembered meeting *her* the year before.

As we were both working on homicide projects, we spent several months working at adjacent tables, comparing trials from the fourteenth and seventeenth centuries. Since then Sarah has been a formative influence, mentor, and friend as I completed graduate school and moved into the life of a working and teaching professional historian.

The community of *Bolognisti* that Sarah has gathered here would like to take this opportunity to express appreciation for her active support of us and our work. I am sure that every contributor has their own story about the impact of Sarah's remarkable work on their thinking about Bologna, about her gracious and kind commentary on their own work, and about the collegiality and friendship that she has brought to the archive in Bologna.

That absolutely none of us hesitated about contributing to this volume speaks to the goodwill which Sarah has earned from the *Bolognisti* community, and the debt that many of us feel toward her for the rigor and exactitude with which she makes our best efforts at scholarship better, and the kindness and friendship which she has shown us all over the years.

Grazie tante, Sarah.

Colin Rose

1

Criminal Justice: Procedures and Practices

Chapter One

Vendetta, Violence, and Police Power in Thirteenth-Century Bologna

Gregory G. Roberts

Over the past two decades,[1] Andrea Zorzi has championed the view that Italy's communes legitimated vendetta.[2] Although vendetta (*vindicta*) is sometimes confused with feud (*faida*) or bloodfeud, medieval Italian sources use the term more narrowly to refer to an act of vengeance within a relationship of hatred (*odium*), enmity (*inimicitia*), or war (*guerra*).[3] As the argument goes, vendetta enjoyed not only cultural legitimacy in a society where it was widely practiced and viewed with moral ambivalence, but also legal legitimacy thanks to communal statutes that sanctioned the practice. To be sure, certain communes' statutes (including Bologna's) placed restrictions on vendetta, but "not a single text banned vendetta" and "civic laws neither prohibited nor prosecuted it." Zorzi accounts for vendetta's legitimacy primarily in terms of its social function. He argues that vendetta, unlike the mass exiles and factional violence that plagued the Italian communes, was a symmetrical response to violence that sought to restore social equilibrium rather than leave one side victorious over the other. It put in place "a temporary balance in the exchange of injury" that could allow parties in conflict to negotiate peace. Consequently, the communes recognized vendetta's "positive value" as a "practice of social self-regulation" and "balancing mechanism" that worked to limit violence rather than spread it.[4] Although a few scholars have challenged this view, Zorzi's reading now enjoys widespread influence in the field.[5]

The rehabilitation of vendetta is part of a broader, functionalist current in medieval history that emphasizes the social uses—and by implication, the social value—of institutions.[6] Whether the subject is hatred, violence, or the public trial, these studies illustrate how institutions "worked" within the logic of the social order.[7] The functionalist paradigm has especially transformed the study of medieval justice through its focus on processes of conflict resolution.[8] This conceptual framework—borrowed from anthropology—has allowed scholars to broaden their understanding of public justice to include extra and infrajudicial processes, such as vendetta, peacemaking, and arbitration, that aimed to resolve conflicts.[9] It has also led them to revise their understanding of judicial practice through a new reading of traditional sources, such as trial records. In both cases, the literature emphasizes community-based practices of negotiated justice, which sought to compensate for offenses, over the state's hegemonic justice, which aimed to punish offenses in accordance with written law, as the dominant mode of justice in medieval societies.[10]

The functionalist approach to vendetta has shed valuable light on the structures of medieval social orders, and helped to correct some long-standing biases in the historiography. In a society where relationships of friendship and enmity determined the order, the pursuit of vendetta was clearly a rational decision, and, in certain situations, culturally sanctioned or even obligatory.[11] Indeed, vendetta is common to many cultures because it addresses the universal need to establish rules for the use of violence.[12] In light of vendetta's social value, historians no longer assume that it suffered a gradual but inevitable decline in the face of growing state power.[13] Historians today are far less likely to speak in terms of the triumph of public over private justice, or the state's progressive claim to a monopoly on the legitimate use of violence.

However, the notion that vendetta enjoyed legal legitimacy in the communes rests on thinner ice. Trevor Dean has already pointed out some of the ways that communes did in fact prohibit or prosecute vengeance. Some communes penalized vendetta outright, while others prescribed severe penalties for secondary vendetta that were double, triple, or even quadruple the norms for assault or homicide. Furthermore, judges and jurists do not seem to have sanctioned the practice. Jurisprudence distinguished between the legitimacy of defending one's self in a single fight and the illegitimacy of starting a new fight in order to take revenge. In legal practice, judges did not accept vendetta as an excuse for violence, nor did defendants and their lawyers—who were generally adept at finding loopholes in the statutes—appeal to vendetta laws to exonerate themselves.[14] Thus, if most communes' laws did not expressly ban vendetta, neither did they grant exceptions for vendetta in prescribing punishments for interpersonal violence. To Dean's critiques can be added a question of emphasis. If vendetta was a deeply entrenched custom in communal society, is it really remarkable that civic statutes did not ban it outright? Is it not more significant that the same citizen legislators who practiced vendetta increasingly sought to regulate it over the course of the thirteenth century? From this point of view, historians who highlight the "legitimation of vendetta" seem to make an event out of historical continuity, while downplaying historical change.

Using Bologna as an example, this chapter highlights an important but overlooked way in which communes sought to suppress violence, including vendetta: the enforcement of weapon-possession laws. By the mid-thirteenth century, Bologna and other communes strictly regulated the right to bear arms through police patrols and a government licensing regime. This proactive law enforcement effort was a novel form of hegemonic justice that resulted in the arrest, trial, and conviction of scores of men, including political elites, each year. Furthermore, the trial records leave little doubt that this new police regime was designed to prevent men who had mortal enemies from expressing their hatred through "war" or violence. The implication for the study of vendetta in medieval Italy is clear: the same men who practiced vendetta made these laws precisely because they did not view the institution as a self-regulating mechanism, or at least one that was self-regulating enough. This chapter suggests that the policing of arms-bearing was part of a broader trend that saw Bologna's citizen legislators attempt to suppress interpersonal violence that occurred outside the context of public collectives. This observation does not require a teleological narrative focused on the rise of the modern state, but it does call for historians to focus once again on explaining institutional change, rather than highlighting structural continuities over time.

THE PREVENTIVE LOGIC OF WEAPON-POSSESSION LAWS

Weapon-possession laws were a standard feature of communal statutes by the mid-thirteenth century. Bologna's weapon-possession laws predate the earliest surviving statutes, as some of the earliest court records of the podestà's office show them to have been in place by the 1230s.[15] Bologna's laws regarding arms-bearing were complicated and frequently amended, but generally they prohibited all individuals—with the exception of select public officeholders—from bearing "offensive arms," which included most types of blade weapons, maces, and polearms. They also restricted the bearing of "defensive arms," which meant various pieces of armor and shields, so that only individuals who had obtained a license from the podestà could wear armor through the city.[16]

Historians have generally either paid little attention to these laws or interpreted them as a type of anti-magnate legislation, which targeted arms-bearing as a defining feature of magnate identity.[17] However, communes began restricting the right to bear arms at least a half century before the *popolo*-magnate conflict emerged. The 1143 *breve* of the Genoese *compagna* prohibited the bearing of arms in the city except for those traveling outside.[18] By the mid-thirteenth century, similar laws also existed in southern Italy and France, where the *popolo*-magnate conflict did not define politics.[19] Indeed, prohibitions against arms-bearing were a common feature of the Peace and Truce of God movements of the late tenth and eleventh centuries. According to the Truce of God decreed by Emperor Henry IV in 1085, no man was to "presume to bear as weapons a shield, sword, or lance—or, in fact, the burden of any armour" on certain days of the week or feast days.[20]

Rather than targeting a specific social group, the regulation of arms-bearing simply aimed to prevent acts of violence. Bologna's lawmakers occasionally made this rationale explicit, as in a 1293 provision that placed new restrictions on *contadini* and *rustici* bearing arms "to restrain" their "many crimes and homicides."[21] Other legislators also left little doubt about their intent. For example, Frederick II unambiguously invoked a preventive rationale in his *Constitutions of Melfi* (1231): "Our aim is not only directed beneficially at the punishment of crimes already committed, but also at preventing the opportunity and grounds for committing them. Therefore, since the bearing of forbidden weapons sometimes is the cause of violence and murder, we elect to resist now rather than to avenge later."[22] Similarly, Henry IV made clear that his 1085 decree was "chiefly for the security of all those who are at feud," and so that "those who travel and those who remain at home may enjoy the greatest possible security." His restrictions on arms-bearing expressly did not exempt men at feud (*faicosi*), and went hand-in-hand with prohibitions against violent crime, namely murder, arson, robbery, assault, and injuring anyone with "any kind of weapon."[23]

Of course, if weapon-possession laws were widespread in the thirteenth century, that does not necessarily mean they were enforced. Bologna's archive offers an extraordinary opportunity to explore the question of enforcement thanks to the richness of the *Corone ed Armi* (Crowns and Arms) series.[24] The notary who oversaw the office of *Corone ed Armi* was responsible for enforcing sumptuary law (hence the "crowns" or tiaras of the title), but also recorded the *familia*'s "discoveries" (*inventiones*) of violations of the curfew, gambling, and weapon-possession laws, as well as the ensuing trials. These patrol and trial records attest a robust police effort by the commune to enforce weapon-possession laws. According to statute, the podestà's *familia* had a special charge "to search for men bearing prohibited arms."[25] One of the podestà's foreign judges or *milites* (knights) led regular patrols, which also comprised a notary and an unspecified number of mercenaries (*berroerii*) and attendants (*domicelli*). The records show that they patrolled the city streets day and night, virtually every day of the podestà's term in office.[26] The *familia*'s patrols also ventured into the *contado* regularly—twice a month by the early fourteenth century—to enforce the weapon-possession laws and capture outlaws.[27] (The *barisellus*, an official from the butcher's guild, pursued political exiles in the *contado* separately.[28]) Case samples from the *Corone ed Armi* registers suggest that the *familia* brought weapon-possession charges against roughly 150 men each year. (They charged approximately the same number of men with violating the curfew and gambling laws in the same span.) Most weapon-possession cases—somewhere between 56 and 71 percent—ended in convictions, which by the 1280s meant a 10-*lire* fine for each assault weapon and 5 *lire* for each piece of armor.[29] The conviction rate was high because the statutes accorded the *familia*'s word the weight of legal proof, and because contumacy was virtually unheard of for these offenses. This proactive policing was a standard feature of Italian communes by the mid-thirteenth century, and wherever we have early enough judicial records—Siena, Perugia, and Orvieto for example—we can see that the cities' foreign police enforced them.[30]

If Bologna and other communes made a concerted effort to enforce their weapon-possession laws, and those laws were aimed at preventing violence, it must be asked whose violence and what kind of violence they were trying to prevent. The *Corone ed Armi* records suggest that the commune's police effort was largely impersonal.[31] Granted, the trial records do not lend themselves to prosopography, because notaries frequently omitted family names and occupations.[32] However, notaries did include family names and other indicators of social status often enough to suggest that the vast majority of people prosecuted on weapons charges were not magnates, or in earlier records, *milites*. Of the more than sixty individuals charged with illegal weapon-possession in the second semester of 1291, not a single one was identified as a noble.[33] Massimo Vallerani has identified the same trend in Perugia in the latter half of the thirteenth century.[34] Conversely, the *familia* showed little regard for the *popolo* regime's leading families. Members of the governing elite—the Pepoli, Gozzadini, Sabadini, Zovenzoni, and Bentivoglio, to name a few of the most prominent—appear throughout the registers of the *Corone ed Armi* office.[35] In the same vein, notaries, whose guild dominated politics in the 1280s, frequently appear in the registers, including three arrested in a 1286 raid on a gambling house.[36]

Of course, the podestarial system was founded on the theory that foreigners, by virtue of their remove from local politics, would be more able to provide impartial justice than the city's own elites.[37] Nevertheless, it is remarkable to observe such indifference to social status in a society where justice remained deeply political in practice.[38] It seems that Bologna's self-governing citizens intended to restrain their own violence, much like Orvieto's sought to restrain their own emotions through funeral law enforcement.[39]

PREVENTIVE POLICING IN PRACTICE

The prevention of criminal acts and the elimination of threats to the social order are the hallmarks of police power.[40] But what threats did the communes seek to eliminate through the policing of illegal weapons? Bologna's judicial sources once again shed light on the issue, suggesting that the repression of vendetta was a major goal of the new police regime. A revealing pair of cases comes from within the context of a war between the Boattieri and Ricci families, who both featured prominently among Bologna's political elite.[41] I have not been able to trace the origins of their enmity, but it surfaces across a range of judicial sources in the early 1290s.[42] In April 1290, Bettino di Megliodeglialtri—almost certainly the son of Megliodeglialtri Ricci—was convicted of attempting to frame Giacomo and Baldo Boattieri for armed assault. According to his sentence, he cut his own hand to make it bleed, found the Boattieri in their neighborhood and provoked one of them to shove him, and then held up his bleeding hand, claiming that they had assaulted him. Bettino contrived this plot with one of Tommaso Ricci's sons after the notary Giacomo Biasmaltorti—later identified as a partisan (*ex parte*) of the Boattieri clan—had Bettino accused by Giacomo and Corso Guglielmi. The record does not say which Giacomo (Biasmaltorti or Boattieri) accused Bettino or for what crime, but these details suggest that Bettino was pursuing a vendetta through criminal accusations instead of direct violence, and that this vendetta involved extended social networks. The podestà punished Bettino by having his right hand cut off, likely in an attempt to prevent the conflict from spiraling further.[43]

Bettino's mutilation evidently failed to lay the conflict to rest, however, because when Rosso della Tosa took office as podestà in January 1292, one of his first orders of business was to place the two families under house arrest. The statutes allowed the podestà to confine warring parties to specific locations in the city or *contado* whenever this seemed politically expedient.[44] Rosso sent eight partisans of the Ricci—including Bettino's likely father, Megliodeglialtri—to stay at the house of Francesco Preti, a leading *popolano*. He also sent nine partisans of the Boattieri—including both Giacomo Boattieri and Giacomo Biasmaltorti—to the house of Delfino del Priore, a belted knight.[45] The podestà ordered the confined men not to stray more than 25 arm's-lengths (*brachia*) from their respective houses under a steep penalty of 1,000 *lire*.[46] Less than three weeks after the initial order, the podestà had the Boattieri relocated to the house of Balduino Balduini, a prominent judge.[47] The record does not indicate how long the two parties remained under house arrest, but their confinement lasted for at least five months.

The podestà also had his *familia* keep a close eye on these houses, as a pair of weapon-possession trials show. That very January, the *familia* charged Bonincontro Boattieri, who was among those confined, with refusing to be searched for illegal weapons, and a certain Bencivenni di Giliolo, who was with him, for possessing one. The *berroerius* Ghino told the following story in court: when he arrived at the house of Delfino del Priore "where the Boattieri are residing in confinement," he saw Bonincontro moving toward the house. He ordered him to stop "in such a way that he could hear him well," but Bonincontro paid him no heed and entered the house. Before long he came back outside wearing armor and carrying a new license for it. Ghino's comrade Faldo added the following: when "he was searching carefully for weapons among the men who were at the house of Delfino del Priore where the Boattieri are residing in confinement," he found a small sword on the ground behind Bencivenni.[48] He testified that Bencivenni was nearest the sword—which by statute made him guilty—but Bencivenni denied in court that it was his.[49] Fortunately for him, Bonincontro came forward and confessed that he was the weapon's owner. After spotting the *familia*, he had laid down the sword and gone inside in order to avoid a weapon-possession charge. In the end Bonincontro was convicted and the charge against Bencivenni dropped.[50] The *familia* evidently continued their surveillance after this case. Just three weeks later in February, they reported finding Bonincontro again, this time standing "under the portico of the house in which he is staying in confinement" with a knife.[51] Again he was convicted and fined 10 *lire*.

Thus, in a two-year window, Bologna's podestà attempted to suppress a war between two elite families through corporal punishment, house arrest, and police surveillance. Any one of these incidents could be dismissed as an anomaly, but together they show a sustained effort by government authorities to prevent the Boattieri-Ricci conflict, which could well have had implications for political stability, from escalating. Even if their enmity was ultimately resolved by a peace agreement or extrajudicial mediation, the sources directly contradict Zorzi's assertion that government authorities "recognized the existence of conflicts and tried to resolve them without repression or punishment."[52]

The *familia* likely used the weapon-possession laws to prevent violence between warring parties more often than the trial records reveal, as in the following, apparently routine case. In August 1298, the *familia* charged Bernabò Gozzadini and a certain Cuscino (*Cossinus*), who lived in the house of Brandelisio Gozzadini, with carrying knives. One *berroerius* reportedly took the knife from Bernabò's hand as he was trying to toss the weapon on the ground; a second claimed to have seen Cuscino throw his knife away before confiscating it. For his part, Bernabò claimed that the *familia* had found the knife not on him but in a shop belonging to the Pegolotti family, and that there were at least fifteen men standing closer to the knife. (Bernabò was evidently familiar with the law that assigned guilt to the person nearest an abandoned weapon.) Cuscino gave a similar story, alleging that the *famil-*

ia had found the knife under a table that some thirty men were standing near. The notary recorded nothing else about their trials except that they were convicted.[53] From this record alone, it looks like little more than a case of the *familia*'s word against the defendants'.

However, other sources reveal that 1298 saw violence erupt between Brandelisio Gozzadini and his sons, on the one hand, and the Pegolotti and Lamandini families on the other. Just three months after this weapons case, their enmity would culminate in the beating death of Guidotto Lamandini. Fearing the outbreak of riots over this murder—an especially grave threat in the midst of Bologna's ongoing war with Ferrara—the city council would remove these Gozzadini from the popular societies, declare them magnates, and place them under house arrest in the countryside.[54] Viewed in this light, an otherwise unremarkable weapon-possession case takes on a whole new meaning. It seems that the Gozzadini were on the premises of their mortal enemies' shop (the Pegolottis), there was a sizable gathering of men, and some of them had weapons. In all likelihood the *familia* deliberately intervened in this volatile situation, using the weapon-possession laws to preempt any violence.

Although the *familia*'s intervention did not resolve the conflict, the episode shows them using the weapon-possession laws to coerce mortal enemies effectively. How many more of the thousands of surviving weapon-possession cases had similar backgrounds, completely glossed over by the formulas of notarial recordkeeping, is impossible to say. But there is also evidence that the *familia* brought weapon-possession and curfew charges against the da Panico and Galluzzi households during periods of conflict between those noble families and the commune.[55] Although the da Panico and Galluzzi were noble families, the examples above show that the *popolo* coalition policed the violence—or potential violence—of its own members with the same vigilance.

When prevention failed, the weapon-possession laws allowed the *familia* to suppress outbreaks of violence, without any regard for whether that violence was taking place within the "legally sanctioned" context of vendetta. For example, in June 1294, the *familia* arrested Don Filippo, the rector of San Geminiano, after they saw him toss a knife on the ground. The priest spent four days in jail before he could post bail.[56] (It seems the commune was reluctant to deliver this cleric to the episcopal court.) In his defense, Don Filippo argued that there had been a street fight in front of his church that day and men had drawn knives. In an attempt to play the role of peacemaker, he had taken a knife from one of the combatants and tossed it away. Two witnesses confirmed this. As one testified, Don Filippo had intervened in the "great *rumor* and *rixa*" in front of his church "lest an evil befall," and the knife's owner had only let Don Filippo have the knife when he noticed the *familia* arriving on the scene.[57] The court acquitted Don Filippo accordingly.

While there are no indications that mortal enmity led to this fight, the *familia* could not have known this at the moment of intervention, nor would they have cared. This was hardly the only arrest they made for an illegal weapon in the midst of an assault or attempted assault.[58]

So far, we have seen the *familia* use the weapon-possession laws to discipline warring parties and quell street violence. These laws allowed the *familia* to police mortal enemies in a third, more sweeping way: through a licensing system for the privilege of wearing armor. The evolution of this system was complex and is difficult to date precisely. The 1252 statutes do not appear to have prohibited "defensive arms" or the long sword (*spata longa*) at all, but a 1262 ordinance alludes to such a ban. The 1262 law lamented that men at war (*habentes guerram*) often fell victim to "assassins and bad men who did not fear the bans of the podestà and commune of Bologna," because they themselves were afraid of the statutory penalties for bearing arms. Lawmakers reasoned that they would not be such easy victims if they were protected, and therefore ordained that all men at war and "all others wishing to bear [arms]" could—at the discretion (*arbitrium*) of the podestà—wear armor and carry a long sword without suffering any penalty.[59] The reference to the podestà's discretion may indicate a permit system, but the 1288 statutes and other sources point to a *reformatio* made under the podestà Giovanni Cari (1263) as the definitive source of the podestà's licensing authority.[60] A 1265 law issued by Loderingo degli Andalò and Catalano di Guido—two members of the military order known as the *frati gaudenti* who had been appointed governors of the city in a time of upheaval—reveals that the podestà's permission came in the form of a written license.[61] It allowed anyone embroiled in "war or hatred" to receive a license to wear armor "for the protection of his person," so long as he gave surety that he would not harm anyone.[62] Furthermore, the 1263 *reformatio* appears to have granted *contadini* and members of the merchants' and bankers' guilds the right to wear armor without receiving any permit or giving any surety, a provision that remained in effect as late as 1288. For its part, the 1288 law prohibited foreigners (anyone not from Bologna's city or district) from receiving a license, with the exception of students, who could secure one for a surety of 300 *lire* if (and only if) they were at war.[63] However, a 1293 provision revised these rules to prohibit anyone—citizen, *contadino*, or foreigner—from wearing armor in the city without a license. It stipulated that any citizen could acquire a license, provided that he gave surety for 200 *lire* and swore an oath before the podestà's notaries that he would obey the podestà's mandates and not harm anyone. The paper license itself was to cost no more than 3 *denari*. *Contadini* could wear armor in the city for three days after their arrival, but beyond that had to receive a license for a surety of 100 *lire*. Foreigners could receive a license for a surety of 300 *lire* only if they could prove through their oath and the testimony of two or more witnesses that they were at war (*gueram habentes*).[64] Finally, a 1295 provision amended the law on *contadini*, prohibiting them from wearing armor in the city at all without a license.[65]

The licensing regime was established to allow men at war to defend themselves, not to sanction violence between mortal enemies. In their oaths, permit recipients swore not to assault anyone during the podestà's reign—to wear armor for the purpose of self-defense only.[66] By the same token, the only foreigners who were allowed to receive permits were those who swore they had mortal enemies.[67] A notarial entry from 1303 records how five Florentines—likely White Guelfs exiled from their city just months before—swore such an oath before the podestà: "They stated that they wished to bear defensive arms since they have hatred and war, because of which it is appropriate to bear these arms, and they fear lest they be struck, and for this they are prepared to give their word."[68] Around the same time, three Bolognese citizens vouched for a man from the nearby rural commune of Medicina that he was at war and had hatred, which made it "necessary for him to guard his person."[69] Perugia had a similar licensing regime that allowed men who had "just cause" to wear armor to give surety for that privilege, swearing not to harm anyone.[70]

The *Corone ed Armi* series shows, once again, that the podestà and his *familia* implemented these laws diligently. Lists of license recipients indicate that, by the late thirteenth century, the issuing of armor permits was a major duty of the podestà's office. Between November 1298 and April 1299, for example, the podestà's notaries issued nearly 1,200 permits.[71] Permits also had to be renewed at the start of every podestà's term (typically every six months), as the heralds reminded city residents on a regular basis.[72] Furthermore, it was the *familia*'s job to make sure that men who wore armor through the city were carrying a valid license and were not in possession of assault weapons, which the permit did not cover. Trial records show that the *familia* frequently did report individuals for wearing armor without a permit or while carrying an expired one. For example, in July 1299, the police reported three men for wearing armor with expired permits (*boleta vetera*). At least two of them, Giacomo Boattieri and Andalò Trentinelli, were from elite political families, but all were convicted anyway.[73] A series of cases from July 1302 are also illustrative. Caza di Duccio, charged with wearing armor in the Piazza Maggiore, told the court that he had forgotten his permit at home. He produced two notarized documents proving his membership in an arms society and was acquitted. (Apparently the court accepted membership in an arms society or guild as proof of license, though it is not clear that legislation had relaxed the requirement for all citizens to carry a written permit.) Answering an identical charge on the same day, Pietro Cardini protested that the podestà's notary had written a new arms permit for him just two days prior to his encounter with the *familia*. The notary in question and two other witnesses confirmed this as well as Pietro's membership in the Society of Drapers, resulting in his acquitttal.[74] A few days later, the *familia* reported finding three men with armor but expired permits. Two of these managed to prove that they had in fact renewed their permits, but the notary Gerardo Bontalenti could not and so he was convicted.[75] All in all, the *familia* on patrol seem to have paid close attention to men wearing armor and, in the absence of a valid permit, made residents prove in court their right to wear armor.

The commune's licensing system was a remarkable departure from custom, which, as late as the 1250s, had allowed anyone to wear armor in the city without appeal to the government. By the 1260s, this customary right had become a privilege to be awarded by the authorities and verified by the police. Indeed, the licensing system enhanced the commune's ability to monitor and police violence in two significant ways. First, it required individuals who felt threatened by mortal enemies to seek the government's permission for the right to protect themselves. Only men who would come before the podestà's notaries and swear an oath—thereby making it public knoweldge that they had mortal enemies or considered themselves likely to have them—were allowed to wear armor in the city. Second, and by extension, the permit system allowed the *familia* to focus their patrols on men who were likely to practice vendetta. By wearing armor in public, an individual both signaled that he had mortal enemies and invited the *familia* to check his permit. When they did check his permit—and searched him for other illegal weapons—the *familia* were in effect reminding him that it was illegal to assault those enemies. Thus, far from legitimating vendetta, the permit system actually sought to limit individuals' ability to pursue it.

Furthermore, judges did not accept mortal enmity as an excuse for ignoring the commune's weapon regulations. Trevor Dean has already made this point more generally about judicial practice in Bologna, and the *Corone ed Armi* registers show this to have been true in weapon-possession cases as well.[76] Indeed, some defendants tried to excuse themselves on the grounds that they had mortal enemies, but I have found no cases where this defense proved effective. For example, in August 1291, Graydano di ser Fantolino explained to the judge that he had been carrying a knife in his stocking for his personal protection since his brother "had died" (i.e., been killed). The judge convicted him nonetheless.[77] In March 1296, the *familia* discovered Giacomino, a resident of Modena's *contado*, in Bolognese territory with an iron helmet (*cervelliere*) and shield, but "had great difficulty capturing him" when he attempted flight. Later in court, Giacomino explained that he had fled because he mistook the police for "bad men," and that he was being especially vigilant at that time because he was in the midst of "a great war" (*magnam gueram*). But as soon as he recognized the armed men for the podestà's *familia*, he had come to them straightaway—or so he claimed. Whatever the truth of the matter, the judge convicted him according to statute.[78] Similarly, in 1295 two brothers from Bologna's *contado* argued in their defense that they had been carrying assault weapons because they had "many mortal enemies."[79] Their witnesses confirmed that they carried weapons "out of fear and for their defense because of the wars that they have," particularly with two members of the powerful Galluzzi family, Lippo and Galluzzo, who had been banned for murdering their uncle a few years earlier.[80] Once again, the judge convicted them according to statute. Simply put, the statutes did not allow men at war to bear arms, and the podestà's judges upheld those laws faithfully.

RESTRICTING THE RIGHT TO WAGE WAR

Bologna's government played an increasingly coercive role in the enforcement of weapon-possession laws over the course of the thirteenth century. For many generations, presumably, there had been no restriction on individuals' right to carry a knife or sword in the city, and certainly no need for a government-issued license to wear armor. By the 1230s, lawmakers had banned combat knives and other assault weapons; by the 1260s, they required a government-issued permit for armor.[81] Later ordinances even attempted to ban all knives with sharp points.[82] In the same period, the podestà's *familia* began patroling the city daily and focused those patrols on men carrying weapons.

The growth of the communes' police power in the thirteenth century is part of a larger story that, decades after William Bowsky's pioneering study, still deserves fuller treatment.[83] For the purposes of this chapter, it is possible to situate the policing of illegal weapons in the context of government efforts to repress interpersonal violence. It would be anachronistic to characterize these efforts as the suppression of "private warfare," a phrase that does not appear in the sources and that assumes the legitimate right to use violence fell along a private-public divide.[84] In reality, the *guerre* of private actors could shade into factional conflict and have public implications.[85] Yet the evidence suggests that Bologna's *popolo* regime increasingly sought to prevent the "illegitimate" interpersonal violence of private collectives such as *guarnimenta* and *consorteria* (in contrast to the "legitimate" violence of public collectives such as communal and *popolano* military organizations). Besides the weapon-possession laws, some statutes denied individuals the tools and tactics of urban warfare. For example, one statute prescribed harsh penalties—up to and including decapitation—for arson, shooting arrows in the city, or throwing stones from one's house at night.[86] Another prescribed a range of penalties for using catapults or similar machines of war to hurl objects at the communal palace.[87] Other statutes placed restrictions on armed groups, denying citizens the right to organize for violence; one statute prohibited anyone from exiting the city armed in the service of someone else without the podestà's express permission.[88] A 1290 regulation (*reformatio*) gave the podestà and *capitano* the authority to prosecute anyone who participated in a military expedition (*andata, guarnimentum*, or *munitio*) without their permission.[89] An ordinance of 1311 gave the podestà jurisdiction over battles involving more than ten persons on each side.[90] In the same vein, lawmakers restricted the right to maintain a personal retinue. According to a 1293 provision, any citizen or foreigner at war could travel with a retinue of armored (but not armed) servants for his protection, but only if he submitted all of their names in writing to the podestà and provided surety for each of them to have an armor permit. The bishop of Bologna could keep up to twelve fully armed *familiares* and the abbot of Nonantola up to six, provided that the podestà's notaries had recorded their names and they wore an indentifying marker (*intagla*).[91]

Conversely, Bologna's lawmakers increasingly reserved the right to take vengeance to the *popolo*'s militias or arms societies.[92] From the 1280s, Bolognese law mandated that whenever a magnate attacked, killed, or kidnapped a *popolano*, the public courts and all shops were to close until vengeance was taken.[93] The podestà was to blazon this order across the city as soon as he learned of such a crime, and fine any public official, merchant, or tradesman who kept his business open in the sum of 25 *lire*.[94] This law expanded an earlier measure from 1259, which had ordered the suspension of business only when an *anzianus* or consul was attacked.[95] Records of the heralds' proclamations show that these laws went into effect on multiple occasions. For example, in the middle of Carnival in 1291, the podestà ordered a halt to all business until "vengeance has been taken for the *popolano* wounded by one of the magnates."[96] On Ash Wednesday at vespers, he lifted the decree "because vengeance has been taken in the aforesaid crisis of the *popolano* wounded by the magnate."[97] By making collective vendetta a legal obligation, the *popolo* ensured not only that vengeance would be taken, but also that an attack on one member would be felt as an attack on all—if only because of the profits they lost when they had to close their shops.

In practice, the organized violence of collective vendetta was hardly distinguishable from warfare. For example, when members of the Baccilieri and de' Berni families killed a member of one of the popular militias in 1286, the *popolo*'s response was devastating. An unspecified number of guilds and militias "ran to burn down and destroy" the properties of Ramberto Baccilieri, the judge Lambertino de' Berni, their kin, and "other persons"—from their towers and homes in the city to their vineyards and woodlands in the countryside. Judging by the podestà's later compensation (using public funds) of several master carpenters and masons who helped to raze the homes of the Baccilieri, this *vindicta* was likely a well-organized and legally sanctioned event.[98] But for good measure, the *consiglio del popolo* passed a resolution in the aftermath granting legal immunity to everyone who had taken part in the arson, robbery, and general devastation on the grounds that it was all "for the honor, good state, and preservation of Bologna's *popolo*."[99] The practice of collective vendetta is also evident in Parma, where in 1294 the notaries' guild avenged the murder of one of its members in the village of Olmo. According to a later chronicle, an *anzianus* of the guild led 100 guildsmen to the village, where they seized two of the alleged malefactors and recovered the corpse of the victim. After Parma's court had hanged one of the captives and sentenced the other to perpetual imprisonment—and after the guild had given its deceased member a proper burial—they returned to Olmo in force to destroy the houses and properties of others banned for the murder. The chronicler even notes that the communal palace remained closed until the notaries had completed their *vindicta* and returned once again to Parma.[100]

The law of collective vengeance made vendetta a political obligation and brought asymmetrical force to bear on magnates who perpetrated violence. The underlying assumption was not that revenge should allow private actors to restore social balance, but that it should be taken by the organs of government to satisfy the ruling party's interest. The same assumption can be seen in the way the sources refer to corporal punishments carried out by the podestà as vendettas (*vindicta*).[101] And it can be seen in the *popolo* regime's punishment of its own members who used violence unilaterally. For example, in October 1300, the *consiglio del popolo* designated Zoenne Beccadelli as a magnate because he had mortally wounded another member of the *popolo* "without any cause, but only because of his power and arrogance."[102] Thirteenth-century communes did not claim a monopoly on the right to use violence, but increasingly they claimed the right to practice vendetta for public collectives and penalized acts of violence that took place outside them.

It is in this context that Bologna's laws prohibiting secondary vendetta, or revenge attacks by anyone other than the original offender and victim, should be read. Zorzi has argued that the "salient element" of these laws—which also existed in Florence—was their "recognition of the vendetta system as a common mode of conflict resolution and as a juridically legitimate institution."[103] Yet the evolution of Bologna's law actually shows the commune's growing intolerance of vendetta. The original 1252 law prohibited the victim of an attack from retaliating against anyone except his assailant, effectively placing kith and kin off limits. It threatened perpetual banishment and the loss of all private property as punishment, but provided for the ban to be lifted by consent of the victim or his heirs, meaning when a peace agreement had been made. This already placed a significant restriction on a practice that customarily required family members to avenge each other. But the penalties for violating this stricture also became progressively more severe. In 1265, the *frati gaudenti* (mentioned above) included a new version of this law in their ordinances to pacify the city. The 1265 law declared that those who killed someone other than the perpetrator in an illicit act of revenge would suffer the same penalty as any murderer (i.e., death) and all their goods would be bequeathed to the victim's heirs except for their houses and towers, which would be razed to the ground, never to be rebuilt. From there the penalties decreased, but they were still severe: 4,000 *lire* for inflicting serious injury, 3,000 *lire* for inflicting minor injury with bloodshed, and 2,000 *lire* for inflicting injury without bloodshed. If the offenders could not be brought into custody, they were to be banished permanently "as for a most serious crime"—regardless of whether the victim was killed or only wounded and regardless of any peace agreement—and all their properties redistributed or destroyed. The *frati gaudenti* passed these extreme sanctions "so that the city and district of Bologna might endure in peace and tranquility, and [so that] such an enormous, most serious, and heinous crime be extirpated by the root."[104] While this law might be interpreted as an emergency measure, it retained full effect—including the threat of perpetual and irrevocable ban—when the *popolo* regime revised the statutes in the 1280s.[105] These laws trended toward the growing repression of vendetta, not its legitimation.

CONCLUSION:
THE PROBLEM OF VIOLENCE IN THE ITALIAN COMMMUNES

The judicial sources thus do not sustain the notion that Bologna's government recognized vendetta as legitimate. On daily patrols, the podestà's *familia* worked to confiscate the tools of violence and ensure that no one walked the city streets arrayed for combat without the government's permission. The permit system also ensured that the *familia* would focus their attention on men who had, or thought they might have, mortal enemies. The podestà also used the weapon-possession laws, in combination with other coercive measures such as house arrest, to target families and individuals in the midst of conflict. The emergence of this new mode of policing should be read as the increasingly strict regulation of a customary practice. The weapon-possession laws emerged not in a police state but in a society where the right to bear arms and use them was widely shared. Furthermore, the policing of illegal weapons seems to have been part of a broader trend that saw government increasingly try to prevent violence from taking place outside of public collectives, and suppress it when it did. Thus, the Bolognese commune did not sanction vendetta in the sense of permitting it, but it did sanction, in the sense of penalizing, behaviors associated with it.

To be clear, this is not to argue for the state's inevitable or progressive monopolization of the right to use violence.[106] The communal "state" was not a unitary actor but an "organization of organizations," and the evolution of public institutions was a highly contingent and dynamic process.[107] Indeed, Bologna's citizen legislators had no concept of a state monopoly on violence; they could scarcely imagine a society where the right to violence was not shared among power centers.

However, it is a call for historians to focus once again on institutional change, rather than continuity in social structures. Since it is widely accepted that the communes were not modern, Weberian states, it should be no surprise that many communes did not expressly prohibit vendetta. Historians can safely assume that these governments did not claim a monopoly on the legitimate use of violence. (Indeed, it is somewhat redundant to highlight the legitimation of an institution that already enjoyed a degree of legitimacy.) What is worth underscoring, however, is citizens' efforts to constrain this institution—and warfare more generally—through new institutions of hegemonic justice. Historians have minimized this change in their reaction against earlier histories that were too teleological. But it remains the historian's task to explain—without the teleology—why this change took place.

If the recent spate of functionalist studies has downplayed institutional change, it may be because the functionalist paradigm is ill-equipped to account for it. By explaining how well institutions worked to maintain social cohesion, functionalism can overlook the drivers of change and even explain it away. In the case of vendetta, scholars' preoccupation with conflict resolution has also led them to misinterpret the social function of the institution. Vendetta is better described as a deterrent than a "balancing mechanism." Insofar as vendetta has a "positive value" in limiting violence, it does not derive from a symmetrical exchange that prevents escalation. Rather, it derives from the threat of retaliation, which aims to deter would-be offenders from acting violently in the first place. Thus, when an act of violence occurs between enemies, the institution has already failed. Moreover, this deterrent often does fail, because people frequently overestimate the advantage they have over their enemies and perceive the harms they suffer as worse than the harms they inflict. These cognitive biases make people prone to risk violence and to escalate conflicts out of proportion to the original offense.[108] Put another way, if vendetta is a "political game," the players often have different understandings of the rules to the game and are likely to miscalculate.[109] Thus, vendetta functions as a self-regulating mechanism more in theory than in practice. Vendetta may be a common solution to the problem of violence, but it is an unstable one. Reading vendetta as a process of conflict resolution effectively de-problematizes its violence and glosses over the instability inherent in the institution.

In reality, the problem of violence is one of the key drivers of social organization and institutional change.[110] Bologna's citizens voluntarily expanded their government's police power in part because they saw their own violence as a problem in need of a better solution. That is, the commune's governing elites knew the destabilizing effects of vendetta all too well, and they did not believe the practices of conflict resolution already in place were adequate for their security. If historians are to explain the growth of police power and hegemonic justice in the communes, they must understand violence the way the communes' elites did: as a challenge to be addressed, not a solution to conflict itself. That growth was neither linear nor inevitable, but it did take place in the context of political and social competition where violence was an omnipresent threat.

NOTES

1. This chapter is based on a paper given at the 2013 Annual Meeting of the Medieval Academy of America in Knoxville, Tennessee.

2. Zorzi, "Legitimation and Legal Sanction"; Idem, "Consigliare alla vendetta"; Idem, "'Fracta est civitas magna.'"; Idem, "La cultura della vendetta"; Idem, "Conflits et pratiques infrajudiciaires"; Idem, "'Ius erat in armis.'" See also his edited volume: Idem, *Conflitti, paci e vendette*.

3. Indeed, the term *faida* does not appear in the sources for medieval Italy; Dean, *Crime and Justice*, 124.

4. Zorzi, "Legitimation and Legal Sanction." Quotes on 44, 47–48.

5. For example, see Massimo Vallerani's recent statement that vendetta was "widely recognized in the communal statutes"; Vallerani, *Medieval Public Justice*, 116. For alternative readings, see Dean, *Crime and Justice,* 123–32; Idem, "Violence, Vendetta, and Peacemaking"; Idem, "Marriage and Mutilation"; Maire Vigueur, "Progetti di trasformazione"; Idem, *Cavaliers et citoyens*.

6. Following Douglass North, this study defines institutions as "the rules of the game" that constrain human behavior. These include both formal rules, such as written laws, and informal norms, as well as the means of enforcement; North, *Institutions, Institutional Change*, 3–4. On the functionalist paradigm, see Netterstrøm, "The Study of Feud."

7. On the social functions of violence and hatred, see Skoda, *Medieval Violence*; Smail, "Violence and Predation"; Smail, "Hatred as a Social Institution"; Throop and Hyams, *Vengeance in the Middle Ages*; Rosenwein, *Anger's Past*. On the function of the law courts, see Vallerani, *Medieval Public Justice*; Wickham, *Courts and Conflict*; Kuehn, *Law, Family & Women*. Smail ties together all three threads in Smail, *The Consumption of Justice*.

8. The literature on conflict or dispute resolution in medieval Europe is vast, but highlights include Esmark et al., *Disputing Strategies in Medieval Scandinavia*; Tuten and Billado, *Feud, Violence and Practice*; White, *Feuding and Peace-Making*; Brown and Górecki, *Conflict in Medieval Europe*; *Le règlement des conflits au Moyen Âge*; Miller, *Bloodtaking and Peacemaking*; Davies and Fouracre, *The Settlement of Disputes*; Bossy, *Disputes and Settlements*.

9. On extra- or infrajudicial institutions, see Garnot and Fry, *L'infrajudiciaire du Moyen Age*; Geary, "Extra-Judicial Means"; Martone, *Arbiter-arbitrator*; Padoa-Schioppa, "Delitto e pace privata." To limit the literature on peacemaking to medieval Italy, see Kumhera, *The Benefits of Peace*; Palmer, "Piety and Social Distinction"; Jansen, "'Pro Bono Pacis'"; Zorzi, "Pace e conflitti"; Wray, "Instruments of Concord"; Sensi, "Per una inchiesta sulle 'paci private'"; Vallerani, "Pace e processo." The seminal work of anthropology is Gluckman, "The Peace in the Feud."

10. Sbriccoli, "Giustizia negoziata, giustizia egemonica." See also Zorzi's commentary: Zorzi, "L'egemonia del penale."

11. Zorzi, "Legitimation and Legal Sanction," 32, 42, 48. More broadly, see Freund, *Sociologie du conflit*; Miglio et al., *Amicus (inimicus) hostis*; Garnier, *Amicus amicis, inimicus inimicis*.

12. All societies face the problem of violence (i.e., the possibility in any group that some individuals will be violent) and devise institutions to manage or contain it; North, Wallis, and Weingast, *Violence and Social Orders*. For a comparative overview of vendetta across cultures, see Boehm, "The Natural History of Blood Revenge." For vengeance in a variety of medieval contexts, see Barthélemy, Bougard, and Le Jan, *La vengeance*.

13. Cf. Rubinstein, *Politics, Diplomacy, and the Constitution*; Heers, *Family Clans in the Middle Ages*; Celli, *Studi sui sistemi normativi*; Martines, *Violence and Civil Disorder*; Cecchini, "L'assassinio del padre del Poliziano"; Niccolai, *I consorzi nobiliari*; Maugain, *Mœurs italiennes*; Enriques, "La vendetta"; Dorini, "La vendetta privata"; Kohler, *Das Strafrecht der Italienschen Statuten*; Pertile, *Storia del diritto*, vol. 5; Burckhardt, *The Civilization of the Renaissance*.

14. Dean, *Crime and Justice*, 126–31; Idem, "Violence, Vendetta, and Peacemaking"; Idem, "Marriage and Mutilation," 7–9.

15. ASB, Podestà, Accusationes, Busta 1a, Register 4, 34v, 35r, 36v.

16. Frati, *Statuti di Bologna*, 268–72; Fasoli and Sella, *Statuti di Bologna dell'anno 1288*, 1:225–28. The statutes made an important exception for travelers, who could carry certain blade weapons (such as a knife) to and from the city gates, so long as they also wore a traveling cap and carried them unconcealed; see Fasoli and Sella, *Statuti di Bologna dell'anno 1288*, 1:227, 568–69.

17. For this argument, see Grundman, *The Popolo at Perugia*, 114; Salvemini, *Magnati e popolani*, 85. Vallerani agrees with Grundman's reasoning but with some reservations; see Vallerani, *Il sistema giudiziario*, 170–71.

18. Imperiale di Sant' Angelo, *Codice diplomatico*, 1:150. By the the 1160s and 1170s, the Genoese *compagna* seem to have relaxed some of these prohibitions, allowing swords and knives but not bows, crossbows, or lances. For a discussion see Epstein, *Genoa and the Genoese*, 36, 66–68.

19. Firnhaber-Baker, *Violence and the State*, 49–51, 77–79; Firnhaber-Baker, "Seigneurial War," 62–63; Gonthier, *Le châtiment du crime*, 55–59; Kaeuper, *War, Justice, and Public Order*, 239–40, 243–46; Toulet, "L'Incrimination de port d'armes"; Perrot, *Les cas royaux*, 152–54.

20. As in Bologna's later statutes, the decree granted exceptions to travelers, provided that they lay down their arms again upon returning home. Doeberl, *Monumenta Germaniae*, 49–51. The translation is from Henderson, *Select Historical Documents of the Middle Ages*, 208–11.

21. Fasoli and Sella, *Statuti di Bologna dell'anno 1288*, 1:569.

22. Piccolo, *Liber Augustalis di Federico II*, 23–27. The translation is from Powell, *The Liber Augustalis*, 15.

23. Doeberl, *Monumenta Germaniae*, 49–51. The translation is from Henderson, *Select Historical Documents of the Middle Ages*, 208–11.

24. On the *Corone ed Armi* series, see Tamba and Zanni Rosiello, "Archivio di Stato di Bologna," 572; Vallerani, "Giustizia e documentazione," 301–2. For studies that draw on the *Corone ed Armi* series, see Lansing, *Passion and Order*; Vallerani, "Giochi di posizione."

25. Frati, *Statuti di Bologna*, 3:392.

26. The *Corone ed Armi* register from 1293I contains a patrol log that records patrols virtually every day of the semester; ASB, Corone ed Armi, Busta 5, 1293I, Liber sive quaternus relationum, 55r–56r. In later years the notary recorded patrols separately from trial records to show the podestà's due diligence in executing his office; see ASB, Corone ed Armi, Busta 27, 1320I, Liber sive quaternus conmissionum (consists of 38 fols.), 2r–23r; Busta 27, 1320I, Liber sive quaternus continens in se conmissiones, 2r–24v; Busta 29, 1324I, 8r–22v; Busta 29, 1324II, 99r–115v.

27. A register from 1320 shows the *familia* patrolling the *contado* roughly twice a month, and trial records bear out that they did in fact make arrests for weapon possession and occasionally gambling on these patrols. See the entries in ASB, Corone ed Armi, Busta 28, 1320II, Liber sive quaternus continens in se conmissiones, 7rv, 19r–20v, 24r–25v.

28. Blanshei, *Politics and Justice*, 60, 93–95, 415–16; Pini, "Manovre di regime"; Vitale, *Il dominio della parte guelfa*, 119–23.

29. The sample registers are: ASB, Corone ed Armi: Busta 1, 1286II; Busta 3, 1291II, Liber de satisdationes armorum; Busta 8, 1296I, Liber continens inventiones and Liber inventionum; Busta 13, 1302II, Liber seu quaternus relationum; Busta 16, 1308I, Liber accusationum and Liber sive quaternus inquisitionum; Busta 20, 1313II, Liber sive quaternus commissionum (48 fols.), Liber sive quaternus commissionum (33 fols.), and Liber sive quaternus testium; Busta 28, 1320II, Liber sive quaternus continens in se conmissiones and Liber inquisitionum. For the rationale behind this selection, see Roberts, "Policing and Public Power."

30. For policing in other communes, see Crouzet-Pavan, "Potere politico e spazio sociale"; Zorzi, "Contrôle social, ordre public"; Manikowska, "Il controllo sulle città"; Eadem, "Polizia e servizi d'ordine"; Sbriccoli, "Polizia (Diritto Intermedio)"; Bowsky, "The Medieval Commune and Internal Violence." For a comparison of Siena, Perugia, and Orvieto with Bologna, see Roberts, "Policing and Public Power."

31. Impersonal institutions treat everyone the same, regardless of personal or social identity; North, Wallis, and Weingast, *Violence and Social Orders*, 23.

32. For example, a certain Bertuccio di Bonaiolo was one of eight men charged with violating curfew one evening in 1294. Only from his defense—a claim to legal privilege—do we know that this Bertuccio was Albertuccio Maranesi, from a preeminent family in the *popolo* coalition. ASB, Corone ed Armi, Busta 6, 1294II, Liber sive quaternus relationum (28 fols.), 7r.

33. Of the more than 200 total *inventiones* contained in the register, the only noble was Francesco Ramberti, convicted for breaking curfew; ASB, Corone ed Armi, Busta 3, 1291II, Liber de satisdationibus armorum, 34v.

34. Vallerani, *Il sistema giudiziario*, 171.

35. To give but one example, Romeo Pepoli was convicted for illegal possession of a knife in September 1294; ASB, Corone ed Armi, Busta 6, 1294II, Liber sive quaternus relationum (58 fols.), 23r.

36. ASB, Corone ed Armi, Busta 1, 1286II, 12r–18v. For examples of notaries convicted on weapon-possession and curfew charges, see ASB, Corone ed Armi, Busta 2, 1288II, 21v; Busta 5, 1293I, Liber sive quaternus relationum, 10r, 42r.

37. Lazzarini and Menant, "Les podestats"; Sabapathy, "A Medieval Officer and a Modern Mentality?"; Maire Vigueur, "L'ufficiale forestiero."

38. Vallerani, *Medieval Public Justice*, 272–305; Blanshei, *Politics and Justice*.

39. Lansing, *Passion and Order*.

40. Dubber, *The Police Power*.

41. The Boattieri and Ricci families included several important political figures among their ranks. Most prominently, Graziolo Boatteri held the office of *anzianus* nine times between 1283 and 1303, and Tommaso Ricci did so eight times between 1287 and 1309. The Boattieri were a family of mixed political status, however, with several magnates and belted knights among them, including Cervo in the note below. See Blanshei, *Politics and Justice*, 173, 285, 560–61.

42. In the examples below, the sources never explicitly use the terms *inimicitas*, *odium*, or *guerra*, but the context is clear. Most notably, the statutes allowed the podestà to confine "men of the city or district having a war"; see Fasoli and Sella, *Statuti di Bologna dell'anno 1288*, 1:186.

43. ASB, Accusationes, Busta 9a, Register 3, 1r. The sentence accorded with the statutory punishment for false testimony in a case of armed assault; see Fasoli and Sella, *Statuti di Bologna dell'anno 1288*, 1:213. For Giacomo Biasmaltorti's occupation as a notary, see Fasoli and Sella, *Statuti di Bologna dell'anno 1288*, 1:392.

44. Fasoli and Sella, *Statuti di Bologna dell'anno 1288*, 1:186.

45. The Boattieri party comprised Cervo and his sons Ubaldo and Niccoluccio, Graziolo and his brother Guido, Bonincontro, Giacomo, and two allies of the family, Giacomo Biasmatorti and Filippo Lisignuoli. ASB, Corone ed Armi, Busta 4, 1292I, Liber sive quaternus preceptorum extraordinariorum, 33rv. The Ricci party comprised Bartolomeo, Megliodeglialtri, Tommasino and his son Paolo, and their allies Giacomino and Giovanni Spavaldi, Gilio Azzi, and Gerardo da Cocca. ASB, Corone ed Armi, Busta 4, 1292I, Liber sive quaternus preceptorum extraordinariorum, 35rv. For Delfino del Priore and the Preti family; see Blanshei, *Politics and Justice*, 139n10, 451, 557.

46. ASB, Corone ed Armi, Busta 4, 1292I, Liber sive quaternus preceptorum extraordinariorum, 3r.

47. ASB, Corone ed Armi, Busta 4, 1292I, Liber sive quaternus preceptorum extraordinariorum, 33v–34r. On Balduino Balduini, see Blanshei, *Politics and Justice*, 245.

48. "Qui Ghinus retulit et dixit quod cum iret ante aliam familiam apud domum domini Dalfini del Priore ubi Bovatterii morantur ad confinia, vidit dictum Bonincontrum [de Bovatteriis] ire versus quandam domum, et cum ipse berrovarius dixisset eidem [illegible word], 'vade plane,' ita quod potuit eum bene audire, ipse Bonincontrus tamen passim passim [sic] intravit dictam domum, et postea cum exivit de dicta domo habebat arma defensibilia tamen sed habebat bulletam novam. Item Bencivenni Gilioli capelle sancte Marie de Karitate quem invenit Faldus ex berrovariis supradictis. Qui Faldus retulit acque dixit quod ipse scrutaretur pro armis inter homines qui erant apud domum domini Dalfini del Priore ubi morantur Bovatterii ad confinia, invenit quendam gradiolum parvum de ferire in terra post dictum Bencivenni, et ipse Bencivenni erat propior dicto gradio aliquo qui esset ibi et habebat arma defensibilia cum bulla nova." ASB, Corone ed Armi, Busta 4, 1292I, Liber sive quaternus preceptorum extraordinariorum, 20v.

49. By statute, whomever the *familia* found closest to an abandoned weapon was presumed to be its owner; Fasoli and Sella, *Statuti di Bologna dell'anno 1288*, 1:227.

50. ASB, Corone ed Armi, Busta 4, 1292I, Liber sive quaternus preceptorum extraordinariorum, 20v.

51. "Berovarii et familiares domini potestatis predicti . . . invenerunt et viderunt Bonincontrum condam Cambii de Boacteriis capelle Sancti Nicholay Burgi Sancti Felicis sub porticu domus in qua moratur ad confinia habentem unum cultellum ad ferire contra formam statuti ad latus. Qui Bonincontrus confessus coram dicto milite et notario se inventum esse cum dicto cultello." ASB, Corone ed Armi, Busta 4, 1292I, Liber inventionum armorum, 2v.

52. Zorzi, "Legitimation and Legal Sanction," 34.

53. ASB, Corone ed Armi, Busta 9, 1298, Liber in quo continentur omnes inventiones (28 fols.), 19v–20r.

54. Blanshei, *Politics and Justice*, 170–71.

55. Roberts, "Policing and Public Power."

56. ASB, Corone ed Armi, Busta 6, 1294I, Liber sive quaternus relationum (118 fols.), 82r.

57. "Dixit quod . . . facta fuit quedam rixa et magnus rumor iuxta ecclesiam Sancti Geminiani per plures homines in quo rumore et rixa traeri fuerunt et evaginari plures cutellos de ferire et quod dominus Dun Phylipus prespiter et rector dicte ecclesie traxit se ad dictum rumorem et rixam causa sedandi et amorcandi dictum rumorem et rixam ne mallum eveniret . . . " ASB, Corone ed Armi, Busta 6, 1294I, Liber sive quaternus testium, 53rv.

58. ASB, Corone ed Armi, Busta 6, 1294I, Liber sive quaternus relationum (118 fols.), 46r; Busta 13, 1302II, Liber seu quaternus relationum (102 fols.), 24rv; Busta 28, 1320II, Liber sive quaternus continens in se conmissiones, 15r.

59. "Cum homines habentes guerram timeant arma portare propter banna potestatis sepe per assasinos et malos homines, qui non timent banna potestatis nec comunis bon., qui feriunt ad postam oculte feriantur, offendatur et occidantur, quas offensiones de facili non recipient si muniti essent, statuimus et ordinamus quod omnes habentes guerram cum aliquibus et omnes alij portare volentes per civitatem et extra abque banno et pena eis auferenda a potestate possint suo arbitrio portare per civitatem et burgos civitatis arma ad defensionem sui, scilicet panceriam, gamberias, collarium, cerveleriam rotellam sive braçarolam et spatas longas pallam et non subtus." Frati, *Statuti di Bologna*, 1:272–73.

60. The published edition of the statutes gives Giovanni Cari's name (in the genitive) as Iohannis Canis; Fasoli and Sella, *Statuti di Bologna dell'anno 1288*, 1:228, 461. In a 1285 weapon-possession case, a *popolano* explicitly appealed to the *riformagio* made under Giovanni Cari in his defense; see ASB, Corone ed Armi, Busta 1, 1285, Liber inventionum portantium arma, 1v. The 1263 law, however, does not appear in the published edition; see Frati, *Statuti di Bologna*, 1:268–72.

61. On the *frati gaudenti*, see Gazzini, "I Disciplinati, la milizia dei frati Gaudenti."

62. Frati, *Statuti di Bologna*, 3:607.

63. Fasoli and Sella, *Statuti di Bologna dell'anno 1288*, 1:227–28.

64. Fasoli and Sella, *Statuti di Bologna dell'anno 1288*, 1:570. These rates—300 *lire* for foreigners, 200 *lire* for citizens, and 100 *lire* for *contadini*—were used in practice in two registers of arms sureties from 1295I: ASB, Accusationes, Busta 16a, Registers 9–10.

65. Fasoli and Sella, *Statuti di Bologna dell'anno 1288*, 1:585.

66. Fasoli and Sella, *Statuti di Bologna dell'anno 1288*, 1:570.

67. In a 1303 book of arms sureties from Bologna, some 83 of the 313 surviving permits, ranging in date from 3 January to 12 February, were for foreigners claiming feuds. Some were students, as one would expect in a university town, but a number were Florentines of the White Guelf party, exiled from their city just months earlier. ASB, Corone e Armi, Busta 13, 1303I, Liber ministralium (70 fols.).

68. "Dominus Mulla quondam Gheri de Florentia forensis, Vanni Zini de Florentia, Bindus Raynucii de Florentia, Lappus Alberti de Florencia sive Lipus, Vanni Resaliti de Florencia omnes comparuerunt coram domine potestate et dixerunt se vele portare arma defensibilia, eo quia habent hodium et gueram propter quod oportet portare ipsa arma, et timent ne sibi offendantur et de hoc parati sunt fidem facere." ASB, Corone ed Armi, Busta 13, 1303I, Liber ministralium (70 fols.), 56v. Another group of seven Florentines who took the same oath that February is explicitly identified as "of the party of the Whites of Florence"; 70v.

69. "Juraverunt [et] dixerunt quod dictus Facius habet geram et hodium propter quod oportet custodire personam suam." ASB, Corone ed Armi, Busta 13, 1303I, Liber ministralium (70 fols.), 49r.

70. ASP, Capitano, Busta 4, No. 1, 15r–33r. For one who had "odium mortalem," see 20r. Between 5 January and November of that year, some fifty-three individuals received armor permits from the capitano. ASP, Capitano, Busta 4, No. 3, 1r–5v. ASP, Capitano, Busta 19, No. 8, 1r–10v. In one month (4 November to 6 December), some sixty-two individuals with two guarantors took this oath.

71. The notaries granted licenses to 1,117 citizens, 33 foreigners, and 48 clerics. ASB, Corone ed Armi, Busta 9, 1298–99, Liber in quo scripte sunt promixiones.

72. New podestà typically sent out heralds to announce that it was time to renew permits. For examples see ASB, Sindacato, Busta 5, 1288I, Liber gridationum (22 fols.), 1v; Busta 10, 1293II, Liber bannorum (50 fols.), 3v. ASB, Corone ed Armi, Busta 7, 1295I, Liber cridationum, 1v.

73. ASB, Corone ed Armi, Busta 10, 1299, Liber inquisitionum (40 fols.), 2rv. The third's patronym is not given.

74. ASB, Corone ed Armi, Busta 13, 1302II, Liber seu quaternus relationum (102 fols.), 10v–12r.

75. ASB, Corone ed Armi, Busta 13, 1302II, Liber seu quaternus relationum (102 fols.), 17v–18v.

76. Dean, "Violence, Vendetta, and Peacemaking," 4–10.

77. "Interrogatus ubi habebat dictum cultelum, respondit in calcca et dixit quod portabat occasione custodie persone sue quia quidam suus frater fuerat mortuus." ASB, Corone ed Armi, Busta 3, 1291II, Liber de satisdationes armorum, 29v–30r.

78. "Qui Jacominus ad eius defensionem dixit quod est forensis et de comitatu Mutine et de terra Bazani et ibi habitat cum familia, quando vidit familiam potestatis credit quod essent malli homines, quia ipse habet atentum magnum et magnam gueram et ipsa de causa afugit, et quando scivit quod erat familia potestatis incontinenti venit ad ipsos, et bene habebat dicta arma ut confesus fuit." ASB, Corone ed Armi, Busta 8, 1296I, Liber inventionum (40 fols.), 15r.

79. "Item quod predicti Ugolinus et Berthollus habent multos innimicos mortales in civitate Bononie et districtu et ideo portabant dicta arma." ASB, Corone ed Armi, Busta 7, 1295I, Liber testium, 72r. The *familia*'s denunciation is in ASB, Corone ed Armi, Busta 7, 1295I, Liber relationum, 14v.

80. "Audivit eis dici quod portabant dicta arma eis inventa propter metum et ad eorum defensionem propter guerras quas habent." ASB, Corone ed Armi, Busta 7, 1295I, Liber testium, 73v. For their enmity with the Galluzzi, see 72rv.

81. Lawmakers may have banned the long sword when they instituted the permit system in 1263; certainly by the time they reaffirmed the permit system in the 1280s, it was listed among the forbidden "offensive arms." Fasoli and Sella, *Statuti di Bologna dell'anno 1288*, 1:225–28.

82. "Item quod nullus habere vel portare cutellum parvum cum ponta vel magnum per civitatem Bononie vel burgos in banno ad voluntatem domini potestatis." ASB, Sindacato, Busta 7, 1290II, Liber continens bandimenta, 4v.

83. Bowsky, "The Medieval Commune and Internal Violence."

84. Firnhaber-Baker, "Seigneurial War," 37–38; Kaminsky, "The Noble Feud in the Later Middle Ages," 55–56. Cf. Shaw, "Honour, Faction and Private Wars"; Carbonnières, "Le pouvoir royal"; Algazi, "Pruning Peasants"; Idem, "The Social Use of Private War."

85. Dean, "Marriage and Mutilation."

86. Frati, *Statuti di Bologna*, 1:278. Fasoli and Sella, *Statuti di Bologna dell'anno 1288*, 1:207–8.

87. Frati, *Statuti di Bologna*, 1:281–82. Fasoli and Sella, *Statuti di Bologna dell'anno 1288*, 1:208–9.

88. In some versions of this law, the podestà could not grant such permission without the approval of the council, *anziani*, and consuls. Frati, *Statuti di Bologna*, 1:273–74.

89. Fasoli and Sella, *Statuti di Bologna dell'anno 1288*, 1:179. An earlier statute had prescribed the death penalty for anyone who led a *guarnimentum* into the city in times of unrest; Fasoli and Sella, *Statuti di Bologna dell'anno 1288*, 1:216. Bologna's heralds also proclaimed a ban against making a *guarnimentum* outside of town in August 1293; ASB, Sindacato, Busta 10, 1293II, Liber bannorum (50 fols.), 22r. The word *guarnimenta* literally meant "garnishments," or in a military context "fortifications," but metaphorically signified the ensemble of men and materiel used in military actions. Antonio Pertile defined the *guarnimentum* as any cavalcade of twenty or more armed men, but Bologna's laws do not seem to have specified a minimum number of participants; Pertile, *Storia del diritto italiano*, 5:487. For two trials that feature *guarnimenta*, see ASB, Corone ed Armi, Busta 24, 1317II, Liber sive quaternus inquisitionum, 72rv; Liber sive quaternus intentionum, 10v–12v. ASB, Inquisitiones, Mazzo 96, Register 2, 21r–29r.

90. ASB, Provvigioni dei Consigli Minori, 4/213, 2r.

91. Fasoli and Sella, *Statuti di Bologna dell'anno 1288*, 1:570. For a case where the podestà acquitted one of the bishop's *familiares* of wearing armor illegally after he showed his license, see ASB, Corone ed Armi, Busta 3, 1291II, Liber de satisdationibus armorum, 42r. For a record of the commune granting an individual license to keep an armed bodyguard on account of his *guerra specialis*, see ASB, Corone ed Armi, Busta 4, 1292I, Liber sive quaternus preceptorum extraordinariorum, 12r.

92. Fasoli, "Le compagnie delle armi." On the popular militias more broadly, see Poloni, "Disciplinare la società"; Artifoni, "Corporazioni e società di 'popolo.'"

93. Fasoli and Sella, *Statuti di Bologna dell'anno 1288*, 1:289, 318, 383.

94. Fasoli and Sella, *Statuti di Bologna dell'anno 1288*, 2:289.

95. Frati, *Statuti di Bologna*, 3:304–5.

96. "Item . . . quod nullus ad pallacium veniat causa jus petendi ex nunc in antea nec alliquis exerceat artem alliquam nec stationes aperiant vel laborerium faciant in civitate Bononie vel burgis contra formam ordinamentorum factorum in pena contenta in dictis ordinamentis donec non fuerit facta vendicta de quodam homine de populo vulnerato per unum ex magnatibus." ASB, Sindacato, Busta 8, 1291I, Liber continens relationes, 18v.

97. "Item . . . in ora vesperi quod quilibet possit laborare et aperire suas stationes et venire ad pallacium causa jus petendi ab inde in antea cum facta sit vindicta de predictis crisis de quodam homine populari vulnerato a quodam magnate." ASB, Sindacato, Busta 8, 1291I, Liber continens relationes, 19r.

98. ASB, Sindacato, Busta 3, Liber preceptorum, 1286II, 106v–7v.

99. ASB, Riformagioni 126, 17r, 24 November 1286. Blanshei mentions this incident in *Politics and Justice*, 384n233.

100. *Chronicon Parmense*, 66. The episode is discussed in Guarisco, "Il 'popolo' e le pratiche della vendetta."

101. One statute, for example, mandated that no *vindicta* or *pena personalis* except flogging was to be carried out within the city limits unless it was deemed necessary; Fasoli and Sella, *Statuti di Bologna dell'anno 1288*, 1:237.

102. "Absque aliqua causa sed solum propter potentiam et superbiam suam." ASB, Riformagioni 153, 254r, 19 October 1300.

103. Zorzi, *La trasformazione*, 168.

104. "Et ut civitas bonon. et eius districtus in pace et tranquillitate persistant. Et tam enorme tanque gravissimum malefitium et nefarium radicitus extirpetur, inviolabiliter observari." Frati, *Statuti di Bologna*, 3:609–10.

105. Fasoli and Sella, *Statuti di Bologna dell'anno 1288*, 1:209–10. The statute made one small modification: there is no 4,000-*lire* penalty for serious wounds inflicted, though the 3,000- and 2,000-*lire* penalties remain.

106. An interpretation criticized in the current historiography, for example, as in Firnhaber-Baker, *Violence and the State*, 3; Zorzi, "Justice," 513.

107. For the state as an "organization of organizations," rather than a single actor, see North, Wallis, and Weingast, *Violence and Social Orders*, 30–31.

108. Pinker, *The Better Angels of Our Nature*, 529-47.

109. For a similar argument, see Hyams, "Neither Unnatural Nor Wholly Negative," 220; Brown, *Violence in Medieval Europe*, 9, 17–20. For vendetta as a "political game," see Zorzi, "Legitimation and Legal Sanction," 49, 51.

110. North, Wallis, and Weingast, *Violence and Social Orders*.

Chapter Two

Criminal Court Procedure in Late Medieval Bologna

Cultural and Social Contexts

Massimo Vallerani

In the middle of the thirteenth-century Bologna was a city in full socioeconomic development, with continuous demographic growth that brought its population to approximately 50,000 in the early years of the Trecento. During these decades (1250–1320) its political institutions were transformed profoundly, with approximately 15,000–18,000 men participating in various roles (communal councils, public offices, societies of the *popolo*); a figure possibly equivalent to all male adults able to bear arms and participate in public life. During the same period the judicial administration of the commune was able to treat in its tribunals approximately 1,600–2,000 cases per year, divided between trials conducted by accusatory procedure and *inquisitio ex officio*, with thousands of persons involved as litigants, *procuratores* (lawyers), and witnesses; and this figure includes only those in the penal sector because no data for the civil courts have survived. Yet Bolognese criminal court procedures can be better understood in a framework removed from these rough quantitative estimates for the very reason that no other public institution demonstrated an equal capacity to control and involve the population both before and after these decades.

Indeed, the interrelationship between participation in public life of such a great number of people and the development of an equally broad judicial system is clear: communal justice was not only a means of controlling urban conflicts; it also was a true instrument at the disposal of the commune for governing the population. Public justice meant, in the first place, recourse to a trial—a form of confrontation regulated according to a procedure developed by judges and judges in the twelfth century, on the basis of Roman models adopted to the demands of large urban communities. It is from procedure and its function in the construction of public justice that we must take our point of departure.

To be sure, at times procedure may seem to project a sense of distance from "real" things and persons, a perception nourished by its linguistic difference (Latin), by the complexity of its theoretical apparatus, and by the intrusive presence of law professionals who act on behalf of litigants.[1] But are these reasons sufficient to categorize procedure as an object remote from people and their lives? Is it conceivable that societies, such as those of the medieval cities, that had assigned great space to conflict and to the jurisdictional dimension of public life, could have elaborated a procedure so far from reality and incomprehensible to the parties involved? Clearly we need a new perspective in order to understand the functionality of procedure and the trial in the construction of a public system for the containment of conflicts.

Procedure is a direct reflection of the logic that rules social ties and the relations of power. For the jurists of the *ancien régime*, who in the absence of civil codes, founded their treatises essentially on the jurisdictional acts of the tribunals, the trial was a great "theater of the world," a collective representation of the reality constructed by a chorus of judges, litigants, advocates, and rulers. Each had a particular design, a characteristic vision of reality and of the interests to be defended. The instruments for reconstructing and imposing this vision were defined by procedure. The final image was indeed due to interactions among the individual actors. We need to ask first of all what was the logic by which these images were able to be reconstructed and then to verify, in the judicial acts of the communal tribunal (the accusations and inquisitions) the picture that emerges.

THE ORIGIN OF BOLOGNESE PROCEDURE AND JURIDICAL CULTURE

I first address the cultural and political context from which the new processual models arose during the course of the twelfth century. The elaboration of procedure in the High Middle Ages, commonly called Romano-canonical, occurred in a very varied cultural context, often outside of the Bolognese law schools where above all judges and advocates, deeply employed in practice, invented the new procedure, reconstructed from Romanist materials long included in the proceedings in use at ecclesiastical courts.[2] The first *ordines* were, in fact, redacted by jurists of the Church, such as the first *ordo* written by Bulgarus for the pontifical chancellor Aimerico (1123–41); a collaboration between civilists and canonists in the matter of procedure, which remained active until the beginning of the Duecento, at least to Roffredo who treated civil and canonical trials jointly, or to Riccardo Anglico, an English canonist who wrote his manual on procedure in 1197 at Bologna.[3] Although toward the end of the twelfth century the signs of a greater autonomy of the canonists becomes evident—for example, the texts on canonical procedure tend not to cite Roman law, depending only on decretals—nevertheless a model of a public trial was established and relatively shared in the civil and ecclesiastical tribunals of the late twelfth century, one based on procedure of an accusatory type.

It was a trial that anticipated at least four large phases: the accusation, with the choice of a juridically relevant fact, one that expressed a violation of a law for which the person (*actor*) sought reparation; a series of citations, which called into court the accused (*reus*); the formal commitment of the litigants to prosecute the trial (*litis contestatio*) and a probative phase, which divided the tasks in a symmetrical manner between the actor who had to present witnesses and the *reus* who could present witnesses in his or her defense; both parties had to furnish a list of the subjects on which the questioning of the witnesses would be made (*intentiones*). The equalization of the parties and the selection of the rational arguments to be proven with witnesses (and documents) were not the fruit of an open and "democratic" political system; they were first of all a response to the need of the Church to find a valid judicial instrument for internal use, one guaranteeing equality before the law, in which all the parties were subject to the same obligations (as occurred between the members of the same institution). It also needed to constrain its own enemies, often lay aristocrats who based their pretexts on their power and recognition of a customary "state of fact"; to find and accept valid legal rules for everyone (for example, on the issue of possession). The *ordines*, in short, served to diffuse a new type of trial that offered a more general and logical legal "order," a useful instrument of governance for those who sought to construct a new form of political community in which internal conflicts were regulated and the litigants of external ones were compelled to follow a shared program to resolution.

The Collective Elaboration of Procedure at Bologna

This practical dimension of the trial remained very much alive during the early years of the twelfth century. Indeed, the range of its diffusion and the circulation of texts relative to procedure were even further amplified. A second generation of *ordines iudiciarii*, this time written at Bologna, often by non-Italian authors, proves the existence of the twofold development of juridical culture: on the one hand Bologna became the center of the production of professional knowledge in the processual field; on the other hand procedure became an object necessary and shared by a great part of European culture—English, German, and French professors were all active in the spread of the new model of the trial in local courts.

Furthermore, and this is a specificity particular to Bologna, the acts of procedure were fixed in written formularies inserted in notarial manuals, called *artes notarie*. The most important of these were redacted by masters of the Bolognese *studium*, first by Raineri da Perugia (ca. 1230) and then by the most renowned of all at the European-wide level—Rolandino Passaggeri.[4] These great notaries did not limit themselves to proposing models of acts, but also furnished examples of procedure, that is to say, they organized the individual acts within a framework of procedural logic. The masters understood that procedure was a sequence of coherent acts and that the validity of the trial depended on the correctness of each individual act, with particular attention to certain apparently secondary passages, such as the citation of the accused person, the threat of the ban in case of failure to present oneself in court, and the hearing of witnesses: three very sensitive passages that often caused the annulment of the trial if executed in an irregular manner.

To this work of collective elaboration were added of course the jurists. The masters of the university of Bologna, from the 1260s and 1270s, employed themselves directly in the redaction of numerous *quaestiones* relative to the trial,[5] above all in points relative to the law and to the duties of the *procuratores* and surety guarantors (*fideiussores*) in their activities representing the accused,[6] and also paid considerable attention to the ban, a processual instrument hardly regulated by the law, which led to numerous discussions relative to its legitimacy.[7] We shall see that discussions were not limited to the schools, since the topics of the *quaestiones* often were taken up in actual proceedings and often resolved with *consilia* by these same jurists.

Finally, procedure was included in the communal statutes of Bologna, especially in the redaction of 1288, which contains a complete exposition of the acts and temporal terms to be fulfilled by the litigants. The rubric considers all the logical nodes of procedure that are also present in the manuals on procedure: qualifications for becoming an accuser; absolute freedom to accuse (not to be constricted to the accuser); economic obligations for one who accepts the trial (commitments and monetary sureties); specific and predetermined terms for the unfolding of the trial.[8]

Duecento Bologna: The Trial as an Instrument of Government

The circulation of procedural models was extensive because procedure interested diverse social actors and especially because the ordered carrying out of the trial had by now become an indispensable instrument of communal government for regulating the collective life of the city. By the mid-Duecento the communal courts were able to accept and execute hundreds of trials, involving thousands of Bolognese citizens as litigants, *fideiussores*, advocates, and witnesses. This public and shared aspect of the trial must be emphasized because it is absolutely central to understanding the social function of public justice as an instrument of the city's governance.

The Model in Action: Its Serial Character and the Coherence of Procedure

The convergence of so many cultural actors in the execution of procedure produced a model of the accusatory trial that was coherent and stable over time. Appearing in the earliest surviving judicial registers, which go back to 1256, the trial unfolds according to phases very similar to those described in the *Artes notarie*.[9] The *libellus* of the accusation is located at the center of the folio, with the names of the accuser and the accused, a brief description of the fact and the request for punishment (*unde peto eum punire secundum formam iuris et statuti*). On the left side are written the acts of the accusation: the appearance of the accused and oath of innocence, the promise to present oneself; on the right side the acts of the accuser: oath of truthfulness, promise to continue to prosecute and fulfill the term of eight days for the presentation of proofs.

After giving the *libellus*, the accuser has to swear to tell the truth (*non animo calupniandi*). The formula is exactly that described by Rolandino in his *Summa*. After the oath comes the first *assignatio terminum*: five days for prosecuting the trial and three for defending oneself in case of a voluntary interruption.[10] The appearance of the accused is the minimal condition for starting a trial. The formula is synthetic, but contains three different acts: denial, equivalent to the *litis contestatio* (*Comparuit predictus accusatus et lecta sibi dicta accusa per seriem negavit omnia que in ea continetur*); a promise to present oneself in response to the precepts of the podestà (*et cavit de presentando se*); and a promise to pay the penalty in case of condemnation (*vel de solvendo condempnationem sub pena in statutis contenta)*; all of which is guaranteed, yet again, by one or more *fideiussores*.

Thirty years later the model is similar, but more complex, above all because of the obligations undertaken by the accuser. In the registers of 1286, when the more complete surviving series of trials begins, the accuser must promise not only to continue the accusation, but must also present a *fideiussor* who commits himself on behalf of the accused to continue the trial and not to present false witnesses. The accused is the recipient of three acts: the *citatio prima, secunda crida e citatio cum tuba ad videndum ordinari terminum*, with the greatest attention to the modality of the citation which has become the first cause for nullification of trials. Then follows the presentation of the accused, his or her oath *de veritate*, and surety. After the assignment of temporal terms, the witnesses are called and also they must take an oath to tell the truth and give *fideiussores* for the very large sum of 300 *lire*.

All these formulas served to certify the wish of the parties to stand in judgment and to discourage the use of instrumentalist and frivolously motivated accusations.

Once these initial obligations were fulfilled, the duration of the trial in general was very rapid. The accusatory trial was relatively swift-moving because the procedure had prefixed terms, which in general were respected: once the parties presented themselves they had eight days in which to bring forward their proofs; the promises and sureties were concentrated within two days; the entire procedure lasted on average twenty days (at least this was true for the trials of the 1280s—during the 1290s the average length of trials expanded to approximately thirty days).

Since the appearance of the accused indeed signified the acceptance of the trial, it should be noted that this was maintained at a relatively high level throughout the Duecento: on average 70 percent of the accused presented themselves with their *fideiussores*. The second aspect that emerges in a macroscopic manner from the registers is the increase in the number of intermediaries in the trial—by the late thirteenth century *procuratores* and *fideiussores* crowded the tribunals and their presence had become indispensable for the functioning of public justice. Without them the trials could not even begin.

Intermediators and Initiation of the Trial

Between 1256 and 1286, as noted above, procedure remained more or less the same, while the number of processual intermediaries was augmented very notably. This element is a particularity of the Bolognese trial: on average for every trial more than ten such persons were involved—trustees (*curatores*), *procuratores*, and *fideiussores*, but there are cases where just the *fideiussores* alone come to more than ten to fifteen persons. The principal circumstances calling for intermediaries were three: a trustee was needed when the accuser was a woman, a minor, or a child (*pupillus*), or if the accuser were absent at that moment from the city; a *fideiussor* to secure the monetary guarantees of the accuser and accused so that the trial could go forward; and a *fideiussor* also when witnesses were present. While the *curatores* are found in approximately 40 percent of the trials (this datum is based on a sample from 1285–88), the *fideiussores* are always present, at least in all the trials in which the imputed presented themselves.[11]

In effect, *fideiussores* had become the hinge of the system and their guarantees served everyone.[12] But who were these persons who offered themselves as guarantors, exposing themselves to the risk of paying very high sums? In contrast to the *procuratores*, who were always notaries and who often exchanged roles with the trustees and notarial redactors of documents, the *fideiussores* present a less clearly defined picture. On the one hand, they appear often in various trials, a sign that they formed a group of professional intermediaries in the processual setting, acting on behalf of both parties (accusers and accused). On the other hand, similarly often, the *fideiussores* were the relatives or friends of one of the parties, who effectively played a role in support of one of the two litigants. The network of intermediaries, whether professionals or family/friends, rendered possible the confrontation in court, because it assured not only the full juridical capacity of the persons who defected (with their *procuratores*), but also the minimum necessary guarantee of "recognizability" to the litigants, by their demonstration of their ability to find guarantors of their cases who would obligate themselves in person with a disbursement of money.

In the urban culture of the communal era, this search for the guarantee of persons was a vital requirement, necessary precisely to render individuals recognizable as socially and economically trustworthy subjects. Numerous passages of public life called, in fact, for the presence of *fideiussores*: from the election to public offices to the assignment of particular administrative posts. In every case, the guarantee played a fundamental role in guaranteeing that the person was known and merited the financial help of other persons. The fact that such a high number of guarantees was obligatory to carry forward a judicial case confirms the determination of the commune to reserve the accusatory trial to persons selected on the basis of their recognizability and trustworthiness. The trial served in certain ways to define and to give legitimacy to one's personal identity. It is also from this perspective that we need to examine the functioning and function of the trial in Bolognese society of the late Duecento.

Litigants and the Reconstruction of the Fact

Consideration of some quantitative data, already noted, is needed in order to understand the conflictual dynamics and role of the trial. The 1280s and early 1290s experienced the greatest development of the accusatory public trial with the highest number of cases, at least according to the data available for medieval cities—from 800 to 1,200 per semester (data confirmed also by registers of acquittals). The explosive expansion of the number of trials seems to have been initiated early, and shows clearly the great capacity of the commune to manage a large number of judicial cases brought by citizens. During the same years, however, the commune put into effect an extremely extensive system of control over persons banned for political reasons, with the compilation of lists of philoghibelline enemies (the Lambertazzi); redesign of the boundaries of citizenship with the urban *estimo* of 1280 and the *contado estimi* in 1282,[13] and experimentation with a new institutional system under corporative leadership, with the *anziani* (elders), elected by the guilds and arms societies, initiating periodic verifications of all the lists that contained and certified the various memberships in urban public life. With all the limitations that can be found in this system,[14] these are the years of the greatest expansion and greatest involvement of the urban population in all sectors of the system of governance. The quantitative expansion of the accusatory trial was very probably connected to this communal-podestarial institutional system, with its nature still relatively open, formed by the councils of the commune and *popolo*, the *ministrales* of the popular societies, the *anziani e consoli*, and other magistrates of exigency (*balìe*).

Another element also confirms the vitality of the judicial system: the high level of acceptance that continued to characterize the accusatory trial. During the 1280s, as noted, between 70 and 80 percent of the accused presented themselves in response to the accusation, bringing with them at least two *fideiussores*. The responses of the citizens to the summons of private accusation is in essence positive: the trial was still viewed as an arena of confrontation worthy to be frequented.

Also, as a third structural element of Bolognese conflictuality indicates, the majority of conflicts of a violent nature occurred between persons who probably did not know each other or live in the same quarter of the city. For the period 1285–94 only a minority of the conflicts happened within the same parish (*cappella*): 25 percent in 1285 (and that is the highest percentage); in the other years the figure oscillates between 15 and 20 percent of the crimes denounced within the city (13.7 percent in 1286—25 of 156 crimes); and 15.8 percent in 1287; 21.9 percent in 1298.[15] These data indicate that in the majority of cases the infrajudicial mechanisms for the containment of conflicts among neighbors were not able to function. The communal tribunal served, instead, as the principal arena for resolution of those clashes, and the rules of confrontation, inasmuch as they were rigid and apparently formal, were considered acceptable by a significant part of the Bolognese population.

To do what? To obtain justice from an efficient system of public punishment? Or to put an enemy into a difficult situation or annoy an adversary? The question has been raised for the medieval era by various scholars, who have noted the contrast between the high number of accusations ("input" of the system) and the low number of trials that ended with a sentence or with a sentence of condemnation. Many trials, for example, at Marseilles (but in the civil sector), remained without sentences.[16] In other cases, as I have established for Perugia and Bologna, the majority terminated with an acquittal for lack of proof or for interruption of the case, that is to say, that the accuser did not terminate the *iter* and the case ended before the probatory phase.[17] Some scholars have hence hypothesized that public justice exhausted itself in an enervating play of accusations and counter-accusations in order to inflict the maximum damage on one's counterpart; or to display an atavistic and uncontrollable hatred, according to a theory that explains actions as reflexes of neuronal emotions refined by humans since the Neolithic age.[18] This openly reductionist vision of the value of the trial even renders superfluous the reading of the sources, since the judicial writings would seem to be no more than the transcription of a series of spiteful acts (tit for tat) that the parties commit in the course of the confrontation.[19] An alternative interpretive key must be found that restores social significance to the recourse of such a great number of people to the public tribunal. For this purpose I shall examine two particular aspects of the communal processual system of Bologna in the Duecento.

In the first aspect I seek to deepen our understanding of what actually happened within the trial. While a strategy of attack on the adversarial figure was ingrained in the processual encounter, it is true that many accusations focused sharply on the identity of the other party, portraying him or her as a possible criminal, guilty of acts against the law in addition to the charge in the accusation. To receive an accusation necessarily compelled one to the defense of one's personal reputation. For this reason the trial became an important act: not so much as an episodic demonstration of an emotion determined by our neuronal structure, but as a pragmatic construction of one's social identity, carried out within the trial. It is necessary to understand with what materials and model of reference this was accomplished.

In the second aspect I investigate the material dimension of conflicts that has yet to be brought to light. It is true that the majority of clashes were violent, but to concentrate only on violence as a constitutive element of conflicts risks creating a tautological circuit: people use violence because they are violent. Reading between the lines of many criminal court writings, one can understand that in reality the use of violence arose from a strong motive: a serried struggle for the possession of goods and properties, of money (loans), for the payment of wages or with respect to contractual relations, all determining components in human life. In short, my aim is to take a series of trials and read them according to an internal logic defined by procedure that translates conflicts into regulated claims over the objects and goods contested by the citizens of Bologna.

Reconstructions of the Fact and Identities of the Persons

As shown above, procedure permitted not only the intervention of more actors, but also a confrontation between more versions of the fact, or rather, between diverse versions of the conflict. The phases of definitions of the fact/crime that procedure provided corresponded, in fact, to the different images reflected in a broader clash. In the accusation, the choice was determined by the selection of the elements that were useful for indicating a *crime*: selected was the element of the fact that was penalogically significant—a physical or verbal aggression, the removal of an object. In the *positiones* (phrases that reconstructed the clash into brief sequences), the spectrum of the conflict was enlarged: the fact was reinserted into the weave of the relations between the two persons and very frequently, in this phase, a substantial movement of the center of interest of the conflict occurred—from the crime to the person. In the *intentiones*, instead, the elements that one party wanted to prove (called *capitula*) rewrote the fact into simple phrases, often very remote from the fact presented in the accusation. In this phase, in fact, the shift of focus of the trial, from the crime to the person who had committed it, had by now taken place. The accuser concentrated further on the negative characteristics of the putative criminal. But the contrary also occurred: the defense of the accused could emphasize the negative aspects of the accuser rather than the details of the crime imputed to him or her. Finally, the chapters of the *intentiones* became direct questions (*quaestiones*) to be submitted to the witnesses of the counter-party in a true cross-examination. It clearly comprised questions prepared with the help of *procuratores*, animated by the explicit wish to render it difficult for the witnesses to prove a fact without uncertainties; but it remained, or rather it consolidated, attention further toward the person rather than toward the facts.

The possibility of reformulating the true object of the conflict is therefore one of the most important elements for understanding the actual function of the trial and it is "Roman" procedure itself that permits it. Nevertheless, it is necessary to utilize an accessory documentation relatively infrequently present in the trial records and rarely studied by historians: above all the *intentiones* and the lists of questions (*quaestiones*) to be asked of the witnesses, which have survived as unbound folios sometimes attached to the *libri accusationum* or inserted in the registers of testimony in the series of *inquisitiones*. Only by broadening (and not by reducing) the documentary spectrum will we succeed in reconstructing the logic of the trial. This logic meant that the parties often found themselves in combat over their own identities and above all over their own good (or bad) *fama* according to the social models circulating widely in the medieval city. We shall see how many and which models were taken up and readapted to particular cases by the parties and how this adherence influenced the trial.

In the first case, a certain Mattiolo Bonacatti accuses a Donna Margherita, wife of Francesco of Prato, of having insulted him before the judge with "bad words": "You are the son of a usurer and thief and if I were a man instead of the woman who I am, I would strike you with a knife in your chest."[20] Margherita, however, was a foreign woman, a vulnerable status in a city that had drawn many immigrants from the *contado* without yet integrating them into a stable network of cognizance. Mattiolo Bonacatti in his *intentiones* (which have not survived) probably insinuated that Margherita was a prostitute and owner of a bordello. The focus of the trial thus moved completely from the initial fact (an offense of *verba iniuriosa* before the judge), to a seemingly accessory issue, that is, the trustworthiness of the woman. Margherita had, in fact, to defend herself from a second defamatory accusation (prostitution), and in the *intentiones* of her defense had to have recourse to models of the good woman of family in order to save and establish her own personal identity:

> [Domina Margherita] intends to prove in her defense that said Francesco holds Margherita as his wife and she holds him as her husband;
> *Item* that said Margherita has three children by said Francesco;
> *Item* that she is a person of good reputation and opinion and the same is true of Francesco;
> *Item* that she and her husband live in that house;
> *Item* that it is not true that she maintains prostitutes and other infamous persons.

In the next phase of the trial, the same elements become questions to be put to the witnesses, naturally with the intention of having them deny the accusation of prostitution. Thus, the witnesses presented by Mattiolo are asked: How did they know that Margherita was a prostitute, where was the house in which she lived located, in which part of the house had they seen prostitutes, what were their names, when had they seen them, and so on, and so on.

There is an analogous attention to the identity and reputation of the parties involved in a trial from 1286, a trial brought by Giacomino Avvocati against Biondo di Giacomino di Torre concerning the possession of a church in the Modenese territory.[21] The accuser maintains that Biondo did not hold the church by a just title because he was a layman; the logic of the *intentiones* of both parties revolves around the lay and clerical status of Biondo, as often happened in communal tribunals. The accusation, therefore, had to construct an image of Biondo as a layman; to prove that Biondo had been walking about as a layman for more than two years; that he wore a layman's clothes for more than two years; that he went every day to a tavern as did other laymen and with other laymen; that he had always resided at Bologna and that he publicly practiced the craft of a goldsmith as a layman.

On his part, Biondo had to defend himself from this portrayal of him as a layman and in his *intentiones* he sought to prove that he was really a cleric and *conversus* of the church of San Nazario. In his questions for the witnesses the encounter centered on what a cleric could or could not do in order not to be confused with a layman; a pure sequence of models of behavior, completely untied from the object of the contest—namely, the possession of the church of San Nazario. To the witnesses of his opponent Biondo asked: what have you seen that leads you to say that Biondo has the gait of a layman; where have you seen him walk like a layman, with whom and how many times; how does a layman walk and how does a *conversus*; and did not *conversi* walk with laymen and have conversations with them. Naturally, there were always questions relative to the fact, but the significance of the fact depended upon the condition of the person who committed it.[22]

The Material Basis of Conflicts: Lawsuits and Contracts

The importance of establishing personal conditions according to current social models depended certainly on the natural tendency of the persons in conflict to discredit their adversaries or to present themselves as a *bonus civis*; but it is explained also by the necessity of representing oneself in tribunal as a trustworthy person who advances a claim based on law or on an asset that belongs to him or her legitimately. Although the court was dedicated to penal crimes (*de maleficiis*), many conflicts were also tied to the possession of goods and properties, to money given in loan, to work to be remunerated. In other words, both the spirit of revenge (*vendetta*) which had given origin to the trial, as well as the surplus of violence generated *by* the trial (called *odium litis* by medieval jurists), did not annul motives that were concrete, material, and sometimes openly economic and often at the origin of the lawsuit.[23] Numerous signs present in various phases of the trial enable one to trace the violent acts of the clash back to a context of economic and work-related relationships which were often formalized with a contract.

The long lawsuit between Margherita and Mattiolo Bonacatti derived from an initial denunciation made by Mattiolo who had accused the woman of having rebuked him as the son of a usurer and a thief and of not being able to make a profit, which had probably occurred in a civil court in which the two had had a case for debts. The accusation of Giacomino Avvocati against Biondo, centered on his allegedly lay status, stemmed from contested rights over a church in the Modenese territory. In other cases as well the material dimension or aspects relating to the economic relations between persons emerge between the lines. In a series of questions to be given to the witnesses in a lawsuit brought forward by Pietro Struccha against two brothers, Martino and Benedetto, sons of Pietro Roagnani, accused of assault, the *procurator* of the two accused, after many other questions, referred to a lawsuit concerning unpaid work:

> *Item*: we affirm that if Martino and Benedetto had accused said Pietro Strunca because of the loss of earnings that Pietro was usually to collect for his work, it is asked how they come to know of it, where they heard this idea circulate, who had put it in circulation and from where it had originated.[24]

Thus, a broader examination of the procedural acts permits us to have a more refined picture of the function of the trial and of urban conflictuality other than that revealed by a simple reading of the initial acts of the accusation. As stated at the beginning of this chapter, accusatory procedure was not artificial and remote from reality, but allowed, at least in two aspects, the reinsertion of data from the real conflict that had provoked the trial. Furthermore, the processual encounter permitted and in certain cases sought to redefine the personal condition of the litigants, initiating a complex dialectical clash concerning their *fama*. Finally, in better documented cases there emerges a substratum of economic relations that already had been "contractualized" at the origin of the often violent disputes (loans, work contracts, tithes). One also finds a disequilibrium between the persons who attacked and better used the contracts and others, often accused, who apparently were less strong in defending their rights.

The trial functioned therefore also as an arena of clashes between segments of the population with different levels of access to resources, and also to the civic resources necessary to defend their rights in an urban context of rapid development. It is possible, in other words, that those who turned to the tribunals were that part of the population no longer subjugated by the violent emotions of hatred, but rather those who were involved in a network of economic and contractual relations of goods and properties and work services that justified a defense through a process open but costly in terms of time and money. The accusatory trial was based on the *voluntas* of the parties to prosecute the trial and their capacity to rely on a network of intermediaries who rendered them credible and recognizable before the court, permitting them in this sense to conduct a regulated encounter.

THE INQUISITORIAL SPHERE OF ACTION

Of course accusation was not the only system for administering justice in the city. Around the 1230s and 1240s one finds the earliest and rare evidence in the Italian communes of trials *ex officio* or *per inquisitionem*—trials initiated by the civic authority (the podestà) after becoming aware of a collective *rumor* relative to a crime. Even if the guilty person were not known, the simple existence of a crime pushed the public authority to intervene because "crimes should not remain unpunished." This initial formula of the inquisitorial trial immediately reveals its origin—the ecclesiastical *inquisitio* formalized by Innocent III in canon 8 of the Fourth Lateran Council of 1215.[25]

Origin and Models

A literal renewal of the canonical text characterizes the first lay manual that inserted the inquisition firmly among the procedures at the disposal of the communal tribunals: the *Tractatus de maleficiis* of Albertus Gandinus, a judge and jurist of importance, who served many times in Bologna, Perugia, and other large Italian communes.[26] Actually, Gandinus was not able to do otherwise than adopt the text of the canon *Qualiter et quando* because he did not have other models available. Only the ecclesiastical *ex officio* trial offered him a procedural plan and a solid ideological justification: public authority had to concern itself with crimes and hence was able (or had to) to do so without an accusation by a party because punishment was in the interest of that authority. Moreover, in the decretal *Licet heli* (which is found in canon 8), *fama publica* took the place of accusation, because it rendered public a scandal provoked by the behavior of a person.

Nevertheless, we must take account of two elements. The first is that this *inquisitio* should not be confused with that in use against heretics. The Innocentian model was born as a "discreet" (or in part secret) procedure against crimes committed by members of the clergy. The pope wanted to achieve a twofold purpose: to verify the consistency of the *rumores* against a given person (a secret inquest before an actual trial) and, if the *fama* were well-founded, to open a formal *inquisitio* against the person, which preserved, at that point, the right of the defense to a proper trial. In short, the pope wanted a filter for selecting which accusations were with foundation and above all which should be followed by a trial and which were better to drop.

Against heretics the trial model was distinctly more severe, because its point of departure was the conviction that to be a heretic was *per se* a crime that allowed only abjuration or punishment; the search for the truth, in other words, coincided with the extirpation of the truth from the body of the guilty person. The most diffused technique for doing so was, as is well-known, violent interrogation and the administration of torture during the proceedings. In the late Duecento, when Gandinus wrote, this model was by then codified into numerous treaties and legitimated by pontifical decretals which, among others, had to be inserted within communal statutes.[27] The connection between ecclesiastical and lay models was therefore direct, but the transfer to lay tribunals of techniques so diverse from the procedures in use in ordinary cases (accusatory trials) could not be direct and painless.

Even Gandinus obviously struggled when he had to justify the superiority of the inquisitorial over the accusatorial trial. To be sure, only inquisition permitted the discovery and punishment of crimes, but it was equally difficult for communal governments to accept the total subordination to the judge of the will of the accuser: to constrain the principle that a trial could be initiated only by the will of the injured party was not something easy to accept for everyone. There was another problem, often neglected by historians of criminal justice: inquisitorial power gave, or was supposed to end by giving, immense power to the judge and the podestà, to two foreign magistrates, from outside the city—an arbitrary power that the governing citizens were not always willing to leave completely in the hands of foreign functionaries. In sum, the theoretical apparatus of Gandinus, adapted in good measure from the Innocentian model and tainted with anti-heretical methods in the chapters on torture, met considerable difficulties once applied in a great commune such as Bologna. Next I will review some aspects of this complex process of the adaptation of *ex officio* procedures.

The Spheres of *ex officio* Procedure at Bologna

From a technical point of view, it is not correct to speak of a single inquisitorial procedure counterposed to the accusatorial. The confrontation-clash between accusatorial and inquisitorial procedures, taken up by many historians,[28] does not take into account a fact that only research into the registers of a great archive permits us to see: the existence not of one, but of multiple procedures of an inquisitorial type, a group of proceedings at the basis of practices in the communal cities.[29] In this sense, the communes already used *inquisitio* before adapting ecclesiastical models, although only in the central decades of the Duecento did they establish a model in use in ordinary criminal justice. But also in this sector, it was never a question of a single model. At Bologna, for example, there existed at least three typologies of trials *ex officio*.

First, collective inquests (called *inquisitiones generales*), in which all the *ministrales* of the urban parishes were interrogated from a list of predetermined crimes: it was a form of collective inquest similar, in certain aspects, to that of the inquisitors of heretical depravity in the villages that they visited periodically (and also similar to episcopal inquests). Despite the great deployment of money and men, from these inquisitions almost no crimes were uncovered; their efficacy was very minimal, but evidently the rituality of the public reading of the list of crimes and the filing past of the *ministrales* who responded out loud before the judge of the podestà were elements of public theater more important than the actual results obtained; they reaffirmed that the commune had responsibility for periodically "purifying" the city of the more serious crimes (heresy, homicide, prostitution, gambling).

A second type of inquisition was that relative to crimes committed in the *contado*, called the *malefici novi*. Denunciations were presented by officials of the *contado* for crimes committed in various villages in the city's territories, possibly a sign that control by the city was penetrating more deeply into the *contado*, and perhaps intentionally so on the part of those governing, but also in this case the results were relatively modest. To be sure, crimes were brought to light, but almost never was the guilty person identified, and when in rare cases, the name of a possible criminal was found, such persons never presented themselves in court and were placed under a ban and condemned in contumacy. Despite the low level of punishment, these inquisitions served, however, to gather denunciations of extra-urban crimes, demonstrating to everyone the existence of an authority responsible for receiving notifications of crimes. Again, rather than to punitive efficacy, it is necessary to pay attention to the symbolic function of confirming the presence of a civic jurisdictional system.

The third type of trial was a true inquisition *ex officio* for a crime committed in the city for which it was necessary to discover the culprit. In appearance, this trial followed closely the Innocentian model: a *vox* reached the podestà, often already with indication of who the guilty person was; he or she was cited three times and if they presented themselves at court the trial continued according to a path in part similar to that for an accusation (promised surety, witnesses in favor); if instead the imputed did not present themselves after three citations, they were placed in ban and, if the crime were one with effusion of blood, a mortal ban, which meant condemnation to death in case they were captured.

The outline of actions was thus a simple one, but hid a more complex one. As I have noted elsewhere, inquisitorial procedure could change according to who the protagonists were.[30] Some procedural mechanisms functioned only under certain conditions: if the imputed presented themselves with *fideiussores*, for example, and there were no negative elements that prejudged in an obvious manner their credibility, in general they were not imprisoned and were granted a suitable period for their defense. Testimony was gathered in the same way as in accusatorial trials, with cross-examination of the witnesses. To be sure, the procedural picture remained more severe, the rules more constricted, but this did not cancel certain guarantees that integrated citizens enjoyed.

This pattern is found in many of the trials conducted by Albertus Gandinus, discussed above, who was a judge at Bologna in 1289 and again in 1294. Gandinus was a severe judge; in 1289 he had already written the first draft of his *Tractatus* and in Perugia had put into practice the inquisitorial procedure that he had so praised. At Bologna he applied it with particular scrupulousness against *delinquentes* who rendered the city insecure. He had prostitutes arrested and expelled from the city if they were found within 30 *braccia* of the cathedral, as called for in the statutes (after having ordered the notaries to measure the distance with the *pertica*, a special pole of measurement). Having had one of these women tortured, he then had her hair shaved.[31] He showed himself to be inflexible with those who committed theft in shops, an act that constituted a direct threat to the class of mercantile shop owners to whom he promised law and order.[32] He was also very skillful in discovering plots to use false accusation to strike an adversary, a crime that he detested and which he punished with severity.[33] When, however, he found himself facing someone of good *fama* and testimony in the person's favor, even if they seemed suspect, he was unable to do otherwise than yield to the evidence and free the presumed criminals. On 11 May 1289 Gandinus received a notification against a certain Tonsolo and Nicolao who were accused of having committed a theft in a house in the rural commune of Castel Brittoni.

The two imputed presented themselves on 16 May, in time to avoid being banned, and promised to appear in court and provided two *fideiussores*. They were not imprisoned. Everything depended on the testimony of witnesses: many confirmed that there existed a *vox* in the village that these two men had committed the theft, but they also attested to the good personal *fama* of the two imputed. The distinction between *fama* of the fact (the theft) and *fama* of the criminal (good) is extremely clear and ultimately won the imputed victory.[34] The next trial shows instead how the inquest could depart immediately from the *fama* of the person. On 16 May Gandinus opened a proceeding against Pagnone, son of Aleotto the tavern keeper, who was accused of having knocked off the hat and struck a certain Filippo. The formulary initiating the trial is explicit concerning the object to be investigated and it is the *fama* of the imputed:

> *Item* June 1 the said judge intends to make an inquiry against said Pagnone who is said to be a public and famous thief and also a man of bad *fama* and condition and infamous for other various and diverse bad deeds.[35]

In other words a condition was the object of the trial, not a crime. When Pagnone presented himself he was immediately arrested and taken to the lower chamber, as usually happened in such cases. On 22 May, however, he was freed, having provided a surety, a sign that he had succeeded in finding guarantors and thereby avoided further imprisonment. Acquittal at this point was probable. More frequent, however, were the cases that were never truly tried because of the absence of the imputed; to be sure, the imputed was placed under ban as a confessed criminal and anyone could kill him or her, but the inquisitorial machinery had not been truly put into operation.

It is difficult to extend these data and compile statistics over time; the data change from year to year, without therefore yielding a true evolution of the forms of justice. Much depended on the judge and the quantity of crimes committed between persons able to present themselves and sustain a trial. Constant, however, remained the "global" dimension of the trials: an average number of approximately 200 cases per year. It could happen that in some years this threshold was passed, but not by much. There were structural limitations that conditioned the activities of the judges *ad maleficia*. In the first place their numbers: two judges and four notaries who were personally responsible for carrying out all the procedural steps, such as citing the imputed, interrogating them, transcribing the acts, finding and interrogating witnesses, and finally determining the sentence. Even an indefatigable worker like Gandinus could not complete more than 100 cases per semester. It is true that in the following years the number of *berroerii* (proto-urban police) was increased, but the investigative apparatus remained limited to two judges and a few notaries. Even the quantitative data of the Trecento, while indicating a certain superiority in the number of cases *ex officio* over those accusatorial, do not seem to present a great discontinuity on average of this range.[36]

In my opinion, however, this is not the principal issue. Of greater importance for portraying the function of *ex officio* procedures is the *flexibility* of the pathways of public justice. Even inquisitorial procedure permitted, as noted above, a plurality of possible effects dependent on the power relations and conditions of the persons involved. In particular, the inquisitorial module can be divided into three possible types of trial: first, an abbreviated trial (the anti-heretical module) of persons already declared suspect and subjected to torture and then, in case of confession, to corporal punishment or a capital sentence. Second, a series of trials never truly initiated that were terminated immediately with banning of the imputed who had never presented himself or herself. Third, a complete trial, with presentation of the imputed, a defense, and cross-examination of the witnesses, whose outcome was not at all foreseen or predetermined.

These three forms reflect the three diverse functions of public justice: first, to eliminate immediately the rejected, the dangerous persons, guilty only of the life they led and their appearance; second, to put to flight those who were unable to sustain a trial and who accepted living under a ban; and third to grant a trial, relatively impartial, to suspect persons who, however, could post sureties and prove their good *fama*. In these last cases, testimony assumed the opposite function it had served in the attacks on the imputed: in the defense they served, in the first place, to prove the good *fama* of the imputed person, showing that he or she could not have (or probably was not likely to have) committed that crime. In this interwoven verification (of the fact and of the person who had committed it), the procedural picture was more severe than in accusations. For example, torture was foreseen and sometimes applied in doubtful cases, although this happened in only a few cases each year. But apart from the quantitative problem, what emerges is that every case had its own history: a pathway tied to the gravity of the crime, to the personality of the individual, to the office that decided if torture was to be applied. Torture was a known instrument, but applied with discretion, adapted to circumstances, and was not automatic.

At the center of the diverse types of inquisition existed a sector where, however, torture was always applied, with regularity—in the case of clearly suspicious persons or banned persons who were captured and condemned to death. Some registers of capital condemnations have survived, with confessions of the guilty who had confessed under torture not only to a particular crime, but to an entire life of crime, confirming the totally antisocial and irredeemable nature of such condemned persons.[37] The long list of admissions made before the judges went beyond the effects of torture: it is obvious that the persons confessed to many more crimes than those which the judges had knowledge of or expected to hear. These sentences, all in all, are limited cases that confirm the necessity of punishment and demonstrate symbolically the capacity of the judicial system to eliminate the worst malefactors through their self-purgation.

It was a function that Albertus Gandinus, in his *Tractatus de maleficiis*, had explicitly assigned to the judge, taking up the maxim of Roman law according to which the *pretor* (magistrate) had to cleanse the city of *delinquestes*.[38] But above all Gandinus had put in the hands of the judges the most powerful judicial tool at his disposal: the capacity to make *fama*—even without direct witnesses of the fact—valid evidence for imposing torture, thanks to an exquisitely ideological rationale: "he who has sinned in the past may also do so in the future."[39] With their reprehensible behavior nailed to their inherently evil nature, the "usual suspects" had to be periodically eliminated from the city without a trial or with a very reduced probatory process, in order to mark the distance from normal trials regulated by norms written for *cives*.[40]

It is difficult to determine whether or not to label this system of justice as efficacious. If efficacy is based on the number of condemnations, then the response, if not negative, is at least in doubt. In the course of the Duecento and even in the century's final years, the number of sentences and trials carried to term was not very high; those in which proofs were found during the proceedings (hence excluding trials that ended in bans) lowers the figure further. It does not seem that the figures from samples studied for the Trecento radically modify this picture.[41] But above all one should address the underlying premise of this issue: to measure the efficacy of justice from the sentences assumes that the entire judicial system was governed by judges and the public apparatus, but that was not the case.

As noted above, the trials, whether by accusation or inquisition, depended in the first place on the presence of the accused/imputed and on their capacity to meet the confrontation, that is, the challenge of *fama* and the amount of help needed from one's network of social relations; and in the second place on the possible actions of the (foreign) judges who had broad discretionary powers, but nevertheless were bound by certain limitations. For example, the intervention of jurists and *procuratores*, which carved out ample space for modifying the trial, before and after the sentencing; or the provisions of the political authorities (the *consiglio del popolo* or the *anziani*) who could—and toward the end of the Duecento did do so often—issue new norms that supplemented or modified the *arbitrium* (discretionary power) of the podestà, or order special inquisitions, suspend condemnations, and direct public justice toward new political objectives. Two factors must now be considered that would at first seem exogenous to the judicial system.

EXTERNAL CONDITIONS: THE POLITICAL ELITE AND THE TRIAL

The broad participation of *procuratores* in trials has already indicated how important and vital the role of juridical personnel was in the functioning of public justice. If, however, the entire arc of the procedural *iter* (accusatory and inquisitorial) is considered, one finds that the typologies of interference and manipulation of the trial were even more numerous. The *procuratores* (who in general were notaries or *iudices*) were able to write "exceptions" (objections) on behalf of those they represented and, if these were accepted, the judge of the podestà asked for a *consilium sapientis* from a jurist or *doctor legum*.

Jurists, Advocates, and the *Consilium*

The system of exceptions-*consilia*, as has been amply demonstrated, represents one of the most incisive forms of interference by local jurists in the administration of justice entrusted to foreign magistrates.[42] This dialectic between foreign and citizen jurists is to be emphasized because in effect the formal monopoly of penal justice in the hands of foreign magistrates generated continuous tensions with the local elites. At Bologna, the *consilium* was a means of bringing, at least in part, penal justice back under the control of the jurists (themselves part of the Bolognese Guelf aristocracy), at least while it was permitted to the jurists to intervene by means of a *consilium*. To be sure, the years between 1256 and approximately the beginning of the Trecento comprised a golden age for processual consultations. Already in the 1250s, in fact, an aggressive nucleus, formed by the greatest Bolognese jurists for giving *consilia*, was active in legitimizing the issuance and management of bans for the responsible administrative office of the podestà.[43] Odofredo, Rolandino de Romanzi, and others wrote numerous *consilia* of this type, almost always choosing annulment of the bans in which they found lacking certain formal normative requirements, above all at the point of citation (such as the absence of witnesses of the neighborhood at the moment of the reading of the ban). The topic remained a sensitive one in subsequent years: the *consilia* for annulment of bans were numerous throughout the Duecento. To be sure, the protagonists changed: in the 1280s the generation of the "moderns" came into the limelight. These were men who were already authors of famous *quaestiones* relative to the trial and active supporters of the rights to a defense of citizens involved in trials.[44]

Particularly rich in anecdotes on these topics is the *Tractatus* of Gandinus, who, when he served as a judge in Bologna, clashed many times with prestigious local jurists over arguments of the defense. The reasons at the bottom of the discord were for Gandinus obvious: multiplying the ranks of representatives with *procuratores* and advocates distanced the judge from direct contact with the imputed and therefore hindered the possibility of finding the truth (that is to say, of obtaining a confession).[45] Furthermore, Gandinus shielded himself behind a prohibition imposed by Roman law of representing a person in criminal trials, opening with jurists (above all those who were Bolognese) a conflict that was not merely technical. In the academic disputes (*quaestiones*), and above all in the *consilia*, the Bolognese jurists attacked this prohibition from every angle. Odofredo wrote that the *procuratores* were able to intervene or present exceptions and requests for delays in the terms assigned. He, along with Guido da Suzzara "et alii doctores" also maintained that a person imprisoned for homicide could name a *procurator* for presentation of witnesses for his or her defense.[46] In another *questio de facto que quotidie occurrit* it was asked if, before being tortured, a culprit could ask to make a defense; Lambertino Ramponi, *doctor legum* of the highest level at Bologna, had given a negative response, in the form of a *consilium*, to Gandinus himself: "On this issue at Bologna, I, Lambertino Ramponi, counseled, that according to the law, [a period to make a] defense was to be granted before [the administration of torture]."[47] Other thorny cases follow in the *Tractatus*, drawn from Gandinus's actual experiences. If the culprit wanted to appoint a *procurator* in his absence, how ought he to conduct himself? Here also a solution is given by means of a *consilium*: Dino del Mugello thought that it was possible to appoint a *procurator*, and affirmed this in a legal consultation requested by the podestà of Reggio Emilia, a sign that the case was an urgent one and needed a definitive learned opinion (evidence in itself that Bologna was the capital of consultations made at a distance).[48]

The fact is that the Bolognese jurists found in the issue of processual representation a justification for their doctrinal and professional activity. The possibility of intervention by a defender, just like that of a consultant in cases of doubt, needed broad guarantees in theory. Thus, the *quaestiones* of the masters amply acknowledge the elementary necessity of a pettifogging practice that had a deep-seated ideological foundation—the defense of the processual *ordo*.[49] This can be seen clearly in another *quaestio* taken up by Gandinus, relative to the possibility of blocking a trial in case the victim of the crime were a person under ban, and therefore not protected by communal law. It was asked, in particular, whether or not the request for suspension of the trial presented by the *procurator* of the accused blocked the *litis contestatio*. Lambertino Ramponi and Iacopo di Arena were of a negative opinion: according to them the trial had to continue because a peremptory exception could not block the *iter*.[50] But the stronger argument that shines through the allegations of Lambertino is of a more general nature: he, like other *doctores*, wanted to apply the guarantees of the civil trial to the criminal trial.[51] Therefore it was imperative to respect the provision of the *ordo iudiciarius* that it was not possible to cancel the entire trial.[52]

Other *consilia* found in the registers of accusations and inquisitions fully confirm this datum with respect to procedure and hence to the formality of the acts. The *consilia* insist often on the correctness of the documents of the accuser, on the presence of the *procurator* (always confirmed), or the suitability of the guarantees presented by the accuser.[53] This can be seen even better in the political trials against the Lambertazzi carried out by the *capitano del popolo*.[54] These cases, often initiated by a party or by an anonymous denunciation, preserve in large measure the characteristics of an accusatorial trial, but in some cases give access to procedural breaches that are far removed from the *ordo*. Concerning these topics the jurists intervened decisively, reaffirming not only respect for the procedural phases on a formal level, but also the correspondence to the *ordo* of the collection of proofs. Twice Lambertino Ramponi centered his *consilia* on the correct modes of gathering witnesses even in political trials, abrogating two trials about which there were doubts.[55] To this topic, in the same year, also turned Tommaso di Guidoni Ubaldini, when he not only admitted the possibility that two *confiniti* (Lambertazzi who were confined to specific territories) could select a defender (again in response to a problem raised by Gandinus), but established as a general principle that also in political cases it was "more fair" to admit a defender than to condemn a person who was absent and "undefended."

This political dimension is of special interest: a method of control existed on the merits of political trials exercised by a class of jurists who, on the one hand, collaborated with the political authorities (the Guelf regime), but, on the other hand, limited or sought to limit its most evident excesses. Emblematic of this two-faced function is the figure of Pace de Pacibus. He was a *doctor legum* (author of numerous *quaestiones*) who had led principal moments in the transformation of Bolognese politics, from the new *estimo* of 1281 (which remained in vigor with some additions to 1296), to the commission on the properties of those banned after the expulsions of the Lambertazzi of 1274 and 1282. Pace was ultra-Guelf in family and conviction; he supported the more radical regimes up to the beginning of the Trecento and succeeded in controlling *de facto* the trials on the assignment of the properties of the banned for the entire twenty years of that activity, furnishing numerous *consilia* to the judges of the *capitano del popolo*; perhaps also rendering almost obligatory the recourse to a *sapiens* (legal consultant) in trials relative to the patrimonial rights of citizens.[56] This use of the *consilium* is a characteristic often undervalued by the historians of Bologna, but if in penal cases the intervention of consultants was irregular, in trials that had property possession as their objective the *consilium* is always present—when property ownership and patrimonial assets of citizens were at play, control passed directly into the hands of local jurists.[57] In these *consilia* the defense of the property rights of the families of banned persons always prevailed. It was they, in fact, who often presented complaints against the awards made by the office that managed the properties of rebels. The jurists, if they verified that a certain property ought not to have been included in the list of properties given out in contract as a penalty for rebellion, arranged in the *consilium* for the restitution of that property to its legitimate owner. Naturally, in this as in other cases mentioned earlier, it was not only a question of an abstract defense of justice and of the law against abuses; rather it was a political choice by a professional class that was "inside" the regime, yet was tied to its own more influential leaders and to more contested decisions.[58]

The Communal Regimes and Justice: Experiments and Attempts of Control

Public justice moved within a complex political system, but one that was fragile in its load-bearing political structures. The communal regime was supported, in fact, by a delicate balance of institutions: podestà and foreign judges held a monopoly over criminal cases; an external procedure carried out and defended by a class of experts, with relative equality of citizens in front of the tribunal. But these parameters were not stable; they were subjected to a profound and prolonged restructuring from the early years of the Trecento. It is the achievement of Sarah Blanshei to have brought to light the nature of these changes and the tight interrelationship between "politics" and "justice"; to have shown the gradual ascent into communal institutions of a *popolare* oligarchy of great merchants and bankers who entered into all the *societates* and sought to condition the actions of the *popolo* government. It was a closure that made itself felt especially on the level, quite sensitive, of political justice—both within the trials against political enemies, identified each time with *ad hoc* provisions, and with a series of normative interventions that had the double effect, on the one hand, of protecting *popolani* from the justice of foreign magistrates, and on the other hand, of making harsher the sanctions against political enemies. A rapid succession of expulsions and readmissions took place between 1303 and 1306, when two different factions of Guelfs alternated in control of the government. In both moments, the victors ordered new inquests against their enemies, labeled the opposition families as "Ghibellines" or "magnates" (even if they were Guelfs and *popolani*) and granted to their own members special immunities from the ordinary tribunals. It was a chain-effect mechanism (penal construction of the enemy-ban-privilege) that could not help but have disruptive effects on ordinary justice.

This can be seen with greater clarity between 1310 and 1315, when the signs of a crisis in the system of ordinary public justice multiplied. On the political level accusations against enemy nobles and magnates increased; in fact, in the accusation registers, political trials appear more frequently, but in a context of the drastic reduction of the volume of accusations; from 800–1,000 each semester to only a few hundred per year.[59] At the same time, the instrument of privilege, first used with generosity but on a limited group of persons, was applied en masse: in 1310 the *consiglio del popolo* ordered a census of the newly privileged which amounted to the incredible number of more than 5,000 persons, who were virtually removed from the jurisdiction of the podestà since they could not be tried for most crimes.[60] Even the few trials that were initiated often ended prematurely, due to an increase in the number of withdrawals of the accusation on the part of accusers—a practice earlier very limited but by now greatly expanded, perhaps because of the increasing role of informal accords taken outside of the official trial.

All of this did not result, however, in an increase in the number of inquisitorial trials, or did so only in part. To be sure, in proportion to accusations, the *ex officio* trials did increase (with respect to the ratio of the 1280s), but in absolute terms it does not seem that inquisitions increased greatly with respect to preceding years.[61] If anything, trials did become more complex, longer, and were often tied to political exigencies of the moment, such as inquests into conspiracies and political crimes. Nevertheless, the significant datum from this restructuring of the judicial system seems to me to lie elsewhere, and again it has been brought into relief by the research of Sarah Blanshei: more than the substitution of one procedural method by another (inquisition over accusation), one finds a multiplication of diverse judicial instruments, not coordinated, but which added up to a tenacious attempt to take control of the requests for justice by the institutional bodies of the *popolo* (the *consiglio del popolo* and the *anziani*). Thus, the appearance of the *querela*, an original instrument for seeking justice put forward by an individual to the *consiglio del popolo*, in which a person could even be denounced for a given crime.[62] Development of the *querele* took place particularly during the 1320s, which together with secret denunciations became a potent weapon in the hands of more radical *popolani*.

Nevertheless, this increase in exceptional instruments did not coincide with construction of a strong and centralized system of justice. Rather, a phase of continuous political and institutional experimentation opened up that also led to the "suspension" of the commune under the regime of Bertrand du Pouget, papal legate and nephew of John XXII. It was during his governance that the supplication presented to the legate, "merciful father" of Bologna, emerged as a new instrument of judicial action. The practice received further development under the regime of Taddeo Pepoli (1337–47), when the practice of the supplication (and of the pardon, if it were granted), not only was superimposed on the ordinary judicial system, penal and civil, constituting a new jurisdictional level, supervised by a vicar. The signorial tribunal, as a result of the pardon, could re-examine or annul trials conducted by the ordinary civic courts.[63] It was a partial execution of the design, for long unfulfilled, of creating a judicial system entirely controlled by political power. To be sure, trials continued to be conducted, to varying degrees, throughout the century, but the social-cultural function of the public trial that had unfolded in the mid-Duecento as the great filter of interpersonal conflictuality involving thousands of citizens of diverse status, no longer rested on the solid ground vital for its continued development.

NOTES

1. Coss, "Introduction."
2. In general see Kuttner, *The Revival of Jurisprudence*, 299–323; Gouron, "L'enseignement du droit"; Cortese, *Il basso medioevo*, 151–58.
3. Fowler Magerl, *"Ordo iudiciorum vel ordo iudiciarius."* The first manual, an anonymous *De Actionum varietate,* goes back to the end of the eleventh century or the beginning of the twelfth; the *Quoniam eorum desideris* dates from 1135, then passes to the more mature *Cum esse Mantue* of Piacentinus, from 1160. On the models of accusation see Cortese, *Il rinascimento giuridico.*
4. Orlandelli, "Appunti sulla scuola bolognese"; Padoa-Schioppa, "Profili del processo civile."
5. Kantorowicz, "The *questiones disputatae* of the Glossators"; Bellomo, *I fatti e il diritto*; Fransen, "Les questions disputées." For Italian examples from the twelfth century, see Belloni, *Le questioni civilistiche*, 3–69.
6. Bellomo, Quaestiones in iure civili disputatae; Vallerani, "Il diritto in questione."
7. Milani, "Prime note su disciplina."
8. Fasoli and Sella, *Statuti di Bologna dell'anno 1288*, 1:169–71, Bk. IV, Rubric 1, "De accusationibus et denuntiationibus et quomodo et qualiter procedi debeat super eis."
9. Vallerani, "Giustizia e documentazione."
10. "Cui assignatus est terminus V dierum prosequendi dictam accusam, et trium dierum si non prosequeratur, ad suam defensionem."
11. Vallerani, *Medieval Public Justice*, 141.
12. There were at least four types of sureties in trials: 1) the guarantee of the accuser after the oath *de veritate* for 20 *soldi*; 2) the guarantee of the accused when they presented themselves—at a rate significantly higher, depending on the severity of the crime—which was guaranteed by at least two persons, but the number often rose to four or six *fideiussores*; 3) the guarantee of the accuser when promising not to present false witnesses, usually comprising two persons; 4) the guarantee of the witnesses before their depositions, from two to four persons.
13. Milani, *L'esclusione*; Smurra, "Fiscal Sources: the *Estimi*."
14. See Blanshei, *Politics and Justice*, 15–42; Eadem, "Aristocratization."
15. For the data, see Vallerani, *Medieval Public Justice*, 135–36.
16. Smail, *The Consumption of Justice*.
17. See the tables in Vallerani, *Medieval Public Justice*, 157 and 160; Dinges, "Usi della giustizia."
18. Smail, *On Deep History*.
19. For the early medieval period this reading in terms of the history of the emotions of justice has brought forward a drastic redimensioning of the significance of the processual sources. For example, in his analysis of the processual documentation of Marseilles, Smail, "Aspects of Procedural Documentation," 150–51, synthesizes well this historiographical interpretation, today undoubtedly prevalent in English-language scholarship: "Like the dust kicked up by a vigorous fist-fight, the writing was no more than a by-product of the emotional gambits."

20. ASB, Carte di Corredo (1286), unbound folio.
21. ASB, Carte di Corredo (1286), unbound folio.
22. In general, see Vallerani, “Justice publique.”
23. It may seem banal to note this, but it is important to insist upon a fundamental interpretive datum: violence is not a feeling that stands alone, but depends on the situations of real competition for material and symbolic resources. For a criticism of the parameter of violence as an end (and not as a means) of the judicial system, see Menzinger and Vallerani, “Giuristi e città.”
24. ASB, Carte di Corredo (1286), unbound folio: “Item si dixerunt quod fama est quod predicti Martinus et Benedictus accusaverunt dictum Petrum Strunca occasione ut admitteret lucra que solitus erat percipere occasione sui laborerii, queratur quomodo s(c)iunt et ubi est dicta fama et per quod et unde habuit horiginem dicta fama.”
25. Fraher, “The Theoretical Justification.” For the early diffusion of the canon, see Fraher, “Tancred’s ‘Summula’”; Kèry, “*Inquisitio-denunciatio-exceptio*”; on precedents see Trusen, “Der Inquisitionprozess.”
26. Edition in Kantorowicz, *Albertus Gandinus*, vol. 2.
27. Padovani, “L’inquisizione del podestà.”
28. Sbriccoli, “‘Vidi communitier observari.’”
29. See for a more complete portrayal of the forms of inquest in the medieval world, Gauvard, *L’enquête*.
30. Vallerani, *Medieval Public Justice*, 106–09.
31. ASB, Inquisitiones, Mazzo 16, Register 2, fol. 25r, 1289: there are more trials that arose from the same inquest made by the notary charged with measuring the distance of the piazza. On 18 April Gandinus personally ordered the custodian of the prison to tonsure and beat Flora, one of the women arrested.
32. The trial, from 1289, is transcribed in Kantorowicz, *Albertus* Gandinus, 1:204–06. A similar case is found in the trial against Gracianus di Camugnano, ASB, Inquisitiones, Mazzo 16, Register 1, fol. 42r, who had been accused of homicide and had been banned in earlier years. He was captured 24 May 1289 and after his confession was condemned to death. The same happened to Balzano di Bindo di Siena, accused of having stolen a skirt. He was captured, confessed to the theft and after a term of three days for his defense, was condemned to the blinding of one eye.
33. On Gandinus and false accusation, see Redon, *Les langues de ll’Italie médiévale*, 137–30.
34. ASB, Inquisitiones, Mazzo 16, 1289, Register 1, fol. 35r.
35. ASB, Inquisitiones, Mazzo 16, 1289, Register 1, fol. 40r.
36. See the chapter by Blanshei in this volume.
37. Vallerani, “La documentazione giudiziaria,” 299.
38. Kantorowicz, *Albertus Gandinus*, 2:6.
39. Vallerani, “Il giudice e le sue fonti.”
40. Todeschini, *Visibilmente crudeli*, 56–60.
41. See the chapter by Blanshei in this volume.
42. Kirshner, “*Consilia* as Authority”; Ascheri, “Le fonti e la flessibilità”; Idem, “I *consilia* dei giuristi.” For Bologna, see Rossi, Consilium sapientis iudicale.
43. The series is published in *Chartularium Studii Bononiensis*, 107–59.
44. Vallerani, “The Generation of the *Moderni*.”
45. Kantorowicz, *Albertus Gandinus*, 2:112, with reference to C. 9.2.6.1 and to Riccardo Malombra; the same passage is found again in paragraph 13: “cum melius noscat veritatem quam ipse procurator, et illa ratione quia dum de rei veritate queritur debet principalis persona venire.”
46. Kantorowicz, *Albertus Gandinus*, 2:114: “Domini Odofredus et Guido et alii doctores dicunt quod procurator ad predicta possit constitui, cum hoc concedatur in civilibus nec in criminalibus videatur esse prohibitur.”
47. Kantorowicz, *Albertus Gandinus*, 2:165: “Et super hoc consuluit Bononie dominus Lambertinus Ramponi, per legem: defensio prius sit danda.” The question had been: “Domine antequam me ad tormenta ponatis, placeat vobis prius mihi dare terminum defensionis,” and the

response in the *consilium* of Lambertino Ramponi was: "Dicatis quod defensio prius sit danda maxime quando tale quid allegatur probari quo probato iste Titius non debet ad tormenta poni. Et super hoc ita mihi consulit Bononie dominus Lambertinus Ramponi."

48. Kantorowicz, *Albertus Gandinus*, 2:120: "Dominus Dynus de Mugello dicit quod sic potest, et ita consuluisse in quadam questione, que sibi fuit commissa Bononie per potestatem Regii." However the response did remain open-ended: "alii plures doctores dicunt contra."

49. Vallerani, "Il diritto in questione."

50. Kantorowicz, *Albertus Gandinus*, 2:121.

51. This must be the sense of the question "*quomodo arguis de civilibus questionis ad criminales? Respondeo legis auctoritate*" with reference to "D 48 19 5" and "D 48 3 2 2." Kantorowicz, *Albertus Gandinus,* 2:122.

52. "Ergo nihil de ordine iudiciario est omittendum ne alias lata sententia contra solitum ordinem iudicario nullius foret momenti." Kantorowicz, *Albertus Gandinus*, 2:122.

53. Vallerani, "*Consilia iudicale,*" 138–39.

54. Studied by Milani, *L'esclusione dal comune*, and by Blanshei, *Politics and Justice*.

55. Milani, *L'esclusione dal comune*.

56. Vallerani, "The Generation of *Moderni*," 141–43.

57. For this practice in Milan, see Padoa-Schioppa, "La giustizia milanese," for a norm of 1330 that made recourse to a *consilium* obligatory if one of the two parties requested it.

58. See Menzinger, "*Consilium sapientum.*"

59. The data given by Blanshei in her chapter in this volume remain in this same range.

60. Vallerani, *Medieval Public Justice*, 296–97; Blanshei, *Politics and Justice*, 387–90.

61. Here I would be less optimistic than Blanshei regarding the possibility of *inquisitio* becoming an ordinary trial. See Blanshei's chapter in this volume.

62. Blanshei, *Politics and Justice*, 441–55.

63. Vallerani, *Medieval Public Justice*, 306–47.

Chapter Three

Bolognese Criminal Justice

From Medieval Commune to Renaissance Signoria

Sarah Rubin Blanshei

The complex apparatus of the criminal trial, as formulated in the course of the twelfth and thirteenth centuries, and the number of trials themselves, increased greatly in late thirteenth-century Bologna, fueled by demographic growth, the expanded authority of communal government, and popular demand for use of the law courts for dispute resolution. Although the number of trials decreased dramatically during the following two centuries, the trial apparatus itself remained a flexible instrument, subjected to significant technical changes attuned to shifting societal needs and governmental policies. Historians traditionally have viewed such developments in evolutionary terms within the framework of state formation, as a linear transition from accusation procedure, representing a trial dominated by dueling private parties with the judge serving as referee, to the triumph of *inquisitio* procedure, in which the trial came under the increasing control of the judge as the representative of public state justice.[1] In recent decades, however, historians such as Chris Wickham, Tom Kuehn, and especially Massimo Vallerani, have employed a processual approach that emphasizes dispute resolution as the driving force of late medieval criminal justice and finds significant similarities between accusation and inquisition procedures.[2] The fate of accusation procedure, however, remains unresolved. On the one hand, Vallerani, Andrea Zorzi, and Joanna Carraway Vitiello see *inquisitio* procedure as adapting many of the features of accusation procedure and accusation procedure itself as remaining vigorous throughout the fourteenth and even the fifteenth century. On the other hand Trevor Dean sees it as virtually disappearing by mid-fourteenth century and Sara Cucini sees it playing a very minor role in the second half of the fifteenth century.[3]

This chapter revisits the issue of the relationship of criminal justice to state formation through the lens of criminal trial procedures by tracing changes between and within accusatory and inquisitorial procedures from the late thirteenth to the early sixteenth century. Did those changes correlate with the many shifts in government between increasingly oligarchical republican and signorial regimes, or were they more related to the impact of war, famine, and pestilence? I show how dramatically accusation procedure did in fact decline in Bologna and document the chronology of that decline; the growth of summary justice; the expanding role of peace accords and poverty pleas in the mitigation of penalties; and shifts in the nature of *inquisitio* trial origins. I also ask to what degree these changes represent a shift in mentality away from criminal justice as "triadic" (that is, as a forum for the resolution of two-party conflicts in front of a judge serving as referee), to one that stressed the law court as a vehicle of social control, and whether that shift signifies implementation of a more repressive form of justice and the loss of due process.

The *ordo iudiciarius* of accusation procedure comprised an *iter* of specific, required steps, the omission of any one of which could invalidate the trial. The process began with submission of the accusation in writing by the accuser or his or her procurator or *curator* (trustee), payment of the *bolla*, provision of proof that the accuser had an *estimo* (that is, that he or she was enrolled in the tax records), and the taking of an oath and provision of *fideiussores* who swore to guarantee payment by the accuser for expenses and any penalties incurred. The judge then ordered a series of summons for the accused to appear in court—usually two *citationes* delivered by proclamation by a herald (*nuncio comunis*) in front of the accused's home, with at least two neighbors present as witnesses, and then a *grida* by the herald at the urban parish (*cappella*) or village church, again in the presence of named witnesses, and to the accompaniment of blasts from a *tuba*, followed by another *grida* by the *bannitor comunis*. At each stage the accused was given one or two days within which to appear in court, and after each summons the herald reported back to the judge that the summons had been delivered, a report that was duly noted in the trial register. If the accused or someone on their behalf failed to respond to the summons, a ban was then proclaimed by the *bannitor comunis* in the Council of 800, with stipulation of an eight-day period before the ban went into effect. It was recorded in the *libri bannitorum* in two stages, the first described as "formatum fuit" and the second as "exemplatum fuit." If the accused were a *forensis* (from outside the city, *contado* and district of Bologna), the process was swifter and the summonses were proclaimed at the *arengheria* on the steps of the communal palace.

If the accused appeared before the ban went into effect, the judge then proceeded to give accusers a series of three *dilationes* of three day-terms in which to appear and present their *intencio* and *positiones* and supply *fideius-*

sores who would guarantee the truthfulness of their witnesses' testimony. The accuser might also present documentation (*instrumenta*) to prove the charge. The judge then interrogated the witnesses on the basis of the *positiones* and interrogatories supplied by the accuser and the accused was given the opportunity to make a defense, again in a series of three *dilationes*. Defendants could respond to the accuser's *positiones* (the notary would write "credit" or "non credit" next to each *positio*) and also present their own *intencio*, *positiones*, interrogatories, witnesses and *instrumenta*, and supply *fideiussores* for the witnesses. The *positiones* could include *exceptiones* in which the accused challenged whether the trial should continue or be suspended (*declinatorie iudicii*), for example, because the court did not have jurisdiction, or because the accuser did not have an *estimo* or had not paid taxes, or did not have the approval of his or her *curator* (if underage). If a trial proceeded through all stages, it could become a lengthy process, lasting months, but as Vallerani has demonstrated, many accusation trials were terminated at an early stage, either because accusers did not prosecute the charge, or more usually, because they appeared at an early stage with a *renuncia* in which they declared they had reached an accord with the accused and did not wish to pursue the charge further. If the accuser presented a *renuncia*, the accused was acquitted and the accuser was "condemned" to pay a fine, usually as low as 12 *soldi.* If the accuser did not make a *renuncia* and also did not prosecute or prove the accusation the fine would be 20 *soldi.* Later in the fourteenth century the amount of the *renuncia* was pegged to the gravity of the charge and could be much higher. Appeals were not permitted in criminal trials, but the parties could contest any step in the process by requesting a *consilium sapientis*, that is, an opinion by one or more local jurists, to which the foreign judges of the courts almost always adhered and which almost always resulted in annulment of the trial.[4]

However, in those cases in which the accuser pursued the charge, the costs of litigation would become of course greater. Indeed, Trevor Dean has postulated that litigants chose *inquisitio* over "costly accusation procedure" in particular because of the expensive nature of accusation trials.[5] Accusers who lost their cases paid not only their own expenses but also those incurred by the opposing party, whose costs were determined based on their statement and then consideration of the validity of those expenses in a *consilium sapientis*. Finally, a judgment by the trial judge decided the actual amount to be paid, the *tassatio*. However, as I have shown in another publication,[6] the expenses of litigation did not change during the fourteenth century and were unlikely to have influenced the relationship between accusation and inquisition procedure.

The essential differences between accusation and inquisition trials were the judge's authority in *inquisitio* to initiate a trial *ex officio* on the basis of *publica fama* without an accuser, to seek the "truth of the facts" concerning a crime "lest crimes remain unpunished" and to bring that trial to a conclusion without the consent of the victim.[7] However, unlike accusation trials, inquisitions might be initiated in diverse ways—*ex officio* on the basis of *fama publica* or from reports of local officials—the *massarius* of a rural commune or the *ministralis* of an urban parish—or from complaints from private individuals who were victims of crimes or others on their behalf. The latter type of trial initiation is often described by historians as an *inquisitio cum promovente*, using the phrase from Albertus Gandinus's thirteenth-century handbook on procedure, and also as "conflictual" (Vallerani's term) or as a "hybrid inquisition" (Vitiello's phrase), which, because it was a dispute between dueling parties, was similar in its processes to an accusation trial. Vallerani and Vitiello stress the importance of such trials, he for the late Duecento and early decades of the Trecento, she for the late fourteenth century. Strongly supporting Vallerani's emphasis on "the involvement of private parties" in inquisition procedure, Vitiello underlines the "agency" of the parties involved and their ability to manipulate the inquisitorial system for their own purposes of conflict resolution. But how frequently were trials actually initiated "*cum promovente*"? Vallerani did not analyze such trials statistically, but Vitiello, equating trials initiated by a "querelant" in her Bolognese sample with trials by a *promotor*, found that 7.5 percent of the trials fit that category.[8] Cucini included in this category all inquisition trials that originated with complaints from non-officials and found that 3 percent of the trials in her sample from 1447–1511 fit this description.[9] But should all trials initiated by private individuals be categorized as trials "*cum promovente*"? In the passage from Albertus Gandinus cited by Vallerani, the judge could initiate a trial when the *mala fama* of the crime was reported directly to him by a private individual, but that person, the *promotor*, then was responsible for proving the *mala fama* of the imputed. Vallerani also refers to Gandinus's adaptation of the concept of the *promotor* in canon law as a person (a non-official) who explicitly requests that the podestà open an inquiry against a particular individual for a specific crime.[10] But does proving *mala fama* or making a specific request for an inquiry carry responsibility for prosecuting the trial and proving the charge? The example that Cucini gives of a trial "*cum promovente*" refers merely to a *denuncia* by the "ministralis cappelle Sancti Iuliani quarterii porte Ravennatis *et ad mandata et per testationem et querelam vicinorum de dicta cappella*" (italics added), not to a specific individual notifier. In fact, on the one hand it is rare to find examples of complainants who actively served in the prosecution of the imputed among the private individuals making notifications (either independently to the judge or in conjunction with a *denuncia* by a local official). Only in exceptional instances did the notifier or a *coadiunctor* actually perform any prosecutorial functions.[11] On the other hand, private notifiers, like accusers, paid a *bolla* or *gabella* when registering the charge and risked having to pay the opposing party's expenses even if the notifier did not play an active role in prosecuting the charge.

The proportion of *inquisitio* trials that were at the opposite end of the spectrum—trials that were "purely" *ex officio*, that is, without *denunce* or notifications—varied significantly, but does not seem to have ever reached a level that would account for the increase in the proportion of inquisition trials. In the second half of 1317, of the sixty-eight trials from three extant registers (of the eight that were originally transcribed), twenty-six of the trials were initiated *ex officio*, without *denuncia* or notification.[12] In 1326, however, the majority of cases in my *inquisitio* trial sample of 132 trials were initiated either by *denunce* of local officials (50.8 percent) or by notifications from individuals (27 percent), with *ex officio* trials comprising 16.6 percent of the 132 trials (with the origins of 5 percent of the trials not given).[13] Trevor Dean found in his sample of inquisition trials from 1347 that the trials were equally divided between those that were *ex officio* and those that originated from denunciations, but in his 1348 data the great majority were *ex officio*, with only fifteen of seventy-five trials initiated by local officials.[14] But that model does not continue and in the 1360s inquisitions initiated by denunciations from local officials once again outstripped trials initiated *ex officio*. In my sample of 611 trials from the 1360s, those initiated by notification or *denunce* comprised 81.2 percent of inquisition trials (438 of 539 trials).[15] However, when the data are broken down between the documentation from 1363–64 and 1365–68, the picture reverses itself. In 1363 and 1364 trials initiated *ex officio* were in the majority, comprising 59 percent of all inquisition trials, possibly because the new government of the papal legate fought two major campaigns against Bernabò Visconti during August and November 1363.[16] Between 1364 and 1368, however, the data flip again with *ex officio* trials sinking to 12 percent of all inquisition trials. In another sample of 624 trials from 1380–1420, there are 129 (20.6 percent) *ex officio* trials and 343 (54.9 percent) *denuncia*-initiated trials.[17] Moreover, the long-term trend was the continued dominance of inquisition trial initiations by local officials. Cucini's sample shows that the majority of inquisition trials between 1447 and 1511 were initiated by denunciations from local officials (239 of 372 inquisitions or 64.2 percent, as opposed to 118 *ex officio* trials, or 31.7 percent).[18] Can the periodic episodes of *ex officio* trial dominance be explained? The phenomenon in 1317 may relate to severe socioeconomic disruptions from the great famine that began in 1315, a pattern similar to that in 1348 as the effects of the Black Death constricted activities of the law courts. However, the shifting pattern of trial initiation between *ex officio* or *denunce* and notifications does not correlate with changes in the type of government. *Ex officio* origin dominated during both the republican regime of 1317 and the *signoria* of Taddeo Pepoli in 1348. Trials by *denunce* and notifications dominated under the communal government in 1326 as well as under the papal *signoria* of the 1360s and the Bentivoglio *signoria* of the second half of the fifteenth century. But what was the relationship of *inquisitio* to the decline of accusation procedure? Did trials initiated by notification from private individuals take the place of accusation procedure?

The decline of accusation procedure between the end of the thirteenth and the beginning of the sixteenth century, once a basic premise of procedural historiography but more recently a disputed topic, as noted above, can be evidenced with clarity in the Bolognese records. To be sure, that decline did *not* take place in the late thirteenth century (as some historians have erroneously claimed was my position).[19] Vallerani has shown conclusively that accusatory procedure presents "a picture of exceptional diffusion" in the second half of the thirteenth century, with a steady increase in the number of trials between 1286 and 1296, rising from 650–700 trials per semester to 2,000 per year in 1291, 2,584 in 1293, and 3,118 in 1294.[20] He specifically noted "the crisis of the accusatory trial in the first twenty years of the Trecento," but considered this development to be a temporary trend. He did not attempt a statistical analysis of the frequency of accusation procedure in the fourteenth century, both because he considered that the strict formula of two trials for each folio (one recto and one verso) no longer held and because the total number of registers could no longer be verified by contemporary inventories from the *camera actorum*. Moreover, he concluded that after 1327 significant registers of accusations were not extant in usable form.[21] The accusation records after 1327 indeed are scattered and sometimes very fragmentary, but there are complete, well-preserved parchment registers in the *Accusationes* series until mid-century (the last complete register is from 1349) and also separate and complete registers in the *Sententiae* series, beginning in 1327, with the last complete accusation register in that *fondo* dating from 1352. After that extant accusation registers are found in the *Inquisitiones* series in paper registers, the first of which are from 1351–52.[22] Moreover, we know the number of notaries for this period (eight until 1376, then six, in the podestà's criminal court, with two in the criminal court of the *capitano del popolo*, which was re-established in that year) and in many instances, beginning with 1346, the registers contain *carte sciolte* (unbound folios) of the notaries' inventories, explicitly describing the number and types of registers each notary passed on to his successor. Using these extant documents and by adopting a strategy of comparing ratios of accusations to inquisitions (where possible by the same notaries), in addition to tracing the absolute number of cases initiated by accusation, it is possible to unveil significant changes that took place over time in the relationship between the two procedures.

After the initial stage of growth in the late thirteenth century, accusation procedure met its first crisis during the major war of 1296–99 between Bologna and the powerful lord of Ferrara, the marchese d'Este. The war disrupted activity of the court in both accusation and inquisition trials, with trials suspended for months because heralds could not deliver summons in the *contado* and men were away at war and unable to initiate or prosecute accusations. In addition, the government expanded the *arbitrium* of the podestà, enlarging the scope of crimes that came under the umbrella of trials he could initiate by inquisition. Nor did court activity return to pre-war levels after 1300. The government's need for money to sustain the war led it to a policy of depriving tax delinquents of their right to initiate a criminal or civil complaint or defend themselves in a trial, a change that had special impact on the use of accusation procedure. Vallerani estimated that on average there were 1,200 to 1,500 accusation trials per year in the late thirteenth century, in contrast to 150–200 *inquisitio* trials, which gives a ratio of eight to one at the lower levels and 7.5 at the higher levels (my calculations).[23] In the decade between 1294 and 1304 that ratio had fallen significantly to three to one.[24]

In the second decade of the fourteenth century, accusation procedure met another crisis with the exploding expansion of privileged status and extensive legal immunities granted in 1310 and 1319 to the thousands of members of the guilds and arms societies that formed the twin components of the *popolo* party. On the one hand privileged *popolani* were empowered to accuse magnates, non-guild and arms society members, and *contadini* by summary procedure. On the other hand they were granted immunity from prosecution for all except capital crimes.[25] The effect of privilege was not only to diminish the frequency of accusation trials but to make accusation procedure a vehicle for interclass conflict rather than intra-class conflict resolution. The immunities granted by privilege meant that thousands of *bolognesi* could not use accusation procedure against each other. Many accusations instead were instituted by privileged *popolano* urban landlords against *contadini*. The dominance of privilege in accusation trials in this period is clear. In a complete accusation register from 1319, 79 percent of the accusations were made by privilege.[26] This one register may be an extreme example, but of the total of ninety-four accusation trials from all extant registers from the first semester of 1319, 54 percent were initiated by privilege. Accusation procedure had largely become the preserve of the politically and judicially privileged classes, and this development significantly diminished the frequency with which accusation procedure was used.[27] By 1326, the last year of the communal government before the advent of the *signoria* of Cardinal-legate Bertrand du Pouget and after six years of privilege-dominated justice, the ratio of accusations to inquisitions once again shifted dramatically—the ratios inverted with more trials initiated by inquisition than by accusation, with a ratio of two to one in favor of inquisitions.[28] Not coincidentally the commune was at war, with parts of its *contado* in the hands of enemies and rebels, and as it had done during the war with Ferrara, the government expanded the *arbitrium* of the podestà, enlarging the scope of crimes that could be initiated by inquisition procedure.

The number of accusations remained lower, at least initially, under the *signoria* established in 1327 by Bertrand du Pouget—there are only seventeen accusations in three extant registers from the first semester of 1329 and sixty accusations from five extant registers from the second semester of that year.[29] Under the restored communal government in 1334, the number of accusations seems to have been similar and the inquisition-accusation ratio still held at two to one in favor of inquisitions.[30] Under the *signoria* of Taddeo Pepoli (1337–47), accusation procedure declined even further. For two of the eight notaries of the *ad maleficia* court, records for both their accusation and inquisition trials survive for the first three months of the first semester of 1342. One notary had four trials by accusation and nineteen by inquisition for a ratio of nearly five to one in favor of inquisition; the other notary had only one accusation but fourteen inquisitions.[31] Accusation registers for other notaries from this period also survive (but not their inquisitions) and the low number of accusations in those registers are comparable to those in these two notaries' registers.[32] By the end of Pepoli's regime, during the first semester of 1347, there are merely forty-seven accusation trials in a sample consisting of six of the eight notaries, which would indicate a 75 percent decline in accusation procedure between 1304 and 1347.[33] The population of city and *contado* was also declining dramatically over those decades, even before the onset of the Black Death in 1348, but the population loss during that period was approximately 30 percent, so the decline in accusation cannot be attributed to demographic loss alone.[34] In a recent study Trevor Dean has shown that the plague of 1348 did cause a virtual collapse in accusation procedure, but as we shall see below, that phenomenon was a temporary one.[35]

The decline of accusation procedure in the first half of the fourteenth century and the further steep reduction under the *signoria* of Taddeo Pepoli stemmed from a series of related developments. The risk of costly expenditures in accusation procedure, the criminalization of tax delinquency, the increased complexity of trials with procurators and *exceptiones*, and the granting of legal privilege, as discussed above, played important roles in the early decades of the century, but the decline continued beyond the introduction of those practices, which indicates other developments were contributing factors. One of those factors, indeed a major one, was the interjection of the executive authority into criminal court activities, which varied in intensity throughout the fourteenth and fifteenth centuries, but was especially acute during the 1320s and under the *signoria* of Taddeo Pepoli (1337–47) and the brief regime of his sons (1347–50). In the 1320s, with the increasing politicization of criminal justice, initiation of trials through a new *querela* procedure became a common practice. The *querela* was a petition to the *consiglio del popolo* in which the querelant asked that the *consiglio* interfere directly in the criminal court on his or her behalf, either by ordering the podestà and his judges to initiate a trial against the querelant's opponents or victimizers, or suspend or annul a trial against the querelant, and usually to do so by summary procedure, that is, without observance of the usual judicial formalities.[36] Approval of the *querela* required a majority vote of the *consiglio*, thereby making an important judicial process subject to political favoritism and animosities. For those allied with the majority of the *consiglio*'s members, the *querela* represented an attractive alternative to accusation procedure since the ensuing trial was pursued by inquisition procedure and summarily in favor of the querelant.

When Cardinal legate Bertrand du Pouget became *signore* in 1327 he abolished the *consiglio del popolo* and the *querela* process and replaced the *querela* with supplications made to him for the granting of a *gratia*. The supplications included requests for tax relief from rural communes or individuals, petitions seeking authorization of the sale of dowry properties, and especially petitions for cancellation of bans, including bans for capital crimes such as homicide, but only exceptionally sought interference in judicial processes, such as the petition from a *scolaris* who had been robbed and sought summary justice.[37] Under the regime of Taddeo Pepoli and then of his sons, however, the supplication became "a new system of governance." Normal legislative activity was replaced by the issuance of decrees from the *signore* and the majority of those decrees were made in response to petitions or supplications.[38] Notations of suspensions of trials are frequently found in the margins of trials, usually by order of Bornio Samaritani (the closest of Pepoli's associates), or by either of Pepoli's sons, or by his wife, the "lady of the lord."

Supplication procedure essentially established a new method of dispute resolution. Instead of lodging an accusation and incurring the expenses associated with it, a petitioner made a supplication to the *signore*, who might render a decision himself or direct the court to initiate an inquisition, with the full backing to the supplicant of the *signore*'s authority and prestige. Moreover, the *signore*'s control of the apparatus of government also empowered the judges to act without fear of penalties for their decisions during their end of term syndication reviews, thereby making a disputant in the law courts, whether accuser or accused, more vulnerable to unfavorable processes and decisions. This vulnerability had already been exacerbated by the exclusion of the *consilium sapientis* in criminal trials. In the late thirteenth and early fourteenth centuries, disputants had been able to challenge the judge's decisions or the motions of the adversarial party by requesting a *consilium* from a local Bolognese jurist, and such a *consilium* was almost always favorable to the party requesting it. The judge received lists of jurists who were acceptable ("non-suspect" of bias) from both accuser and accused and appointed one or more jurists from those lists. Vallerani found fifty *consilia* in his sample of accusation records from 1286 to 1301, but the Statutes of 1335 specifically forbid the use of *consilia* in criminal cases.[39] Similarly, other city-states sought to curtail the use of *consilia*. In 1341 the *signore* of Milan attempted unsuccessfully to forbid the use of *consilia* in the criminal courts.[40] However, Giangaleazzo Visconti (1378–1492) did succeed in doing so "because recourse to consultants led to the avoidance or reduction of penalties."[41] The practice was also forbidden in the Florentine statutes of 1355 and 1415.[42] Nevertheless, collections of *consilia* for criminal trials continued to be commissioned and compiled, although Trevor Dean found they usually comprised a minority of the *consilia* he consulted in printed collections.[43] In the court records from Bologna after the middle of the fourteenth century, their appearance in criminal trials is very limited and is used consistently only for the establishment of the *tassatio* in cases where the complainant had to pay the imputed party's expenses, as noted above.

Accusatory procedure was based on the principle of the absolute equality of the litigating parties, and by the middle of the fourteenth century legal privileges under communal regimes, loss of the protection of the *consilium sapientis*, and interference in the courts by both communal and signorial governments had greatly corrupted that principle and undermined the integrity and function of accusation procedure. But the virtual disappearance of accusation in the 1340s did not mark the end of the process of decline. Use of the procedure revived sporadically, albeit very modestly, in the following decades, paralleling a concurrent diminution in the use of supplication procedure and direct interference in the courts by the executive body.[44] In my sample of 611 trials between 1363 and 1368 I found only fifty-four trials initiated by accusation—8.8 percent, although in 1363 and 1364 there was a brief but significant resurgence of accusation trials, which comprised thirty-nine of the 115 trials (33.9 percent). There were no instances of interference in the courts by the papal legate during 1363 and 1364 and only six such instances between 1365 and 1368. For the period 1380–1420 there are seventy-five accusation trials (12 percent) of the 624 trials in my sample. Moreover, the trend was downward in the period of intense factional strife and proto-*signorie* after the initiation of government by *balìe* (special commissions) in 1394.[45] Between 1395 and 1420, there are only nine accusation trials (3 percent) of 265 trials in my sample. These accusation trials typically were limited to minor charges such as *verba iniuriosa*, property disputes, adultery, minor theft, an assault that occurred outside of Bologna (in Ferrara) and an assault without weapons.[46] Finally, during the years of comparative stability during the Bentivoglio *signoria* Cucini found that only forty of 440 trials (9.5 percent) were by accusation in her sample from 1447–1511. As she notes, the process of change had come full circle: the ratio of eight to one in favor of accusations in the late thirteenth century had reversed to almost the exact opposite, a ratio of seven to one in favor of inquisitions.[47]

The dominance of *inquisitio* procedure after the crisis of the mid-fourteenth century derived from a growth of state power in criminal justice, whether under a republican or signorial regime, a change made possible by the great reduction in population combined with an increase in the number of officials available for surveillance, enforcement of dispute settlement, and control of the streets. To supplement the existing street patrols by *sbirri* of the podestà, the sixteen *gonfalonieri* were entrusted in 1376 with patrolling the city streets and additional street patrols were provided by *milites* under the re-established office of the *capitano del popolo*. Mercenaries were also used for that purpose.[48] In 1397 the number of *familiares* or *sbirri* assigned to the podestà was raised from thirty-three to fifty-eight. He also had ten *domicelli* and four *conestabiles*.[49] In contrast, for a much larger population in the late thirteenth century (probably twice the size),[50] the podestà usually had twenty *sbirri*, a figure raised to forty in 1295 as the commune prepared for war with Ferrara, and fifty police on foot with another twenty-five on horseback in 1306 after the major regime change and factional turmoil of that year.[51] New officials were appointed, such as an *esecutore* or *conservatore di giustizia* in 1441 and 1445 who had authority to act *ex officio* and apply any sentence.[52] The government seems to have gained better control over crime in the *contado*, and the office of the *vicarius* judge of the *capitano delle montagne*, formerly viewed as an exploitative office, seems to have more than doubled its effectiveness or at least the level of its prosecutorial activity between 1370 and 1409.[53]

At the same time the executive branch of government expanded its control over the judiciary and simultaneously broadened the *arbitrium* of the criminal courts. In 1376 the *bolognesi* overthrew the *signoria* of the papal legate and re-established a republican government, but it was vastly more oligarchical and restrictive than the government of the late medieval commune, and a major emphasis of the criminal courts was on protecting the existence of the regime, not the rights of citizens. Executive control of the judiciary, characteristic of prior signorial governments, continued under the restored republican regime and indeed was institutionalized by entrusting oversight of the judiciary to the executive council of the nine *anziani* and their associated colleges of sixteen *massari* and sixteen *gonfalonieri*, who intervened in court trials, suspending or initiating them and deciding procedural issues. To be sure, these interventions could be based on principles of equity and mercy, as in the trial against Johannes Muzoli of the parish (*cappella*) of S. Felice, which the *anziani* ordered suspended. The suspension was justified for two reasons: because the imputed was a herald of the *massari* and *gonfalonieri* who had struck a person with his weapon in the face in the course of performing an official assignment and because the herald had been earlier charged and acquitted by the alleged victim in an accusation trial.[54] But in other instances the *anziani* ordered an investigation and trial against specific persons, as in the inquisition against seven men who had been captured and presented to the court at the mandate of the *anziani*. The men were charged with having robbed and attacked Frosinus domini Andree de Perutiis of Florence and his mercenary associates. The podestà as well as his judge presided over the investigation and after finding circumstantial evidence in the testimony of five witnesses against one of the men, Jacobus Chichi, proceeded to order that he be submitted to torture. After he was tortured an *inquisitio ex officio* was initiated against him, a trial that lasted for two months and ended with the *anziani* ordering not only suspension of the trial against Jacobus but also the dropping of charges against the other six men.[55] The *anziani* also not only ordered that trials be held but granted the courts authority to act summarily in specific cases, especially in cases of sedition and treason, as in the three-day trial and execution of six men charged with conspiring with the exiled Pepoli to enter and take control of the city in 1386. In this trial the *anziani* also intervened by commuting the sentence of execution from hanging which had been issued by the *capitano del popolo* to decapitation.[56] The *anziani* also intervened in accusation trials and on procedural issues, essentially performing the function fulfilled earlier by the *consilia sapientis*.[57]

Interference also could be made for diplomatic reasons. Thus, in 1395 the *anziani* and their colleges intervened in a trial against Biagio di Giovanni de Calvis of Imola and six other men, all with one exception described as *forenses* and *vagabundos* and all charged with three instances of kidnapping and robbery. Two of the imputed were in custody and on 18 June confessed to the crimes and renounced all terms for presenting their defense. The judge issued a capital ban against the others. On 24 July, however, the judge received a mandate from the *anziani* and their colleges that they had decided, in response to a request from the powerful mercenary captain Count Giovanni da Barbiano, that all the imputed, including the two men who had confessed, were to be acquitted.[58] The *anziani* intervened in homicide trials as well. On 16 March 1396 two *contadini* received a capital ban for arson and the killing of a young girl who had been trapped and burned to death in the fire. However, the ban was not finalized after the usual eight-day waiting period because on 25 March an *inhibitio* from the *anziani* suspended the trial for fifteen days and a second *inhibitio* on 7 April mandated another suspension of an additional eight days. Finally, on 17 April the *anziani* and their associated colleges suspended the trial for a third time, which ended all recorded action against the culprits.[59] Not only did the *anziani* suspend trials and commute sentences, they also removed cases from the courts and formed special commissions to act as courts of law whose members were drawn from the ranks of the *anziani*, *gonfalonieri*, and *massari*. In 1395 Bartolomeo di Jacopo and Giovanni di Perondelli de Tassis were charged with assaulting Vanne of Florence and his son Lapo with lances. The trial began with the first summons of the imputed on 20 October but seven days later the trial was suspended because the *anziani* had received a petition from the imputed, had set up a commission to investigate the case, and had concluded that rather than being punished, the two imputed men should be commended for having attacked the alleged victims whom the commission had determined were themselves guilty of having committed an assault.[60]

However, it should be noted that the frequency of such *anziani* interventions remained low in the podestà's court. Between 1380 and 1420 I found only ten such instances out of a sample of 624 trials, although the frequency of such instances in the court of the *capitano del popolo*, which treated most of the conspiracy cases, may have been higher—the four trials in that court in 1386 were all mandated by the *anziani*. Nevertheless, the potential for and reality of such interference by a small group of forty-one officials contrasts sharply with the politicization of justice in the early decades of the fourteenth century when interference in the courts required a majority vote from the 1,200 members of the *consiglio del popolo*. The nature of interference had also become more intrusive, in contrast to the earlier more limited directing of the courts to hold trials in response to petitions from individuals seeking court action.[61] Cucini found that in the second half of the fifteenth century, at least until the Malvezzi conspiracy of 1488, the *Sedici Riformatori* intervened especially in the case of political crimes, using the courts as a means of consolidating signorial power.[62]

The ruling regime of the restored republican government of 1376 asserted control over the judiciary in other ways as well. The *anziani* appointed two foreign notaries (the *notai forensi*) who attended the criminal courts of the podestà and the *capitano del popolo* (one notary per trial) and transcribed the responses of the defendants and the trial outcomes. If the transcripts of the podestà or *capitano*'s notaries contradicted those of the *anziani*-appointed *notai forensi*, the records of the *notai forensi* were deemed the authoritative version.[63] Ilaria Prosperi favors viewing this new institution as a reform initiative, one intended to prevent judicial abuses. However, she also admits that the appointment of these notaries by the *anziani* means that the innovation could be interpreted negatively.[64]

The 1376 government also re-established the office of the *capitano del popolo*, a magistracy eliminated under the prior signorial regimes, but the *capitano* and his judges played a very different role from the one they had exercised in the late medieval commune. In the earlier period the *capitano* did not have authority over crime, but the court of his *vicarius* judge served as a safety net for citizens who believed they were being treated unjustly by the podestà's judges. Instead of waiting until the syndication review at the end of the podestà's term, citizens could appeal for immediate relief from perceived injustice to the *capitano*. The podestà was accountable to the *capitano* and the *capitano* was entrusted with upholding the rights of citizens, and especially with protecting members of the guilds and arms societies from judicial torture.[65] In the restored republic of 1376 the podestà and the *capitano* were co-equals with no subordination of the podestà to the *capitano*. Both shared jurisdiction over crime, but the *capitano* was particularly entrusted with cases of treason and conspiracy; in short, his primary charge was to protect the regime, not to guard the rights of citizens. In creating the new criminal court of the *capitano*, the government did not expand judicial resources against crime; rather it redirected its efforts. The number of notaries assigned to the podestà's *ad maleficia* court was reduced from eight to six and two new notaries were appointed to serve the *capitano*, one of whom served the *officio mallificiorum* of the *capitano* and its special responsibility for protecting the regime.[66] Although a person indicted for a crime could not make a *protestacio* for immediate assistance to the *capitano*, he or she could petition the *anziani* for interference and redress, as did the procurator for six men in 1398 who had been charged in the podestà's court with the homicide of Michael Jacobi. The procurator, citing the statute on how many persons could be convicted for the homicide of one person, claimed in his supplication that only one of the imputed, Antonius de Brissia, had struck a mortal blow and should be convicted. The *anziani* suspended the trial against the six men in the podestà's court and remanded it to the *capitano*'s court, where a new trial against three of the six men, including Antonius, was held and then suspended, precisely on the grounds that only one mortal blow had been inflicted upon the victim.[67]

Greater social control was exerted by expanding the *arbitrium* of the podestà and his judges and the instrument for that increase was inquisition procedure. The late medieval commune had tried to expand the podestà's jurisdiction in 1295 by giving him authority to initiate a broader list of crimes by inquisition procedure, but the *ad maleficia* court had been overwhelmed by the volume of trials and the legislation was quickly rescinded.[68] In the second half of the fourteenth century, however, the courts faced a much reduced population, and freed from the heavy burden of adjudicating hundreds of accusation trials each semester, successfully implemented legislation that significantly increased the scope and function of inquisition procedure. The broadening *arbitrium* of the podestà has been documented by the cumulative efforts of various scholars who have analyzed the Bolognese statutes of 1248–67, 1288, 1335, 1376, 1389, and 1454.[69] The jurisdictional scope of the podestà's *arbitrium* was generally set by 1335. Crimes that had been outside the purview of the podestà's jurisdiction, such as *verba iniuriosa*, for which he had authority only in cases of magnate acts against *popolani* and acts against officials, became part of his *arbitrium* between 1288 and 1335.[70] Forty-eight categories of crime are described in the statutes of 1335 as those in which the podestà was *required* to take action and another twenty-two as those in which he *could* initiate an investigation (for a total of at least seventy different crimes).[71] Trevor Dean similarly found in the statutes of 1454 that the podestà could initiate an investigation and trial for seventy-eight separate crimes, "ranging from treason and murder to blasphemy, bigamy and moving boundary marks" (the same range as in 1335).[72]

Did the expanded *arbitrium* and enforcement resources of the late fourteenth century signify more repressive policies and procedures in criminal justice? Historians have traditionally emphasized the brutality of medieval justice. Certain crimes that were regarded as particularly outrageous did receive special, gruesome penalties, such as piercing of the flesh with hot pincers or implantation (death by burying the culprit alive head first into the ground), but such cases were very rare.[73] Trevor Dean concludes that "by the end of the fourteenth century, the more atrocious forms of punishment . . . had become rare" and that "[c]apital penalties were usually commuted into imprisonment, banishment or corporal punishment."[74] The more lenient policies of punishment significantly affected the function and processes of inquisition procedure and can be seen most clearly in the courts' treatment of the many more minor cases of assault, no longer dependent upon accusation procedure, that had come under the inquisitorial jurisdiction of the courts. In expanding inquisition procedure to include minor acts of violence, the government aimed not to punish or ban those charged with assault, but rather to ensure that brawls did not escalate into further reprisals and violence. To achieve this goal it employed a technique that historians have traditionally associated with weak government and with accusation procedure—the *pax* or peace accord.[75] In late thirteenth- and early fourteenth-century Bologna the peace accord was widely used in accusation trials, usually with the *renuncia* of the charge by the accuser. It also was necessary, especially in capital crimes, for a banned person to have made an accord with his or her victim in order to have a ban annulled at the end of the ban period, but it was not used to mitigate a penalty or suspend a trial before sentencing as was done elsewhere.[76] Use of a peace accord to mitigate a penalty became an option in the 1330s under the *signoria* of Bertrand du Pouget, but was not frequently used under his rule, when most trials ended in bans. For example, in 1339, in the five extant inquisition registers from the first semester, four of the 146 trials have peace accords (2.7 percent). Under the Pepoli *signoria* of the 1340s the peace accord rarely appears in the trial records.[77] But by the 1350s, with the establishment of the new *signoria* of the Visconti, the peace accord was regularly used in inquisition trials to mitigate penalties for non-capital crimes.[78] The role of the peace accord had shifted from an instrument that was part of the process of reconciliation between the accuser and accused in accusation procedure to an instrument for the mitigation of penalties or even for gaining an acquittal in an inquisition trial. Moreover, it was used in "purely" *ex officio* trials as well as those initiated by *denuncia* of a *ministralis* or *massarius*. In sixty-two inquisition trials from the three extant registers in the first semester of 1351, eighteen of the trials (29 percent) were resolved with presentation of a peace accord.[79] Occasionally the peace accord is dated and is prior to the initiation date of the trial, indicating that the trial was not serving as a vehicle for reconciliation on the part of the parties, as in accusation procedure, but as an instrument of the government and courts that combined punishment and reconciliation for purposes of social control. It was a policy that lowered the number of trials that ended in bans. Such trials and bans, even for a minor crime, meant that the *bannitus* could be attacked and even killed with impunity, thus opening the door to escalation of disputes, which in turn could lead to riots and endanger the stability of the government. Indeed, a common defense in trials for homicide, arson, and robbery was that the victim was under a ban and therefore that the trial had to be suspended. The many *banniti* who remained secretly in the Bolognese *contado* also presented a potent threat to security of the regime, especially when they allied with its exiled political opponents.

The compatibility of the peace accord with more repressive procedures can be seen in a trial in 1362, brought to court by *denuncia* of a *ministralis* against a certain Jacobus for an assault with flow of blood. The imputed responded to the second summons and was imprisoned because he could not provide a *fideiussor*. After interrogating the witnesses provided by the *ministralis*, the judge gave the imputed a term of eight days to show why he should not be tortured. The imputed's procurator provided a defense of six *capitula* and supporting testimony of witnesses, but the judge decided to have Jacobus tortured, after which Jacobus confessed and promised to pay his penalty. But then two weeks later he returned to court and presented a peace accord that he had made with the victim. The peace accord in this case was not a sign of the weakness of the court and the strength of infrajudicial justice but part of a prosecution policy that combined aggressiveness with reconciliation and mitigation of penalties.[80]

The policy of social control through mitigation of penalties was significantly strengthened by the introduction into the courts of another procedure for mitigation of penalty—the poverty plea. To be sure, poverty had been the basis for pardons granting mitigation and annulment of penalties and bans in response to supplications under Bertrand du Pouget, Taddeo Pepoli, and the Visconti *signori*.[81] The poverty plea, however, was not an act of clemency originating outside the judicial process but was an integral part of the inquisition trial procedure. The imputed appeared in court, usually confessed to the charge, and had a procurator (but not always) who on his or her behalf presented a poverty plea (often, but not always, with a peace accord), with the names of witnesses who gave evidence of the imputed's poverty, for example, that he was without material goods worth more than 25 *lire*, was gravely burdened with sustaining a family, and worked by the sweat of his brow for daily nourishment.[82] Trevor Dean observed the existence of the poverty plea in mid-fifteenth-century trials in the podestà's court, and thought the procedure was "rare before 1440." But he also noted that further research was needed to discover when it became a part of the court system.[83] In fact, it became a regular and frequent judicial procedure beginning in October 1368 in the court of the podestà with the advent of a new papal legate, and the mitigation duo of peace accord and poverty plea were also normal procedures in the courts of the *capitano del popolo* and *capitano delle montagne* by 1379 and 1381, respectively. In the podestà's court in the first semester of 1368, in six extant registers with 165 trials, there are twenty trials with poverty pleas (12 percent) and in some cases in the same trials, sixty peace accords (36.3 percent).[84] Testimony to prove the defendant's poverty became so common in the ensuing years that they comprise a large portion of the testimony in cases in the *inquisitiones* records and those of the *notai forensi*. For example, in a *Liber Testium* of 1379, five of the thirteen sets of witnesses' testimony concern poverty pleas.[85]

The new procedures of the *pax* and poverty plea, by encouraging those charged to come to court, confess their crimes, and pay reduced penalties, were also part of a longer-term trend to streamline the inquisition trial process and to make justice swifter and more effective. Inquisition trial in the late thirteenth century was a much more elaborate process than it was to become in the second half of the fourteenth century. After the judge became aware of a crime, either by notification or *denuncia* from a victim or a local official or by *publica fama*, he had to choose from among the different ways of proceeding. If the crime had taken place in the *contado*, and especially if it originated from a private or anonymous notification, he might send an order to the judges and notaries of the *malefici novi* court to initiate a trial. That court, in contrast to the podestà's *ad maleficia* court, was staffed by Bolognese judges and notaries. After the reforms of 1295, its responsibilities were reduced to offenses of minor property damages, disputes over court-confiscated properties and supervising the destruction of properties of those condemned or banned for certain capital crimes such as homicide.[86] If the *ad maleficia* judge decided to try the case directly, he sent his *miles* and one of his notaries to initiate the trial by an investigation at the scene of the crime, or less frequently, went to the scene himself, whether the crime had taken place in the city or in the *contado*. That investigation involved the interrogation of witnesses in the presence of the *ministralis* or *massarius* and two "good men" of the urban *cappella* or the rural commune who could vouch for the integrity of the witnesses and their age (at this point they had to be forty years or older). The trial might be completed by the *malifici novi* officials or by the *ad maleficia* judge.[87] The interrogations at the scene of the crime, whether carried out by the *miles* or judge of the *ad maleficia* court or by the officials of the *malifici novi* court, involved many witnesses (usually at least seven or eight but sometimes dozens). The judge would also order a medical report in cases of severe injuries or homicide. Only after receipt of those reports and completion of the interrogation of those witnesses would the judge issue a summons for the imputed to appear in court. If the imputed were in custody, and if the interrogations had supplied sufficient circumstantial evidence ("indicia") and the imputed had denied the charge, the judge might then and only then, decide to submit the imputed to torture. This process was followed in the 1280s and 1290s even in the case of infamous thieves and killers. If the imputed confessed not only at the scene of torture (the podestà's dining room) and a second time in court, or if without torture, once in court, they were then given a set of terms within which to make a defense. After confession, however, such a defense was rarely made and the imputed would renounce all periods for their defense and quickly be subjected to payment of a fine or corporal punishment. In the case of a notorious thief and killer, all steps of the process would be followed, but usually swiftly, as in the trial against Bernardinus quondam Gratiadei who was also convicted as a blasphemer and hanged. His trial was conducted in the presence of the podestà as well as the judge within two days, even though it included testimony from seventeen witnesses.[88]

The practice of interrogating witnesses at the scene of the crime at a pretrial stage of the proceedings and before the issuance of summons or bans was continued in most trials until the *signoria* of Bertrand du Pouget.[89] The importance and persistence of this procedure derives from the proofs needed for conviction: the *ordo iudiciarius* called for two eyewitnesses but the 1295 *Ordinamenta* provided for conviction on the basis of one witness and *publica fama* if the evidence for the latter was obtained at the scene of the crime.[90] The significant discontinuation of this practice was maintained in the briefly restored republican government of 1334–37 and under the governments of Taddeo Pepoli and then his sons, but by the end of their *signorie* and the transition to the *signoria* of the Visconti in 1350 yet another stage in the streamlining of *inquisitio* process was initiated.

Trevor Dean has shown that by 1351 witnesses were no longer necessarily interrogated before issuance of a ban against the imputed—that the mere denunciation by a local official (coupled with non-appearance of the imputed in court) was considered a sufficient basis for assuming guilt, even in cases that carried capital bans. The witnesses named in the *libelli* submitted by local officials were summoned only in trials in which the imputed appeared in court and denied the charge. Dean attributes his important finding to the dissolution of the *vicarius domini* judge's court. That court had been a special tribunal under Pepoli and had dealt particularly with criminous acts related to public order and office (especially by and against foreign mercenaries) and had done so using summary procedure. Dean suggests that it was the influence of these cases moving into the podestà's court after the abolition of the court of the *vicarius domini* that was responsible for the change to non-interrogation of witnesses before issuance of a ban in the podestà's court.[91] The change marks a significant stage in the development of inquisition procedure but it had more than one influential precedent. As noted above, summary justice procedure, including not only a more rapid process but also the omission of testimony from witnesses before issuance of a ban, was used in the 1320s in certain *querela*-initiated trials in the podestà's court. In the 1320s and 1330s trials against infamous thieves and assassins were sometimes conducted without a probative stage of witness interrogation and moved immediately on the basis of *publica fama* to the appearance of the imputed in court and their confession, almost certainly as a result of torture. In other cases the witnesses testified only to *publica fama* and hearsay, but the judge issued the summonses and the trial concluded with a ban.[92] In a sample of eighty-two trials from 1336, twenty-nine of the trials (35.3 percent) skipped the interrogation of witnesses, in charges that included kidnappings, rape, homicide, *guarnimenta* (attacks by armed bands in the *contado*), and serious assaults.[93]

Three further innovations completed the process of streamlining *inquisitio* procedure: the *licentia*, the *requisitio*, and the *circumdatio*, all established in the second half of the fourteenth century. The *licentia* was permission granted by the imputed to the judge to proceed, after the imputed's initial appearance in court, through all the stages of the trial, including interrogation of witnesses, up to final sentencing without further appearance in court of the imputed. The formula appears sporadically in the trial records of the early 1360s and consistently beginning in 1368, the same year in which the poverty plea was introduced.[94] The *licentia* meant that the imputed did not have to appear in court to hear the testimony of witnesses and signifies a further departure from the accusation procedure mentality of the trial as a confrontation of two dueling parties. The *requisitio*, established in the 1380s, was a complaint from a victim or on behalf of a victim that accompanied the *denuncia* of a local official, either a *ministralis* or a *massarius*. The complaint was also termed a *querela* or *protestacio* (but is to be distinguished from earlier procedures of the first two decades of the fourteenth century with the same names). By means of the *requisitio* local officials could report minor crimes outside the jurisdiction given them by the statutes. On the one hand it thus represented an expansion of the court's *arbitrium*, but on the other hand it was hedged with an important limitation against frivolous charges. If the imputed were acquitted, the complainant was responsible for trial expenses. The *requisitio* is included in the statutes of 1389 but was in effect by 1388. Eleven of the thirty-two inquisitions in one register from the first semester of that year were initiated by a *requisitio* accompanying the *denuncia* of a local official. The importance of the *requisitio* to authorization of the *denuncia* is demonstrated in one of the trials in which the *massarius* reported the charge of a brawl among three men "ad querelam partis contrarie." But the procurator for the defense of two of the imputed claimed that none of them had made a complaint and therefore the trial should not proceed against his clients because their offenses (striking without a weapon and without shedding blood) were not "de casibus et mallificis" for which *ministrales* and *massari* were responsible for reporting crimes. The judge agreed and suspended the trial against two of the imputed.[95] The *circumdatio* of the mid-fifteenth century further extended the practice of mitigating penalties for minor crimes by means of a payment of 1 to 25 *lire*, made before sentencing in order to avoid conviction and thereby making the process of justice swifter.[96]

The criminal justice system that emerged after the changes in the structure of criminal trials between the thirteenth and late fifteenth centuries culminated in a definite, albeit not linear, shift from accusation to inquisition procedure, a change closely tied to the capacity of the state to take the initiative in law and order. It was a system more attuned to preservation of the political regime than protection of due process and the rights of the imputed, a system that combined aggressiveness with leniency and transformed the nature and function of inquisition procedure. It was not, however, the result of a transition from commune to *signoria*, from one stage of progressive state formation to another.[97] To be sure, the *signorie* of Du Pouget and Taddeo Pepoli marked significant stages of procedural change, but we have also seen that those changes had already begun under the commune during the early decades of the fourteenth century and continued during the restored communal government of the mid-1330s and again in the restored republic of 1376, indicating that fundamental socioeconomic developments, especially the increasingly oligarchical nature of state formation, whether signorial or republican, strongly exerted pressure on the policies, purposes, and functions of criminal justice.[98] The changed system was swifter and more repressive, but was it more effective? Chroniclers of the mid-fifteenth century complained that the podestà was unable to enforce the law because many powerful families and their followers were protected by the Bentivoglio government, a lament that strongly and eerily echoes the complaint of the podestà Corso Donati in 1288 that he could not enforce the law because of the impunity of privileged *popolani* who had no fear of retribution from his office.[99] Criminal justice may have become swifter and more repressive, but perhaps not more effective in providing peace and security to the community.

NOTES

1. Pertile, *Storia del diritto*; Kantorowicz, *Albertus Gandinus*; Levy and Rousseaux, "Stato, giustizia penale e storia."

2. Wickham, *Legge, pratiche e conflitti*; Kuehn, *Law, Family and Women*; Vallerani, *Il sistema giudiziario*; and Idem, *Medieval Public Justice*.

3. Vallerani, *Medieval Public Justice*, 171–72, sees a "crisis of the trial" not a "crisis of the accusation" in the early decades of the fourteenth century and firmly opposes the idea of "an unstoppable affirmation of the inquisition as justice of the state. The action is still in play in the fifteenth century." Zorzi, *L'amministrazione*, 78–79, moreover, asserts that there was an increase in accusation procedure and a decrease in inquisitions during the fifteenth century in Florence. Vitiello concludes that accusation procedure "was alive and well at the end of the fourteenth century" at Bologna, although in contrast at Reggio Emilia she found only 1 percent of trials were initiated by accusation. Vitiello, "Trial Procedure"; Eadem, *Public Justice*, 79–80. Dean describes accusation procedure in mid-fourteenth-century Bologna as "rare" and notes there were just four accusations in the records of 1351. Dean, *Crime and Justice*, 37. In an earlier work he set the date for decline later, noting that "accusations had become very rare" by the mid-fifteenth century. Dean, "Criminal justice," 17. Cucini notes that the descriptions of the two typologies of trials are no longer presented in separate rubrics in the statutes of 1376, 1389, and 1454 and in her sample of 440 trials from 1447–1511 for which the trial origin is known she finds only forty or 9.5 percent of the trials were initiated by accusation. Cucini, "Législation statutaire," 1:95–96, 1:337–48.

4. Vallerani, *Medieval Public Justice*, 114–73 and Idem, "La documentazione." For examples, see Kantorowicz, *Albertus Gandinus*, vol. 1. For an example of a more expensive *renuncia* (for 5 *lire*) in an accusation trial in 1364, see ASB, Inquisitiones, Mazzo 200, Register 3, fol. 62r and Accusationes 49b, Register 53, (1331) where the fine for a *renuncia* varied between 2 and 5 *lire*. The requirement that an accuser have an *estimo* was legislated in 1281–82, after a major compilation of the tax rolls completed that year. ASB, Inquisitiones, Mazzo 8, Register 6, fol. 3r, 14 August 1286.

5. Dean, "Criminal justice," 17.

6. Blanshei, "Cambiamenti e continuità."

7. Vallerani, *Medieval Public Justice*, 73–113; Idem, "La documentazione," 292–97.

8. Vitiello, "Trial Procedure"; Vitiello, *Public Justice*, 79.

9. Cucini, "Législation statutaire," 1:330.

10. Vallerani, *Medieval Public Justice*, 51–52. For the pertinent passages in Gandinus's *Tractactus* (e.g., if a person is reported as infamous for the crime by a promotor and denies that he is "de dicto crimine infamatum," then "nec prius poterit iudex super criminis probatione per inquisitionem procedure, donec constiterit de obiecto crimine infamatum eum esse; unde promotor inquisitionis debet probare, quod ille, contra quem inquiritur, sit de illo crimine infamatus"), see Kantorowicz, *Albertus Gandinus*, 2:40–41. At issue is the role the promotor plays *before* the judge initiates a trial reported by a private party on the basis of *mala fama*.

11. Blanshei, *Politics and Justice*, 343–44.

12. ASB, Inquisitiones, Mazzo 193, Registers 1–3, 1317 II.

13. Blanshei, *Politics and Justice*, 344.

14. Dean, "Plague and Crime."

15. The sample consists of complete registers from 1363 II, 1364 I, 1365 I, 1367 II and July 1368, and 1368 II, from ASB, Inquisitiones, Mazzo 197 (Registers 1 and 4), Mazzo 199 (Registers 2, 4, 6, 7), Mazzo 201 (Registers 1–5), Mazzo 204 (Registers 1–3, 5, 7–9, 12, 14, 15), Mazzo 206 (Registers 1, 4, 6–8, 10).

16. Ghirardacci, *Della historia di Bologna,* 2:265–74.

17. The sample is from the following semesters: 1380 I and II, 1381 II, 1388 I, 1390 II, 1395 II, 1398 II, 1400 II, 1419 I, and 1420 II.

18. Cucini, "Législation statutaire," 1:337.

19. Dean, "Criminal justice," 17. He cites my article of 1982 "for the reduction of accusation in the thirteenth century." Prosperi, "Il quadro politico-istituzionale," 50, expresses her disagreement with what she describes as my description of the decline of accusation in the late

thirteenth century. However, in that article, while I contended that inquisition procedure became dominant in cases of serious crimes, such as homicide, robbery and arson, as reflected in the ban and condemnation records, I also maintained that accusation was the method used in the majority of assault cases, which in turn comprised the great majority of all trials. Blanshei, "Crime and Law Enforcement."

20. Vallerani, *Medieval Public Justice*, 126–27.

21. Vallerani, *Medieval Public Justice*, 161–62. Changes in the physical aspect of the registers reflect the decline in the number of accusations. In 1313 the accusation parchment registers became smaller but thicker as the notaries ceased to write various notes such as *citationes* in the margins but rather included them in the body of the text itself, thereby dedicating more space to each trial.

22. ASB, Inquisitiones, Mazzo 173, Registers 2 and 10 (1352).

23. Vallerani's data can be used to indicate the impact of war at the end of the thirteenth century and that of factional strife in the early years of the fourteenth century since he gives the number of extant accusation registers and the total number of trials extracted from the extant registers for 1294 II, 1298 I, 1300 II, 1301, 1303 I, and 1304 I. The average number of trials per register by my calculations declines from 160 in 1294, the year before the war, to seventy-seven in 1298, forty-six in 1300, fifty-eight in 1301, sixty-six in 1303, and twenty-eight in 1304. The data are particularly suggestive since the 1294 figure according to Vallerani represents 20 percent of the hypothetical total number of trials and the 1298 figure 50 percent. Given the lack of extant inventories from the *camera actorum* for the later years Vallerani does not calculate the percentage of the hypothetical total after 1298, but since each notary probably had one register of accusations and we know there were eight notaries after 1295, we can estimate that the percentages were 50 percent for 1300, 25 percent for 1301 and 1303, and 75 percent for 1304. Vallerani, *Medieval Public Justice*, 121 for the trial data and 294–95 on tax delinquency "a true 'criminalization' of tax evasion."

24. I derive the 1304 ratio from the trial records of two notaries for whom we have both inquisition and accusation records. Francischus de Justenpoli recorded thirty-four accusation trials and eleven inquisition trials for a ratio of three to one. Antonius condam Marchexini de Padua recorded twenty-six accusations and ten inquisitions, for a similar ratio of 2.6 to one. ASB, Inquisitiones, Mazzo 86, Registers 3 and 6, January-June 1304. For another four of the eight notaries of this court only accusation records survive, which nevertheless permits us to see that the accusation trial averaged approximately twenty-three trials per semester, or possibly forty-six per year per notary, which yields an estimate of 184 accusation trials per semester and 368 trials per year, in sharp contrast to the peaks of 2,000 and over 3,000 accusations per year that Vallerani found in 1292 and 1294. ASB, Accusationes, Busta 26a, Registers 1–3 and 6.

25. Blanshei, *Politics and Justice*, 386–93.

26. ASB, Accusationes, Busta 41a, Register 1, 1310, first semester. It should be noted that this register, while it is complete for the first three months of the year, does not cover the whole six-month semester. There were two podestà for that semester, the first one dying at the end of March, and the new podestà did not have his judges finish the trials pending from his predecessor. The records for the second podestà are archived in separate registers for April, May, and June. However, to confuse matters even further, the podestà appointed in June for the second semester had his judges return to the pending cases of the first podestà of semester one and complete those trials, issuing sentences in July that are recorded in the original register of the first podestà, that is, in Register 1. That action has confused archivists and historians into thinking that Register 1 was complete for the entire semester when it actually represents only the first three months.

27. ASB, Accusationes, Busta 41a, Registers 11–14 cover only the brief regime of the second podestà for the first semester of 1319, with trial initiations from 27 April to 31 May, but have a large proportion of trials by privilege: Register 11 has thirteen trials, of which five are by privilege; Register 12 has thirteen trials, of which six are by privilege; Register 13 has twenty-five trials, of which ten are by privilege; Register 14 has nine trials, of which three are by privilege.

28. ASB, Inquisitiones, Mazzo 118, 1326 I, Registers 1 and 2 have forty-nine and fifty-five trials each. Register 3 has only twenty-five trials but is missing data from part of April and all of May and June. The five extant accusation registers, however, have only a total of seventy-three trials, ranging from twelve to twenty-one each. ASB, Accusationes, Busta 48b, Registers 755 (twelve trials), and 757 (twelve trials), Register 766 (twenty-one trials) Register 713 (fifteen trials), and Register 734 (thirteen trials). There is also a fifth register that is misfiled in ASB, Accusationes, Busta 50b, Register III.1. It is by the same notary, Turschus domini Dominici de Anchona, whose inquisitions are found in Inquisitiones, Mazzo 118, Register 2. His accusations extend from February to the end of June and comprise six accusation trials, three of which were by privilege, in contrast to the fifty-five inquisitions he recorded from January through July.

29. ASB, Sententiae, Busta 1, 1327 I: Register 784—six accusations; Register 29—seven accusations, Register 830—four accusations. Sententiae Busta 2, 1327 II: Register 850—six accusations; Register 847—twenty accusations; Register 851—six accusations, Register 848—five accusations; Register 827—twenty-three accusations (of which one is a continuation from the prior semester).

30. ASB, Inquisitiones, Mazzo 143, Registers 1 and 8, with thirty-six and thirty-four *inquisitio* trials each and nineteen accusations combined for the same two notaries, Salvus Gay and Laurentius, who shared a register for the semester, one doing the first three months and the other the last three months. ASB, Sententiae 11, Register 434. The number of accusations in three other registers (two notaries each for a combined six-month period) is twenty-four, nine, and twelve, in Registers 426, 418, and 425.

31. ASB, Inquisitiones, Mazzo 146, Register 2 (704) and Register 3, and Accusationes Busta 50a (1341–42), Register V.5 and Register V.18. The notaries were Gerardus condam Tecti Ser Burgi de Prato and Bertus condam Andree de Sancto Miniato. The inquisitions register for Bertus contains the *carta sciolta* inventory he made of all his registers, showing that his surviving accusation register was his one and only record of accusations, as is the case with all the surviving *carte sciolte* inventories.

32. ASB, Accusationes, Busta 50a (1341–43), Register V.10 has eleven accusations for the notary Leonardus Ser Jacobi de Sancto Miniato for an entire six-month period, twice the time period for Gherardus and Bertus. Register V.11, again for six months, for the notary Lucha condam Jannis de Vulteriis has nine accusations. Register V.17 has five accusations from the notary Matheus condam Ser Muczi Ser Pieri de Vulteris for the first three months of 1342 and Register VII.9 has seven accusations by the notary Symon Ser Bindi de Sancto Miniato for the entire six months of the first semester of 1342.

33. ASB, Sententiae, Busta 19 (1346–48), Registers 931, 933–37.

34. Dondarini, *Bologna medievale*, 164–71 for the demographic data.

35. Dean, "Plague and Crime."

36. Blanshei, *Politics and Justice*, 418–55. The term "querela" refers to the specific procedure here described but is not to be confused with the same term as used in the second half of the fourteenth century and later as synonymous with a complaint, for which the terms *requisitio* and *protestacio* were also used, as described below.

37. ASB, Riformagioni e provvigioni serie cartacea, Busta 222 (1327–28) and Busta 223 (1328–30); ASB, Riformagioni e provvigioni, serie miscellanea, Busta 2 (1301–35), folder "Suppliche del Bertrando del Poggetto." Petitions could also be made to the Council of the *Anziani*. Orlandelli, *La supplica*.

38. Vallerani, *Medieval Public Justice*, 306–47.

39. Vallerani, *Medieval Public Justice*, 151–56 on the *consilia* in general and 154n72 for the number of *consilia*. Also see Vallerani, "*Consilia iudicialia*"; and Dean, *Crime and Justice*. The *consilium* continued to be used in the first three decades of the fourteenth century, for example, in 1324 in which case the judge *ad maleficia* ordered the procurator of the victim "ad allegandum quicquid allegare voluit" before the *sapientes* who were to prepare a *consilium*. ASB, Inquisitiones, Mazzo 112, Register 4 (642), fol. 16r. For the forbidding of *consilia* by 1335, see Trombetti Budriesi, *Lo Statuto del Comune di Bologna dell'anno 1335*, 2:628–35, especially 635: Bk. VIII, Rubric 20, "De modo et forma procedendi contra accusatos vel

inquisitos non contumaces." The pertinent part of the rubric is retained in the statutes of 1389. ASB, Statuti 47(formerly XIV), Bk. V, Rubric 15, fols. 287r–89r, especially fol. 289r.

40. Lucchesi, *Si quis occidit occidetur*, xii-xiii.

41. Dean, *Crime and Justice,* 108.

42. *Statuta populi et communis Florentiae,* 1:180–81, Bk. I, Rubric 81, "De petitione consilii sapientis," "In causis et super causis et questionibus criminalibus, vel aliqua earum vel aliquot articulo earundem, non petatur nec petitum dari debeat consilium sapientis, et datum sit ipso iure nullum." And Archivio di Stato di Firenze, Statuti del Comune di Firenze 10, fols 51r–52r, Rubric LXVIII, De petitione consilii sapientis, "Et quod in causis vel super causis et questionibus criminalibus non petatur nec dari debeat consilium." I am grateful to Julius Kirshner for the Florentine citations.

43. Dean, *Crime and Justice,* 98.

44. The two points made (the principle of absolute equality in accusation procedure and the argument that the shift from accusation procedure to inquisition procedure "was neither unidirectional nor overall") are also made by Esther Cohen for developments in France. Cohen, "Inquiring Once More."

45. See Tamba, *Il regime del popolo*, for a fundamental study of the *Dieci di balìa* and the establishment of the authority of the *Sedici Riformatori*; also Lantschner, *The Logic of Political Conflict*.

46. ASB, Inquisitiones, Mazzo 274, Register 2 (1398), fols. 36r–37v, fols. 127r–29r, fols. 57r–70r; Inquisitiones, Mazzo 278, Register 2 (1400) fols. 45r–46v. Trevor Dean found that the charges in accusation trials were usually for "insult, trespass or adultery" in 1424–25, 1444, 1450, and 1469. Dean, "Criminal justice," p. 17.

47. See above, endnote 3.

48. For the colleges of the *gonfalonieri* and the *massari artium*, see Braidi, *Gli Statuti del Comune di Bologna,* 1:cxix–cxxiv. For the authority of the *milites* of the *capitano*, see ASB, Giudici, Register 805, Officium extraordinariorum. In 1377 the *gonfalonieri* were authorized to identify crime with help from men in their parishes, including crimes such as homicide. De Benedictis, "Da confalonieri del popolo a tribuni della plebe," 299.

49. ASB, Sindacato, Mazzo 25 (1396–99), Register 1, fol. 7v for the thirty-three *familiares* in 1396, and Register 3, fols. 4r–5r for the fifty-eight *familiares* in 1397.

50. In the 1370s the population of the city was 32,000 and probably descended to 25,000 after the epidemics of that decade. It was 50,000 in the late thirteenth century. Ginatempo and Sandri, *L'Italia delle città.*

51. Roberts, "Policing and Public Power," 52.

52. Dean, "Criminal justice," 30. A similar official with summary justice authority and his own court, the *vicarius domini*, was established by Taddeo Pepoli, for which see Antonioli, *Conservator pacis et iustitie,* 140–41.

53. ASB, Capitanato della Montagna, Mazzo I (1336–88), Liber Inquisitionum 1370 and Mazzo III (1406–09), Liber mallificiorum, 1409 II.

54. ASB, Inquisitiones, Mazzo 237, Register 1, fols. 7r–12v, 5 May–13 June 1380. Similarly, in response to a supplication, they ordered suspension of an inquisition against Nanne condam Casini de terra Castri Britonum on a charge of *verba iniuriosa* because the imputed was over eighty years old. ASB, Inquisitiones, Mazzo 238, Register 4, fols. 95r–97r, 5–15 October 1381.

55. ASB, Inquisitiones, Mazzo 237, Register 6, fols. 88r–90v, 92r–97v, 8 August–27 October 1380. For another trial suspension by the *anziani* that year, see Register 7, fols. 59r–61r, 30 March–5 April. The trial was an inquisition for property disturbance (cutting down trees) against twenty men and the *anziani* ordered that this trial and an accusation lodged separately by the alleged victim both be suspended.

56. ASB, Giudici, Register 824, fols. 2r–5r, 14–16 May. In this particular case, but not in others, the *anziani* and the colleges acted in conjunction with the Council of 400 for the initiation of the trial and the granting of summary justice (but acted alone for the commutation of the sentence from hanging to decapitation).

57. ASB, Giudici, Register 808, fols. 95r–98r, April 1377.

58. ASB, Inquisitiones, Mazzo 268, Register 1, fols. 46r–52r, 18 June–24 July 1395. For the role of Count da Barbiano in Bolognese affairs, see Cantelmi, *Bologna fra Trecento e Quattrocento,* 65–67.

59. ASB, Inquisitiones, Mazzo 268, Register 3, fols. 41r–45v, 26 February–17 April 1396.

60. ASB, Inquisitiones, Mazzo 268, Register 2, fols. 177r–78v, 20–27 October 1395. On the appointment of members of the *Sedici Riformatori* to special committees charged with addressing specific types of crimes or particular individuals from 1394 through the middle of the fifteenth century, see Dean, "Criminal Justice," 31.

61. For the politicization of justice in the early fourteenth century, see Blanshei, *Politics and Justice*, chapter 5. For a discussion of intervention of a broader type in the courts, see Dean, *Crime and Justice*, 42–43.

62. Cucini, "Législation statutaire," 1:324–27. This political use of the courts should be compared to the policy of government by supplication and decree that Vallerani found in the *signoria* of Taddeo Pepoli.

63. ASB, Notai Forensi, 1379–1531.

64. Prosperi, "Il quadro politico-istituzionale," 41–43. Also on the *notai forensi*, see Albertani, "Al cospetto dei giudici."

65. Blanshei, *Politics and Justice*, 369–77.

66. The 1295 *ordinamenta* and the statutes of 1335 and 1352 list eight notaries for the podestà's *ad maleficia* court. The statutes of 1376 list six notaries and the 1454 statutes list four. Fasoli and Sella, *Statuti di Bologna dell'anno 1288*, 1:576–92, Bk. V, Rubric CLIII, "Ordinamenta facta sub anno Domini millesimo ducentesimo nonagesimo quinto"; Trombetti Budriesi, *Lo Statuto del Comune di Bologna*, 1:7–10, Bk. I, Rubric 3 "De familia et salario domini potestatis et hiis quos secum ducere prohibetur"; Braidi, *Gli Statuti del Comune di Bologna*; 1:5–9, Bk. I, Rubric 2 "De familia et salario domini potestatis et hiis quos secum ducere prohibetur"; Cucini "Législation statutaire," 1:298.

67. ASB, Giudici, Register 844, fols. 103r–4v, 19 September 1398. The original trial in the podestà's court is in ASB, Inquisitiones, Mazzo 272, Register 2, fols. 14r–16v, 24 May–10 June 1398.

68. For the December 1294 legislation and its 24 January 1295 annulment, see ASB, Riformagioni, 139, fol. 139r.

69. Vestrucci, "Un confronto"; Venticelli, "Normative medievali bolognese"; Pini, *Le giustizie dipinte*; and the introductions to Trombetti Budriesi, *Lo Statuto del Comune di Bologna* and Braidi, *Gli Statuti del Comune di Bologna*; Venticelli "Metodologie elettroniche," and Cucini's Introduction (vol. I) to her edition of selections from the 1454 statutes, including all of Book IV, the "Liber quartus causarum criminalium," Cucini, "Lègislation statutaire." For a more general analysis of *arbitrium* see Vallerani "L'arbitrio." Vallerani makes a sharper distinction between republics and lordships in their respective relationships between the political and judicial spheres. My interpretation is closer to that of Moritz Isenmann for Florence during the same period. Isenmann, "From Rule of Law to Emergency Rule." I thank Maria Venticelli for making her dissertation available to me.

70. Fasoli and Sella, *Statuti di Bologna dell'anno 1288*, 1:191–92, Bk. IV, Rubric XXIIII, "De pena eius qui iniuriam vel obprobrium vel contumeliam fecerit domino potestati vel eiius familia," for the authority of the podestà in verbal attacks against officials. In the 1288 statutes, the rubrics on assault do not include injurious words. Fasoli and Sella, *Statuti di Bologna dell'anno 1288*, 1:206–7, Bk. IV, Rubrics XXXVIIII–XXXXI, In the statutes of 1335, however, penalties for *verbis iniuriosis* against anyone are specifically included, with the penalties to be determined by the judge. Trombetti Budriesi, *Lo Statuto del Comune di Bologna*, 2:689–91, Bk. VIII, Rubric 64 "De pena vulnerantis seu percucientis vel insultantis alliquem."

71. Trombetti Budriesi, *Lo Statuto del Comune di Bologna*, 2:607–12, Bk. VIII, Rubric 15, "De casibus in quibus dominus potestas tenetur inquirere,"; 2:612–16. Bk. VIII, Rubric 17, "De casibus in quibus dominus potestas possit inquirere,"

72. Dean, "Criminal justice," 19–20. The difference between the statutes of 1335 and 1454 lies in part in the shifting proportions of crimes for which the podestà was required to act or had the option of acting, with more in the first category in 1454. I count forty-eight required and twenty-two optional in 1335 and fifty-five required and eighteen optional in 1454.

73. Blanshei, "Homicide in a Culture of Hatred."
74. Dean, "Criminal justice," 26–27.
75. Wray, "Instruments of Concord"; Kumhera, *The Benefits of Peace*; Jansen, "'Pro bono pacis.'"
76. Blanshei, "Criminal Law." It was used at the turn of the century to mitigate a penalty for a captured *bannitus*, but that practice was annulled and the pertinent rubric removed from the statutes in 1311. Blanshei, *Politics and Justice*, 366–67, footnote 176.
77. ASB, Inquisitiones, Mazzo 151, Registers 1–5 (1339 I). ASB, Inquisitiones, Mazzo 143, Register 1, 1336, has three peace accords in assault trials during the communal regime between the *signorie* of Du Pouget and Pepoli. Given the relatively low proportion of minor crimes in the 1340s it is not surprising to find only two peace accords (both in assault trials) in the extant records from that decade. ASB, Inquisitiones, Mazzo 156, Register 2, fols. 16r–17r, 21 March–8 April 1342 and fols. 43r–45v 26 April–17 May 1342. In 1347 I, before the onslaught of the Black Death, seven of the hypothetical eight inquisition registers have survived as well as two *Libri prosecutionum*, or continuations of trials from the prior semester. There are no peace accords in those registers, but there is a high proportion of homicide trials—twenty-eight of eighty-one trials (34.5 percent). ASB, Inquisitiones, Mazzo 166, Registers 1–8 and Mazzo 166bis (which contains only one register).
78. ASB, Inquisitiones, Mazzo 172 (1351), Register 2, fols. 3r–5v; Register 6, fols. 24r, 58r, Register 10, fol. 38v, Register 12, fol. 8v, Register 13, fol. 20v.
79. ASB, Inquisitiones, Mazzo 173, Registers 4, 5, and 9. The probable use of a peace accord is almost never explicitly recorded in an accusation (just the *renuncia*), but for an exception, see Mazzo 173, Register 10, fols. 57r–58v, 22 January–17 March 1352. In this case the accuser charged his wife with adultery, then made a peace accord with her and ended the case with an "instrumentum pacis renunciationis et remisionis dicte accuse." The accuser received a condemnation of 10 *lire*.
80. ASB, Inquisitiones, Mazzo 195, Register 1, fols. 5v–8v, 13rv, 23r–24r, 9 September–14 November 1362.
81. Vallerani, *Medieval Public Justice*, 306, 331–32, 339–46. ASB, Inquisitiones, Mazzo 184, Register 1, fol. 61r.
82. For the 25-*lire* figure, see ASB, Giudici, Register 825, fols. 28r–33v, May–June 1386.
83. Dean, "Criminal justice," 28.
84. ASB, Inquisitiones, Mazzo 206, Registers 1, 4, 6, 7, 8, and 10.
85. ASB, Inquisitiones, Mazzo 233, Register 2.
86. Fasoli and Sella, *Statuti di Bologna dell'anno 1288*, 1:576–92, Bk. V, Rubric CLIII, "Ordinamenta facta sub anno Domini millesimo ducentesimo nonagesimo quinto." At the same time the number of *ad maleficia* judges was increased from one to two. The last record of the *malefici novi* acting as a criminal court under the mandate of the *ad maleficia* judge is a two-folio fragment of a rape case from the second semester of 1294. ASB, Inquisitiones, Mazzo 31, Register 4.
87. Kantorowicz, *Albertus Gandinus*, 1:244–47.
88. ASB, Inquisitiones, Mazzo 8, Register 1, fols. 25r–31v, 26–27 August 1286. For another example, see Kantorowicz, *Albertus Gandinus*, 1:203–18 for the 1299 trial against Menghus, Nicholaus, and Sandrolus. Menghus was in custody and was hanged; Nicholaus and Sandrolus were banned as public and famous thieves. This trial was initiated by the *miles* and notary at the scene of the crime at a *stacio* in *capella* S. Bertholi on 5 December and concluded on 14 December. Menghus was captured when the three attempted a theft at that *stacio*, and was tortured, but only after nine witnesses testified against him and after the *miles* and notary, together with some *beorariis* and *familliaribus* of the podestà and two heralds of the commune, at the order of the judge, went to Menghus's house and there found certain of the stolen goods.
89. ASB, Inquisitiones, Mazzo 112 (1324 I), Register 1 (612). Trials in 1324 still included interrogation of witnesses at the scene of the crime, for example, fols. 5r–6v, fols. 18r–21v, 58r–64r, 78r–81r, 86r–88r, 89r–92r, 98r–96r, 96v–100r. The same is true for trials in 1324 II and 1326 I and II. ASB, Inquisitiones, Mazzo 114 (1324 II), Inquisitiones, Mazzo 117 (1326 I) and Mazzo 118 (1326 II). There are exceptions, for example the trial against Maghinardus filius condam Turdini comitis de Panico and several others, a trial initiated by *querela* and a grant of

summary justice authority to the podestà, but this is not typical of *querela*-initiated trials. ASB, Inquisitiones, Mazzo 118, Register 2, 56r–59r, 10–15 February 1326.

90. Fasoli and Sella, *Statuti di Bologna dell'anno 1288*, 1:576–92.

91. Dean, "Plague and crime."

92. ASB, Inquisitiones, Mazzo 129, Register 2 (1330 I). This register has twenty-eight trials, of which eight are without witnesses. In two of the trials against famous thieves there are no witnesses (fols. 20r–22r, 39r–40r), but in other such trials there are witnesses. In one trial for homicide the witnesses are all only *publica vox* and hearsay but again the judge proceeds on the basis of their testimony (fols. 2r–4v).

93. ASB, Inquisitiones, Mazzo 143, Registers 1, 7–9. (The probative stage is missing in ten of the trials because they are *prosecutiones*). The number of witnesses given by the local officials and interrogated by the judge had also been reduced, usually to four or five witnesses.

94. ASB, Inquisitiones, Mazzo 195, Register 4, fols. 13r, 32v–33r. 41r, 44r, September 1363. However, the formula is not found in the records of 1364 (Mazzo 200), 1365 (Mazzo 202), 1366 (Mazzo 203), or 1367 (Mazzo 204). It appears again and becomes an integral part of trial procedure in 1368 (Mazzo 205, Register 11).

95. ASB, Inquisitiones, Mazzo 253, Register 3, fols. 45r–50r, 9–23 April 1388. The trial proceeded, however, against the third person, Nardolus, whose procurator produced a peace accord and a poverty plea on his behalf. Nardolus had inflicted a blow with a lance and with effusion of blood to the head of one of the others. For the statute of 1389, see ASB, Statuti 47 (formerly XIV), fols. 281r–82r, Bk. VIII, Rubric 10, "De notticationibus mallificiorum per Ministrales vel Massarios fiendis." For the *requisitio* in 1454, see Dean, "Criminal Justice," 18 and Cucini, "Législation statutaire," 1:90.

96. Dean, "Criminal justice," 28–29. Cucini found five examples of *circumdatio* in her sample of ninety-one trials that were not completed. Cucini, "Législation statutaire," 1:370.

97. The classic article on this theme is by Philip Jones, "Communes and Despots." For overviews of the topic, see Zorzi, *Le signorie cittadine,* and Scott, *The City-State,* 51–56, 230–34.

98. Blanshei, "Aristocratization."

99. Ghirardacci, *Della historia di Bologna,* 107, 116, 129, 130. Also cited by Dean, "Criminal justice," 25 and Vallerani, *Medieval Public Justice*, 278.

Chapter Four

Investigating Homicide

Bologna in the 1450s

Trevor Dean

On Christmas Eve 1453, the local official of the village of Saliceto traveled the 45 km to Bologna to report the discovery of a dead man in a ditch in woodland on the riverbank.[1] A servant herding some oxen had come across it when his dog began to bark loudly: he went to the tavern, informed his master, who called some neighbors and they all went to look. No one knew who it was or who had killed him. Having received this notification, the head of the judiciary in Bologna, podestà Giovanni Leonelli da Spoleto, sent one of his notaries to inspect. He reported that the dead man was wearing a cloak and red hose, his hands were tied behind his back with a belt, he was about thirty years old, of middling stature, with a thick beard ("he appeared to have been shaved two or three days before his death"). The veins of his throat had been cut with a knife, which was found in the ditch by his head. Noteworthy is the very precise description by the notary, in order to assist in identifying this unknown victim (clothes, usual appearance, age), as well as the manner and timing of his death. Inspection of the body, the number and size of wounds, the likely weapon, and the location, were all essential first steps in establishing that a homicide had occurred.[2] One fifteenth-century jurist insisted that the judge must take care to ensure that this information was recorded "in bastardello"—in the daily journal of the court—so as to avoid later challenge.[3] Accordingly, it is in the *bastardelli* for 1453–54 that this report of the inspection of the corpse at Saliceto is to be found, along with all the subsequent stages in the investigation. Within a month, the podestà had a chief suspect, one Giovanni di Boldrino, alias Grillo. How did he arrive at this outcome?

This is a chapter in understanding how late-medieval Italian judges conducted criminal investigations, specifically into alleged homicides. The history of medieval crime is usually written with the trial or its outcome (sentence, petition for pardon) as the starting point. This is an effect of the type of source usually available: either trial records, which begin with an indictment,[4] or sentences, issued at the trial's end,[5] or fines paid or unpaid,[6] or pardons, requested at later dates,[7] or lists of executed convicts.[8] The documentation is thus mostly post-investigative. Only rarely do documents from the investigative stage survive.[9] Fortunately, the judicial archive in Bologna contains numerous journals (*bastardelli* or *vacchettini*) of the criminal court notaries, in a characteristic long and narrow format.[10] It was these journals in which judges were encouraged to ensure that every stage in a criminal trial was recorded.[11] Though this Bolognese archival series starts in the late fourteenth century, the early registers lack consistency of focus, and some of them are not judicial records at all. It is only from the mid-fifteenth that they come to focus exclusively on recording the day-by-day hearings in the criminal court, a mixture of complaints, depositions, interrogations, inventories of sequestered goods, and promises to appear when summoned. The value of this source lies in the fact that, as a manual for criminal-court notaries stated: "many things are noted down in the *bastardello* which are not later put into the ordinary criminal register."[12] One of those things was the infliction of torture on suspects, such that the *bastardelli* help fill an important gap in judicial sources, namely the lack of material regarding the practice of torture.[13]

The *vacchettini* constitute the least used and studied of the major sources of criminal trials in Bologna, the others being the much more extensive trial registers, the collection of sentences, and the court's "repository papers" (*carte di corredo*) consisting of all the documents and parchments submitted to the court in the course of a trial. The city's podestà, and his subordinates as criminal judges, were always non-Bolognese professionals on short-term contracts. They were appointed and paid by the government of the city, which at this time consisted of a combination of the representative of the city's papal overlord (legate or governor) and the civic councils of the *Sedici Riformatori* and the *anziani* (elders: members of the executive council), within a political evolution of shifting balance between external-papal and internal-oligarchical and signorial politics, and the growing dominance of one family, the Bentivoglio.[14] The decade in question here, the 1450s, opened with a major oligarchical advance, as the ruling *Sedici Riformatori*, having been confirmed in office annually since 1447, were then prolonged indefinitely, the trend being toward life-terms and inherited office.[15] During the decade, the regime leader, Sante Bentivoglio, "managed to accumulate . . . many of the trappings of 'lordship,'" such as grants of property and economic privilege, a new urban palace, and alliance with external powers such as the Medici in Florence and the Sforza in Milan.[16] Politically, the decade was relatively tranquil, marked until 1455 by the presence of Cardinal Bessarion as papal representative,[17] and marred only by the occasional conspiracy or attempt by exiles to re-enter the territory.

The *vacchettini* for the 1450s—nineteen registers covering mainly the period 1451–56—contain twenty-two cases of homicide, in various phases of reporting and inquiry.[18] Some are complaints from relatives of the victim, with supporting testimony: thus, for example, the *bargello* (captain of the guard), Raffaele da Pistoia, lodged a formal complaint (*querela*) for the killing of his son in a fight while on police duty.[19] Some are depositions from witnesses following denunciation by local officials.[20] Some are confessions: Alessandro confessed to killing his brother-in-law "because he was abusing his wife Clara," Alessandro's sister; and Agostino Galluzzi revealed the identity of the killer of a goldsmith in March 1455, taking advantage of an appeal for information, which offered rewards (money and pardon), even to an accomplice. Some are investigations following formal denunciation, as in the case of two men who "suddenly and unexpectedly" came to blows at celebrations on the feast of Saint Peter, 1459, and killed each other;[21] others follow notification by private citizens implicated in the antecedents to the crime, and presenting incriminating evidence, as in the case of a woman found dead in a man's "studio" in 1453.[22] There are also several investigations into unexplained deaths: two students attested that a man, Filippo da Napoli, had been unwell and had died from failing to take sufficient care; a man who pulled a woman's body out of a well explained how he thought she had died; a widow was found drowned in the river and there were reports of her enmity with a tailor and of her possible abduction by masked men.[23] An inquiry was also launched into the disappearance of a man, presumed dead, as he had not been seen at home for weeks yet his house was full of bread and wine.[24] These, together with the five cases discussed in detail below were probably not the sum total of homicide investigations in Bologna in this decade, as not all the *vacchettini* survive and as the surviving trial registers—sixteen, covering the years 1450–53 and 1455–58—contain 136 homicide trials, or roughly twenty per year. There does seem to have been some selectivity of cases in the *vacchettini*: investigations were carried out where there was doubt whether a crime had taken place, or doubt over the identity of either the victim or the killer, or where extensive examination of witnesses was required or, especially, torturing of suspects. Such also seems to be the case in the late fourteenth century.[25]

In examining five cases in detail, one area of modern criminology and one area of medieval jurisprudence will be brought together: research on interrogative techniques in modern forensic linguistics, and medieval works on the theory and practice of criminal justice. From the first, I draw conceptual distinctions regarding questions (types and sequences) in police and court interrogations. Against a background distinction between open questions ("Tell/Explain/Describe") and closed (allowing a "Yes/No" answer), researchers have classified investigators' questions in various ways (open and closed, productive and unproductive, probing and facilitative as against leading, suggestive, or hypothetical).[26] This has the advantage of providing a specific repertory of question-types which offers a means of categorizing and conceptualizing the rather generic recommendations of medieval jurists on the form that interrogation should take. In his treatise of 1495, Francesco Bruni urged that interrogation should be "general, not descending to details or to naming individuals," as that would be suggestion not inquiry,[27] while Lodovico Bolognini (1446–1508) added that the judge must be careful not to "instruct" the suspect by loading a question with detailed information about the crime, but must follow an interrogative hierarchy, from the more general to the more specific.[28] From this body of medieval juristic writings I have also drawn an understanding of how judges were trained to conduct criminal investigations, particularly in the area of the value and weight of pieces of incriminating evidence.

NAME THE LOCAL VILLAIN

In the case of the corpse found on Christmas Eve, the podestà's first step was to order the local officials of four villages closest to the crime scene to appear, with all the men of their villages, in Bologna on 30 December. Consequently, over 150 *contadini* assembled in the podestà's palace, and were told not to leave without permission. The podestà then ordered his criminal judge to question them all, to discover the identities of the victim and his killer, and the public reputation (*fama*) of the inhabitants. With an open invitation to talk about neighbors, the first villager to speak very promptly named Giovanni alias Grillo, though without implicating him yet in this killing: instead, he stated that two years previously Giovanni had robbed a traveler in that district and had been convicted for it, but the penalty had been remitted because Giovanni had killed a Bolognese bandit (a contumacious and banned suspect who could be killed with impunity and the killer rewarded). The second villager to be questioned added that Giovanni was a man of ill-repute who lived just half a mile from the crime-scene. A succession of other informants repeated these assertions. One, asked if there was anyone of ill-fame in the village, said that "Giovanni Grillo is used to doing such things." Asked if Giovanni had any associates in his crimes, the villagers produced other names and other stories: one Bartolino had engaged in some thieving, along with a shoemaker; Bartolino's son "could not stay in Bolognese territory" and was said to be in prison in Ferrara; another Giovanni who had stolen a pig; a family once resident in the village, "of great ill fame of this sort of crime, of whom only one survives, in Ferrara, and the others are dead." With this information, the judge took to one side Bartolino and the two Giovannis, and questioned them. This interrogation at once went into a closed mode, with yes/no answers. Bartolino denied having stolen anything. Giovanni Grillo denied previously robbing or killing anyone. Nevertheless, they were all detained, and that evening the podestà himself took over the interrogations.

This was a textbook case of how to identify an unknown killer. Jurists' treatises advised commencing with a "special" inquest regarding the fact of the crime, and a "general" inquest regarding the person responsible.[29] Regarding the first, Baldus de Ubaldis hypothesized the case of a man found drowned in the river Po: the judge should ascertain, he advised, whether the man was in the habit of bathing, whether he had enemies, or whether there were robbers active in the area.[30] Regarding the second, jurists listed the various incriminating signs (*indicia*) that could suggest culpability: whether suspects were used to committing such actions, whether they had fled, whether they had enmity with the victim and had recently threatened him, what sort of places the suspects frequented, what their reputation (*fama*) was, and so on.[31] In the sixteenth century, Francesco Casoni drew all these signs together into a single "Table of *indicia*," with seven chief categories, including the person, the cause of the crime, and what was said and done before, during, and after the crime.[32] In the case of an unidentified killer, *fama* and past actions were a good place to start.[33] As the Bolognese jurist Lodovico Bolognini advised, "anyone's ill-fame in the past creates presumption about the present."[34] Bolognini also referred to an opinion of the earlier jurist Angelo Ubaldi: if a corpse is found near the house of a certain person, should it be presumed that he was killed by that person? Yes, is the answer, if that person is used to committing homicides.[35] So it is unsurprising that the judge enquired into the *fama* of local inhabitants. What is surprising is that the inhabitants gathered in the podestà's palace already knew this script: they immediately pointed to a man who lived close to the crime-scene and who had killed before. As has been noted in other contexts, inquests were prepared for.[36]

Giovanni Grillo was quickly put to torture, because of his "manifest vacillation, changing color and trembling and rambling speech."[37] This "rambling speech" was not, however, recorded, and putting to torture on the basis of pallor was questionable.[38] The jurist Francesco Bruni advised that, though a judge could torture on the basis of trepidation, trembling and vacillating responses, he should be careful to have these responses fully written down, in order to avoid being accused later of torturing without *indicia*.[39] It is possible that Podestà Leonelli was in a hurry to close the case, but this does represent a departure from the textbook. Raised on the rope-hoist, Giovanni at first maintained that he had never done anything wrong and was totally innocent, but after a while asked to be let down, promising to tell the truth. Meanwhile, the other suspects were released, according to one witness, because "half the men of Bologna rose up asking for them."[40] Giovanni Grillo was not questioned again until 3 January, when he reverted to denying any knowledge of the dead man. Tortured once more (though with no sign of the additional *indicia* required by statute law for repetition of torture), he admitted that over a year ago, in the same place, he had robbed a traveler of a sword and some coins. Then on 7 January it was reported by one of the podestà's staff that some bloodstains had been found on Giovanni's clothing. Asked where the blood had come from, Giovanni at first said he did not know, then that it could have come from a pig he had killed in his own house. Eventually, toward the end of January, Giovanni's wife confirmed that about a month before Christmas, he had brought in a dead pig, but she did not know where it had come from.

Meanwhile, other leads had also been pursued. The story about a stolen pig, related by the local taverner at the first questioning of the villagers, led to the torturing of two men, one of whom eventually admitted killing and eating it as part of a neighborhood quarrel. Information about the identity of the dead man came at last when Giovanni's mother-in-law, Bartolomea, was questioned. She reported a conversation in the house of Giovanni Scaccani. Giovanni had said "It seems that the poor man who was killed had a sack of merchandise," and Bartolomea's daughter said, "It would be the one who came here and asked me for some heat and food for the love of God, and he had a sack of nice things, textiles and bags."[41]

Finally the outline of a solution to this Christmas killing took shape: an itinerant pedlar, whom no one in the village would have recognized; a suspect of ill-repute with a track record for robbing and killing on the very same spot; bloodstains on his clothing. However, none of this was sufficient to lead to a formal trial. Giovanni's ill-fame, along with his physical reactions (trembling, changing color), were sufficient to subject him to torture, but not sufficient to convict. Under torture, Giovanni maintained his denials. The speed and directness of the investigation are impressive. The podestà was able to command the assembly, in midwinter, of scores of villagers. They cooperated willingly, keen to name the ill-famed. By open-ended questioning, several names, and some other crimes, were immediately identified. The men spoke freely about public events—a previous robbery, a release from penalty, local thieving, a man in prison. However, the women close to two of the suspects in fact knew more about the possible identity of the victim than did their menfolk, but the failure to question them at the beginning excluded their more domestic information: female testimony was more voluble and detailed, presenting different facts differently, but was less trusted.[42] Perhaps the podestà had identified the killer, perhaps he had not; what is important to focus on is the means by which he conducted the investigation, its strengths and limitations. The villagers were keen to point to someone who had killed before, and the podestà was trained to follow their indication. Blood was found on that man's clothing. Other suspects were released, allegedly by popular demand. Convicting Grillo became the only goal: a recipe for false confession and wrongful conviction.[43] Had the judge got his man, or was this an example of co-construction, by judge and witnesses, of a likely suspect on the basis of the medieval equivalents of "recurring storylines, familiar genres . . . and typical characters"?[44]

SUSPICIONS OF KILLING TO ORDER

A similar thoroughness was exhibited in the inquiry into the murder of Elena, wife of Gregorio delle Garzarie from the village of Sant'Agata, who was killed with an axe on All Saints' Day 1456 in the urban parish of San Martino.[45] The sequence of thirty depositions opens on 12 November at an already advanced state of the investigation, when a man with the nickname Gatto, from Carpi, had been incriminated by the parish official in a formal denunciation. The questioning of these witnesses aimed to establish the movements and contacts of Gatto, on the assumption that he had killed Elena at the request of others, namely Ugolino da Sassuolo, of Sant'Agata, and Rolandino Romanti, of Bologna. This assumption seems to have been created from the responses of the first witness to be questioned, Ugolino's own brother-in-law. In addition to providing a physical description of Gatto—about twenty-five, black hair, middling stature, no beard, fleshy face—this witness provided the information linking him to Ugolino, who had employed him as a day-laborer in the summer, and to Rolandino, as he had heard that Gatto was staying on his farm, though not working there. He reported hearing a conversation in the village about the murder: "There's talk that it was the servants of Ugolino."[46] Asked about Ugolino's *fama*, he related that Ugolino had directly told him that he had killed his own cousin ten years previously and was banned for it, then later released. It was also common report, he said, that twenty-eight years ago Ugolino had killed a merchant and robbed him. The next witness, also from Sant'Agata, reported that Ugolino had already fled the village into the territory of Modena, ruled by the duke of Ferrara, "out of fear lest his body be destroyed by torture, because he is weak and has long been unwell . . . and if he did not fear torture he would come and defend himself from incrimination as he regards himself as not guilty."[47] With the third witness, a tanner (*pelacanus*) in Bologna, the judge asked again about Ugolino's *fama*: Ugolino had killed his cousin in a dispute over a small debt, the tanner said, and had become rich by killing the merchant; he also had a recent lawsuit with Elena and her husband and had several times sworn, "al corpo di dio," that he would have one of them killed.[48]

Again, the focus was quickly tightening on a likely suspect: a man who had killed before, who had fled the village, and who had previously threatened the victim. Actions before and after a homicide were treated as indicative of participation: similar crimes in the past, flight, and threats were all standard elements in the repertory of incriminating signs. Within a few days the judge ordered Ugolino's goods to be impounded, including considerable quantities of grain, wine, and hay.[49]

The judge next moved on to investigating the possible involvement of Rolandino Romanti, and in particular whether Gatto or any other *contadini* had recently stayed in his house. This would have rested on the assumption that such closeness—the juristic sources would say "domesticity and familiarity"—was a possible sign of instigation to kill.[50] First he interrogated Rolandino's wife, who denied all knowledge of Gatto or of other *contadini* staying there. Then his daughter-in-law, who was more forthcoming about the servants and domestic arrangements, and confirmed that they had two axes in the house. Then his son, who admitted that Gatto had been his father's servant two years previously, and had been in Sant'Agata again recently, working for Ugolino; he also confirmed that they owned two axes, but denied that his father had any enmity with Elena or her husband.[51] Then Rolandino's servant, Lisa, who had been there for five weeks during the daughter-in-law's labor, and his tenants (*socide*), who responded to questions about Gatto or other foreigners staying there. No one mentioned the fact that Rolandino's son Niccolò had been convicted of murder in 1450, which might have been in their minds.[52]

Alongside this, the judge questioned other villagers about the movements of both Gatto and Rolandino on the day of the murder: one man had seen Gatto on the road into the city, another had seen him pass the church of San Martino Aposa in Bologna, a third had seen him pass in front of Elena's house, and a fourth had seen him going toward Ugolino's house, "pallid with sweat and muddied"; while Rolandino was spotted in Ugolino's house on the day after the murder, and one witness recalled hearing a conversation between them: "Because I've been ill I wouldn't want to go to those prisons or to torture"; "You're making a big mistake in taking flight if you're not guilty."[53] Again the judge's action seems structured by juristic discussion of possible *indicia*: being seen in the area at the time of a killing was one argument for connecting suspect to crime when direct evidence was lacking;[54] and the reference to pallor was not an incidental detail.[55]

Finally, he interviewed Rolandino himself, who explained his long association with Ugolino, and his temporary employment of Gatto two years ago, but denied hearing that Ugolino had threatened Elena or her husband or that he had had any recent contact with Gatto, and accounted for his movements around the feast of All Saints. Rolandino promised to reappear if summoned, and was released. Consequently it was Gatto alone who was charged with this murder: the trial formally opened on 27 November with the indictment stating that Gatto—only now is his real name, Niccolò di Manfredino, given—killed Elena with three wounds to the head with an axe, in the street outside her house, and naming two witnesses, a priest and a married woman (neither of whom were interviewed).[56] Gatto did not appear, and was banned with a sentence of decapitation.

Contract killings were among the most difficult to prove.[57] As one French historian has put it, they existed in the shadows and were hard to unveil.[58] The "processus cloisonné" by which assassinations were organized, meant that the judge had to seek out the weak link who could lead the inquest up the shadowy chain of command.[59] This judge was certainly tenacious in his search for evidence of association between the supposed killer and his supposed hirers. He was led to this by reports of Ugolino's own murderous past, of his dispute with the victim, and his threats against her and her husband. Previous history was seen as determinative. His interviewing technique combined the initial open questions posed to villagers about Ugolino's *fama*, with the probing questions put to Rolandino, his family and servants. However, no one was tortured, and the occasion for closed questions did not arise. In other such cases, the judge had more success: in March 1456, a Bolognese woman, Maddalena, was sentenced to death for ordering the killing of her son-in-law.[60]

CHERCHEZ LA FEMME

On 11 August 1453, the local official of the city district of Santa Lucia informed the judge that Gaspare Tibaldi had died in the street overnight from wounds to his head.[61] At once, some witnesses were questioned, "to inform the court," regarding what they knew of Gaspare and if they knew who killed him. The questions were open-ended, designed to elicit information, and the witnesses responded cooperatively with lengthy narratives. The first witness, from the victim's parish of San Mamolo, said that, on his return from accompanying one of the *anziani*, he and three other men had encountered Gaspare, "and they stood and sang together" nearby and then dined. Meanwhile, Alberto Boccadiferro, armed with a sword, had appeared and called Gaspare aside. They spoke together secretly, but the witness and his companions then left, so he did not know what happened next, though he did know that Alberto had not been found. So, the first witness already indicates a possible killer: a man with a sword, a private conversation, a disappearance. The second witness provided a complementary account: he was at his doorway the previous evening when he saw Alberto pass, sword in hand, and saw him go to Gaspare's house and knock. Gaspare not being in, the witness said to Alberto "What are you doing here?" to which Alberto replied "I'd like to talk to Gaspare." The witness then saw the group of singers arrive and saw all of them, Gaspare and Alberto included, move off. The questioning of this witness then took a sudden turn, both in form and content: Did Alberto visit Gaspare's house to have sex with his wife? The shift to a closed question was evidently purposed to reveal a possible motive for the murder. With this shift, the witness became less cooperative: certainly he visits the house, he replied, but he did not know the reason. And what is the reputation of Gaspare's wife? "It is commonly reputed ill by all the neighbors." How and why the judge introduced this line of questioning is unclear. This time there is no juristic discussion to act as a guide. Was the judge following a hunch, or was there some off-the-record gossip? Whichever it was, after just two interviews, the judge clearly believed he had identified both killer and motive.

From this point, the gathering of information accelerated. Matteo Gazzoli da Piumazzo (near the border with Modena) attested that, on his way to Bologna, four miles outside the city, he had met Alberto, and he reported the following conversation:

> Matteo: "God give you good day, *compare*. Where are you going?"
> Alberto: "I'm going yonder. Recommend me to Misser Carlo Malvezzi. I've done something that I shall always be unhappy about, but I've done to him what he wanted to do to me."
> Matteo: "What have you done?"
> Alberto: "I've wounded a man, and if he isn't dead, he can't survive, because I've given him three or four sword-blows."[62]

Matteo asked who it was, but received no reply.

Carlo Malvezzi himself (a member of the ruling *Sedici Riformatori*) then appeared and said that Gaspare's wife, Giovanna, had another lover (Melchiore da Vizzano) and had been pressing him to throw Gaspare down a well so that he would die. With the judge returning to open questions ("What do you know of Giovanna?"), further information on a relationship between her and Alberto came from Francesco Caravita, who reported it as *publica vox* that they were having sex. Showing familiarity with the technical vocabulary, he said he knew this by presumption and *indicia*, for every day Giovanna passed four or five times in front of Alberto's workshop, and Alberto was always overjoyed to see her, saying "Here she is, here she is," and going after her. This witness, who worked in Alberto's shop in San Mamolo, also said that he had heard that Alberto entered her house by a window and stayed all day. Two female witnesses from the parish confirmed that Alberto frequented Giovanna's house, and that Giovanna was ill-famed ("she does things her own way"), but they were uncertain about what constituted ill fame.

Finally, still on 11 August, the time had come to interrogate Giovanna. On the basis, presumably, of her reported ill-fame and the secondhand information from Carlo Malvezzi, the judge had already decided to torture her, as she was brought directly into the torture room. It is questionable whether the judge had sufficient *indicia*—jurists' opinions varied on whether ill-fame alone sufficed—but he was perhaps following the line of reasoning, suggested by Baldus de Ubaldis, that in concealed crimes the judge should be "easier and more ready" to torture.[63] It is important to stress that this happened before the trial was formally initiated, and that both the criminal judge and the podestà were present, indicating the seriousness of the decision. The interrogation of Giovanna shifts into a firmly closed mode (yes/no), and her responses were correspondingly brief: the judge was no longer seeking information, but confirmation of guilt. She was first asked a standard question: did she know why she had been arrested? No, she replied, unless it was about the killing of Gaspare last night. Did she know who killed Gaspare: No. She was then questioned under torture—one "cavaleta," then two pulls (*tractus*) on the rope, followed by another three pulls. About her relation with Alberto: did she know him, has he ever had sex with her? She admitted to knowing Alberto, as her husband had introduced him, but she denied ever having sex with him. Faced with these denials, the podestà sent her back to prison, with the order "to think about telling the truth," a clear indication that he did not accept her answers, a mode of interrogation that is identified in modern studies as likely to produce false memories.[64] Before her next interrogation on 13 August, one further witness reported a conversation with Melchiore da Vizzano, who had claimed to have had sexual relations with Giovanna, and who had said that "this devil of a woman wants me to kill her husband."[65] This additional evidence legitimated further torture, according to the legal regulations.[66] So Giovanna was questioned again, after having been given three "moderate" drops on the rope. This time the question was more open, though presumed her guilt ("Tell the truth about the death of Gaspare"). In response, she insisted that she was unhappy at Gaspare's death, "as she had good times with him and he let her do what she wanted,"[67] and that Alberto only ate in their house on a few occasions. Given this continued profession of innocence, the podestà declared the *indicia* against Giovanna to be "purged" and ordered her release.

Consequently it was against Alberto alone that the trial began on 21 August. He was charged with going, armed with a sword, to the house of Gaspare, where three or four companions had dined, and, calling to Gaspare, "with such familiarity and closeness that he seemed to be a friend," after which they both left, going to an alley where Alberto drew his sword and "treasonably" (*proditorie*) hit Gaspare five times to the head, causing his death. Alberto did not attend court to enter his defense, and was banned with a sentence of decapitation.[68] The first part of the indictment clearly draws on the testimony gathered—the sword, the place, the private conversation—but then departs from the evidence in interpreting the character of the conversation (intimate, seeming-friendly), as a support for the subsequent presentation of the killing as "treasonable", that is, deceptive and probably signaling that the blows were inflicted from behind. The indictment also narratively connects the attested sighting of Alberto and Gaspare in conversation to the location of Gaspare's corpse: Alberto led Gaspare to the secluded spot.

What is striking about this investigation is its speed. The day after the killing, a suspect is immediately indicated. Witnesses are assembled who saw the victim and suspect together, who saw the suspect on the road and who had information about the character, behavior, and conversation of the victim's wife. The judge also solicited the information that suggested a motive: that Alberto killed Gaspare at the request of Giovanna. This murder had some of the hallmarks of assassination (the timing at night, the location in an alley-way, the swift but certain kill, the "treasonable" blows), but lacked secrecy, as Alberto was reported to have sought Gaspare openly and to have spoken about his crime during his flight. However, the case against Giovanna could never be substantiated, as she successfully denied it. The suspicion attests to a belief that adulterous women could order the killing of their husbands, a belief perhaps constituting what has been called a "folk psychological narrative script," to which prosecutors appealed in constructing their versions of events, to make them persuasive.[69]

Such suspicions arose in other cases. In 1457 Bartolaccio Calli from Saliceto confessed to killing the husband of Margarita with a single blow to the head with an axe: Bartolaccio admitted that he and Margarita had begun to have sex after her first husband died, but her relatives insisted on marrying her to an old gardener called Tonio, which she accepted reluctantly and on the private understanding, between herself and Bartolaccio, that if she did not like Tonio, Bartolaccio would kill him and they would run away together.[70] Bartolaccio was prosecuted for adultery and for killing Tonio. As he had confessed, he was condemned, though the precise penalty is not recorded.[71] The following decade produced two further examples of suspected female instigation: Lucrezia, wife of Niccolò da Siena, for the revenge killing of her "enemy" Benedetto della Rate; and Margarita from the village of Riosto, for the killing of her husband ("Get rid of this husband for me, and let's leave here"), who was cut down with an axe and fell into the river.[72]

NO CRIME

In mid-June 1453 a notification arrived—not a formal denunciation—from an inhabitant of the city district of Sant'Arcangelo, that a shoemaker, Guglielmo from Germany (later described as coming from Holland) had killed his pregnant wife.[73] The informant nominated two witnesses, both men from Flanders, one of them a carpenter, to prove this. Asked an open question, what did he know of this, the first witness said very explicitly that Guglielmo had beaten his wife, Joan from Scotland, so hard (*acriter*) that she had died. He had heard from one of the podestà's own *sbirri*, and from others, that Joan was ill, and he had gone to visit her, and she had told him that Guglielmo had beaten her with punches and kicks all over her body, and that "she had sensed that the birth (*partum*) she had in her belly was dead from these blows and beatings," and she showed him her arms and chest, all "bruised and battered" ("lividam et amachatam"). She died that very day. Asked when this was, he said "in the summer at the time of the Jubilee" (i.e., in 1450). The second witness, again cooperative, started his narration further back in time, on an occasion when he heard that Guglielmo had beaten Joan and she "wanted to leave him because of the beating." Guglielmo had asked him to intercede and make peace between them, which he did, with Guglielmo promising not to hit her again. Two months later, he heard that Guglielmo had hit her while she was pregnant, and Guglielmo again sent for him to re-pacify them. The witness visited Joan, who said that Guglielmo had hit her "stronger" than before; and she died a few days later. At this stage, a German witness also attested that, at Guglielmo's request, three years ago he had visited Joan to treat her for an "infirmity," and had found her lying in bed, her head "bandaged with bloody pieces" ("fasciatum cum peciis sanguinolentis"), but he could not get to the bottom of her infirmity because she was from Scotland and he did not understand her. He did advise on some medicine, but heard that she died the following day.

On the basis of this notification and testimony, Guglielmo was taken into custody. Meanwhile, two other witnesses were summoned. This time, the questioning started in open mode, before moving to closed (yes/no, and multiple choice), while their answers adopted the narrative-expansion mode, which has been seen as defensive.[74] Thomas from Flanders recalled that Joan came to Bologna from Rome at the time of the Jubilee,[75] and after a few days began to complain of pains in her chest, then she became ill "from the pestilence, which she had in her groin," and she died of this. What does he know of this disease? He saw it, he said (presumably meaning the bubo), and touched and palpated it, and placed a poultice on it. Did he see Guglielmo beat her? Yes: on one occasion she said in Guglielmo's presence "that no German was good enough to kiss a Scotsman's ass," for which Guglielmo slapped her in the face.[76] A second witness, a neighbor of Guglielmo's, when asked if he beat her, said that he had never heard it—if it were true he would have heard the "clamor and lamentation." Did she die of a beating or of plague? He believes of plague, as it was then active.

The judge decided that there was insufficient evidence to proceed and ordered Guglielmo to be released. At this distance of time (no one explained, or was asked, why this allegation came after three years), he could probably see the difficulty of establishing a cause of death: inspecting this corpse was not an option.[77] With no one having seen Guglielmo beat Joan, and with two witnesses opining that her death was due to pestilence, the *indicia* were weak or nonexistent. Guglielmo was not even questioned. The judge seems to have followed the advice of the treatises to be careful of torturing before the fact of the crime was established.[78] It remains of course a possibility that Guglielmo got away with murder: wife-battering and wife-killing were not uncommon;[79] epidemic disease could act as a screen.[80]

There were similar cases among the investigations of the 1450s. Two students were interviewed about the death of a third student, from Naples, in October 1456, but they provided only information on illness and treatment.[81] Four witnesses were questioned when the son of a builder was reported as "murdered" in August 1459, but he had survived for over three weeks after an unprovoked attack one night in the portico outside his daughter's house, and did not seem to have sustained "any ill, except that fevers later came upon him": he was even reported to have pardoned the man who had hit him, and to have given him a drink.[82]

This analysis has used one source from the Bolognese criminal court to investigate interrogative techniques. The *vacchettini* of the court notary were not just a useful aide-memoire, but a subscribed, authenticated record. So the structure and content of the document contain a rhetorical force, purposed to display that correct procedure had been followed. Hence the *vacchettini* show us judges apparently following the manuals when searching for *indicia*, such as neighbors with criminal pasts, previous threats, existing enmities, and what suspects said before or after the crime. They also show us judges following the rules on torture: there were always existing *indicia* before initiating it, and sometimes fresh evidence before repeating it. Forensic linguistics helps in categorizing the ways in which judges followed recommendations to sequence their questioning of suspects, and draws attention to the precise moment when judges ceased searching for information and began pressing for confession. However, there are gaps or inconsistencies in the evidence that might be considered as signs of momentary tension between actuality and public record, such as the failure to record "rambling speech" before putting trepid suspects to torture, the occasional absence of supplementary evidence before repeating torture, the introduction of speculative questions, and the decision to torture on the basis of ill-fame alone. By repeating torture, by rejecting suspects' denials, judges did construct pressures likely to produce false confessions. That they always did so, however, is open to doubt. In discussing an Inquisition trial in Venice held in 1570, Brian Pullan resisted the claim that Inquisition records were of use only in addressing questions such as "What are the most effective methods of obtaining false confessions?"; he did this on the grounds that torture was rare, and not intensive, and that suspects could show "resourcefulness and tenacity" in their defense.[83] The evidence from the secular court in Bologna is reason to be less sanguine: torture could be extensively applied and repeated (as in the case of Grillo), and was known to be so (as attested by Ugolino's reported comments). However, some suspects, such as Giovanna, resisted torture and successfully asserted their innocence.

This analysis has profound implications for our conception of the criminal trial in the fifteenth century. In an earlier period, the late thirteenth and early fourteenth centuries, an allegation or notification of a crime, along with a list of witnesses, would be presented to the court, and the judge would question the witnesses on their knowledge of the crime as alleged. This preliminary stage was included in the records of the trial. After the mid-fourteenth century, this preliminary stage was omitted, in what looks like a simplification or acceleration of the criminal process: the named witnesses were summoned only if the suspect appeared in court and denied the charge, otherwise the judge proceeded directly to convict and ban the suspect.[84] However, by the mid-fifteenth century, process seems to have changed yet again: when information on a suspicious death was presented, the judge conducted a free-ranging inquiry, up to and including questioning all the inhabitants of a village, or all the family and associates of a suspect, and torturing suspects, ignoring the witnesses eventually named in the indictment—and all before the formal trial actually began. The trial became the moment and forum where the results of the investigation were publicly stated and recorded, and the investigative process, especially the torture of suspects, was occluded.

NOTES

1. ASB, Vacchettini, Busta 5, Register for December 1453–January 1454, unnumbered folios (24 December). And, for what follows, entries dated 26, 30, and 31 December, and 3, 7, 8, 17, 18, and 22 January.
2. Casoni, "Tractatus maleficii praemeditati," fol. 281v. On Casoni: Martin, "Francesco Casoni."
3. Bruni, da Suzzara, and de Ubaldis, *Tractatus de indiciis et tortura,* fols. 35v–36.
4. As in my previous studies, of which specifically relevant here is Dean, "Eight Varieties."
5. Verga, "Le sentenze criminali" 98–99; Bonfiglio Dosio, "Criminalità ed emarginazione," 113; Giuffrida, "Giustizia e società," 553; Cohn, "Criminality and the State," 213. And in general: Vallerani, "Conflitti e modelli procedurali," 267–68.
6. Pene Vidari, "Sulla criminalità e sui banni," 160–62; Constant, "La justice dans une châtellenie savoyarde," 392; Barbero, "Gruppi e rapporti sociali," 190–91.
7. Muchembled, *La violence au village*; Gauvard, *"De grace especial."*
8. Gundersheimer, "Crime and Punishment," 110.
9. Apparently the case at Rome, where nine registers of "investigations" survive from the later fifteenth century: Cherubini, "Una fonte poco nota," 159–60. For some early fourteenth-century investigations in Bologna: Blanshei, *Politics and Justice*, 339–42. For investigations at

Venice, which seem limited to the questioning of witnesses: Ruggiero, *Violence in Early Renaissance Venice*, 21–32.

10. On the format: Brogi, "Il fondo Giusdicenti dell'antico Stato senese," 865–66.

11. De' Cerchi, *Libellus qui vulgari sermone nuncupatur el Birracino*, fols. A. iii–iiiv.

12. De' Cerchi, *Libellus qui vulgari sermone nuncupatur el Birracino*: "quia multa notantur in dicto bastardello quae postea non mittuntur ad librum ordinarium maleficiorum."

13. Cohen, *The Modulated Scream,* 67, 74–75, 79; Vallerani, "Giustizia e documentazione," 299; Graziotti, *Giustizia penale*, 59.

14. De Benedictis, "Lo 'stato popolare di libertà.'"

15. Robertson, *Tyranny under the Mantle,* 41–42.

16. Robertson, *Tyranny under the Mantle,* 130.

17. Nasalli Rocca di Corneliano, "Il card. Bessarione." On Bessarion's interventions to mitigate penalties, see Bacchelli, "La legazione bolognese," 140.

18. The period from December 1451 to December 1456 is fully covered. There is then a gap until the next register covering July–November 1459.

19. On Raffaele da Pistoia, see Dean, "Criminal Justice," 30.

20. ASB, Vacchettini, Busta 6, Register for July–November 1459 (28 August).

21. ASB, Vacchettini, Busta 5, Register for July–October 1456 (11 and 18 September); Register for July–December 1456 (12 November, 28 December); for July–November 1459 (1, 10 and 28 August, 19 September).

22. ASB, Vacchettini, Busta 5, Register for June–November 1453 (20 November).

23. ASB, Vacchettini, Busta 5, Register for July–December 1456 (8 November); Register for September–December 1457 (13 September); Register for January–June 1456 (26 February).

24. ASB, Vacchettini, Busta 5, Register for July–December 1458, fol. 5v.

25. For rare examples of late-fourteenth-century investigations—a body had been discovered, but there was no report of a suspect; a highway robbery had been reported—ASB, Inquisitiones, Mazzo 235, Register 7, fols. 31–35 (1380); 236, Register 6, fols. 88–90 (1380).

26. Oxburgh, Myklebust, and Grant, "The Question of Question Types"; Shuy, *The Language of Confession.*

27. "Generaliter non descendendo ad speciem et ad nominationem certae personae": Bruni, da Suzzara, and de Ubaldis, *Tractatus de indiciis et tortura*, fol. 13v.

28. Bruni, da Suzzara, and de Ubaldis, *Tractatus de indiciis et tortura*, fol. 71.

29. Thus Francesco Bruni: Bruni, da Suzzara, and de Ubaldis, *Tractatus de indiciis et tortura*, 35v-36; also Gambiglioni, *Angeli de Aretio legum doctoris tractatus*, unnumbered folios (but fols. 3v–4).

30. Baldus de Ubaldis, *Consilia* 3, *consilium* 77.

31. Thus Guido da Suzzara in Bruni, da Suzzara, and de Ubaldis, *Tractatus de indiciis et tortura*, fol. 72v.

32. Casoni, "Tractatus maleficii praemeditati," fol. 281.

33. On the role of *fama* in trials, see Stern, "Public Fame"; Vallerani, "La fama nel processo."

34. Bruni, da Suzzara, and de Ubaldis, *Tractatus de indiciis et tortura*, fol. 73: "quod mala fama alicuius de praeterito facit praesumi de praesenti"; a judicial commonplace: Vallerani, *Medieval Public Justice*, 108–9; and a modern axiom: Felson, *Crime and Everyday Life*, 43.

35. Bruni, da Suzzara, and de Ubaldis, *Tractatus de indiciis et tortura*, fol. 73v.

36. Provero, "Dai testimoni al documento," 76.

37. "Cum manifeste vacillaret et variis coloribus transmutando et tremulente vite et varia loquendo": ASB, Vacchettini, Busta 5, Register for December 1453–January 1454, 31 December.

38. Casoni, "Tractatus maleficii praemeditati," fol. 288v.

39. Bruni, da Suzzara, and de Ubaldis, *Tractatus de indiciis et tortura*, fol. 15v.

40. "Quia medietas hominum Bononie commota fuit rogando pro eis," according to Grillo's mother-in-law: ASB, Vacchettini, Busta 5, Register for December 1453–January 1454, 17 January.

41. "Seria quello che venne qui che me domando un pocho de focho e da manzare per amore de dio. Et avie una sachetta de belle cose ciò le tessuti e borselli": ASB, Vacchettini, Busta 5, Register for December 1453–January 1454, 17 January.

42. Verdon, *La voix des dominés*, 46; Reyerson, "Le témoignage des femmes," 155.

43. Leo and Ofshe, "The Consequences of False Confessions," 440.

44. Sherwin, "Law Frames," 40. On the systematic isolation of "judicial marginals" in Italian medieval justice, see Vallerani, *Medieval Public Justice*, 111–12.

45. ASB, Vacchettini, Busta 5, Register for July–December 1456, fols. 29–58.

46. ASB, Vacchettini, Busta 5, Register for July–December 1456, fol. 30v.

47. ASB, Vacchettini, Busta 5, Register for July–December 1456, "Timore ne distrueretur de persona cum tortura quia est debilis et stetit multum infermus . . . tamen dicit quod nisi timeret de dicta tortura quod ipse veniet ad se deffendendum et excusandum de dicta imputacione . . . quia tenet se non esse culpabilem": fol. 32.

48. ASB, Vacchettini, Busta 5, Register for July–December 1456, fols. 33–34.

49. ASB, Vacchettini, Busta 5, Register for July–December 1456, fol. 133 (24 November).

50. Guido da Suzzara in Bruni, da Suzzara, and de Ubaldis, *Tractatus de indiciis et tortura*, fol. 87.

51. ASB, Vacchettini, Busta 5, Register for July–December 1456, fols. 38–39.

52. He was one of six men indicted for killing an agricultural laborer in the city: ASB, Inquisitiones, Mazzo 355, Register 1, fols. 129–30 (13 April 1450). He was released from the penalty on petition: ASB, Libri Partitorum, Busta 383, Register 1, fol. 45 (Dec 31, 1451).

53. ASB, Vacchettini, Busta 5, Register for July–December 1456, fol. 52v: "perche mi suto mali io non vorava andar in quelli presone ne ala corda" and "Tu fai gran mali a meterti in rota si tu non ai colpa in questo."

54. Francesco Bruni in Bruni, da Suzzara, and de Ubaldis, *Tractatus de indiciis et tortura*, fol. 20.

55. Kantorowicz, *Albertus Gandinus*, 2:97; Martin, "Francesco Casoni," 107–8.

56. ASB, Inquisitiones, Mazzo 361, Register 2, fol. 181.

57. For discussion of the legal difficulties: D'Anagni, *Consilia, consilium* 59; Baldus de Ubaldis, *Consilia* 1, *consilium* 98, and 3, *consilium* 424; Angelus de Ubaldis, *Consilia*, *consilium* 22; Capra and Bolognini, *Consilia domini Benedicti Caprae*, *consilium* 8; Cipolla, *Consilia criminalia* (1531), *consilia* 34–38.

58. Gauvard, "La violence commanditée," 1006, 1014, 1020–21. Cf. however Dean, "Eight Varieties."

59. Bubeniceck, "Dénoncer son maître." 149.

60. Dean, "Domestic Violence," 539–40.

61. ASB, Vacchettini, Busta 5, Register for July–November 1453, unnumbered folios.

62. "Dio te dia il bon dì compare, dove vai tu?"—"Io vo in za. Ricomandimi a misser Carlo Malvezzo. Io ho fato cossa che ne sero sempre mal contento ma io o fato quillo a lui che lui volea fare a me"—"Che ai fatto?"—"Io o afrido uno e se non e morto so che non po scampare perche io date tre o quatro spadazate." ASB, Vacchettini, Busta 5, Register for July–November 1453, unnumbered folios.

63. As reported by Lodovico Bolognini: Bruni, da Suzzara and de Ubaldis, *Tractatus de indiciis et tortura*, 78v.

64. Brainerd, "Murder Must Memorise," 549; Leo, "False Confessions," 333, 335.

65. "Questa diavolo de femina vorebe pura che io facesse morire Gasparo suo marito" ASB, Vacchettini, Busta 5, Register for July–November 1453, unnumbered folios (12 August).

66. See Cohen, *Modulated Scream*, 70, who implies that this rule was ignored.

67. "Pessima contenta cum haberet bonum tempus secum et dimitteret ei facere quidquid volebat." ASB, Vacchettini, Busta 5, Register for July–November 1453, unnumbered folios.

68. ASB, Inquisitiones, Mazzo 359, Register 2, fols. 92–94v.

69. Heffer, "Narrative Navigation."

70. ASB, Vacchettini, Busta 5, Register for September–December 1457 (9 and 14 September).

71. ASB, Inquisitiones, Mazzo 362, Register 2, fols. 55–56.

72. ASB, Vacchettini, Busta 6, Register for February–May 1461 (16, 19, and 29 March); Busta 7, Register for January–June 1465, fols. 13v–17.
73. ASB, Vacchettini, Busta 5, Register June–November 1453, unnumbered folios (13, 14, 15, and 17 June).
74. Galatolo and Drew, "Narrative Expansions."
75. For the general context of Scottish pilgrimage to Rome, especially in 1450, see Ditchburn, "'Saints at the Door,'" 85–87.
76. "Quod nullus Alimanus erat dignus osculari culum uni de Schozia." ASB, Vacchettini, Busta 5, Register June–November 1453, unnumbered folios.
77. For contemporary methods of diagnosis of causes of death, see Carmichael, "Epidemics and state medicine."
78. For example in Gambiglioni, *Angeli de Aretio tractatus*, fol. 54.
79. Dean, "Domestic Violence," 527–30.
80. Collard, "Quand l'épidémie sert d'alibi."
81. ASB, Vacchettini, Busta 5, Register for July–December. 1456, fol. 15.
82. ASB, Vacchettini, Busta 6, Register for July–November 1459 (28 and 31 August, 5 September).
83. Pullan, "'A Ship with Two Rudders,'" 33–34.
84. Dean, "Plague and Crime."

Chapter Five

Violence and the Centralization of Criminal Justice in Early Modern Bologna

Colin S. Rose

A centralized criminal court, the *Tribunale del Torrone*, was the papal answer to the violence that gripped sixteenth-century Bologna. After Pope Julius II conquered the city of Bologna in 1506 and expelled the Bentivoglio oligarchs, he was faced with the difficult task of restraining the city's nobility and curbing their independence. The pope, after the failed Bentivoglio rebellion of 1509, vowed to strip the noble families of their traditional and usurped rights and privileges. In particular this meant removing the nobles' influence over the operations of the podestarial court within the city, and their administration of justice through the direct operation of criminal and civil courts of first instance in their feudal territories in the city's hinterland.[1] The urgency and importance of this task reflected the papal conquest's unique characteristic as both an episode of the Italian wars of the late fifteenth century and as a rebellion of the city's *popolo* against what the pope labeled as the tyrannous rule of the elite families.[2] The city's papal sovereign needed to curb the noble class's hereditary privileges of justice, while its inhabitants, as they had under the medieval courts, wanted an efficient and reliable vehicle for conflict resolution.

The first decades of the sixteenth century found the courts in Bologna in flux as a result of the conquest. Gradually, the papal legates—cardinals installed as city governors by the papal overlord—increased the power and reach of the criminal court and inserted papal representation firmly into the system of criminal justice. The inefficiencies of podestarial justice drove plaintiffs, lawyers, and jurists toward a centralized legatine court. The *Tribunale del Torrone* cemented *inquisitio* and summary procedures and claimed a monopoly over criminal justice in Bologna and its environs. As a project of papal absolutism, the *Tribunale del Torrone* represents the ideal goal of the early modern prince; the court became perhaps the most functional arm of papal absolutism, more efficient and effective at its task than the Senate was at legislating, but the process was a slow one. By the end of the seventeenth century, the *Torrone* finally secured its judicial monopoly. Paradoxically, it was able to do so because of, not despite, the continued resistance of the nobility to the court's jurisdiction, which culminated in a wave of violence in the late seventeenth century. Rural *bolognesi* increasingly brought their conflicts to the *Torrone* for resolution, rather than to the courts operated by local feudal powers; the less capricious and more efficient solutions provided by the central court made it the better option for *bolognesi* of all social strata. The mixed use of summary justice and *inquisitio* process made this victory possible.

While the medieval period was marked by significant changes in judicial process and featured a decisive but non-linear evolution from accusatorial to *inquisitio* procedures, the basic structure and functioning of the *Torrone* was established by the mid-sixteenth century, in a period when similar courts were developed elsewhere in Italy, and it persisted in much the same shape until the eighteenth century. In response to the presence of a powerful and rebellious nobility, the Bolognese court established a more professional structure than the courts operating in contemporary states. In Florence, for example, Cosimo I had effectively redirected the Florentine nobility away from oligarchical competition and toward bureaucratic service as the route to political power. John Brackett sees the centralized criminal court as an important aspect of sixteenth-century Florentine governance and surveillance, extending the reach of the Medici dukes into the *quartieri* of the city and the many *ville* of the Tuscan state, much as Cosimo I had used patronage and clientage to staff major charitable institutions and hospitals.[3] In Rome, despite the continued existence of multiple criminal courts through the sixteenth century, the increasing centralization of Roman political power around the College of Cardinals brought these courts into closer operation and influenced the use of *inquisitio* procedure by all. Nevertheless, Roman criminal tribunals remained, as Irene Fosi argues, inefficient, ineffective, and incapable of delivering justice.[4]

Other states faced similar problems in establishing the effective control of centralized courts over the hinterlands of their territories. Venice operated central urban courts but was unable to establish a reliable jurisdiction in its vendetta-ridden *terra ferma* empire.[5] In the Kingdom of Naples, representatives from the royal court served as a court of second appeal for rural plaintiffs whose feudal overlords retained, in southern Italy, a robust local privilege of justice.[6] Gregory Hanlon and Angelo Torre have argued that Lombard nobles enjoyed extensive jurisdictional privileges well into the eighteenth century.[7] In Bologna prominent urban *popolano* aristocrats gained feudal fiefs and jurisdictions, for example, the Pepoli family, which in 1340 acquired Castiglione dei Gatti (today Castiglione dei Pepoli) from Ubaldino dei Conti Alberti.[8] The process of "refeudalization" continued after Bologna reached its concordat with the papacy in the mid-fifteenth century, and as Ian Robertson notes, "the development of the oligarchs' *contado* estates were frequently blessed by direct papal concession" and the popes "sealed the 'neo-feudal' aspects of these developments with the title of count."[9] In these rural fiefdoms Bolognese nobles exercised illegitimate powers of arbitration and judicial decision-making. No matter the structure of local and feudal justice, all the states that instituted centralized *inquisitio* courts did so at the expense, in both reduced potency and income, of the hereditary nobility who enjoyed extensive power under the existing systems—podestarial, feudal, or legatine.

The consolidation of the *Torrone* in Bologna was a process that lasted almost a century and a half, from at least 1525, the court's earliest mention in documentary evidence, to the late 1660s when, following a decade of noble violence, the city expelled the leading members of the nobility; indeed it was only in the eighteenth century, with significant reforms instituted by Benedict XIV, that the court truly eliminated the last vestiges of feudal jurisdiction.[10] An explanation for the long and arduous nature of this process may be found in the functional use of criminal justice in early modern Italy. The theoretical purpose of the court, according to the Bolognese *Constitutiones* of 1556, was to prosecute and punish malefactors.[11] However, analysis of the records of judicial proceedings and sentences indicates that, as under the earlier courts, its functional purpose was different: officials, plaintiffs, and defendants viewed the court as a forum for conflict resolution. Accusatorial procedure, as Sarah Blanshei notes in her chapter on procedure in this volume, traditionally placed the judge as an arbitrator between two parties. The *Torrone* served a similar role, although it made dispute resolution a public matter between the court, the imputed criminal and his or her kin, the victim and his kin, and the communities around them. *Ex officio* proceedings, initiated at the instance of a local *massaro* or *mestrale* through a *denuncia* to the court, drew entire communities into an elaborate process in which men, women, and children explained to the notaries and themselves the circumstances of a murder, an arson, or a simple brawl in a tavern. Through this process they confronted and discharged strong emotions, such as the impulse to revenge, and were guided, by the skillful questioning of notaries, toward reconciliation and, perhaps following a period of enforced separation of the parties through a ban, finally toward forgiveness. The goal of the *Torrone* was not to execute every murderer, but to prevent cycles of revenge violence from breaking out in both urban and rural contexts, and among all levels of Bolognese society. Indeed, analysis of the court's execution patterns reveals that the state executed killers at a very low rate, compared to the number of condemnations of those in custody. *Inquisitio* procedure in Bologna thus allowed the state to expand its role in conflict resolution into the daily life of the most remote rural communes. While subject to occasional reform, the court retained its basic structure throughout the sixteenth and seventeenth centuries and grew in power as *bolognesi* resolved quarrels through its channels rather than through the violent sponsorship of the feudal nobility.

Tracing the emergence of the *Torrone* in the early sixteenth century is difficult, but the issues that ultimately cemented its authority are clearly visible in the extant documentation. There is no foundational legislation establishing the court, although its earliest appearance in documentary evidence is somewhere around 1525.[12] During the initial decades of the court's operation, it existed alongside a podestarial court and other vestiges of late medieval justice in Bologna.[13] A *bando* of 1535 detailing the process and punishments to be enacted against homicides bears the authority of the podestà, an authority that was certified by the legate Innocenzo Cybo.[14] Cybo's *bando* clearly shows that the podestà still held primary criminal jurisdiction in the 1530s, but that Cybo recognized the problems with access and objectivity in the podestarial courts. In early 1536, he published ordinances for access to justice for the poor under the podestarial system.[15] By this *bando*'s provisions, every Saturday the podestà chose one member of the *auditori di Rota* to dispense summary justice in the podestarial court for the following week. He also selected a procurator to act in defense of the poor, and reserved to himself the right to select an advocate for anyone who did not have one. Perhaps most importantly, the names of those selected for duty were posted on each and every *palazzo* in the city, as well as in the main piazza and churches, so that all *bolognesi* would know who their agents were. Although still operating primarily under a podestarial judicial regime, in the early sixteenth century Bolognese officials were already addressing the problems of access and fairness that centralized justice was supposed to resolve.

The 1540s seem to be the critical decade in which the *Torrone* fully emerged. Indeed, the first appearance I have found of the *Torrone* in the *bandi* and proclamations of the legate came on 14 February 1541 under the legateship of Bonifacio Ferrara. In a *bando* entitled *Reformationes Turroni Bononiae*, Ferrara clearly laid out the procedure and emoluments of judges and notaries in criminal cases falling under the *Torrone*.[16] Bonifacio stipulated the fees notaries could charge for receiving and inscribing a denunciation from a *massaro* (45 *soldi* for a homicide, 3 *soldi* for all others), the protocol for payment to notaries (absolved killers paid a 10-*scudi* fee, while false accusers were responsible for all court fees of the accused) and the quality of persons hired to assist the court (doctors performing autopsies had to be registered with the *Torrone*). A year later, the new vice-legate Fabio Mignanelli released a comprehensive list of "the salary and emoluments of the judge and notaries deputed to the criminal office" without specifically referring to the *Torrone*.[17] In 1542 the legate Contarini published a *bando* written by a notary of the "Turroni Bononiae" calling for the arrest of two men who had killed their enemy in a church.[18] In 1545 Contarini released a *bando* in the name of the *auditore del Torrone* referring to the court's 1542 banishment of all prostitutes from the *contrada* of *Cento Trecento* and exhorting all landlords to rent rooms only to honest people.[19] Finally, a 1548 *bando* illuminates the participatory and public aspirations of the *Torrone*, as the court gradually inserted itself into the daily life of the city and *contado*.[20] This *bando* exhorted all *contadini* to take note of any crimes, to rouse their communities to alarm, and to chase evildoers as a community with intent to bring them to justice. This practice, with deep medieval roots, of *inquisitio* process initiated by community action, became a crucial aspect of *Torrone* procedure and a hallmark of its legitimacy.

The structure of the *Torrone* differed significantly from those of contemporary courts such as the *Otto di guardia e balìa* in Florence. Brackett argues that the Medici dukes maintained a policy of non-professionalization, drawing the eight judges of their criminal court from the broad pool of general applicants who staffed the Florentine bureaucracy as a whole.[21] These judges served in teams of three and were served by a staff of notaries and bureaucrats who knew the system intimately and ensured its smooth functioning under what Brackett terms "citizen-judges."[22] In Venice, the major courts such as the *Dieci della notte* and the *Cinque alla pace* were presided over by the aristocrat-merchants who made up the Venetian political class.[23] In the multiple courts with criminal jurisdiction in Rome, the *procuratore fiscale* co-ordinated the activities of a diverse body of judges with various professional backgrounds.[24] By the 1550s, the *Torrone*'s structure was more formalized and more professional than any of those courts.

At the apex of the *Torrone*'s hierarchy of authority was the judge, always a foreigner, known as the *auditore del Torrone*, who served with independent authority and whose office attracted a reputation for autocracy.[25] Unlike their medieval Bolognese and contemporary Florentine counterparts, who served in rotating terms of between two and six months, the chair of the *Torrone* was a permanent post limited only by the judge's age and interest.[26] *Torrone* judges appear to have taken their posts quite seriously, unlike the *Otto* officials who may have seen the post merely as an opportunity to increase their personal incomes. *Torrone* judges could serve long terms, gaining a wide knowledge of and deep investment in the daily life of city and *contado*. For instance, the Senate on 24 May 1661 celebrated the retirement of *Signore* Giuliano Laureti, who served as the *auditore* of the *Torrone* for ten years beginning in 1551.[27] His encomium reveals the ideal qualities of the *Torrone* judge: he was praised for observing the *Constitutiones* that governed *Torrone* procedures and financing, for ensuring that poor *contadini* were not extorted and terrorized by *sbirri* (law enforcement officials), and for curbing abuses of power by *Torrone* officials in the investigative visitations known as *cavalcate*. The *Torrone* judge was supposed to be bound by the rules, compassionate to the city's helpless poor, and just in the application of laws: the Senate heaped high praise on Laureti for dispensing impartial justice to all.

Beneath the *auditore* were the *sotto-auditori*, or *giudici*, whose function was primarily to assist the *auditore* with cases requiring the on-site presence of a judge outside the city. They, like the *auditore* above them, were theoretically bound by the 1566 *Constitutiones Turroni Bononiae* that structured the court and its officers' duties.[28] The document does not specify the number of *sotto-auditori*, but there seem to have been between two and four of them at any given time. Primarily acting to deliver judgments when plaintiffs were unable to appear in Bologna, the *sotto-auditori* could dispense judgments, which were reviewed and confirmed by the *auditore*, but they were functionally eclipsed in importance by the notaries of the *Torrone*, who constituted its working core and performed most of the work of investigating, interrogating, and collating evidence during the court's proceedings.

The brunt of the *Torrone*'s work fell on the notaries of the court, who were responsible for recording all the documentation relating to the court's investigations, from denunciations to final sentencing, supplications, and pardons. The *Torrone* employed eight notaries, seven of whom shared equal competency to hear cases and one of whom was designated the *caponotaio*. These men performed most of the court's daily work, and were often responsible themselves for the investigation of crimes in the *contado* when a *sotto-auditore* was not present. They received a salary based on their seniority as well as emoluments and fees for the variety of services they performed, such as copying a supplication into a criminal proceeding record or inscribing a letter of safe conduct.[29] The notaries of the *Torrone* developed an early reputation for unfairness and partiality, as well as openness to bribes, as indicated by *bandi* and reforms concerning the notaries.[30] Much of the reform work done throughout the *Torrone*'s hold over Bologna was aimed at eliminating notarial abuse from the court, and providing better justice for *bolognesi* who did not have the resources to influence the judicial process. The earliest attempt to ensure a standard of professionalism and dedication, as well as fiscal responsibility, among the *Torrone*'s notarial staff was the subjugation in 1560 of the office of *caponotaio* to the officials of the *Monte di Pietà*, who were henceforth responsible for his selection and his salary.[31]

This move had two major effects. The first was that the notarial staff of the *Torrone*, already adept and drawn from the ranks of the city's university graduates, became instantly more professionalized and authoritative with the oversight of one of the city's oldest and most venerable charitable bodies. Henceforth notaries of the *Torrone* were a prestigious body of men with a great deal of power. The integration of the office of *caponotaio* with the *Monte* drew together two large administrative bodies. Justice became inextricably linked to both debt and charity through the nexus of the court and public finance. Money flowed from the *Torrone*, via fines, into the *Monte*, and the *Monte*'s longstanding presence in the city linked the new court to a respected city tradition. The *Monte* raised the *Torrone*'s stature while the *Torrone* buttressed the *Monte*'s fundraising.

The second major impact of the integration of the *caponotaio* into the *Monte* was the reverse of the first. While the court's stature and authority were raised, it was linked closer than ever before to the household of the legate and his administrative staff, who governed the *Monte* and thus exercised a great deal of influence over the selection of the *Torrone*'s *caponotaio*. The *Monte*'s governance of the notarial staff—the *caponotaio* appointed all the others—drew the court closer to the city government and also afforded the legate the power to approve or negate the selection of staff. For instance, in 1588, the city's ambassador to Rome protested the legate's choice, via the *Monte*, of a *caponotaio*. The legate conceded that he would not decide alone, but then nominated instead a candidate favored by his sister; the *Torrone* was forced to accept the result.[32] The governance of the court's notarial staff by the *Monte* both increased the staff's professional status, and probably ensured a supply of well-trained and experienced notaries, and also decreased the court's judicial independence, by drawing the notaries under the authority and purview of one of the city's most powerful and centrally governed bodies.

Beneath this administrative structure of *auditori*, *sotto-auditori*, and notaries, the *Torrone* was supported by a staff of *sbirri*, who were tasked with keeping order, as in many of Italy's cities, and who attracted a reputation for violence, corruption, and being "one step removed from the criminals they captured."[33] Chief among these was the *baroncello*, sometimes called the *barigello*. As defined by the *Torrone*'s *Constitutiones*, the *baroncello* was responsible for maintaining an armed force of *sbirri*, both mounted and on foot, to keep order in the *contado*, to arrest delinquents, collect witnesses, and transport them to the *Torrone* for imprisonment, interrogation, and possible torture.[34] Unlike his medieval antecedents, the *baroncello* did not have limits on the number of men he could employ and enjoyed broad discretion in choosing their weapons, both offensive and defensive.[35] Other *sbirri* were responsible for delivering citations and summons to imputed criminals and witnesses in the city, for patrolling the streets at night to ensure compliance with weapons regulation and public decency ordinances, for guarding the city's gates along with the militia of the Senate and legate's household, and for protecting the notaries and judges of the *Torrone* as they went about their often unpopular work of investigating local crimes in areas that were feeling the impact of the centralizing efforts of the *Torrone*. While noble clans retained households of *famigliari* and high-ranking officials were afforded the right to a retinue of *bravi*, the *sbirri* of the *Torrone* constituted the official forces of law and order in Bologna, as much responsible for keeping the peace as they were for arresting delinquents.

The urban *sbirri* were supported in their pursuit of criminals by a network of informers and "friends of the court" who provided information on crimes recently committed or the location of fugitives. They worked almost exclusively in the city, leaving rural crime reporting to local officials. Some worked openly as couriers, collecting emoluments for shuttling information from the streets to the court, as did Alessandro Rubiano, who reported two separate killings on 24 and 25 July 1660.[36] They could be long-time contacts of the court: Lorenzo Mazzoni, a *cursor curius Turroni*, reported three killings in 1660 and three homicides a decade later, in 1670.[37] Others, perhaps more similar to a confidential informant than a courier, appear only anonymously in the records as "amic[i] della corte"[38] or, when they had ties to a particular *sbirro*, such as the *baroncello* Pietro Zanotti, as "suo confidente."[39] These anonymous informants were more likely to report on events in the *contado*, if their local *massaro* had failed to do so.[40] Whether anonymous or named, the couriers of the court formed a crucial link in the network of communications and information-gathering that allowed the *Torrone* to operate and to consolidate its exclusive criminal jurisdiction during the seventeenth century.

In challenging the feudal nobility for jurisdiction over the villages and hamlets in the Bolognese *contado*, the *Torrone* continued the medieval office of the *massaro*. The *massari* were elected by their local communities on an annual basis. As in the Bolognese podestarial courts and in other medieval and early modern Italian cities, they brought notice of crimes from the *contado* to the city and under the *Torrone*'s purview. Their duties for the *Torrone* were outlined in the *Constitutiones*, which stipulated that each *comune* should have one *massaro* and one only, or the extras would face a fine of 10 *scudi*.[41] This allowed the *Torrone* to have one point of access and information in each of the major communes of the *contado*. Each *massaro* was responsible for reporting crimes in his jurisdiction, usually a village but sometimes two or three, to the court offices in the palazzo comunale, where a notary would decide whether it was dealt with summarily or whether a full process was warranted. This direct access to information allowed *contadini* to bring even minor conflicts directly to the central court, significantly eroding the hold of feudal nobility over the resolution of disputes in the most isolated mountain hamlets as well as those in the densely populated agricultural plain surrounding the city.

The essential elements of inquisition procedure, common across Italy by the fourteenth century and employed by the *Torrone* since its inception in the first half of the sixteenth century, were *ex officio* initiation of a trial on the grounds of denunciation by a local official or *publica fama*, a concern with the "truth of the facts" over the relative weight of arguments, and a resolve to punish crimes rather than resolve conflicts.[42] The *Torrone* incorporated these elements and shaped them to create a powerful court. Particular crises engendered reforms to the *Torrone*'s procedures to make it more fair and accessible to all *bolognesi*. The banditry crisis of the 1590s and the great plague of 1630 provided the opportunity to expand its framework of social control over rural militias and urban curfews. This great expansion of power, achieved primarily through the *Torrone*'s efficient use of *inquisitio*, was contested for well over a century by the leading families of the Bolognese oligarchy. The *Torrone* finally succeeded in quashing their unsanctioned feudal courts in the 1660s, with the banishment of a large swath of the nobility following a decade of vicious public violence. Each of these episodes allowed the *Torrone* to incorporate additional elements of social control, conflict resolution, and governance of everyday life into its competence. While the shape of its procedures—from denunciation, investigation, interrogation, torture, sentencing, to petition and pardon—remained essentially unchanged, the evolving complexity of the court's documentation and shifts in its pattern of punishment demonstrate how the *Torrone* came to dominate criminal jurisdiction in Bologna, almost two centuries after Julius II first quelled the oligarchs.

A series of reforms in the 1590s enhanced the credibility of the court by forcing its notaries and officials to be more transparent in their dealings with the public, condemning the practice of taking bribes by notaries and *sbirri*, and publicly advertising the strictly regulated fees that they charged for various services. These reforms were designed to bring ordinary *bolognesi* further into the *Torrone*'s fold. Finally, the court's limited use of violence—torture in interrogation and corporal and capital punishment—demonstrates how the *Torrone* strayed from *inquisitio*'s lofty goal of ensuring that all crime was punished and indicates that the court was far more interested in containing and suppressing cycles of revenge violence than it was in punishing individual acts. Even its treatment of theft was meant to dampen the victim's impulse to revenge by providing satisfaction through the court's channels. These aspects of *Torrone* procedure made it a useful option for *bolognesi* seeking resolutions to conflicts that otherwise might have been arbitrated by local feudal nobles, and allowed the court's control of everyday life to expand throughout the seventeenth century.

Fundamentally, the *Torrone* relied for its success on the participation of ordinary people in this elaborate network of information. Simply put, for *inquisitio* to function, the court had to be made aware of crimes. The *massari* and *mestrali* of Bologna's *contado* and city played a crucial role in this first phase of criminal court proceedings—the denunciation. Homicide trials, because the act was heinous and engendered strong emotions within whole communities, provide the clearest and fullest view of criminal trials in action.

But how was the court made aware, for example, of a killing in Castiglione, when a man was robbed and killed on his way to sell some livestock in Bologna?[43] Or of the murder of a landlord by his delinquent tenant, who had refused to pay the arrears on his rent?[44] The *massari* and *mestrali*, as local bailiff figures, provided the first response to such major crimes. Upon the commission of a crime, the victim or any witnesses were obligated to inform the local official, as in the case of the robbery-homicide noted above. Here, the victim's wife first went to the local *massaro* to report the crime. The *massaro* served both as the *Torrone*'s contact in the area and also as the font of public participation in justice: upon hearing of a crime, he was obligated first to ring the tocsin and gather all the local men in the square. With all the men gathered, the *massaro* led a search party to apprehend the delinquent, which in the vast majority of cases was a fruitless attempt. (The thirty minutes it would have taken to ring the bell and gather the men provided a window of escape to killers, who were generally local and against whom the community bore no particular animus.) They would typically search his home and those of his parents and brothers, if they lived in the same town. With the criminal having fled, typically into a self-imposed exile in Modena before the trial process even began, the *massaro*'s second obligation was to inform the court of the crime with or without the consent of the victim or his or her relatives.[45] Traveling to the court's central office in Bologna's palazzo comunale, the local official presented either orally or in writing his *denuncia* to one of the *Torrone*'s eight notaries, who were seated around the courtyard.

A typical denunciation went as follows:

> The *massaro* of Roffeno, by virtue of his office, reports and denounces how last night in the middle of the night a loud knocking on his door brought him to his window, where he saw there were two armed men. He asked them who they were and one of them responded "I am Giovanni Battista della Becara and here I denounce to you that this night we were assaulted by men who pointed guns at us but they did not fire. We pointed guns at them and we killed one of them, and we know him as Giovanni Maria Stanzati from Modena, banned from the state of Bologna." They did not say anything else and they left, and the *massaro* went and looked for the said dead man and found him beneath a market stall in the place called the Little Field in the said commune of Roffeno and he did not know the dead man and did not know the men who had called on him that night, and they said they had cut one of their shirt sleeves as a signal to him.[46]

This denunciation from 1652 appears in two written versions, the original brought to the notary by the *massaro* of Roffeno and the version copied into the trial record by the notary. Whether given orally or in writing, the denunciation was first reported by the *massaro*, *mestrale*, or any of the other officials and semi-officials who might be involved in transmitting news of a crime to the court. As the denunciation above indicates, the system relied at its base on the voluntary participation of individuals and communities—in this case, two men self-reporting that they had killed another man. The men obviously knew the law that *banniti* could be treated with impunity, and were confident that they had committed no legal wrong. Indeed, they were not reporting the homicide that they had committed but rather the assault by bandits that they had endured.[47] While most often submitted in an official capacity, *denunce* were also given by a variety of other actors.

Chief among these semi-official sources for information on crimes were the physicians and barbers of the city's major hospitals and villages. Peter Blastenbrei has argued that the *relazioni dei barbieri* of Rome are a unique source for that city, but they are present from an early period in Bologna, collated among the other stages of *Torrone* proceedings which, in a boon to historians, are grouped together in dedicated *fascicoli* rather than separated among dispersed archival *fondi* as are the podestarial records.[48] In Bologna the physicians and barbers were required to make denunciations sometime before 1588, as evidenced by a 1588 decree against "the doctors and barbers who do not denounce."[49] Physicians at the Ospedale di Santa Maria della Morte (known as the Ospedale della Morte) and that of Santa Maria della Vita were required to, and generally did, submit reports of all suspicious wounds that they treated, noting their nature, judging the wound's seriousness, and suggesting what type of weapon caused it. They submitted these descriptions for simple assaults as well as wounds that became fatal. If the notary deemed it appropriate, the surgeon's report initiated a full *Torrone* proceeding; at the very least, the notary was usually dispatched to interview the victim in the hospital before he was released or died. Like the *massari*, the urban physicians and rural barbers permitted the *Torrone* to penetrate the dense community networks that might work to occlude crimes. This intelligence and surveillance network of *massari, medici,* and *amici* gave papal officials the information necessary to make the *Torrone* an effective instrument of state control.

A *denuncia* having been made, the notary decided whether the case warranted summary procedure or a full inquisition. For simple assaults, minor *danni dati* (property damages), and other small quarrels, the notary recorded the *denuncia* in his casebook (of which a notary might produce twenty a year, between 300 and 600 folios each, for a total archive of some 15,000 casebooks between 1500 and 1700), assigned a fine according to the infraction, and sent the *massaro* back with the decision. For more serious cases, such as robbery, serious assault, rape, arson, theft, and public disorders, the notary was dispatched to investigate the crime *in situ* and gather information such that the judge could make a decision. In urban cases, a judge or *sotto-auditore* often went directly to the investigation as well. For rural crimes, the notary and a group of *sbirri* embarked on a *cavalcata* to the village. Thus far

I have found 170 of these *calvacata* investigations recorded between July and December 1689, which gives a sense of how busy these notaries were.[50] The dispatch of a notary and *sbirri* constituted the initiation of a full inquisition, beginning with an investigation of the immediate facts of the crime.

In cases of serious assault or homicide, this meant an inspection of the wounds or the body. If the victim was in the hospital, this was usually performed by the doctor who denounced the wounds and two witnesses, the notary and a medical assistant. If the victim was in the streets, his house, or outside the city, this inspection was performed by the notary and two locals who knew the victim. Generally in groups of three, sometimes of four, these men described the victim's appearance, clothes, and possessions; the nature, location, and cause of all visible wounds; and the victim's name, age, and origin. In cases of poisoning and other ambiguous deaths a physician might perform an autopsy.[51] If the victim was not a local, the notaries might order that the body be left exposed in a public area until someone could identify it.[52] They noted where the body was found, where locals had moved it, and where the crime was alleged to have taken place. These body inspections were extremely important as they allowed the *Torrone* to track who the victims of violent crime were in a fairly comprehensive fashion. More importantly, they drew members of rural communities into the judicial process by holding villages accountable for the identification of victims of crime. This brought the victim's close friends and relatives into direct contact with the apparatus of justice that was to resolve their claim against those who had injured their kin. The body inspection phase of a trial doubled as both an information-collecting phase and an opportunity for the notary to assess the local community's attitude toward the victim, the imputed, and the crime itself. This attitude could then inform the notary's approach to the third phase of the trial.

The interrogation of witnesses was a highly varied affair dependent on the nature of the crime, the witnesses being interviewed, the victim and his or her status, and the notary's personal preferences. Some crimes warranted the interrogation of three witnesses, others hundreds. If the victim was of a high-enough status to afford a lawyer, this phase might well be doubled by the provision of witnesses for the accused after the initial phase of notarial interrogation. Despite the multitude of ways in which interrogation of witnesses might proceed, a few general patterns stand out. Interrogation was never a piecemeal approach: the notaries always had a plan and a list of both witnesses and questions to be pursued. The initial list of witnesses was formulated on the basis of the *denuncia* and the initial investigation, and usually included the immediate kin (particularly mothers and sisters) of the victim and imputed criminal in order to establish a firm sense of *publica fama* and each person's role in his or her community. Citations were issued to both witnesses and suspects to appear before the notary on a given day, with increasingly severe fines for those who did not appear at the appointed times. Several prepared lists of questions survive as *miscellanea* in the casebooks, such as that prepared for the interrogation of Domenica Bertazzori, a former servant of Giulia Zaccaria, in 1600.[53] Like many others, Domenica's interrogation proceeded from simple to complex questions: did she know why she had been called by the notaries? Had she spoken to any other witnesses who were called by the *Torrone*? How did she know the victim? Why did she leave her service? How long did she work for her mistress before leaving? Did she know if there had ever been any arguments between her mistress Giulia and her killer Giulio? Did she know if he had repeatedly offered her 4 *ducatoni* for a broken *cetera*? Again, what was the nature of her service to Giulia, where did she stay after leaving her, and why did she leave? Was she aware that if she was lying, she would be sent to prison, and did she admit that Giulio had fired her from Giulia's service? Had Giulia told her many times to go to Giulio's and get either the *cetera* or the money? The list concludes with the open-ended phrase "and other questions at the discretion of the interrogator depending on what seems important in the answers given." The interrogation of witnesses, a technique used by the notaries to investigate the social network of entire communities, rather than isolated crimes, was both highly orchestrated and extremely flexible, making it very useful for compelling the loyalties of *bolognesi*.

Of course, recalcitrant witnesses could be threatened with worse than prison if they refused to co-operate. As part of the interrogation phase, witnesses as well as accused criminals could be tortured by the court, which maintained records of torture sessions. The *Torrone* only used the *strappado* but its effectiveness at attaining reliable information may have been problematic at times, overwhelming and breaking prisoners rather than causing them to confess deep secrets, and consequently torture was used with decreasing frequency.[54] In cases when it might have been effective, witnesses were often sufficiently cognizant of the legal strictures surrounding torture that they could avoid it, for example by having a doctor certify to the court that one's back was already too injured by labor and age to sustain a torture session.[55] The legal restraints on torture were followed when it did occur, and authorities were careful not to maim or permanently disfigure suspects or witnesses, as in the case of Anna Trevisana, whose torture was abruptly ended when a doctor declared that her arms could not sustain another drop of the rope.[56] Torture was used at least into the 1630s as a means of proof in interrogation.

With an initial round of witness interrogations completed, further citations were issued. *Sbirri* posted citations in the larger and border rural communes calling the imputed to appear for interrogation and sentencing. Three citations were issued before suspects were declared contumacious, at which point they could be killed with impunity and, indeed, a cash reward or a grant of freedom be given to the person who killed them.[57] With the citations dispensed and the suspect either having fled into exile or having been interrogated, possibly with torture, the notary collated the evidence and handed it to the judge, who reviewed the evidence and presented his view of the crime, including the imputation of guilt and the sentence that he would give. If present, advocates for the accused were then given the opportunity to review the evidence and present counter-arguments and technicalities. The vast majority of trials, however, were resolved without the input of lawyers. The judge determined every step of the process, evaluated the evidence, and pronounced sentence.

Judges had a wide *arbitrium* with which to determine punishments according to the qualities of the crime, the victim, and the criminal. The death sentence could be applied in cases of theft, assault to officials, homicide, sodomy, counterfeiting, heresy, rebellion, banditry, and spying. However, the actual application of capital punishment declined significantly over the seventeenth century, following a significant spike in the 1580s during the campaign to cleanse bandits from the *contado*.[58] Throughout the early years of papal rule of Bologna, until the 1540s, the legates used the power of the podestá's court to summarily execute exponents of the anti-papal opposition, but with the legate established and the *Torrone* integrated into the judicial system by the late sixteenth century, capital punishment began to lose its usefulness and become another emblem of inefficient and ineffective medieval justice. While the period 1540 to 1600 saw Bologna execute 917 men and women, from 1600 to 1700 this number was only 556, an average of 5.5 a year compared to the average 15.25 from 1540–1600.[59] In the final three years of the seventeenth century, one person was executed annually, and no one was executed in 1696. A large spike in executions in the 1640s reflects the increased presence of disbanded armies and deserters in north Italy following the Thirty Years War; a similar spike in 1630 reflects the increased hold of the *Torrone* over the city during a major crisis of plague, and most of the eleven men executed in 1653 were involved in the brazen and public murder of the *Torrone sotto-auditore* Giacinto Pungelli. The pattern is clear: the *Torrone* executed criminals who represented a threat to the security of the state and the court's hold over that state. As the *Torrone* grew more powerful with each of the crises noted above, execution was less useful as a demonstration of its authority, which by the late seventeenth century was better represented as mercy, demonstrated in the exile, rather than execution, of the last remaining *bentivoleschi* in the 1660s.

With capital punishment on the wane, the *Torrone* instead used convicted criminals to man the oars of the papal galleys in the Mediterranean. Sentences could range from one year to perpetual galley service, which was a functional death sentence.[60] Punitive incarceration was possible but rarely employed, since it was both expensive and considered extremely cruel. Corporal punishment could be employed for minor quarrels and disputes, while mutilation and maiming were reserved for heresy and other deviant categories. However, most people who committed simple infractions received a fine, the amount of which was determined by the judge. Since pecuniary punishment was flexible and at the judge's discretion, it was possible to avoid overly harsh punishment of poor *bolognesi* while making some kind of exchange—even a few *quattrini*—the basis for the court's accepting the criminal back into society's fold.

This drive to balance offenses—through pecuniary punishment or corporal vengeance—may largely explain the prevalence and importance of outlaws and contumacious bandits in north Italy in the later sixteenth and well into the seventeenth century. Contumacy became, under the *inquisitio* system of the *Torrone*, the *de facto* punishment for a wide swath of crimes. Some criminals in custody were explicitly punished with banishment, such as a gang of young men following a murder in 1700.[61] Others were banned because they were contumacious, with the provision that they would be executed if they were found, such as a certain Sabbatino, who had fled into the *contado* after robbing and murdering the priest who employed him as a servant.[62] Lombard and central Italian bandits had a deserved reputation for theft, murder, rape, and robbery, and the *Torrone* first took significant action against them in the 1580s and 1590s, resulting in the late-century spike in executions noted above. The 1580s and 1590s saw considerable legislation exhorting *bolognesi* to assist in reporting and capturing bandits whenever possible; employing a carrot and stick approach, these *bandi* promised significant rewards to those who turned in bandits while threatening heavy punishments against individuals and communities who failed to do so.[63] The campaign to purge the Bolognese *contado* of violent bandits was part of a broader project in the Papal State, and thus some of this legislation appears in the pope's name.[64]

The success of the late-sixteenth-century campaign against bandits was considerable, if the numbers of captured and killed bandits is any indication, but was transitory and depended to a large extent on the continued participation of those *bolognesi* who were least under the *Torrone*'s control—the *contadini* who earned their living on *poderi* near the borders with Modena and Ferrara, the most popular destinations for exiled and banned *bolognesi*. The need to maintain the vigilance of these *contadini* and their capacity to repel bandit incursions led the *Torrone* to decree, on 17 June 1614, the obligation of all *contadini* in these borderlands to keep in their houses at all times at least one, and preferably two, loaded wheel-lock archebuses, and to carry one with them at all times when out in their fields and around their villages.[65] This obligation made the *contadini* the first line of defense against invading bandits, but also resulted in a flood of firearms to the *contado* that plagued the *Torrone* throughout the rest of the century. Within two and a half years the decree was reversed due to the many disorders and homicides that accompanied the sharp rise in firearms ownership.[66] Most important, and often left out of historiographical discussion, banditry was often a temporary stage in a criminal process that could last for years, even decades. While under ban killers could be killed with impunity, as noted above, unless they were able to make peace with their victims' families, and thus receive pardons from the legate. The final stage of the *Torrone*'s process, the crucial acts of peacemaking and pardon, allowed the offended party and his or her kin a period of separation in which the violent emotions engendered by social conflict could be tempered, and hatred turned first into forgiveness and then even to friendship. Here the *Torrone*'s goal to prevent the outbreak of cycles of violence and to ensure conditions of peace is most obvious. While not explicit in the documentation, many trials imply that notaries and officials of the *Torrone* applied considerable pressure on victims and their kin to accept the overtures of their enemies for peace accords. The peace accord, forged with the sponsorship of the court and ratified in its archive, brought the temporary state of outlawry to a close and re-integrated the offender into Bolognese society.

A peace accord could be difficult to obtain given that contumacious offenders could be punished with impunity if they returned to negotiate an accord, and thus bandits had to seek ways to influence the course of events from beyond the borders. The most common means for this to occur was through the sponsorship of a noble family. In 1600, the Ronchetti and Tozzi clans of the district of Aiano, in the mountains south of the city, engaged in a vendetta exchange that left at least three dead and many others assaulted and wounded.[67] By November the violence had moved from Aiano and into the city as the two families brought their networks of kin and friendship into the conflict, and the quarrel attracted the attention of the *Torrone*, whose notaries arranged for a peace conference between the leading members of the families in the *palazzo* of *Signore* Galeazzo Paleotti, a member of one of Bologna's leading noble families.[68] This conference was ultimately unsuccessful because one of the young scions of the Ronchetti family, Battista, the nephew of the *capofamiglia*, refused to make peace along with his other male relatives; nevertheless, a peace accord was signed between the two families and young Battista was confined to house arrest in Bologna until such time as he capitulated to the peace. In fact, he and his cousin Nicola fled into contumacy rather than face that punishment.[69]

In many cases the process was much less fraught, and the peace accord became a regular aspect of criminal justice. In my sample of 658 homicide trials from the records of the *Tribunale del Torrone* for every ten years between 1600 and 1700,[70] at least 212 of the trials were settled with a notarized peace accord granted by the victim's kin to his or her killer, thereby allowing the killers to have their sentences of banishment, galley service, or death commuted to a pardon, and permitting them to return home to their communities. Often these pardons stipulated a further period of separation between the parties, for instance, a period of three years in which the killer could not return to the village where the homicide had been committed, but was free to move about elsewhere in the territory governed by the *legato*. The formulation of peace became such an important part of criminal court proceedings in Bologna that by the 1650s a new government council, the *Assunteria di Liti e Paci*, was formed to facilitate peacemaking between high-ranking noble families. Although it does not seem to have been a very active council, the *assunteria* was involved in forging a peace in at least one major conflict, which involved the Ghisilieri, Bentivoglio, Ercolani, Malvezzi, and Calderani. It was mediated by high-ranking members of the Fibia and Pepoli families.[71] These formal structures for making peace and ending conflict gave the *Torrone* potent instruments of social control, which supplemented its use of summary and inquisition procedures and increased the court's effective hold over *bolognesi* in all areas of the legatine territory.

If the *Torrone* was instituted in order to bring a measure of regularity and reliability to the complex judicial system that existed in the early decades of the sixteenth century, the ambitions of legates, judges, and notaries made it a much more powerful instrument of control and coercion than its founding members had envisioned. A document printed sometime after the death of Paul V in 1621 reveals the growing ambitions of its judges in a "proposal-response" format. This document, entitled *Ricordo di alcuni pastori da trattarsi dagl'Illustrissimi Signori Confessori et Assonti del Torrone col molto Illustrissimo et Eccelentissimo Signore Auditore di esso Torrone, con le rispose da esso Signore Auditore date a capo per capo*, establishes the parameters of the *Torrone*'s responsibilities, as seen by the court's judge.[72] The judge's responses to the suggested limits on *Torrone* activity indicate his view of the court as the primary office of social control in the state.

Each of the proposals addresses a topic of the *Torrone*'s authority that was contentious, and provides the *Torrone*'s justification for its use of that authority. From his first response that the *Torrone* had authority to insert itself directly into even the most minor quarrels of *contadini*, to his fourteenth—that the *Torrone* was a repository of sensitive information, over whose publication the court held responsible custody—this judge declared the court's sweeping competence and independence and downplayed its corruptions. In his conclusion he displayed his increasing impatience with the criticisms and proposed limitations on his court.

Moments such as the plague of 1630, when increased jurisdiction of daily life allowed the *Torrone* to augment its power and justify its expanded authority, were tempered by a series of reforms to mitigate the court's independence and ensure a transparent fiscal as well as judicial structure. The first of these was the subjugation in 1563 of the *Torrone*'s finances and the office of the *caponotaio* to the officers of the *Monte di Pietà.*[73] Another series of reform attempts took place in the 1590s and 1600s, when the court's eager campaign to gather information about banditry in the *contado* gave rise to notarial corruption. In 1595 vice-legate Annibale Rucellai published his *Ordini da Osservarsi nel Foro Criminale del Torrone di Bologna*, both as a broadsheet posted in public spaces around the city and *contado* and as a document provided to the *Torrone* as its guiding orders.[74] This document defined the scheme of payments and emoluments and the procedures with which notaries had to comply in keeping records of cases. It was supported in 1596 with a bull by Pius V giving the *Monte* authority over all the *Torrone*'s notaries in addition to the *caponotaio*, and confirming the court's jurisdiction over all areas of the legatine territory.[75] Another reform, published in 1602 reproduced the same schedule of fees, which dated back to 1580.[76] The first fifty years of the *Torrone*'s operations witnessed repeated efforts to professionalize and standardize its notarial staff and eliminate the types of petty corruption for which they were known in many public offices.

Five years later, in 1607, the legate Benedetto Giustiniani pushed the reforms further, making the *Torrone*'s casebooks as well as its finances transparent and accountable. A new set of *ordini* concerned the documentation of cases and the preservation of evidence.[77] Notaries were ordered to transcribe testimony word for word, instead of in shorthand; to bring evidence to judges at an appropriate time in the investigation, not before or after; to interrogate witnesses singly rather than in pairs or groups; and to record their testimony directly into the casebooks. They were not to conduct interrogations for "serious crimes" without the assistance or order of a judge, nor to accept any payment greater than stipulated in the rubrics for defense examinations. Notaries were not to interrogate every person who came to make a denunciation, but were to take their names, and write the denunciations in full with their dates. These rules managed the relationships of notaries with witnesses and suspects, regulating the dynamic between the parties to ensure that notaries did not abuse their positions. The next series ensured that cases would be preserved adequately and be accessible for future use: copyists must not write on original trial records in any way; as soon as the notary has finished a proceeding ("in neat, legible writing") he must record the case in the *caponotaio*'s notebook; similarly, denunciations and quarrels must be sent immediately to the *caponotaio*, who reported daily to the *legato*; every two weeks, or when they completed a casebook, notaries must report to the *caponotaio* the names of everybody processed at their bench, and must turn over all their books as soon as they were filled; finally, they must retain a full inventory of their own papers and turn this inventory over to their successors. A third set of orders publicly regulated the scheme of payments notaries might receive for making copies of pardons and registering peace accords, and stipulated situations when they were forbidden to charge for these services (such as when a proceeding was canceled, but a full pardon not granted). These fees were low, a matter of *soldi* and *quattrini* for the most part, and many were dependent on the person's ability to pay.

Further reform efforts occurred in 1627, although these were not published. A supplication written to the legate entitled *Considerationi sopra gli abusi del Torrone* echoes the criticisms made in the *Ricordo di alcuni pastori* disputation cited above, and likely emerged around the same time, perhaps even provoking its printing.[78] With its technical and informational apparatus thus completed by the end of the sixteenth century, the seventeenth-century reform movements aimed to publicly encourage *bolognesi* to use the *Torrone*'s channels to resolve disputes rather than turn to the sponsorship of nobles. By presenting itself as regular, reliable, and accountable, the *Torrone* began to undermine the influence of nobles in the city and especially the illegal courts of dispute resolution that continued to operate in the *contado* until the 1660s.

The *Torrone* thus emerged as the singular dominant court in the legatine territory of Bologna, the response of a frustrated papal overlord to the continued violent resistance of a powerful nobility. When the *bentivoleschi* were expelled in 1506, control of the courts and the criminal law became an extremely important element of the city's governance, and were used for the first thirty years to eliminate vocal elements of the noble opposition to papal rule.[79] By the 1540s papal control was more solid, and the *Torrone* emerged as the institution attempting to cement that rule among all sectors of society, including rural laborers, urban artisans, and feudal nobles. Its dense informational network, a necessary function of its procedures, allowed the court to maintain detailed records of activities in the entire *distretto*. This network served as the bureaucratic face of *inquisitio*, providing the judges and notaries with the necessary background to resolve disputes to the satisfaction of all parties. Its staff were not perfect, and were subject to a series of reforms that culminated in the early eighteenth century under Benedict XIV.[80] Those reforms sought to bring further clarity and accountability to the work of its notaries.

The sheer volume of the *Torrone*'s archive, and its long tenure as the central criminal court in Bologna, indicate that it achieved some success, perhaps limited, in these aims. In part, this is because it functioned well as a forum for the public, not private, resolution of disputes that involved entire communities as well as the victims and criminals themselves. Here the *Torrone*'s complex informational apparatus and the vigor with which its notaries interviewed dozens of witnesses for petty crimes truly made its mark, as the *Torrone* brought relative peace to an unruly and conflict-ridden society. Revenge violence was lessened, although not eliminated, and was much less likely to become cyclical. As the city's governance stabilized through the sixteenth and seventeenth centuries, and was solidified with the final expulsion of fractious nobles in 1664, the *Tribunale del Torrone* modified *inquisitio* procedure to ensure that it upheld state power while also increasing the penetration of that state power into all corners of the territory controlled by the *legato*, and into the minutiae of Bolognese daily life. With papal rule came centralized criminal justice, both to empower the city's new sovereign and to reduce the hold of its violent nobility over the conflicts and concerns of the *contadini*, blacksmiths, and wool-sellers of the legatine territory.

NOTES

1. Angelozzi and Casanova, *La giustizia criminale in una città*, 21.
2. De Benedictis, *Una guerra d'Italia*.
3. Brackett, *Criminal Justice and Crime*; Terpstra, "Competing Visions of the State and Social Welfare"; Waquet, *Corruption*. Waquet in particular notes how the Medici dukes allowed nobility a certain leeway in graft and other opportunities for private profit off the public purse, in exchange for absolute loyalty to the Medici regime in what he terms an exercise of "machine politics." Terpstra notes that Cosimo's patterns of cronyism and patronage in charitable staffing and funding played a similar role, drawing formerly restive noble families into a domesticated Medici household in which the duke played the benevolent father to all.
4. Signorotto and Visceglia, *Court and Politics*; Blastenbrei, "Violence, Arms and Criminal Justice"; Fosi, *Papal Justice*. Blastenbrei argues that the ineffective justice of Rome was a result of "the lasting refusal of the great majority of the Roman population to cooperate with the organs of the papal criminal justice, and the predilection of the average Romans for arms," but does not provide reasons why these two situations should have prevailed.
5. Ruggiero, *Violence in Early Renaissance Venice*, 18–40; Muir, *Mad Blood Stirring*, 13–50.
6. Astarita, *Village Justice*.
7. Hanlon, "In Praise of Refeudalization"; Torre, "Feuding, Factions, and Parties."
8. Antonioli, *Conservator pacis et iustitie*, 109–11.
9. Robertson, *Tyranny under the Mantle*, 109–11.
10. On the *Torrone* see Angelozzi and Casanova, *La giustizia criminale in una città*; Idem, *La nobiltà disciplinata*; Idem, *La giustizia criminale a Bologna nel XVIII secolo*; Cavina, "I luoghi della giustizia"; Di Zio, "Il tribunale del Torrone"; Eadem, "Il tribunale criminale."
11. ASB, Constitutiones Turroni Bononiae, 1566, fols. 1r–4v.
12. Angelozzi and Casanova, *La giustizia criminale in una cittá*, 33–34.
13. Angelozzi and Casanova, *La giustizia criminale in una cittá*, 24.
14. ASB, Bandi e Notificazioni, Series 1, no. 3, fols. 6–8r.
15. ASB, Bandi e Notificazioni, Series 1, no. 3, fol. 13.
16. ASB, Bandi e Notificazioni, Series 1, no. 3, fol. 95.
17. ASB, Bandi e Notificazioni, Series 1, no. 3, fol. 108.
18. ASB, Bandi e Notificazioni, Series 1, no. 3, fols. 111–12r.
19. ASB, Bandi e Notificazioni, Series 1, no. 3, fol. 123.
20. ASB, Bandi e Notificazioni, Series 1, no. 3, unnumbered.
21. Brackett, *Criminal Justice and Crime*, 12–14.
22. Brackett, *Criminal Justice and Crime*, 14–20.
23. Ruggiero, *Violence in Early Renaissance Venice*; Davis, *The War of the Fists*.
24. Blastenbrei, "Violence, Arms and Criminal Justice in Papal Rome, 1560–1600," 69.
25. Angelozzi and Casanova, *La giustizia criminale in una cittá*, 43.
26. Brackett, *Criminal Justice and Crime*, 10.
27. ASB, Senato, Diari, no. 8, 1656–71, fol. 31r.
28. ASB, Constitutiones Turroni Bononiae, 1566.
29. These salaries are listed in ASB, Constitutiones Turroni Bononiae, 1566, fols. 14r–19v.

30. ASB, Constitutioni e Bolle del Torrone, 1488–1623, "Ordini da Osservarsi dalli Notari del Torrone, così intorno alle Cause more alle Mercedi loro," 1607.

31. Angelozzi and Casanova, *La giustizia criminale in una città*, 37–40. On the *Monte di Pietà* and its prominence as a Bolognese institution, see Terpstra, "Apprenticeship in Social Welfare."

32. Angelozzi and Casanova, *La giustizia criminale in una cittá,* 39.

33. Hughes, "Fear and Loathing," 98.

34. ASB, Constitutiones Turroni Bononiae, 1566, fols. 20r–25v.

35. ASB, Constitutiones Turroni Bononiae, 1566, fol. 20r.

36. ASB, Atti e Processi, 6812, *in fine*; 6796, *in fine*.

37. ASB, Atti e Processi, 6787, fasc. 16; 6789, *in fine*; 6798, *in fine*; 6953, *in fine*; 6953, *in fine*; 6956, *in fine*. Giovanni Mioli was also working as a *cursore di Torrone* for a decade or more, from 1670 to 1680. 6936, fasc. 3; 7175, fasc. 37.

38. ASB, Atti e Processi, 6948, fasc. 7; 6634, *in fine*.

39. ASB, Atti e Processi, 6947, fasc. 16.

40. ASB, Atti e Processi, 6947, fasc. 16.

41. ASB, Constitutiones Turroni Bononiae, 1566, fol. 27, section 124.

42. Vallerani, *Medieval Public Justice*, 73–113.

43. ASB, Atti e Processi, 5840, fol. 384.

44. ASB, Atti e Processi, 6782, *in fine*.

45. This was not a popular task. Locals angry at seeing a friend or relative reported to the court harassed and sometimes assaulted these rural bailiffs as they traveled to Bologna. For an edict exhorting people to let their *massari* execute their duties in peace, see ASB, Bandi e Notificazioni, Series 1, no. 5, unnumbered, *bando* of 21 August 1585, " Bando che non sipossi gridar dietro alli Contadini che conducono Delinquenti in mano della Corte." The *Torrone* also expected these *massari* to act as first-line surveillance, particularly with regard to bandit activity, ASB, Bandi e Notificazioni, Series 1, no. 5, unnumbered, *bando* of 5 September 1584, "Bando che li Massari debbano quando passano li Banditi per li loro Communi venire Subito a denonciarli."

46. "Comparisse il Massaro di Roffeno e per vigore del suo officio denoncia qualmente a meza notte in circa col batere a la sua porta e facendosi a la finestra vide che erano doi homini armati e domando chi e la risposero uno di loro 'io son Gio Batista della Becara e cosi vi denunciamo che questa note siamo stati assaltati da gente che siano tirati delle archibugiate ma non siano colso e noi li stiamo tirato a loro e ne abiamo amazato uno e lo abiamo conosciuto et è Gio Maria Stanzati modenese bandito del Stato di Bologna' e non dissero altro et andorno via e il Massaro è andato a cercare il sudetto morto e lo ha ritrovato soto una comercia in loco detto il Campedino in detto commune di Roffeno e non si cognose il morto e anco quelli che di note lo ano chiamato non li ha conosciuto e dissero che l'aveno taliati con pezo di manica del giupone per segnale." ASB, Atti e Processi, 6611, *in fine*.

47. Contumacious banditry, usually temporary, continued its role as an important stage in the judicial process. See below for more on contumacy's role as a "cooling off period."

48. Blastenbrei, "Violence, Arms and Criminal Justice," 69. Blastenbrei makes a persuasive case that these *relazioni* can give a rough idea of levels of violence, and they play a significant role in his larger study of crime in Rome.

49. ASB, Bandi e Notificazioni, Series 1, no. 5, unnumbered, *bando* of 31 December 1588, "Bando sopra quelli che non perseguitano li delinquenti e li medici e barbieri che non denontiano." Importantly, this also reiterates the long-standing requirement that all citizens had a responsibility to report crimes to their local officials.

50. ASB, Registro Cavalcate, 1689–91.

51. ASB, Atti e Processi, 5876, fols. 432v–35v.

52. ASB, Atti e Processi, 5869, fols. 395–400.

53. ASB, Atti e Processi, 3232, unbound folio.

54. ASB, Atti e Processi, 4216, fols. 83r–85v; 3202, fol. 286.

55. ASB, Atti e Processi, 3270, fol. 153r.

56. ASB, Atti e Processi, 5904, fols. 437v–40v.

57. ASB, Bandi e Notificazioni, Series 1, no. 5, unnumbered, *bando* of 31 October 1584.

58. Terpstra, "Theory into Practice," 123.
59. Terpstra, "Theory into Practice," 121; ASB, Gonari delle Giustizie seguite in Bologna dal 1030 al 1750.
60. See Damasio Zavagli's sentencing to ten years of galley service at the age of twenty-two. ASB, Atti e Processi, 6592, *in fine*.
61. ASB, Atti e Processi, 7535.2, fasc. 8.
62. ASB, Atti e Processi, 7536, fasc. 31.
63. Cf. the latest of the sixteenth century, which promises *contadini* 200 *scudi* for killing a *capobandito* and 400 for turning him in alive. ASB, Bandi e Notificazioni, Series 1, no. 5, unnumbered, *bando* of 6 July 1590.
64. ASB, Bandi e Notificazioni, Series 1, no. 5, *bando* of 23 July 1585.
65. ASB, Legato, Bandi, 1600–1700, *bando* of 7 June 1614.
66. ASB, Legato, Bandi, 1600–1700, *bando* of 20 December 1616.
67. ASB, Atti e Processi, 3173, fol. 147; 3184, fols. 298–418; 3185, fols. 162–326r; 3246, fol. 176. For more on this feud, see Rose, "Justice in the *Contado*."
68. ASB, Atti e Processi, 3246, fols. 176–85v.
69. ASB, Atti e Processi, 3185, fol. 218r.
70. ASB, Atti e Processi, 3171–7532.
71. ASB, Assunteria di liti e paci, Atti dell'Assunteria e di Paci, 1658–72, fols. 1v–53r.
72. ASB, Bandi e Stampe, "Ricordo di alcuni past.ri da trattarsi dall'Ill.mi SS.ri Conf.e et Assonti del Torrone col molto Ill.mo et Ecc.mo Sig. Auditore di esso Torrone, con le rispose da esso S.r Auditore date a capo per capo," without date, unnumbered.
73. Angelozzi and Casanova, *La giustizia criminale in una città*, 36.
74. ASB, Constitutioni e bolle del Torrone, 1488–1623, "Ordini da Osservarsi nel Foro Criminale del Torrone di Bologna," 1595, unnumbered.
75. ASB, Constitutioni e bolle del Torrone, 1488–1623, "Per il Torrone," 1596, unnumbered.
76. ASB, Constitutioni e bolle del Torrone, 1488–1l623, "Ordini di NS Papa Clemente Ottavo Sopra l'osservanza delle Constitutioni del Torrone, e Altro," 1602, unnumbered.
77. ASB, Constitutioni e bolle del Torrone, 1488–1623, "Ordini da Osservarsi dalli Notari del Torone, cosi intoro alle Cause, come anco alle Mercedi loro," 1607, broadsheet.
78. ASB, Bandi e Stampe, "Considerationi sop. Gli abusi del Torrone," 1627, unnumbered.
79. Terpstra, "Theory into Practice," 121–23.
80. Angelozzi and Casanova, *La giustizia criminale a Bologna nel XVIII secolo*.

2

Typologies of Violence

Chapter Six

Contra Ribaldos Proditores

From Factional Conflict to Political Crime in Renaissance Bologna

Sara Cucini

The *governo misto* and the *signoria* of the Bentivoglio family are commonly considered the two main political features of Bologna in the second half of the fifteenth century. The *capitoli* of 1447, approved by Pope Nicholas V upon the request of the Bolognese authorities, created a political system in which power was shared by the *Sedici Riformatori dello stato di libertà*—a local council, at this stage comprising members of preeminent Bolognese families,[1] among whom the Bentivoglio held a primary role—and the papal representatives in Bologna.[2] Despite the juridical recognition of the *governo misto* and the undoubted supremacy of the Bentivoglio on the *Sedici*, the relationship between the council and the papal representatives and, in particular, the nature of the effective role of the Bentivoglio in the Bolognese governmental elite have been subject to historiographical debate.[3] Stressing the significant participation of the local patriciate in the handling of political and economic aspects of government, some scholars define the Bentivoglio as *primos inter pares*, considering their capacity as *signori* as merely symbolical, and diverging in essence from the other signorial experiences of the fifteenth-century Italian peninsula. More recently, the limitations on Bentivoglio supremacy have been reviewed and widened. While the perception of contemporaries and their definition of Bentivoglio power has been taken into broader consideration, a similar extensive involvement of the patriciate in civic government has also been observed in other Italian regimes traditionally recognized as "fully signorial."[4] Some scholars have gone as far as defining the Bentivoglio *signoria* as the epitome of a para-*signoria*, that is, a regime in which the *signore* obtained a "partial formalization" of his preeminent role.[5]

Symbolic or effective, the preeminent role of the Bentivoglio in Bologna was achieved by virtue of the dynamic relationship that the family maintained with the Bolognese oligarchy. The position of Annibale Bentivoglio, the "hero of Bologna,"[6] was consolidated in 1443, after his imprisonment by Niccolò Piccinino—the foreign ruler associated with the Milanese Visconti lord—who saw in him a threat to his personal power. However, other members of the Bolognese patriciate shared the stage with Annibale during the events that led to the affirmation of his personal supremacy. Gaspare and Achille Malvezzi were imprisoned with Annibale, and both, together with another member of a patriciate family, Galeazzo Marescotti de' Calvi,[7] participated in the adventurous events that resulted in Annibale's triumphant return to the city and the consequent stabilization of his leadership.[8] The same families were crucial to the definitive affirmation of the Bentivoglio *pars* that followed the assassination of Annibale in 1445. The result of a long-lasting rivalry between the Bentivoglio and another elite family, the Canetoli, the conflict peaked after an attempt at pacification.[9] Invited to be the godfather of a Canetoli associate's son, Annibale attended the christening in the cathedral of San Pietro on 24 June 1445.[10] As he left the church, he was surrounded by a group of Canetoli partisans and, unable to escape, was stabbed to death by Baldassarre Canetoli.[11] Execution of the plot acted as a call to arms for the Canetoli supporters: the subsequent insurrection was intended to kill other members of the Bentivoglio *pars*—and indeed at least three members of the Marescotti family perished in the riots—and overturn its current domination,[12] but the uprising was bloodily repressed by the prompt action of Bentivoglio supporters. Associates of the Fantuzzi and Pepoli families occupied the main piazza in the name of the Bentivoglio,[13] the houses of the Canetoli were burned down;[14] and Battista Canetoli, the brother of Baldassarre, found hidden in a hole in the ground, "was cut into pieces by many citizens, then dragged by his feet into the Piazza Maggiore, thrown onto a pyre, and completely consumed by the flames."[15] Later, while immunity was granted to everyone admitting his involvement before an *ad hoc* commission, a ban for rebellion and the confiscation of all properties was issued against the other perpetrators,[16] and a reward of 1,000 *ducats* was set for the capture of the murderers.[17]

As repercussions from the Canetoli plot of 1445 were experienced for several years, all the families who had intervened in favor of the Bentivoglio during those events and who later participated in the government became, throughout the second half of the fifteenth century, protagonists in new political conflicts aimed at overturning the personal power of the Bentivoglio.

The resolution of this type of conflict, animated by polarized factions, resulted in the attainment of a stronger political position for the winning party, thereby allowing the newly prevailing *pars* to put into action a judicial response. This frequently entailed the exclusion of its opponents from civic society and served as a further tool for consolidation of its power.[18] The nature of this judicial response, the juridical tools that sustained it, and the authorities that were mobilized in its enactment are fundamental elements for clarifying the relationship between the signorial family and the local patriciate, as well as, in the case of Bologna, the dynamics of power between the local oligarchic organs and the papal authority. This essay aims to bring to light these elements through an exploration of the major Bolognese political conflicts of the second half of the Quattrocento: the Canetoli plot of 1445 and its later developments, and also the Fantuzzi and Pepoli insurgency of 1449–50, the Malvezzi conspiracy of 1488, and the Marescotti plot of 1501, in order to analyze how the Bentivoglio turned these conflicts into "political crimes" and managed punishment of the culprits.

In this context, the occupation of the Bolognese *contado* by the Canetoli and their supporters after issuance of the bans of 1445 against them constituted an event of particular importance: the *provvigione* of 9 August 1447 that defined the punishment for this occupation was turned into the official legislative text establishing the method for dealing with the crimes defined as "rebellion." The text describes in detail the circumstances that prompted its promulgation:[19] despite the assassination of Annibale, which aimed to usurp the Bolognese *stato di libertà*, the Canetoli and their supporters did not succeed in their plan and were exiled "by the honest and esteemed citizens of the city of Bologna." Nevertheless, their criminal goal was not repressed by their expulsion. Together with the Milanese troops sent by the Visconti to regain control over the city, which had been lost when Annibale Bentivoglio came to power, they invaded the Bolognese *contado* "occupying numerous castles, [. . .] capturing men, [. . .] stealing livestock, crops and other objects and goods, and setting several fires, and causing damages." The *Sedici,* after "a long meeting, counsel and wise deliberation on how to take action *contra ipsos ribaldos proditores* (against those deceitful traitors)," unanimously decided to declare all the Canetoli and their supporters "rebelles communis Bononie." The status of "rebel" entailed a perpetual ban from the Bolognese territory—and a capital penalty for a banned person found within Bolognese boundaries—the confiscation of all properties, exclusion from all public office, as well as extension of the aforementioned provisions to all descendants up to the fourth masculine generation. A list of the banned culprits was compiled under the supervision of the council, which prohibited the concession of any pardon, except for those receiving favorable votes by at least four fifths of the council's members meeting in plenary session.[20]

With these provisions, management of the political crisis was fully assumed by the *Sedici*, who acted as the responsible judicial authority, determining the nature of the criminal action—implicitly conceptualizing it as a crime against the state—identifying the culprits, fixing their penalties, and controlling the process of pardon, all through a procedure clearly defined as collective and involving all the council's members. In November 1449, a "self-regulatory" *provvigione*[21] was promulgated by the *Sedici* themselves to define the decision-making procedure of the council. When discussing the minimal vote requirement for approval of new provisions, this text recalled the necessity of having four-fifths of the votes when deciding upon pardons for rebels. In doing so, it officially extended the validity of the provisions of 1447 "ad omnes rebelles futuros," henceforth turning the *Sedici* into the solely competent authority for political crimes.

The attribution of this competency to the *Sedici* significantly transformed the nature of the Bolognese judicial authority managing political crimes. During the late thirteenth century, the *capitano del popolo* and his courts supervised the expulsions and confiscations that followed major political conflicts.[22] Suppressed during the Visconti and the ecclesiastical regimes between 1350 and 1376, that responsibility was restored with the reestablishment of the *stato popolare di libertà* in 1376, and the Bolognese statute of that year specifically attributed jurisdiction over political crimes to the *capitano.*[23] His office was suppressed again in 1377 and his criminal jurisdiction converged into that of the podestà, who began to be defined as *potestas et capitaneus* in the late fourteenth century.[24] However, at the beginning of the fifteenth century, the specific task of prosecuting political crimes was entrusted to a new officer, the *executor iustitie*, who first appears in the documentation in 1402. That magistracy, which in the 1420s had its name changed to *conservator iustitie*, was elected extraordinarily and appointed several times until 1446.[25] The *capitano*, the podestà, the *executor*, and the *conservator* who managed the judicial response to political crimes until 1446 were foreign officers, while the transfer of their tasks to the *Sedici* conferred this competency to a local council composed of members of the Bolognese elite. This appropriation of competency by the *Sedici* coincided with the normalization of the relationship between Bologna and the papal sovereign: the *capitoli* with Pope Nicholas V—which established, among other things, the exclusive papal right to nominate foreign officers—were officially approved only a few days after the promulgation of the 1447 text that defined the prerogatives of the council.[26]

The Bolognese governing patriciate thus assumed direct control over local dissidence, thereby preventing any possibility of direct interference by the papal authorities in managing the repercussions of internal political conflicts. The statute of 1454, which aimed to act as validation of the renewed harmony between Bologna and the papacy,[27] officially extended the validity of all the normative texts promulgated by the *Sedici.*[28] This extension, together with the allusions to the *provvigione* of 1447 in several normative texts promulgated by the papal authorities over the course of the late fifteenth century,[29] indicates that the *Sedici*'s self-attributed prerogatives over political crimes were tolerated by the pontificate, despite the fact that sovereignty over Bologna would have guaranteed to the papal representatives the right of intervention in every case that could be conceptually associated with the *crimen laesae maiestatis*.[30] Moreover, the exercise of these prerogatives, with the tacit accord of the papacy, provided the council with the opportunity to extend its interference over the sanctioning of common crimes, through a group of provisions that identified certain criminals as rebels—for instance the murderers of relatives, culprits breaking a peace accord with violent actions, those under ban who unlawfully reentered Bolognese territory, and those found guilty of illicit revenge[31]—submitting them to the *iurisdictio* of the council.[32]

Despite the extension of *Sedici* jurisdiction over some criminal cases and their direct management of political conflicts, the records of the podestà's court *ad maleficia* show how this court also remained involved in the sanctioning of political crimes. For instance, several trials concerning certain Canetoli associates can be found in the podestà's court until the 1470s,[33] while a cluster of such trials in 1451–52 was connected to one of the Canetoli's attempts to return to Bologna.[34] These trials, regarding suspects who had minor involvement in the plot and its aftermath, appear to have been conducted by the podestà's court without a direct involvement of the council. The only exception, for which the mandate of the *Sedici* was openly mentioned, was a procedure of March 1462 concerning Ludovico Bartolomeo di Castello, accused of conspiring with the Canetoli for the assassination of Sante Bentivoglio.[35] The *Sedici* reserved their direct action for those crimes that they considered to be direct attempts at disruption of their supremacy. However, trials against individuals who had a marginal role in those attempts or were protagonists of such events—sometimes clearly defined as *crimen laesae maiestatis*[36]—if those events did not directly concern the Bentivoglio government in force, were, officially or informally, delegated to the autonomous management of the podestà's court.[37]

The conflict between the Bentivoglio and the Canetoli thus contributed crucially to forging the extension of the *Sedici*'s political power as a collective entity and establishing the pattern of judicial action for political crimes. The *Sedici* created the juridical conditions for assuming a direct judicial function that they exercised when the consequences of the political conflict required "extraordinary" means of action, but which they delegated to the regular judicial authority for minor occurrences or for implementing the council's decisions once the "extraordinary" sanction had been established.

This pattern of action, defined during the events of 1445–47, was tested only a few years later, when the *Sedici* had to deal with the rebellion of some of its own members—Giovanni Fantuzzi and Romeo Pepoli and their associates. The growing tension between Sante Bentivoglio[38] and the two families who contributed to the consolidation of his personal power,[39] materialized into a conflict presented by Fantuzzi and Pepoli as a defense of Bolognese *libertas* and papal sovereignty over the city. During the summer of 1449, members of both families voluntarily left Bologna—under the pretext of a plague outbreak that was ravaging the city—for Castel San Pietro in the Bolognese *contado.*[40] From there, Pepoli and Fantuzzi contacted the banned Canetoli and representatives of King Alfonso I of Naples, who at that time was in the Romagna, and bribed the captain of the gate of Strada Maggiore,[41] in the hope of gathering military support, reentering the city, and overturning the Bentivoglio regime.

However, betrayal by one of those involved thwarted the plot; the conspirators present in the city were executed in the main piazza with a symbolic set of forged keys hanging around their necks.[42] The members of the Fantuzzi and Pepoli families remained in the *contado,* attempting to extend their control over other fortifications. Escalation of the conflict having been made clear by the discovered plot, the *Sedici* sent Carlo Malvezzi, one of their number, to negotiate, in the name of the council, the surrender of the rebels. The response of the conspirators fully revealed the political nature of their actions: Romeo Pepoli was said to have declared that he was "more than a little surprised by the arrogance of the *Sedici* and the insane audacity of Sante Bentivoglio in delivering such an order [of surrendering] and that in said *castello*, where he was to be found with his associates, they had as much authority as they [the *Sedici*] did."[43] The conspirators were claiming their right to control the fortifications on the basis of their belonging to the *Sedici*, which had been invested in its entirety with governmental authority by the papacy through the *capitoli* of 1447.[44] The two families described their action as a legitimate expression of disagreement within the *Sedici*, justifying their occupations in the *contado* in the name of respect for superior papal sovereignty.[45] For this reason, in order not to appear to be opposing papal sovereignty, the response of the *Sedici* to this conflict had to be formally concealed behind the action of other authorities. The trials against the conspirators of August 1449 were delegated to the podestà's court,[46] which one month later also carried out proceedings against the leaders of the rebellion[47] and their associates[48] for their occupation of the *contado.* None of these trials record any reference to direct intervention by the *Sedici,*[49] and further measures against the Fantuzzi and Pepoli rebels were officially taken by the papal representatives in 1450.[50] The role of the *Sedici,* invisible in the trial records and never mentioned by the narrative sources, becomes evident only in the *Libri Partitorum*, where the votes of the council were recorded: the *relegationes* (confinement of culprits in specific cities as determined by judicial authority) of all the accused were fixed by the *Sedici* on 10 September 1450,[51] while other votes concerning the culprits were recorded in 1452.[52] The approach used in the repression of the Fantuzzi and Pepoli rebellion is not only remarkably different from that used in response to the events of 1445–47 involving the Canetoli, but also in comparison to another plot in which the latter were again protagonists. Late in 1453, Galeotto Canetoli, together with Battista Manzoli, *decretum doctor* and canon of the cathedral of San Pietro, organized a new attempt to return to Bologna early in 1454.[53] The plot having been discovered and reported,[54] Manzoli was imprisoned, and the *Sedici* themselves ordered the confiscation of all his properties on 3 January 1454, and delegated, this time officially, their *arbitrium puniendi et condemnandi* to the podestà.[55] Despite this official delegation of jurisdiction, the matter was taken in hand by one of the *Sedici*, Paolo della Volta, who personally mandated the hanging of Manzoli without waiting for a trial by the podestà, or further official instructions from the council.[56] Since della Volta belonged to the *Sedici*, it was possible to consider his technically extrajudicial action as the concretization of the council's prerogatives, and therefore the only reaction to his violent intervention was a mild protest by Cardinal legate Bessarion, possibly related to Manzoli's clerical status.[57]

The self-justifying premises of the Fantuzzi and Pepoli rebellion forced a major change in the pattern of judicial response that had been established in 1447. At that time Sante was consolidating his personal power after the sudden death of Annibale, and was fully supported by the Bentivoleschi *Sedici*, whose political force was strong enough to allow open and direct judicial action. Two years later, the Fantuzzi and Pepoli challenged the very legitimacy of the *Sedici* and the nature of Bentivoglio supremacy, reaffirming the position of the Bolognese political class in relation to papal sovereignty. As members of the patriciate defending their class interests, the Fantuzzi and Pepoli justified their actions in the *contado* by the fact that they were members of the *Sedici* and thereby entitled to a "share" of the political power of the council.

Hence the *Sedici*, whose legitimacy of action had been questioned, had to restrain their own capacity for judicial action, leaving fulfilment of this judicial response to the podestà, an official elected by the papacy and technically invested with this task by the statutes. Only in November 1449 after the trials were concluded, and once papal support had been openly expressed, were the Bentivoleschi *Sedici* able to officially confirm their prerogatives concerning political crimes with promulgation of their self-regulatory *provvigione*. In 1454, when the favorable legation of Bessarion certified papal backing of the Bentivoleschi *Sedici*, actions by the council that constituted an abuse of their own self-established prerogatives could be openly condoned.

After 1454, the consent of the political class to Bentivoglio supremacy remained stable, resulting in the absence of major political conflicts within the governmental elite for more than three decades. The consolidation of Sante's personal power led to the splendor of the Bentivoglio era, fulfilled in the first decades of the regime of Giovanni II,[58] the son of Bologna's hero

Annibale. One contributing factor to this stability was the role played by the Malvezzi family in the council of the *Sedici*.[59] Members of this family functioned as "antagonists" who balanced Bentivoglio influence, creating what has been defined as a "power diarchy,"[60] in which Virgilio Malvezzi, who had actively worked to guarantee the succession to Giovanni II, incarnated the opposition to the Bentivoglio inside the governmental faction.[61] This role was played by the Malvezzi until the late 1480s, when this family devised a plot that revealed a rupture in the balance within the "power diarchy."

According to the narrative sources, the origins of the fracture between the two families were to be found in trivial circumstances.[62] However, a conflictual dynamic that characterized the Malvezzi "opposition" had already emerged in the late 1450s, after members of the family acted, against the wishes of Sante Bentivoglio, on behalf of a Canetoli associate, to commute his death penalty into a permanent ban.[63] Sante created a further reason for confrontation when he attempted to designate his son, Ercole, as his successor to his council seat, originally destined for Annibale's son, Giovanni.[64] Despite these early clashes, the growing tension culminated only at the end of November 1488,[65] once the *Sedici* were informed of the imminent conspiracy.[66] The Malvezzi, possibly with the help of some members of the Marescotti family[67] and the Florentine government,[68] planned to slaughter Giovanni II, his wife and sons. A crossbowman at the service of the family[69] was supposed to open the doors of the Bentivoglio's palace to the conspirators during the family dinner on 28 November, the day after the conspiracy was revealed to the council.[70] Once the assassination was carried out, the conspirators planned to overturn the government by killing the main supporters of the Bentivoglio *pars* and occupying the Piazza Maggiore and the palazzo comunale.[71] The plot having been disclosed, Giovanni II, who finally had succeeded in 1463,[72] summoned the *Sedici*, and the council ordered the incarceration of Battista Malvezzi's four sons who had been involved in the conspiracy.[73] Three of them having fled the city, only Giovanni Malvezzi was brought before the council, where he confessed. Transferred to the urban prison, he was questioned again by the podestà, who was assisted by the papal delegate, two members of the *Sedici*, two members of the council of the *anziani*, and three members of the *collegi*; he reiterated his confession and revealed the names of his accomplices. He was then executed that very same day, together with several other culprits.[74] The fugitives were instead officially summoned to appear before the podestà, to whom the *Sedici* transferred their "authority, jurisdiction, capacity, and power of any sort."[75] In spite of this official delegation of authority, the *Sedici* themselves decided the *relegationes* of each member of the Malvezzi family.[76] For some the council established a generic edict of banishment from Bolognese territory,[77] for others they chose specific cities such as Naples, Venice, Trento, and

Rimini,[78] while they declared all of them rebels and had their properties confiscated.[79]

The management of the Malvezzi plot of 1488 thus appears to be an act of cooperation between the main Bolognese political and judicial authorities, conducted under the direct supervision of the *Sedici*.[80] The involvement of the papal representative and *anziani* and the formal transfer to the *ad maleficia* court of the podestà were intended to define the attempt on Giovanni Bentivoglio's life as a crime that would have affected the stability of civic society as a whole. However, the preponderant role of the *Sedici* in conducting the judicial response to the crisis of 1488 is evident: the council summoned the suspects, supervised the podestà and extended his *arbitrium*, decided the final sanctions, and was fully empowered to do so by the prerogatives established in 1447 and confirmed in 1449. In contrast to the events linked to the Fantuzzi and Pepoli, who presented themselves as supporters of papal sovereignty and champions of the prerogative of the oligarchic political class, the Malvezzi plot specifically targeted the life of the Bentivoglio *signore*. In this circumstance, application of the prerogatives of the *Sedici* could therefore be openly executed, aiming, through the collegial exercise of the council's judicial power, to reunite around the Bentivoglio the political class disrupted by the plot.

Even if the judicial response to the Malvezzi conspiracy constituted an emblematic example of the prompt reaction of the *Sedici* in the management of political crimes, further provisions were taken to implement more incisive governmental action in dealing with those banned *pro rebellionis*, for instance, the negotiation early in 1489 of treaties with the Florentine and Ferrarese governments. For "any person banned as a rebel for the crime of *lèse-majesté*, that is, for a crime concerning the state, and similarly for any person, confined for this reason, who would cross the boundaries of his confinement,"[81] the two treaties prescribed that any rebel found within the respective boundaries could be freely executed by any authority that had such a person in custody.

These further provisions against rebels reveal the perceived need to expand the means of control over political opponents, and are indicative of the radical transformation unveiled by the Malvezzi plot in Bolognese civic society,[82] as attested to by the words of a contemporary chronicler: "from this conspiracy, this evil in our city occurred, so that from when we were without divisions two factions were created. This was because the Malvezzi had many supporters and relatives in the city, some called *Segantes*, others *Malvezeschi*. And in this way, the harmony of the city was lost."[83] The narrative sources are, in fact, of particular importance in reporting other significant aspects of this situation. The chronicler Fileno dalla Tuata, for instance, mentions several examples of extrajudicial action related to political opponents, reporting numerous assassinations of Malvezzi's partisans, executed by unknown offenders, usually completing his description of the events with the formula" and it was not discussed in the courts, because he was a *malvezzesco*."[84]

While the *Sedici* never reprised their judicial role against the Malvezzi and their supporters after 1488, a few significant cases appear in the records of the *ad maleficia* court. One trial of 1499 and a sentence of 1502 concerned individuals who never had an active role in the conspiracy, but publicly displayed their preference for the banned family over the current Bentivoglio *pars* ruling the city.[85] Earlier, in 1490, a proceeding involved a resident of the *contado*, accused of "a plot, conspiracy, and crime of treason, transgression, and crime of lèse-majesté" in reference to his alleged participation in the events of 1488: the trial ended in acquittal, as the witnesses' testimony supporting the accusation was found to be untruthful.[86] Fileno dalla Tuata reported at least other two cases of false accusations for alleged relations with the banned Malvezzi, one in 1494 and another the following year.[87] The latter cases manifestly constituted self-serving accusations designed to shape the *mala fama*[88] of an individual and, in attempting to do so, referred to events that clearly evoked a major disruption of civic life, while the former cases show how, even over more than a decade later, the simple public expression of support on behalf of the Malvezzi corresponded to a criminal offense that had to be officially punished. Significantly, though—and in contrast to the Fantuzzi and Pepoli insurgency which saw its leaders personally tried, or to the Canetoli plot, whose protagonists continue to appear in the court's records until the 1470s—no trial concerning any person with a direct involvement in the Malvezzi conspiracy survives.[89] Extrajudicial activity against the *malvezzeschi*, to which Fileno dalla Tuata bears witness, seems to have been the only model for management of the aftermath of the 1488 events. While the immediate reaction to the conspiracy of 1488 constituted an exemplary response of the Bentivoglio council, during the last period of the Bentivoglio supremacy conditions were lacking that might have enabled the *Sedici* to exercise their prerogatives. Consequently, management of the judicial responses to political crimes had to cross the boundaries of regulations that the council itself had established some decades earlier.

Conditions for another major conflict were created when external factors were added to local political dynamics after the election of Pope Alexander VI. The conquest of Milan by Louis XII offered the papacy the opportunity to gain submission of the Romagnol territories and turned Giovanni II Bentivoglio, subject to papal sovereignty and ally of Ludovico Sforza, into an enemy of both the pope and the French king.[90] Pacification with the latter, after the conquest of Milan, required a toll of 43,000 *ducats*, another reason for the decline of local support for the Bentivoglio government.[91] The threat posed by the expansionist ambitions of Cesare Borgia contributed to this critical political framework, and his march on Bologna was stopped only by the opposition of Louis XII.[92] The last conspiracy to strike Bentivoglio domination, instigated by the formerly allied Marescotti, developed during the negotiations between the city and Cesare Borgia.[93] Paolo Orsini, the Borgia delegate in Bologna, revealed the plot to Giovanni II by sharing the private correspondence between Cesare and Giasone and Agamennone Marescotti.[94] Heirs to the Galeazzo Marescotti who had been one of the main supporters of the Bentivoglio during the events that led to the death of Annibale, they supposedly would have offered control over the city to Cesare Borgia, hoping to liberate Bologna from the "tyranny" of the Bentivoglio.[95] Despite suspicion that the letters might have been forged in an attempt to fuel discords in the governmental elite, Giasone and Agamennone Marescotti were imprisoned, together with their nephews Agesilao and Ludovico,[96] in the palazzo comunale. The incarceration, never officially authorized by the council,[97] lasted four days before the adoption of a completely extrajudicial solution, related exclusively by the narrative sources: Giovanni II's son, Hermes, assassinated the suspects on 3 May 1501, when "all four poor fellows were cut into pieces like dogs," with the help of several scions of other members of the *Sedici*,[98] who continued the slaughter the following day against other associates of the Marescotti.[99] While Ginevra Sforza, wife of Giovanni II and mother of Hermes, was identified as the instigator of the action, the involvement of Giovanni II himself was excluded by contemporary chroniclers.[100]

The notoriety of the conspiracy would have sufficed to legally justify direct action by the *Sedici* in the light of a reform of the 1447 provisions, dated 2 March 1496 which aimed, as did the treaties of 1489 with Florence and Ferrara, to reinforce the juridical tools of the Bentivoglio government against political rebels. As voted by the *Sedici*,[101] and officially promulgated by the papal representative,[102] this text of 1496 opened by deploring the absence of a law that defined the bans *pro rebellionis*, noting, however, the remarkable exception of the 1447 *provvigione* condemning the Canetoli. As this latter text had established the sanction in relation to a specific case, the reform of 1496 intended to universally determine the nature of the crime of rebellion and the punishment associated to it. The *provvigione* of 1496, therefore, defined as *rebelles* "those who conspire and carry out an attack against any person with the aim of damaging and unsettling the present state" and "anyone who, instigated by an evil impulse, dares to kill or murder somebody with a dagger or poison or in any other way, to the damage and disturbance of the present state."[103] In this way, the assimilation between the political crime and the attempt to overturn the personal power of the Bolognese *signore*—hinted at in 1447 with the implicit association of the concept of rebellion with the violent death of Annibale Bentivoglio—was made explicit. Moreover, the text updating the provisions of 1447 changed the quorum of the *Sedici* for votes on political crimes, requiring unanimity instead of four-fifths of the ballots for granting a pardon. This modification effectively guaranteed the right of veto, and consequently full control over the readmission of unwanted individuals to the Bentivoglio, *de facto* removing any power of action to any opposition within the council. As a result of this reform, the Bentivoglio openly defined attempts against their power as political crimes, excluded other members of the governmental oligarchy from the process of control over rebels, and obtained an official papal confirmation of these prerogatives, which were, nevertheless, never exercised against the Marescotti.

The extrajudicial resolution adopted for the Marescotti plot, described by the narrative sources as the result of the reckless act of bravado by a Bentivoglio scion instigated by a mother lacking political clairvoyance, was instead a logical outcome of a period of internal crisis characterized by clashes within the governmental elite. The assistance given by the younger members of several other patrician families in the assassination of the alleged Marescotti schemers was, therefore, not casual. It suggests, instead, a careful planning of the events, as the involvement of several members of the oligarchical families would have guaranteed the support of these families for the action of Hermes,[104]—which in fact was never punished—and simultaneously assured the fulfillment of an exemplary castigation that might not have received the seal of approval if voted by a divided council. The plot supposedly planned by the Marescotti was not different in essence from the Malvezzi conspiracy: in both cases a scheme aimed at overturning Bentivoglio supremacy was organized by one of the most prominent families belonging to the governmental circle and discovered before its completion. The difference between the two circumstances lies in the judicial reactions. On the one hand, the answer to the Malvezzi conspiracy was organized a few hours after the plot was discovered, displayed a clear exercise of the *Sedici* prerogatives, involved all the governmental councils as well as the papal delegates and the criminal court of the podestà elected by the pontificate, and stressed the maintenance of civic unity and the standing support of the Bentivoglio despite the Malvezzi betrayal. On the other hand, the Marescotti were imprisoned for days while no official decision was taken concerning their plot; inaction that indicated a strong reluctance to exercise the same prerogatives that, indeed, had been officially confirmed only a few years earlier with the reform of 1496. Respect for the legislative provisions concerning political crimes was thus exchanged for a different modus operandi, culminating in the process started in the years after the Malvezzi conspiracy when the extrajudicial executions of the persons suspected of being *malvezzesca* became the only form for management of the aftermath of the plot, implementing a mode of political conflict resolution that situated itself outside the boundaries of all ordinary or extraordinary jurisdictions. The disruption of the collegial dynamics within the *Sedici* deprived the Bentivoglio of the political force needed for acting within the normative system that had been built during their period of supremacy. The legislative provisions concerning political crimes, elaborated at the beginning of their domination as a result of the assassination of Annibale and the attempted return of his banned murderers and their associates, provided a regulatory solution that involved jointly all members of the restricted patrician council sharing power with the *signore*. In judicial practice, the regulatory solution allowed the *Sedici* to function as an extraordinary court specifically dealing with situations that directly imperiled the *signoria* and the *pars* that supported it, while the jurisdiction of the *Sedici* on political crimes was delegated, under council supervision, to the podestà's court for those cases that could be associated with that type of crime, but involved a minor role in disrupting the political system of the *signoria*. Therefore, despite the normalization of the judicial function of the *Sedici* through the normative provisions of 1447–49 and 1496, partial delegation to the podestà of some of the prerogatives of management of political crimes contributed to keeping the action of the *Sedici* within the boundaries of "extraordinariness."

This system, based on parallel streams of action, became unusable after the loss of internal stability caused by the Malvezzi conspiracy, revealing the depth of the interconnection between the Bentivoglio and the oligarchic system that sustained their power. When this interconnection was shattered by a strong interior crisis, the signorial family defended its preeminent position by acting independently, outside the normative regulation that, elaborated together with the *Sedici*, created a system based on the concerted action of that group. The conflict incited by the Fantuzzi and Pepoli had already demonstrated, in 1449–50, the limits of this normative regulation, forcing the Bentivolesca *pars* and its governmental body to hide its judicial action behind a superior authority to confront the question of legitimacy posed by members of the system who came into conflict with it. Papal intervention supporting the *bentivoleschi* was crucial to overcoming that conflict which had revealed how the limits imposed on the local *signoria* were embodied in the Bolog nese governmental elite and not in the papacy itself. Management of the *malvezzeschi* opponents in the years that followed the conspiracy of 1488 and the sanguinary repression of the Marescotti plot of 1501 exposed the extreme consequences of what had been glimpsed in 1449–50: the oligarchic system was effective only in a context of concerted action, while the same system turned into a limitation on the exercise of signorial power when that collaboration failed. In these situations, the Bentivoglio had to bypass the juridical structure, abandoning the system and, at the same time, igniting further reasons for conflicts within the *Sedici* oligarchy.

The management of political conflicts shows how the strongest limitations on the personal power of the Bentivoglio were a direct consequence of the dynamics that the family had with the oligarchic group that had supported its regime and favored initially its ascension—during the events tied to the Canetoli and, most of all, to the former members of the *Sedici*, the Fantuzzi and Pepoli—and later its patently despotic turn after the Malvezzi conspiracy. The adoption of an exclusively extrajudiciary response to the political crisis that followed this plot shows that cohesion within the prevailing faction constituted a necessary condition for implementing the normative regulations elaborated within the governmental system and wielding the authority of the Bentivoglio regime to its full extent.

While papal support had been fundamental in overcoming the conflicts of the mid-fifteenth century, the beginning of the Cinquecento saw a tense relationship between the Bolognese government and the pontificate, adding to the factors that led to the Marescotti plot. In this context, an extrajudicial resolution was turned into the only possible form of response, revealing the final collapse of the dialectical dynamic within the governmental faction. From this collapse papal authority profited: one of the reasons given in support of the *iusta causa* by Julius II for his recapture of Bologna was, significantly, that "noble families of citizens had become totally extinct as a result of the prescriptions and persecutions of the Bentivoglio."[105] Canetoli, Malvezzi, and Marescotti preceded the members of all the civic councils—*anziani*, *gonfalonieri del popolo*, and the new Senate—in the parade that accompanied the solemn entrance of the warrior pope in Bologna on 11 November 1506.[106]

NOTES

1. This act contributed to the later development of a civic nobility, as noted by Gardi, "Making of an Oligarchy."

2. On the *capitoli*, see De Benedictis, *Repubblica per contratto*, 107–36; Duranti, *Diplomazia e autogoverno,* 56–61. On the Bentivoglio, the work of Ady, *The Bentivoglio,* remains fundamental. On the origin of the council of the *Sedici Riformatori* see Tamba, "I XVI Riformatori"; on the council during the fifteenth century, see Duranti, *Diplomazia e autogoverno*, 67–104.

3. On the *governo misto*, see Colliva, "Bologna dal XIV al XVIII secolo"; De Benedictis, "Il governo misto," Eadem, *Repubblica per contratto*, 87–105.

4. On this reinterpretation see Duranti, "*Libertas*, Oligarchy, Papacy." On the relationship between the Bentivoglio and the Bolognese patriciate, see De Benedictis, "Quale 'corte'"; Duranti, "Un compromesso."

5. Somaini, "The collapse," 252.

6. Duranti, *Diplomazia e autogoverno*, 111.

7. He left us a precise account of the events: see Marescotti, *Cronica come Anniballe Bentivoglij fu preso*. On the context of its production see Roversi Monaco, *Conflitti oligarchici*, 41–45. On the diffusion of the text, which did not take place until the 1480s, see Quaquarelli, *Memoria Urbis*, 136–41.

8. For an analysis of the description in Marescotti, *Cronica come Anniballe Bentivoglij fu preso,* see Roversi Monaco, *Conflitti oligarchici*, 77–86.

9. In the words of Machiavelli: "There were in Bologna two very powerful families, Canetoli and Bentivoglio: of the latter Annibale was the leader, of the former Battista. For improving their trust in each other, they became one family, but men who aspire to the same

greatness can easily become family, not friends." Machiavelli, *Istorie Fiorentine*, chap. 9, 2–3, 551. See also Duranti, *Diplomazia e autogoverno*, 113.

10. Ady, *The Bentivoglio*, 28. Dalla Tuata, *Istoria di Bologna*, 1:286.

11. Marescotti, *Cronica come Anniballe Bentivoglij fu preso*, 42–43.

12. As described by both "Cronaca Rampona" and "Cronaca Varignana," 4:126.

13. Dalla Tuata, *Istoria di Bologna*, 1:287–88.

14. "Cronaca Rampona" and "Cronaca Varignana," 4:128.

15. Dalla Tuata, *Istoria di Bologna*, 1:291. Also see Marescotti, *Cronica come Anniballe Bentivoglij fu preso*, 51.

16. De Benedictis, "'Sendo la parte,'" 443–45.

17. ASB, Liber Fantini, fols. 175rv, edited in Cucini, "Législation statutaire," doc. 37, 2:421–22.

18. For Bologna, on the dynamics of political conflict in the late fourteenth and early fifteenth century, see Lantschner, *The Logic of Political Conflict*, 95–130; on the process of exclusion see Milani, *L'Esclusione dal comune*.

19. ASB, Liber Novarum Provisionum, fols. 177r–80v of the modern pagination; Cucini, "Législation statutaire," doc. 1, 2:306–13, see also 1:428–30.

20. This requirement would be modified in 1451, authorizing voting on pardons also during non-plenary sessions of the council: ASB, Libri Partitorum 383, Register 1, fol. 35r; Cucini, "Legislation statutaire," doc. 78, 2:487.

21. As defined by Duranti, *Diplomazia e autogoverno*, 78–81. An edition of the text is at 277–79.

22. For instance, he played a major role in the expulsion of the Lambertazzi in the second half of the thirteenth century, Milani, *L'Esclusione dal comune*, 292–97. More generally, in the civic society governed by the *popolo*, "the capitano's *arbitrium* stemmed from his primary role as protector of the *popolo* from external and internal enemies, both for the *popolo* as a political entity and for the individuals that comprised that entity." Blanshei, *Politics and Justice*, 525.

23. ASB, Statuti 46 (formerly XIII), fols. 78v–82v (1376).

24. Montorsi, "Involuzione del capitanato," 166–67 and 196–98. Despite the suppression of the charge, the statutes of 1389 and 1454 reported the articles concerning the *capitano*, respectively ASB, Statuti 47 (formerly XIV), fols. 88r–91v; 50 (formerly XVII), fols. 50v–54v, with adjustments aimed at extending his competencies to the podestà. See Cucini, "Législation statutaire," 1:289–93.

25. For a list of the *executores* and *conservatores* between 1402 and 1446 see Montorsi, *La Giustizia*, 485–501; on their offices and jurisdiction see Montorsi, "Involuzione del capitanato."

26. The *capitoli* were officially promulgated on 24 August 1447. In point eight, the pope reserved the right to appoint the podestà. De Benedictis, *Repubblica per Contratto*, 115. As noted by Lantschner, "Revolts and Political Order," 36n82, the *capitoli* marked a significant change in Bologna's system of conflict—for a study of which, see Lantschner, "The Nourisher of Seditions."

27. Duranti, *Diplomazia e autogoverno*, 91.

28. Duranti, *Diplomazia e autogoverno*, 93–94.

29. For example: ASB, Liber Novarum Provisionum, fols. 396r–97r of the modern pagination (1467) and, most of all, the text of 1496 that officially reformed the content of the *provvigione* of 1447: ASB, Liber Novissimarum Provisionum, fols. 171r–72r of the modern pagination; Cucini, "Législation statutaire," docs. 13 and 35, 2:341–43, 2:413–17.

30. The pope was formally the temporal sovereign of Bologna. Moreover, the juristic reflection identified in the papal authority a primary holder of *maiestas*: Sbriccoli, *Crimen Laease Maiestatis*, 204–5, 219.

31. Respectively: ASB, Liber Novarum Provisionum, fols. 396r–97r of the modern pagination (1467); Liber Novissimarum Provisionum, fol. 12r of the modern pagination (1472); fol.111r of the modern pagination (1480)—the original 1461 text of the provision against the banned is lost and its content is known through a later *provvigione*—Libri Provisionum 311, Register 2, fols. 36v (1498); Cucini, "Législation statutaire," doc. 13, 341–43; doc. 17, 2:358–59; doc 32, 2:408–9, doc. 42, 2:431.

32. On other means of intervention of the *Sedici* in trials for common crimes see Cucini, "Législation statutaire," 1: 312–27. See also Dean, "Criminal Justice."

33. See Cucini, "Législation statutaire," 1:443–45. The last trial for political crime concerning the Canetoli dates to 1470: ASB, Inquisitiones 377, fols. 22r–23v.

34. Described by the "Cronaca Rampona" and "Cronaca Varignana," 4:176–79; Ghirardacci, *Della historia di Bologna*, 137. For the trials see ASB, Inquisitiones 356, Register 2, fols. 58r–59v, 60r–64v, 116r–18v,182r–86r; 357, fols. 60r–61v; 358, Register 2, fols. 69r–70r, 73r–74v.

35. ASB, Inquisitiones 364, fols. 89rv.

36. The individuals indicted in ASB, Inquisitiones 356, Register 2, fols. 116r–18r and 358, Register 2, fols. 73r–74v, respectively in March 1451 and July 1452, are accused of "tractatum et etiam crimen lese maiestatis."

37. Cucini, "Législation statutaire," 1:436–38 and 1:481–83.

38. Ady, *The Bentivoglio*, 31–34; Duranti, *Diplomazia e autogoverno*, 113–14.

39. Ady, *The Bentivoglio*, 36.

40. Dalla Tuata, *Istoria di Bologna*, 1:301.

41. ASB, Inquisitiones 354, Register 2 bis, fol. 3v: "'How could we have those keys to open this gate for said Giovanni Fantucci and other people to enter Bologna? Would you like to forge these keys?' To which Giovanni, known as el Mosca, responding to the said Cristoforo, declared and promised that he would make those keys."

42. "Cronaca Rampona," 4:164–65; "Cronaca Varignana," 4:166–67.

43. As reported in the sixteenth-century history of Bologna by Ghirardacci, *Della historia di Bologna*, 131. "Rispose Romeo che non poco sì maravigliava della prosontione del reggimento et del folle ardire di Santi Bentivogli, che gli facessero un simile comandamento, sendo loro più legitimi cittadini, che non era Santi, et che nel detto castello, ove esso con li suoi compagni era, havevano tanta autorità quanto che essi."

44. As effectively noted by De Benedictis, "'Sendo la parte,'" 444–45.

45. See Ady, *The Bentivoglio*, 48–49. According to "Cronaca Rampona" 4:165 and "Cronaca Varignana," 4:167: "*Messer* Romeo Pepoli and his brothers, with Giovanni Fantuzzi and his associates, all shouted in the said *castello* 'Long live the Church!'"

46. ASB, Inquisitiones 354, Register 1, fols. 59r–60v, 62r–64r; Register 2 bis, fols. 3r–4v, 5r–6v. Fileno dalla Tuata, reports the destruction and pillage of the culprits' houses: Dalla Tuata, *Istoria di Bologna*, 1:301.

47. The trial of September 1449 involved Giovanni Fantuzzi and his son Antonio: ASB, Inquisitiones 354, Register 1, fols. 66r–69r. At the beginning of October 1449, a second trial (fols. 79r–81v) saw Antonio Fantuzzi accused, with others, of provoking the uprising of the *castello* of Medicina. The same register reports (fols. 118r–21r) a third trial about another attempt to return to Bologna through the gate of Strada Castiglione. None of the Pepoli family members were indicted in these trials.

48. ASB, Inquisitiones 354, Register 2 bis, fols. 7r–8r., f. 37r–39r.

49. This absence is all the more striking, considering that in the same period at least two trials for *crimina contra statum* unrelated to the Fantuzzi and Pepoli were litigated by the podestà's court, and in these occurrences the competencies of the *Sedici* were specifically mentioned in the trial records. See ASB, Inquisitiones 354, Register 2, fols. 18r–20r and 21r–23r.

50. See for instance "Cronaca Rampona" and "Cronaca Varignana," 4:173, which, referring to the dismissal of Romeo Pepoli, declare "his departure happened in this way, that Pope Nicholas V sent a priest to him as a representative, who came the 19th of March; and as soon as he entered the said *castello*, he requested to be given the keys of the said *castello* by the *castello* keeper; and this done, he ended the occupation of the fortress, and dismissed *messer* Romeo [. . .] with the authority of Pope Nicholas V, and dismissed the foreigners, and so everyone left."

51. ASB, Libri Partitorum 383, Register 1, fol. 7v, Cucini, "Législation statutaire," doc. 75, 2:485, "10th of September. It was voted with twelve favorable ballots that *dominus* Romeo Pepoli and his brothers, *dominus* Nanni and Francesco da Vizano, Giovanni Fantucci, his sons Antonio, Pietro, and Iacopo, Iacopo Fantucci, Alberto, and Nicola, known as Maiazo, brothers

and sons of Pietro Masotti, are to be confined in the coming three days somewhere at least sixty miles far from Bologna, and their properties are considered seized by the treasury of the commune."

52. ASB, Libri Partitorum 383, Register 1, fols. 49v, 59v.

53. See "Cronaca Rampona" and "Cronaca Varignana," 4:195–98, Dalla Tuata, *Istoria di Bologna*, 1:310.

54. The denunciation was made for a substantial reward established by the *Sedici*: ASB, Libri Partitorum 383, Register 1, fols. 128v–29r.

55. ASB, Libri Partitorum 383, Register 1, fols. 129v.

56. "Cronaca Rampona" and "Cronaca Varignana," 4:194.

57. Ady, *The Bentivoglio*, 49.

58. Basile, *Bentivolorum Magnificentia*.

59. The self-regulatory *provvigione* of 1449 established the exclusive rights of Virgilio Malvezzi and Galeazzo Marescotti to substitute for their fathers in the council's sessions, while Achille Malvezzi obtained the privilege of attending the session even in the presence of his father. Moreover, Achille was invested with several crucial roles during the period of Bentivoglio dominance, for instance, in 1454 he was sent as ambassador to the pope to request the confirmation of Bessarion as papal legate in Bologna, see Duranti, *Diplomazia e autogoverno*, 79, 90. Together with the Bentivoglio, the Malvezzi were the only family to obtain a double representation inside the council, Ady, *The Bentivoglio*, 54.

60. Belvederi, "I Bentivoglio e i Malvezzi," 63.

61. Ady, *The Bentivoglio*, 53–54.

62. According to Alberti, for instance, members of the Malvezzi family were said to have accused Giovanni Bentivoglio of not supporting them during the aftermath of a minor quarrel against some foreigners and lower-class citizens: Alberti, *Historie di Bologna*, 52–53.

63. As reported by Ady, *The Bentivoglio*, 55.

64. Duranti, *Diplomazia e autogoverno*, 116.

65. Although peremptory summoning orders for some of the conspirators appear in the documentation already during the month of July, proving that the tensions between the two families was not sudden: ASB, Libri Mandatorum 401, Register 20, fols. 210v–11v; Cucini, "Législation statutaire," doc. 61–63, 2:467–69.

66. According to Alberti, this occurred only because of fortuitous circumstances, such as a word-of-mouth exchange between guards at the services of the Malvezzi and Bentivoglio: Alberti, *Historie di Bologna*, 60.

67. Alberti, *Historie di Bologna*, 57–58, mentions the involvement of Agamennone Mare scotti.

68. Again, Alberti reports that Giovanni Malvezzi was said to have had a private audience with Lorenzo the Magnificent who, about the plot, had suggested "that one should follow the example of the tailor, who, having to cut a piece of fabric, would have drawn the pattern so many times and then, after having it properly outlined, would have proceeded to cut." Alberti, *Historie di Bologna*, 56. Ultimately, a request for help to Florence would have been a possibility, considering the tense situation between Lorenzo and Giovanni II following the deaths of Galeotto Manfredi of Faenza and Girolamo Riario of Forlì, two events in which the Bentivoglio had a major involvement, causing a direct conflict with the Florentine ruler: see Pellegrini, *Congiure di Romagna.*

69. Alberti, *Historie di Bologna,* 56.

70. Dalla Tuata, *Istoria di Bologna*, 1:359.

71. "Continuazione della 'Cronaca,'" 505.

72. Duranti, *Diplomazia e autogoverno*, 116–17.

73. *Cronica gestorum ac factorum*, 907.

74. *Cronica gestorum ac factorum*, 907–8.

75. ASB, Libri Mandatorum 401, Register 20, fols. 218rv; Cucini, "Législation statutaire," doc. 64, 2:470–71.

76. ASB, Libri Partitorum 388, Register 9, fols. 224r–26v, the decisions were confirmed with a second vote, at fols. 227r–29v; Cucini, "Législation statutaire," docs. 83–84, 2:495–503.

77. ASB, Libri Mandatorum 401, Register 20, fols. 220rv, Cucini, "Législation statutaire," doc. 70, 2:477.

78. ASB, Libri Mandatorum 401, Register 20, fols. 218v–21v; Cucini, "Législation statutaire," docs. 65–67, 69–73, 2:472–74, 2:476–80.

79. A special commission including several members of the *Sedici* was created for disposing of the properties: ASB, Libri Provisionum 310, Register 1, fol. 110v; Cucini, "Législation statutaire," doc. 39, 2:424.

80. "Continuazione della 'Cronaca,'" 505–6. Christine Shaw considers the reaction to the Malvezzi conspiracy, together with the Pazzi conspiracy in Florence, a perfect example of conjoint action between the political authorities and the podestà's court: Shaw, *The Politics of Exile*, 60.

81. ASB, Libri Provisionum 310, Register 1, fols. 110v–11v and 111v–13r; Cucini, "Législation statutaire," docs. 40–41, 2:425–31. The treaty with the Florentine government proved to be ineffective, according to Dalla Tuata, *Istoria di Bologna*, 1:383–84, who relates that in 1495 the Florentines captured Giulio Malvezzi and then released him after discovering that the *bolognesi* sheltered some members of the Medici family, banned after the institution of the Florentine Republic in 1494.

82. As described by De Benedictis, "Lo stato popolare," 923–24. Trombetti Budriesi, "Alessandro VI e i Bentivoglio," 671n22, highlights the fortification of all the Bentivoglio's residences as another possible symptom of the changed situation after the conspiracy of 1488.

83. "Ex hac conjuratione hoc malum in nostra civitate sequutum est, quod cum sine partialitatibus esset, partes duae factae sunt. Cum enim magna affinitatem, et consanguinitatem in civitate haberent Malvitii, aliqui Segantes, aliqui Malvezeschi dicti sunt, et sic est amissa unio civitatis." *Cronica gestorum ac factorum*, 908.

84. "Et non se ne parlò per la giustizia, ché era malviçescho." Fileno dalla Tuata reports at least twenty-one cases: six in 1500, five in 1491, three in 1499, two in 1497 and 1502, and one in 1491, 1493, and 1501, Dalla Tuata, *Istoria di Bologna*, 1: 361–63, 394, 397, 403–4, 415–17, 419, 429, 433.

85. ASB, Inquisitiones 402, fols. 268r–70r; ASB, Sententiae, Busta 42, podestà Iohannes Benedictus de Barattanis de Nursia, bound register, fols. 19r–20r.

86. ASB, Sententiae, Busta 41, podestà and capitano Amelius de Parisianis de Asculo, unbound fols., 16 April 1490.

87. Dalla Tuata, *Istoria di Bologna*, 1:372, 381.

88. On the concept of *fama* see Théry, "Fama. L'opinion publique"; Migliorino, *Fama e infamia*; Kuehn, "Fama as legal status"; Bettoni, "Fama, Shame Punishment."

89. Nevertheless, no trial records survived and only one sentence is conserved between October 1488 and July 1488: ASB, Sententiae, Busta 41, podestà Petrus Franciscus de Advocatis de Lucha, unbound fols., 21 March 1489.

90. Dondarini, "Il declinio," 197. On the relations between Bologna and the Sforza see Covini, "Milano e Bologna"; Idem, *L'esercito del Duca,* especially 296–98; Duranti, *Il carteggio,* 1:xiii–cxxxii.

91. Trombetti Budriesi, "Alessandro VI e i Bentivoglio," 667, Ady, *The Bentivoglio*, 121, Dondarini, "Il declino," 197.

92. Trombetti Budriesi, "Alessandro VI e i Bentivoglio," 663–64.

93. A treaty was stipulated 30 October 1501, see Trombetti Budriesi, "Alessandro VI e i Bentivoglio," 668.

94. Besides the suspicions of his direct involvement in the conspiracy of 1488, in 1496 Agamennone had also been accused of keeping in contact with the banned Malvezzi: Ady, *The Bentivoglio*, 128.

95. The events are reported by Ghirardacci, *Della historia di Bologna*, 304. See also Trombetti Budriesi, "Alessandro VI e i Bentivoglio," 671n21.

96. As referred to by the chronicler Giacomo Gigli: *Cronica*, 65.

97. No votes are registered between 24 April and 11 June 1501: ASB, Libri Partitorum 389, Register 12, fol. 6r.

98. Ghirardacci, *Della historia di Bologna*, 305 reports the names of the other families involved: Bargellini, De Poeti, Fantuzzi, Orsi, Da San Piero, Marsili, Aldovrandi, Ariosti, Bianchi, and Montecalvi.

99. Gigli, *Cronica,* 65.

100. As reported later by Ghirardacci, *Della historia di Bologna*, 305

101. ASB, Libri Partitorum 389, Register 11, fols. 121v–22r; Cucini, "Législation statutaire," doc. 86, 2:507–8.

102. ASB, Liber Novissimarum Provisionum, fols. 171r–72r of the modern pagination; Cucini, "Législation statutaire," doc. 35, 2:413–17.

103. "Eos qui tractaverunt et attentaverunt contra personam alicuius, et in preiuditium et perturbationem presentis status" and "quicunque, diabolica instigatione impulsus, auderet aliquem in preiudicium et perturbationem presentis status ferro vel veneno vel alio quovis modo occidere vel interficere."

104. As noted also by Ghirardacci, *Della historia di Bologna*, 305: "Nor did Hermes lack caution in this malefaction, because he wanted to have with him a company of many scions of first citizens, for later, forever keeping them opposed to the Marescotti."

105. De Benedictis, *Una guerra d'Italia*, 101–11, quote at 104.

106. Ghirardacci, *Della historia di Bologna*, 355.

Chapter Seven

The "Enormous and Horrendous" Crime of Poisoning

Bologna, ca. 1300–1700

Margaux Buyck

Plus est hominem extinguere veneno, quam occidere gladio.[1] With this formula a Roman law issued under Emperor Antonius Pius (138–61) defined criminal poisoning as an act more heinous than homicide by the sword. Perception of the severity of the crime had earlier led to significant repressive measures, such as the *lex Cornelia de sicariis et veneficis*, declared by Sulla in 82–80 BCE, which was long to exert great influence on Western legal thought. Since Antiquity, the criminal use of poison has raised questions and sparked intense debate among jurists.

Bologna's university was renowned in the late Middle Ages for its law school whose jurists actively participated from the late eleventh century in the rediscovery of Roman law. Extant legislation from this ideal intellectual climate, together with records from the city's criminal law courts, offer a profitable source for study of the evolution and application of criminal law to what was viewed as one of the most violent and atrocious of crimes.

In this chapter I investigate the emergence and evolution of the crime of poisoning in Bolognese legislation and statutes between the late thirteenth and seventeenth centuries. I also compare it to that of neighboring cities in the territories that today comprise the region of Emilia-Romagna in order to identify the distinctive features of the Bolognese normative corpus. The final section is dedicated to the actual application of the legislation in the criminal law courts.

THE LEGACY OF THE *LEX CORNELIA*

The contents of the *lex Cornelia de sicariis et veneficis* are known to us thanks to Cicero and the comments of Roman jurists that were collected, six centuries later, in the *Digest*, one of the sections in which the *corpus Iustinianeum* is subdivided.[2] At the time of its promulgation, the *lex Cornelia* had as its primary objective the re-establishment of public order and safety in a period of political instability.[3] It defined the sanctions against homicide, with special reference to those acts perpetrated by "hired assassins" and "poisoners," and linked poisoning to the broader categories of homicide or magic. Franck Collard maintains that this linkage blocked or rather slowed down the emergence in the medieval West of a legal statute specific to criminal poisoning.[4] Nevertheless, the *lex Cornelia* does provide a first form of legal recognition to poisoning, since article 5 is dedicated exclusively to poisoners.

The penalty imposed on poisoners belonging to the nobility was decapitation; those of the less wealthy social classes were left to the mercy of the savage animals of the circus. The Roman jurist Aelius Marcianus notes that initially the penalty was deportation to an island and the confiscation of properties, however, as the customs of his era (second century AD) became less lenient, the law was changed to capital punishment for poisoners and their accomplices.[5] The *lex Cornelia* also refers to the ambiguous nature of poisons since their effects could be either fatal or curative.[6] Poisoning is then defined as the intentional use of poison, or of substances dangerous to health, or of medicines used to cause death. Given the severity of the crime, the *lex Cornelia* prescribes the death penalty both for the person who physically administered the fatal poison as well as for those who prepared and supplied toxic substances for criminal purposes.

Regardless of the final outcome of the criminal action—whether the victim survived or not—the *lex Cornelia* focuses on the issue of *dolus* (malice aforethought) in order to justify the severity of the penalty for poisoners: intention, rather than the mere act, needed to be punished.[7] With the rediscovery of Roman law beginning in the eleventh century, the *lex Cornelia* had considerable impact, as described below, on debates among jurists seeking to formulate the legal penalties for poisoning.

POISON AND THE CRIMINAL STATUTES OF THE DUE AND TRECENTO

In the 1288 statutes, poisoning is mentioned only in the rubric "De tondolo et tormento," which establishes the use and modalities of torture. Torture could be practiced during trials for homicide, in order to unmask a false witness, or in trials against highway robbers, infamous thieves, hired assassins, arsonists, sodomites, kidnappers, those who consorted with the enemies of the commune, and poisoners, be they man or woman.[8] In the 1335 statutes there is also a reference to poisoning in the rubric "How some men may be accused of homicide and of one or more lethal wounds, and of the report of medical doctors." This rubric establishes the role of doctors in defining the cause of death (strangulation, suffocation, or poisoning) or the extent of the injuries suffered by the victim.[9] These rubrics are repeated in the statutes of 1352 and 1357, but poisoning is also mentioned in a rubric on assassination that establishes a capital penalty if the crime by an assassin was "a homicide or wounding with flow of blood or poisoning even if death does not follow."[10]

This new reference to poisoning is particularly significant, given its appearance in a rubric on assassination, not homicide, since the latter crime implies premeditation, that is *dolus*, possibly reflecting the influence of *lex Cornelia*. More likely, however, its appearance is linked to the political conditions of the 1350s, which were similar to those in the period in which the *lex Cornelia* was promulgated. In 1352 Bologna came under the domination of the Visconti and in 1354 Giovanni d'Oleggio, called by his detractors the "tyrant of Bologna," came to power. In 1356 he escaped a conspiracy to assassinate him fomented by Bernabò Visconti together with Giovanni Pepoli and many other members of great Bolognese families.[11] As we shall see, however, this association of poisoning with assassination changes in the statutes of 1376.

During the same period, the *Constitutiones Aegidianae* of 1357 dedicate a rubric, albeit a very brief one, to poisoning. The *Constitutiones* were a collection of the legislation in civil law in force in the Papal State, promulgated in Fano by Cardinal Albornoz during an assembly of all the vicars of the papal territories. Building on previous legislation, their objective was to bring order to the voluminous legislative material available, and eliminate superfluous and obsolete norms. The *Constitutiones Aegidianae* were, in theory, the only compilation of general law in effect in the Papal State, to which Bologna belonged at the time of their publication.[12] The brief rubric "De veneficis" provides that "in cases of poisoning the punitive regulations in place for homicide should be followed," but uses language that insists upon the greater gravity of poisoning.[13] As in Roman law, *dolus* remains a concept of primary importance regarding the punishment of poisoners.[14] Preventative measures are also included against the suppliers of toxic substances. If an individual were to knowingly sell a fatal poison, that person was to be punished the same way as the poisoner. However, if this individual was not aware of the criminal purpose of the transaction, he or she would be condemned for homicide *sine dolo*. The reference to poisoning in a chapter of the *Constitutiones Aegidianae* may in part explain why at the end of the Trecento new rubrics dedicated to the criminal use of poison appear in local law codes in the territories of the Papal State. However, the complex political-constitutional situation of the Italian communes, particularly that of Bologna, subject as they were to papal authority but claiming their autonomy over the centuries, makes it difficult to perceive effective interactions between the *ius comune* of the Papal State and local statutes.

The earliest rubrics in criminal statutes dedicated to poisoning in the territories of Emilia-Romagna appear roughly during the same period—in the second half of the Trecento. The first one is found in the statutes of Imola in 1341 and is rather brief: "Poisoning and the poisoner are condemned to the most extreme punishment [capital punishment]."[15] The fifteenth-century vernacular transcription of the 1341 statutes includes the provisions adopted against poisoning. However, even though its contents do not change, the rubric loses its autonomy, becoming integrated into a more general rubric dedicated to criminal sanctions.[16] In the Forlì statutes of 1359 there is a rubric "On poisonings and their punishments." In comparison to the Imolese rubric, the one from Forlì is much more detailed (its contents are not modified in the later redaction of 1373):

> As it is more serious to kill by poison than by the sword, for this reason we establish that if any man or woman were to kill another using poison, he or she will suffer immolation; that is how the accused must die. The same punishment is to be applied to the purchaser, the perpetrator, and the supplier of the poison should they have knowingly provided the poison and the victim dies. And whosoever procured the poison for the purpose of homicide, even if the act is not followed by the death of the victim, shall be condemned to the same punishment.[17]

The statutes from Imola are consonant with the provisions described in the *lex Cornelia*: the intent to poison is severely reprimanded and a failed attempt, even if the victim survived unhurt, is punished with immolation.

In Bologna, the earliest "De pena venenantis" rubric is from the statutes of 1376. The redaction of this rubric took place within a wider environment of normative dynamism in Emilia-Romagna. Bolognese legislation called for capital punishment both for the individual who implemented the act and for the instigator, but in contrast to the statutes of 1352–57, only if the victim died. Moreover, this provision appears not in the rubric on assassination, but in the one on homicide and without the implication of *dolus*.[18] The offender's properties were to be confiscated and divided between the Bolognese commune and the victim's heirs. The same penalties were to apply to poisonings perpetrated without *dolus* or if the victims survived, but with irreversible damage to their health.[19] In contrast to the 1373 statutes of Imola, however, if the victim survived without ongoing health problems, then the poisoner was to be condemned to a fine of 200 *lire*.[20] With these provisions, the Bolognese statutes depart from the *lex Cornelia* and from the *Constitutiones Aegidianae* of 1357. Rather than focusing on the concept of *dolus* when establishing punishment, the statutes concentrate on the consequences of the poisoning, a notable difference that fueled many debates among jurists up to the end of the early modern era.[21]

In 1389, with the redaction of a new statute, the rubric "De pena venenantis" underwent only minor modifications. The fine for a failed attempt of poisoning, however, was increased considerably, from 200 to 500 *lire*. Certain preventative measures were also included to control the sale of toxic substances for criminal purposes:

> In order to halt the activity of poisoners we establish that spice merchants, cured meat merchants, and apothecaries not sell or provide any form of poison without the express and special license from the *massari* of their guild, under penalty set at the discretion of the podestà, with the quality and condition of the accused considered.[22]

A few years prior to this new redaction of the Bolognese statutes, the city of Mirandola enacted a lengthy rubric, "De poena venenantis vel maleficiantis aliquem." The almost contemporary drafting of the statutes of Mirandola and Bologna, even if the cities were of different size and importance, offers an opportunity to compare their legislation against poisoners. In contrast to the Bolognese statutes, those of Mirandola associated poisoning with witchcraft:

> It is thus established and ordained, that if anyone gives to another person in the form of food or drink any type of poison or other medicine, or undertakes or has another undertake any form of witchcraft against a person or persons, or it is said by others that a person must die, then such a delinquent and the person ordering the act are equally condemned to capital punishment by immolation [. . .].[23]

The legislation from Mirandola provides a much broader definition of poisoning than the Bolognese statutes: poisoning is considered as both a human and a magical action. Historians have shown that the link between poison and witchcraft persisted in the mentality of the medieval and early modern West, particularly in legal culture.[24] Georges Duby, for example, maintained that poisoning was the "relative" of enchantment.[25] Nonetheless, in contrast to Mirandola, the statutes of other cities in Emilia-Romagna do not yield evidence of a link between witchcraft and poison. Poisoning is much more frequently compared to homicide or assassination, of which it was considered a particularly grave form. Its magical aspect is not emphasized in Bolognese legislation nor in that of its neighboring territories—we find instead a kind of "disenchantment" in the laws against poisoners.

FIFTEENTH–SEVENTEENTH CENTURIES: TOWARD A MORE REPRESSIVE LEGISLATION?

In the 1454 Bolognese statutes, the crime of poisoning and its punishment remains closely tied to that of homicide.[26] Although the 1454 rubric retains several provisions from the 1389 version, it also adds defamatory and corporal punishments for the first time for attempted poisoning:

> If, in fact, the above-mentioned death or debilitation does not ensue [from the deed], the poisoner will nonetheless be condemned to a fine of 500 *lire* and also the amputation of both hands and the branding by fire of both cheeks of the face with a stamp of flaming iron so that the scar deforming the criminal is visible publicly and in perpetuity.[27]

Although the 1454 rubric thus increases the corporal punishment for attempted poisoning and emphasizes the infamy of the crime, it does not reach the level of capital punishment.[28]

One year after the drafting of the 1454 statutes, a *provisio* was issued by the papal legate that modified the contents of the rubric "De pena venenantis."[29] The tone of the *provisio* is very "aggressive": poisoning is described as an enormous and horrendous crime, highly dangerous, of a gravity far superior to that of homicide *cum gladio* (reprising the terminology used in the *Constitutiones Aegidianae* of 1357). Despite the vivid language, which would suggest an increase in sanctions against poisoners, in fact the modifications appear to be relatively light. The *provisio* above all confirms the rubric "De pena venenantis." If the victim dies, the poisoner is still condemned to capital punishment. However, instead of confiscation of all the offender's properties, the *provisio* mandates a fine of 1,000 *lire*. There are no changes concerning attempted poisoning. The principal legal "novelty" is forbidding establishment of a peace accord if offenders confessed to their crimes; with this condition the authorities rendered extrajudicial negotiations between the parties involved in the trial more difficult. Faced with such minor changes, one might question the effective purpose of a *provisio* published only a year after the redaction of the new criminal statute; a statute that was harsher than its predecessor concerning attempted poisoning. In the preamble, the legate mentions a notable increase in this sort of crime in Bologna, which could well have justified the publication of a *provisio*.[30] A climate of political and social tension existed in mid-fifteenth century Bologna: "the city was prey to a thousand difficulties" during a period in which the Bentivoglio family was increasing its power.[31] Various changes in alliances among the most important Bolognese families of the time engendered fear of factional conflict, in particular between the Bentivoglio and Pepoli families. In September 1451, Romeo Pepoli died under suspicious circumstances: according to some chroniclers he was poisoned by his barber on behalf of the Bentivoglio.[32] Such events may have instigated the perceived need to maintain order in Bologna and discourage potential assassins by means of corporal and defamatory punishments. Similarly, as noted above, the *lex Cornelia* also had been established by Sulla during a period of high tensions bordering on civil war.[33] The aim of the *provisio*, which was to be disseminated throughout the Bolognese territory, seems to have been, first and foremost, to spread widely knowledge of the penalties that had been adopted against those who were prepared to kill by using the occult and pernicious method of poisoning.

Bologna underwent great changes at the political and institutional level in the early sixteenth century when the city came under direct papal rule with Pope Julius II's expulsion of the Bentivoglio. This fracture in the history of Bologna gradually was reflected in the Bolognese legal system, as described in the essay by Colin Rose in this volume, resulting by the 1530s in replacement of the podestarial system by a new criminal court—the *Tribunale del Torrone*, governed by a judge (*auditore*) who functioned under the authority of the papal legate. The 1454 edition remained the final redaction of the criminal statutes, but was later republished. In the 1525 and 1735 editions, the contents of the "De pena venenantis" rubric remain identical to the 1454 edition, with the addition of the 1455 *provisio*.

Other types of normative sources concerning the repression of poisoning also survive from the early modern era. In the Bolognese archives four *bandi generali* (general edicts) set forth a number of articles dedicated to poisoners. The *bandi* of September 1586, April 1588, and December 1596 contain a specific chapter entitled *Veneno*.[34] In 1610, however, consideration of poisoning is treated in other chapters.[35] In the chapter "Of homicide or attempted homicide, of parricide, of doctors, surgeons, barbers, and pharmacists and alike: and prohibition of poison," poisoning is viewed as a variant of intentional homicide perpetrated by means of poison. Although poisoning is thus recognized juridically, it is very difficult to distinguish it from the larger categories of homicide and assassination and returns to simply being mentioned in the chapters dedicated to homicide, parricide, or to the sale of toxic substances by doctors or spice merchants, as it had been treated in the Duecento and early Trecento. This was not a development distinctive to Bologna. In fact, numerous criminal statutes from the region of Emilia-Romagna attest to this ambiguity: the criminal statutes of 1527 from Faenza and the 1609 statutes from Cento define the punishments for poisoners within the rubric dedicated to homicide.[36] In the 1509 statutes of Parma, provisions regarding poisoning are mentioned in the rubric "De assassinis et veneficis."[37] Singling out the crime of poisoning with an "independent" statute in Bologna, and in the whole of Emilia-Romagna until the seventeenth century, moreover contrasts with the situation in France. From 1682, following the famous *affaire des poisons*, an edict was published, issued by Louis XIV, in which a statute clearly defining poisoning was recognized in French legislation.[38]

In the Bolognese *bandi generali* dedicated to poisoning there is stigmatizing language similar to that used in the *provisio* of 1455, where poisoning was already defined as an "enormous crime." Furthermore, poisoning was now also linked to the notion of betrayal.[39] These terms appear in normative texts issued primarily by the papal legate or vice-legate. Originally used in the West by the Church, the concept of *enormitas* implies reference to a moral and sinful dimension of the crime.[40] This idea is clearly developed in the Bolognese *bandi*, as in the one promulgated in 1596: "not only do a thirst for death, or of other people's belongings stem from the disorder created from poison, but also other unbridled desires."[41] The *bandi generali* were designed to be published and delivered orally across the entire Bolognese territory: the use of moralizing vocabulary was not irrelevant but contributed to reinforcing the dissuasive effect of the *bandi* on the community. The article from the 1586 *bando* that treated poisoning specifically and exclusively was republished repeatedly in the following decade. But after this brief interval, references to poisoning again are found only in the chapters of *bandi* dedicated to homicide, parricide, or medical practices.[42] One might ask whether during this brief interval the authorities had again found themselves faced with an increase in the crime that earlier in 1455 led to the drafting of the above-discussed *provisio*. However, my research in the criminal court archives of Bologna neither validates nor rejects the possibility of an increase in the number of poisonings during this period.

In these late-Cinquecento *bandi* we find a distancing from the statutes of 1454. For the first time in Bolognese legislation, the use of poison for abortion is mentioned. Indeed, the *bandi generali* of the early modern era refer to the principles of the *ius comune* such as the *lex Cornelia* which concern the use of poison for the purpose of abortion or *ad amorem*.[43] In the *bandi generali* of 1586 and 1596 the authorities demonstrate greater rigidity concerning poisoning, in radical contrast to the norms incorporated from the medieval statutes: "Thus if anyone with poison tries in any way to poison any other person, undertaking the act of giving it to them, either in food, or in drink, or in any other way, furthermore, if [the victim] does not take the poison or if it has no effect, [the poisoner] needs to be treated as a traitor and condemned to the death penalty."[44]

Bolognese legislation from the sixteenth and seventeenth centuries reevaluates the importance of *dolus* (malice aforethought) in establishing punishment. The terms "scientemente" and "volontariamente" or the expression "assolutamente dolo" appear in the *bandi generali*: *dolus*, a fundamental principle of Roman law, once again becomes the determining element in pronouncing punishment.[45] It is possible that a succession of political upheavals in Bologna over the course of the Seicento were at the origin of the changes found in the *bandi generali*. At the beginning of the sixteenth century, as noted above, Bologna lost its autonomous status and found itself once more under the more pressing control of the Church. Justice and finance were the main areas in which papal authority was exercised. The *bandi generali* served to extend and reaffirm the presence of the papal representative in the city. There is, on the one hand, a disjuncture between the early modern *bandi* and the legislation in the medieval statutes, but on the other hand, there is also a similarity with the provisions taken from the *Constitutiones Aegidianae* of 1357 and updated in 1544.[46] Irrespective of the outcome of the crime, in all cases the poisoner was condemned to capital punishment. As noted above, in the fourteenth century, the *Constitutiones Aegidianae* had become, in theory, the only compilation of general law in force in the Papal State; in reality, they were blocked by the important obstacle of local law (the statutes)—symbol of the Italy of the *comuni*—which defended communal autonomy. One may ask whether Bologna's return to the direct authority of the Church led to a reaffirmation of a model of general law common to the territories subject to papal domination. However, the rubric dedicated to poisoning in the *Constitutuiones Aegidianae* was not the only source of inspiration for the *bandi generali* of the sixteenth and seventeenth centuries—in these *bandi* the papal legate defended the idea of continuity with local laws and expressed a desire to update them. Furthermore, the *bandi generali* were also signed by representatives of communal authority: the *consiglio degli anziani*, the *consiglio dei Sedici Riformatori*, and the *gonfaloniere di giustizia*.

A constant reference to *dolus* and the legacy of the *lex Cornelia* in order to establish sanctions against poisoners had, nevertheless, been discussed in Italian judicial literature since the Middle Ages.[47] In fact, in cases of poisoning in which the victim died, jurists agreed on the punishment of maximum severity—the death penalty. Attempted poisoning, however, engendered bitter debates. In the Trecento, Bartolo da Sassoferrato and Baldus de Ubaldis maintained that aggravating factors (*dolus*, *proditio*, *enormitas* of the crime) justified the death penalty even in attempted poisonings.[48] From the fifteenth century, however, various Italian jurists argued that such a punishment could not be applied in cases of attempted poisoning in which the poison did not have a lethal effect. This opinion was upheld by Bartolomeo Cipolla, a jurist from Verona, who justified his argument with reference to Italian customs of his day: "and these above all are the true premises for the consideration of what is being spoken of everywhere in Italy, since it is correct that the laws punish the effects and that a second universal practice does not take place"—a viewpoint shared over the centuries by various jurists, for example, by Pietro Barbo and Tommaso Grammatico.[49] Nevertheless, throughout the sixteenth and seventeenth centuries, jurists such as Tiberio Deciani[50] continued to maintain that the importance of *dolus* in the perpetration of poisoning justified the death penalty even if the crime had not resulted in a fatality. The writings of these jurists regarding the determination of sanctions for poisoners, at times privileging the notion of *dolus*, but at other times focusing on the effects of the crime, do not in any way demonstrate a contrast between medieval and early modern views. Rather, from the fourteenth to the seventeenth century, the two legal positions contested each other in a continuous confrontation with the legacy of the *lex Cornelia* and with the problematic application in juridical practice of the laws of the *ius comune* and local law.

Legislation on poisoning was not limited to punitive measures: the prevention of the crime through control over the sale of toxic substances is attested beginning in the Duecento. The *bandi generali* of the sixteenth and seventeenth centuries were harmonized with statutory legislation while various revisions were also proposed. In the sixteenth century, for example, there was a focus on the spice merchants as particularly open to suspicion: their shops were identified as ideal places for supplying lethal substances.[51] In the 1610 "Bando dei medici, cirugici, barbieri, speciali, et simili: et prohibitione del veleno," three of the four articles are dedicated to preventive measures linked to the sale of potentially lethal poisons. The list of potential suppliers is much more detailed than in the *bandi* of the Cinquecento:

> No doctor, surgeon, barber, distiller, or any other person, even if without evil intention, should make up poisons or other substances which could lead to death or madness. They may not sell, or buy, or by any other means give or receive, or hold such concoctions or simple or mixed poisons without a license signed by the hand of S.S. Illustris. on pain of death.[52]

Both in terms of prevention and punishment, Bolognese legislation, with one exception, underwent progressive evolution—in fact, there was no absolute caesura between the late medieval and early modern eras. The exception and principal difference distinguishing the two periods concerns the treatment of attempted poisoning. Whereas the medieval criminal statutes concentrate on the effects of the crime in order to determine punishment, laws in the early modern era appear to turn to the principles of the *lex Cornelia*, making *dolus* the key element for imposing more severe penalties against poisoners. Bolognese laws, and those across the territory of Emilia-Romagna, reflect the bitter debates concerning the punishment for attempted poisoning that are also found in the writings of many Italian jurists until the Settecento.

POISONING IN BOLOGNESE JUDICIAL PRACTICE

Study of the evolution of Bolognese legislation across the late medieval and early modern periods clarifies many issues regarding the perception of criminal poisoning, but it remains of fundamental importance to compare the legislation with its application in judicial practice. My sample of ninety-seven cases from the Bolognese archives constitutes the basis for this analysis of the contrast between theory and practice.[53]

According to the *lex Cornelia*, recognition of the atrocity of poisoning had to push magistrates to sentence culprits to harsh and exemplary punishments. In part, this was to compensate for the perception that many perpetrators acted with impunity since their misdeeds could not be uncovered by the justice system.[54] At issue is whether in judicial practice the majority of presumed poisoners were condemned to death and the answer is clearly negative. Only 26 percent of those accused of poisoning in the sample were condemned to capital punishment. This rather low figure is in part due to a large number of cases, approximately 54 percent, that were in fact failed attempts or simply suspected cases of poisoning. In the majority of cases in which the death penalty was issued, the victim had died from the potency of the poison.

Nevertheless, five offenders were in fact condemned to death for attempted poisoning.[55] In 1300, in Pianoro, in the rural outskirts of Bologna, Giovanni Ciappelli was arrested as he fled the scene of a crime and was found in possession of a powder suspected to cause severe dizziness in anyone who inhaled it. Although his victim survived with no permanent injury, the carrier of the "poison" was hanged and his accomplice condemned to have his eye gouged out.[56] In 1369, Giacomo Gherardi of Ferrara attempted to poison the wife of his friend during a dinner; the guests immediately noticed the unusual taste of the cabbages and they all survived the poisoning. Giacomo was nonetheless decapitated.[57] The punishments pronounced in the other cases from the Trecento were related to assassination. Punitive measures against this type of crime were reinforced in the 1352 statutes, during the Visconti rule in Bologna. Originally punished with a fine, attempted assassination with loss of blood or through the use of poison by now had become a capital crime.[58] The gravity of poisoning is underscored, but in this instance it is viewed as comparable to a crime of bloodshed. It seems that the increasing harshness of sanctions against poisoners stemmed not from a specific statute, but rather from consideration of the motives in particular cases, the status of the imputed, and the climate of tension in Bologna in this period. In 1485 Pietro de Barbieri, a recidivist, was condemned to death for a number of thefts and for having attempted to poison his father.[59] In 1641 a delinquent was condemned to death for having been convicted of eleven different crimes, one of which was a failed attempt at poisoning.[60] In these last two cases of attempted poisonings, the conviction for numerous crimes in one instance, and the recidivist nature of the other, probably explain the severity imposed by the Bolognese authorities.

In practice, apart from these five cases, attempted poisoning was rarely punished with the death penalty. The severity expressed in early modern legislation thus was not reflected in practice. Furthermore, great continuity can be seen in the number of executions for such cases throughout the late medieval and early modern periods, which remained stable, without the occurrence of any anomalous increases. The evolution of the legislation toward increasingly severe punishments that can be identified in the normative sources of the early modern period is entirely absent in judicial practice, which was instead characterized by continuity in its treatment of the crime.

As noted above, for poisoners who killed their victims, legislation and statutes called for capital punishment and this was the norm not only in Bologna but throughout the territories of Emilia-Romagna. However, until the beginning of the seventeenth century, the normative corpus does not provide specific information concerning the modes of execution. In most cases, we find general expressions such as *delinquentes puniantur ad mortem* (delinquents are punished by death), *capitali sententia* (with a capital sentence), or *pena capitis* (with capital punishment).[61] Some historians mention immolation as the preferred means of execution in Italian statutes.[62] Indeed, this mode of execution is stipulated in Mirandola and in Forlì.[63] In these cases, the choice of this form of torment in punishment may be due to the association between poisoning and witchcraft. Execution of this type, however, was definitely not widespread across the territories of Emilia-Romagna.

In practice, at Bologna poisoners were sentenced to two types of punishment—decapitation or hanging. From the Trecento to the beginning of the Cinquecento, poisoners were executed by decapitation. However, from the sixteenth to the seventeenth century, hanging was the preferred mode and decapitation became a prerogative reserved for the nobility. In contrast to witchcraft, the death penalty for poisoning was the same as that for homicide and assassination.

There are, nevertheless, some exemplary cases in which the death penalty was associated with extraordinary corporal and defamatory punishments. In 1622 and 1648, for example, poisoners were hanged and their cadavers quartered. In the first case, Pellegrino Benzi was executed for having poisoned his wife and children.[64] In the second case, a certain Francesca and her lover had tried three times to poison her husband, Fulvio Sirani, a spice merchant. The first two attempts failed, thanks to the intervention of the serving maid who merely pretended to pour the poison into the food and drink of the intended victim, but in fact otherwise disposed of it. On the third attempt, the spice merchant himself realized what was happening and took various antidotes. When her attempts at poisoning did not work, Francesca paid an assassin to murder her husband in his workshop.[65] In these cases, characterized by deep hatred against their victims and determination of the guilty parties to carry out their crimes, the severity of the punishment seems to have been a way of making the penalty comparable to the cruelty of the perpetrators.[66] To a crime already considered "enormous," a "hierarchy of horror" was established with additional defamatory punishments. This "ultra-violence" in execution was not specific to the crime of poisoning, but was also used for assassination.[67]

In practice, accomplices were often punished the same way as instigators or perpetrators of the crime, with the exception of suppliers. Yet in statutes from the Trecento and Quattrocento, condemnations were given for all accomplices to the crime that were identical to those against the poisoners themselves.[68] In the early modern period the *bandi generali*, reflecting an acute awareness of the problems surrounding the sale of poisonous substances, set out very severe punishments for those who knowingly supplied poison.[69] Nevertheless, in practice very few suppliers were accused or condemned by the courts. From the Trecento to the Seicento they are mentioned in various trials but almost never condemned. In 1336, Niccolò, a spice merchant from Ferrara, despite having sold an ounce of arsenic to the person ordering a poisoning, was not punished; in fact, he apparently was not even called to court.[70] From the Cinquecento, the judicial authorities seem to have taken great care in investigating the origin of toxic substances used in crimes. Yet there is no evidence of suppliers having been condemned even after the severity of their punishment was increased in legislation. In 1637, Niccolò Guerrini, an alchemist distiller, confirmed before the judge of the *Torrone* that he had sold to Caterina de Rubeis liquids allegedly poisonous that had, in fact, been prepared with innocuous ingredients, but her husband nevertheless died. The trial concluded without the supplier condemned to any form of punishment; not a surprising outcome since throughout the period it was difficult for the authorities to prove the guilt of those who had supplied the poison.[71] In fact, many sellers did not seem to be aware (or at least systematically pretended not to be) of the criminal aims of their customers. Indeed, many poisons, such as arsenic, were openly sold in apothecaries and spice merchants' shops. Arsenic was often used in the city against mice and fleas, but also as a beauty product. It is clear, therefore, why it was so difficult to assess the guilt of the suppliers of these substances.

Finally, in contrast to what was called for in statutory legislation, in practice very few monetary penalties were issued against poisoners condemned to the death penalty. In some cases, extreme poverty may have prevented the offender's family goods from being confiscated. This possibility fails, however, to explain why the fines were not levied, since even the wealthiest of those convicted of poisoning were not subjected to them.

THE PROBLEM OF ATTEMPTED POISONING AND ITS PUNISHMENTS

Attempted poisoning is probably the most complex phase of the crime both in juridical and judicial terms. In practice, the percentage of such attempts is high (28 percent).[72] From the fourteenth to the seventeenth century the records show clear diversity in the application of punishments for attempted poisonings. As we have already seen, capital punishment for these attempts was very rare and limited, for the most part, to the Trecento. In 1454, the statutes provided corporal and defamatory punishment for attempted poisoning. In practice, sentences of bodily mutilation pre-date the legislation authorizing such penalties. The mutilated body parts varied: the amputation of the right hand was frequently adopted; in other cases the removal of an eye, the tongue, the nose, or the mouth. Mutilation branded the guilty parties and made their crimes visible to all, depriving them of the basic attributes of their humanity.[73] Moreover, in the records examined, I found no cases of corporal punishment after 1412. Trevor Dean notes that there was a significant reduction of corporal punishments in Bologna at the end of the fourteenth century and that they became extremely rare during the fifteenth century.[74] His findings are in sharp contrast to the rubric: "De pena venenantis," in place during that period, which authorized mutilation as a punishment. It is possible that during the Trecento a "legislative void" and the resulting frequent sentencing at the discretion of the judge, favored the use of this repressive penalty. From the fifteenth century, however, the establishment of a specific framework of corporal punishments in statutory legislation may have served to limit mutilation as a punishment for attempted poisoning.

From the fourteenth to the seventeenth century, however, punishments for attempted poisoning seem to have been based on the circumstances of the crime and particularly the status of the offender. Many of the punishments issued are not even mentioned in local legislation. The sentence most often imposed in practice to punish attempted poisoning was exile (39 percent of cases). The *lex Cornelia* had established exile to an island for notables, however, it is not possible to establish whether Roman law influenced late-medieval and early modern magistrates to prefer sentences of exile.[75] In fact, nobles were the most numerous of exiles, although convicts of the lower social classes were also given this punishment. In 1665, for example, Lucia Tolomelli, a servant, was accused of poisoning her mistress, the famous painter Elisabetta Sirani, and was exiled.[76] Frequently, exile was the penalty in cases in which the guilt of the accused could not be proven, or to avoid vendetta by the victim or the victim's family.[77] That the cause of death was from poison could not be established in the trial against Lucia Tolomelli. Of the six doctors present for the autopsy of the painter's body (an exceptional case since usually only two doctors were required for the medical report), two concluded that the presumed victim had died from a perforated ulcer. Nevertheless, the servant suspected of poisoning was exiled in order to appease the painter's father who was inconsolable at the loss of his eldest daughter, and who was supported by powerful patrons. Exile could also stem from political motives since offenders were usually stripped of their political offices as well as having their properties confiscated.[78] The alleged poisoner thus endured both a social and political death. In addition, exile was often accompanied by a monetary penalty. The amounts of the fine varied considerably, and rarely corresponded to those established in the statutes, but were tied to the social class of the accused. In some cases the guilty parties were forced to pay double the fine set by law, evidence that the offender's social status was a determining factor throughout the trial process.[79] In short, these variations in the application of punishments attest to the preponderant influence of the judges' discretion in medieval and early modern justice.

Despite the impression of a harsh and implacable system of justice that one derives from the penal legislation, not all trials ended with an effective and irrevocable condemnation of the accused, even in an atrocious and enormous crime such as poisoning.[80] First of all, 20 percent of the trials concluded without any sentence issued. Trials were frequently suspended, for example, because of a lack of evidence, false accusation, or agreement between the two adversarial parties. Furthermore, approximately another 20 percent of the alleged poisoners were contumacious and were subsequently sentenced *in absentia*—flight was seen as proof of guilt.[81] However, removing themselves from Bologna often made it possible for the accused later to obtain remission of their penalty or to negotiate a peace accord with the victim's family.

In fact, the negotiation of a peace accord constituted a possible penal resolution, even for serious crimes like poisoning.[82] The rubrics on poisoning in medieval statutes and the early modern *bandi generali* do not mention this contingency. The 1455 *provisio* forbids negotiations for a peace accord between the two parties if the offender confessed to the crime.[83] In practice, however, a peace accord between the two parties was possible either before or after sentencing.[84] In theory, a peace accord drafted by a notary ended a more general conflict and often maintained the social balance of the city.[85] For more humble persons, a *rinuncia* could alternatively be arranged in which the offended party renounced legal action in exchange for financial compensation.[86] In 1570, Alessandro Salandri, a tailor, who had accused his wife of poisoning him, stipulated that she provide him, in order to obtain a pardon, monetary compensation equivalent to sixteen months of work and also payment of his medical and trial expenses.[87] The peace accord and *rinuncia* were essential but only preliminary stages in gaining a pardon, which was the prerogative of the representatives of governing authorities; in the Papal State, it was the papal legate who, in theory, could grant pardons.[88]

The granting of pardons, however, was strongly linked to oscillations in political power. In the fourteenth and fifteenth centuries, in certain trials for poisoning, intervention by local *signori* or their representatives from the Bolognese oligarchy took place: *supplica* and *gratia* effectively became elements in the affirmation of power. [89] In the mid-fifteenth century, collaborations developed between the papal legate and the civic council of the *Sedici Riformatori* in deciding whether to approve a pardon.[90] In the case of medieval trials for poisoning, my sample is too small to reveal the dynamics that allowed convicts to obtain a pardon (four of seventeen trials). However, the important role played by the Bolognese *signori*—the Pepoli in the Trecento or the Bentivoglio in the Quattrocento—can be noted. Frequently the *signori* of Bologna or their representatives played the role of intermediary in the peace accord negotiations, but on occasion they also assumed an authoritative stance and intervened in the judicial process. In 1342, for example, Bartolomeo Pepoli, acting on behalf of the *signore*, ordered Agnesia de Galluzzi, accused of poisoning her father-in-law, released from the commune's prison.[91]

More sources are available for the early modern period; supplications are attached to some trial records, and on occasion the notaries make note of the sum paid in order to obtain a pardon. The legate remained the primary recipient of the supplications, which often came from those who were contumacious. At the end of the century, however, the *congregazione criminale* was instituted, which was responsible for sentencing or, in the case of disputes, requests for pardons.[92] Intervention by the *congregazione* was sought in only one trial from my sample, that of Benedetta Malagodi, a resident of the rural commune of Crevalcore, accused of having poisoned her husband, who requested a pardon in order to avoid the death penalty. The family of the victim had refused to negotiate a peace accord. The poisoner, however, at the time of the exhumation of her husband's body, had obtained a grant of (temporary) immunity from the Church.[93] Benedetta was young (eighteen years old) and interrogation during the trial had revealed how she had been manipulated by her lover, the true instigator of the misdeed. Given all these factors, her defenders sought the intervention of the *congregazione criminale* in order to obtain a pardon, but without success.[94]

Peace accords and pardons in trials for poisoning were not provided for by the normative corpus, but the perceived gravity of poisoning did not preclude an extra-judicial settlement of such cases. It was the social status of the imputed, more so than the criminal statute, that determined the application of punishment. In my sample, the more humble members of society were pardoned only in cases of failed attempts or in those in which they were merely suspects. In these trials the good reputation of the accused, his or her place within the community, and the protection offered by the community played a determining role.[95] Some wealthy offenders managed to avoid capital punishment even if they were guilty, as for example, in the case of Camillo Bolognetti who, in a letter sent to the legate of Bologna, confessed that one April evening in 1606 he had attempted to poison his wife, Dorotea. Immediately after her meal, the victim noticed the initial effects of the poison and was taken to her bed by the servants. During the night, Camillo, helped by one of his male servants, entered his wife's bedroom and began beating her with bags of sand. Leaving her unconscious, he fled the house into the countryside where he joined his accomplices, who included the victim's brothers. Dorotea meanwhile had escaped death a second time, only to be strangled a few days later by one of her own brothers who returned to the house in order to kill her. One year after the extremely violent murder of Dorotea, her husband, a member of the nobility, was pardoned.[96] Powerful people were often willing to negotiate a peace accord with perpetrators in order to avoid a condemnation that would damage the family's prestige—the good name of the clan surpassed the importance of "obtaining justice." Finally, even when considering crimes of the utmost gravity such as poisoning, judicial authorities privileged the preservation of the *pax urbana* over the ideal of impartial justice.[97]

CONCLUSION

In the medieval statutes of Bologna, the drafting of a rubric dedicated to criminal poisoning took place in a context of debate and reflection concerning this type of crime. The Bolognese statutes have a conflicting relationship with Roman law, in particular with the *lex Cornelia*: they differ from the Roman tradition by emphasizing the effects of the crime rather than the concept of *dolus* in determining the punishment to be imposed on poisoners, even if malice aforethought constituted an aggravating factor. A form of "disenchantment" of the crime can also be noted in the Bolognese statutes as well as in judicial practice: whereas witches were often accused of poisoning, poisoners in Bologna were almost never accused of witchcraft.

Study of the early modern *bandi*, however, indicates that increased repression against poisoners took place. Normative measures seem to return to the principles of the *lex Cornelia*, such as the pre-eminence of *dolus* for imposing much harsher punishments. And yet the evolution of legislation on poisoning also seems to have varied and depended primarily on political circumstances or the development of the judicial process rather than on the implementation of the statute on the crime. Although poisoning had been identified almost immediately by jurists as an atrocious and enormous crime, for the early modern period it remains difficult to find poisoning distinguished from the main categories of homicide and assassination.

In judicial practice, great continuity can be observed from the Trecento to the Seicento in the way poisoners were brought to justice. There were differences, to be sure, but the greatest lay between the law and its application. Capital punishment remained the principal sentence when the victim did not survive the violence of poison, but attempted poisoning constituted a complex case whose treatment varied over time. Judicial practice reflected the uncertainties of jurists but also the ambiguities within penal legislation that did not provide a univocal punitive response to the crime. Judicial practice, however, demonstrated less severity than legislative norms: corporal punishment was limited to the Trecento and obtaining a pardon, an outcome not provided for in legislation, was a possibility for poisoners despite the enormity of their crime. This difference between theory and practice also demonstrates the importance of the magistrates' discretion in sentencing in both the medieval and early modern periods. Penalties, but also even procedures, were determined more by the social status of the accused than by the importance, for all its perceived gravity and enormity, of the poisoning itself.

NOTES

1. Krüger and Mommsen, *Corpus juris civilis*, vol. 2, IX.18.
2. Cicero, "Pour Cluentius," 146–47, LIV. 148; Collard, *Pouvoir et poison*, 55–57.
3. Demuro, *Il Dolo*, 1:38.
4. Rivers, "Magic, Religion, and the Law."
5. Hulot, Berthelot, Tissot, and Berenger, *Les cinquante livres du Digeste*, 350, "Ad legem corneliam de sicariis et veneficis," Bk. XLVIII *titulus* 8, paragraph 1.
6. Pastore, *Veleno. Credenze, crimini*, 161–62.
7. Hulot, Berthelot, Tissot, and Berenger, *Les cinquante livres du Digeste*, 354, "Ad legem corneliam de sicariis et veneficis," Bk. XLVIII *titulus* 8, paragraph 14.
8. Fasoli and Sella, *Statuti di Bologna dell'anno 1288*, 2, 184–85, Bk. IV, Rubric XVII: "De tondolo et tormento."
9. Trombetti Budriesi, *Lo Statuto del Comune di Bologna,* 604–5, Bk. VIII, Rubric 12, "Quot homines possint inculpari de morte et mortiffero vulnere uno vel pluribus, et de medicorum transmissione."
10. ASB, Statuti 44 (formerly XI), fols. 152–54. Bk. XI, Rubric 61, "[. . .] homicidum vel vulnus cum sanguinis effusione, vel venantio etiam si mors non sequat."
11. Buyck, "Crimes de poison," 322–23.
12. Sella, *Costituzioni egidiane*; Colliva, *Il Cardinale Albornoz*.
13. Pastore, *Veleno. Credenze, crimini,* 61. The formula, used by Emperor Antoninus Pius, is "veneno aliquem nechans, quod plus est quam gladio perimere." Krüger and Mommsen, *Corpus juris civilis*, vol. 2, IX.18.
14. Demuro, *Il Dolo*, 1:31–38.
15. "Veneficius et venenans ultimo supplicio tradantur." Benatti, *Gli statuti del contado*, 430–31.
16. Benatti, *Gli statuti del contado*, 430–31.
17. "Quia plus est aliquem veneno perimere quam gladio occidere, ideo statuimus quod si quis vel si qua veneno aliquem occiderit, igne cremetur, ita quod penitus moriatur. Eadem pena puniatur si quis hoc fieri mandaverit vel fecerit aut ad hoc fatiendum venenum scienter concesserit ex quo aliquis sit mortuus. Et qui venenum prebuerit causa necandi, licet mors sequuta non fuerit, eadem pena plectatur." Rinaldi, *Statuto di Forlì*, 240–41, Bk. III, Rubric 46, "*De veneficis et eorum pena.*"

18. "Ordinamus quod quicumque alium venenaverit ex quo veneno mors sequatur puniatur pena capitis tam qui venenaverit quàm etiam quilibet cuius mandato vel dolo venenum datum fuerit." ASB, Statuti 46 (formerly XIII), fols. 236, Bk. V, Rubric 59, "De pena venenantis."

19. "[. . .] idem si venenatus non moreretur ex ipso veneno sed sit toto tempore suae vitae verisimiliter remansurus debilitates" ASB, Statuti 46 (formerly XIII), fols. 236, Bk. V, Rubric 59.

20. ASB, Statuti 46 (formerly XIII), fols. 236, Bk. V, Rubric 59.

21. See Buyck, "Crimes de poison," chapter 5, "Crime de poison et pensée juridique."

22. "Et ad compescendum venenandi facultatem statuimus quod speciarij, salaroli, & apotecharij nulli vendant, seu tradant aliquam speciem veneni sine expressa & speciali licentia eorum Massarij Artis sub pena arbitrio D. Potestatis imponenda considerata qualitate personarum & conditione." ASB, Statuti 47 (formerly XIV), fol. 315, Bk. IV, Rubric 57, "De pena venenantis."

23. "Item statutum et ordinatum est, quod si quis dederit alicui persone ad comedendum vel ad bibendum de aliquo genere veneni vel aliquo medicamento vel fecerit seu fieri fecerit aliquam incantationem contra aliquem ex quibus seu ex quorum altero dicta talis persona decesserit, tunc talis delinquens et fieri faciens igne cremetur ita et taliter quod penitus moriatur." *Statuta Mirandulae*, 92.

24. Collard, "Veneficiis vel maleficiis"; Pastore, *Veleno. Credenze, crimini*, 70–71.

25. Duby, *Dames du XIIe siècle*, 3:29.

26. ASB, Statuti 50 (formerly XVII), Bk. IV, fol. 315, Rubric 57, "De pena venenantis."

27. "Si vero mors vel debilitatio praedicta non sequatur condenetur omnimodo venenans in quingentis libris bononinorum et etiam in pena amputationis utriusque manus et bullationis in utraque gena faciei cum bulla ferrea ignita ex qua sit perpetuo et verisimiliter evidens et deformis cicatrix remansura quae habeat ipsum huiusmodi criminis reum manisfestum omnibus publicare" ASB, Statuti 50 (formerly XVII), fol. 304r, Bk. IV, Rubric 56, "De pena venenantis aliquem."

28. On defamatory punishments, see Azzara, "Pene 'infamanti.'"

29. ASB, Liber Novarum Provisionum, 1400–70, 306, fols. 231r. The *provisio* was one of the means of updating statutory legislation. For this process, see Dean, *Crime and Justice*, 84–85. On this particular *provisio*, see Cucini, "Législation statutaire," 1:261 and 2:314–15.

30. Cucini, "*Législation statutaire*," 1:261 and 2:314–15.

31. De Benedictis, "Lo 'stato popolare di libertà,'" 911–22.

32. Dalla Tuata, *Istoria di Bologna*, 306–7; BUB, ms. 1107, Giovanni Francesco Negri, *Annali della città di Bologna dall'anno 1001 al 1600*, 6.1, fol. 236.

33. Collard, *Pouvoir et poison*, 55–57.

34. ASB, Legato, Bandi speciali, bobina 67, vol. 5 (31 March and 1 April 1588), "Bandi generali dell'Illustrissimo et reverendissimo Monsig. Anselmo Dandino Prothonotario apostolico di Bologna," 19. For the other *bandi*, see end notes 40 and 45 below.

35. ASB, "Bando generale dell'illustrissimo, e reuerendissimo sig. Benedetto card. Giustiniano legato di Bologna. Publicato alli 23 di giugno, & reiterato alli 24 di luglio 1610" (23 June and 24 July 1610), 15, 16–17, and 64–65, respectively chap. VI, art. 2, chap. VII, art. 17, chap. XXXI, art. 2, 3 and 4.

36. *Magnificae ciuitatis Fauentie*, 40; *Statuta terræ Centi*, 127, Bk. VI, Rubric 29, "De poena venenantis aliquem."

37. *Statuta magnificæ ciuitatis Parmae*, 122v, Bk. III, "De assassinis et veneficis."

38. Bibliothèque Nationale de France, "Édit du Roy pour la punition de différents crimes [magie, sortilèges, empoisonnement]. Registré en Parlement le 31 aoust 1682," http://gallica.bnf.fr/ark:/12148/btv1b8607061d (accessed 7 September 2017).

39. ASB, Legato, bandi speciali, bobina 67, vol. 5 (27 and 28 September 27 1586), "Bando generale dell'Illustrissimo et reverendissimo sig. Henrico Caetano Cardinale di S. Chiesa, e legato di Bologna, suo contado, territorio, e distretto," 41.

40. "L'*enormitas* est à la fois criminelle et pénitentielle." Théry, "*Atrocitas/Enormitas*."

41. "Non solo la sete della morte, o robba altrui, e causa delli disordini che nascono dal veneno, ma anco qualch'altra sfrenata voglia." ASB, Legato, Bandi speciali, bobina 65, vol. 2

(6 December 1596), "Bandi generali dell'illustrissimo e reverendiss. Monsig. Antonio Gianotti, arcivescovo d'Urbino e di Bologna vicelegato," 152.

42. ASB, "Bando generale dell'illustrissimo, e reuerendissimo sig. Benedetto card. Giustiniano legato di Bologna. Publicato alli 23 di giugno, & reiterato alli 24 di luglio 1610" (24 June and 24 July 1610), 64–65, chap. XXXI, art. 2, 3 and 4.

43. Hulot, Berthelot, Tissot, and Berenger, *Les cinquante livres du Digeste*, 350, "Ad legem corneliam de sicariis et veneficis," Bk. XLVIII *titulus* 8, paragraph 1.

44. "Ité se alcuno con veneno procurerà in qualche modo di attossicare qual si voglia persona, venendone all'atto prossimo con porglilo inanzi, ó in vivande, o in bevande, o in altro modo, ancorche, o lui non lo pigliasse, o non faccia l'effetto, debba subito come traditore esser condānato alla pena della morte naturale." ASB, Legato, bandi speciali, bobina 65, 2:152.

45. Demuro, *Il Dolo*, 1:36.

46. *Aegidiane constitutiones*, cap. LXVIII, 298. The content of the article on poisoning is not modified. However, various jurists are cited. The text insists also on the importance of *dolus* and *animus necandi*, in particular at the moment of sale of poison.

47. Buyck, "Crimes de poison," 383–89.

48. Lucchesi, *Si quis occidit occidetur*, 105–11.

49. "Et sunt haec maxime vera praesupposita consideratione quae dicitur esse per totam Italiam quod licet iura puniant effectus non habet locum secundum consuetudinem universalem Italiae." Cipolla, *Consilia criminalia* (1575)*, consilium* 80. 267; Barbo, *Criminalium consiliorum atque responsorum, consilium* 98, 1:236; Grammatico, Decisio II, in *Clarissimi iuriscons. Thomae Grammatici, decisio II,* 4.

50. "[. . .] scilicet dandi & propinandi venenum, sed fuit impeditus dare vel detectus, ut supra dicebā. at si omnia consumasset, quae ipse in hoc facere poterat, quia scilicet venenum ipsum propinauit, & ille cui propinauit, ebibit totum, sed vel quia non erat potens venenum, vel quia remediis & medicinis repentine adhibitis sanatus fuit, hoc casu puto talem dignum morte [. . .]; Deciani, *Tractatus criminalis*, cap. XXIII, 2:220.

51. Collard, "Les risques d'un métier."

52. "Non doverà alcun medico, cirurgo, barbiero, distillatore, o altro qualsivoglia, quatunque senza mala intenzione comporre veleno, o altra cosa, dalla quale ne possa seguire morte, o alienatione di mente ad alcuno. Nè anco vendere, o comprare, o per qualunque altro titolo, dare, ricevere, o tenere tali compositioni, o veleni, semplici, o composti senza licenza, sottoscritta di mano di S.S. Illustris. sotto pena della morte." ASB, "Bando generale dell'illustrissimo, e reuerendissimo sig. Benedetto card. Giustiniano legato di Bologna. Publicato alli 23 di giugno, & reiterato alli 24 di luglio 1610" (23 June and 24 July 1610), 64–65, chap. XXXI, art. 2, 3 and 4.

53. The sample consists of a total of 173 cases from all sources. Of these ninety-seven are from judicial records, of which forty four trials are from the Middle Ages and fifty three from the early modern era. Most of the cases are from the records of the *Curia del Podestà*, in the series *Giudici ad Maleficia.* For the early modern era many trials derive from the *Tribunale del Torrone* series and other secondary archival series such as that of the *Ospedali*. The works of Ottavio Mazzoni-Toselli and also Gian Carlo Angelozzi and Cesarina Casanova, *La giustizia criminale in una città di antico regime*, were utilized to identify some of the ninety-seven judicial cases.

54. Collard, *Le crime de poison*, 216.

55. Three are from the Trecento, the other two concern events from the sixteenth and seventeenth centuries.

56. BCA, Fondo Ottavio Mazzoni-Toselli, Busta III, fasc. 1, fols.24v–26v.

57. ASB, Sententiae, Busta 21, 1369, trial against Giacomo Gherardi.

58. ASB, Statuti 44 (formerly XI), fols. 152–54. Bk. VI, Rubric 61.

59. ASB, Inquisitiones, Mazzo 385, Register 1 (1484–85), fols. 172r–73v.

60. ASB, "Catalogo di tutte le giustizie seguite in Bologna dall'anno 1030 sino al 1539 estratto da varie croniche e manoscritte e stampate, come si vede dalle note in margine. Dall'anno 1540 sino al tempo presente (1751) dalli libri della Conforteria."

61. *Statuta civitatis Caesenae,* 128; *Statuta urbis Ferariae*, 146v, Bk. III, Rubric LXXV, "Poena venenantis, vel venenum habentis, vel venenari facientis aliquem"; ASB, Statuti 47 (formerly XIV), (1389), Bk. V, Rubric 57, fol. 315.

62. Lucchesi, *Si quis occidit occidetur*, 105.

63. *Statuta Mirandulae,* 92, Bk. IV, "De poena venenantis vel maleficiantis aliquem," 92; Rinaldi, *Statuto di Forlì*, 240–41, Bk. III, Rubric 46, "De veneficis et eorum pena."

64. BCA, Fondo Ospedali, Ospedale Santa Maria della Morte, "Libro dei giustiziati dall'anno 1540–1673," Bk. 1.

65. ASB, Atti e Processi, 6461–1.

66. Zorzi, "Dérisions des corps," 237.

67. ASB, "Bando generale dell'illustrissimo, e reuerendissimo sig. Benedetto card. Giustiniano legato di Bologna. Publicato alli 23 di giugno, & reiterato alli 24 di luglio 1610" (23 June and 24 July 1610), 16–17, chap. VII, art. 1 and 11.

68. ASB, Statuti 47 (formerly XIV), (1389), fol. 315r, Bk. V, Rubric 57; ASB, Statuti 50 (formerly XVII), (1454), fol. 304r, Bk. IV, Rubric 56.

69. ASB, Legato, Bandi Speciali, bobina 65, 2:152.

70. ASB, Sententiae, Busta 21.

71. ASB, Atti e Processi, 7000, *in fine*, fasc. 7.

72. Half of the cases refer to the fourteenth century. Comparison with normative sources is not possible since the first rubric dedicated to poisoning does not appear until 1376.

73. Ortalli, "Pingatur in Palatio," 13.

74. Dean, *Criminal Justice*, 27.

75. Hulot, Berthelot, Tissot, and Berenger, *Les cinquante livres du Digeste*, 350, "Ad legem corneliam de sicariis et veneficis," Bk. XLVIII *titulus* 8, paragraph 1.

76. ASB, Atti e Processi, 6868, fasc. 10, *in fine*.

77. Dean, *Criminal Justice*, 12–14.

78. Gonthier, *Le châtiment du crime*, 111–72.

79. ASB, Inquisitiones, Mazzo 231, fols. 120r–21r; BCA, Fondo Ottavio-Mazzoni Toselli, Busta 1, fasc. 10 (1390), fols. 469v–70r.

80. Collard, *Le crime de poison*, 217–21.

81. Gauvard, *"De grace especial,"* 1:163–65.

82. Gauvard, "Grâce et exécution capitale," 281. A peace accord is mentioned in seventeen of the ninety-seven trials in my sample. Fourteen date from the sixteenth and seventeenth centuries. This does not mean that the granting of a pardon occurred more frequently in the early modern era since it remains extremely difficult to locate supplications for pardon from the medieval period.

83. ASB, Liber Novarum Provisionum, 306, fol. 231r.

84. Sbriccoli, *Storia del diritto penale*, 1:5.

85. Niccoli, *Perdonare. Idee, pratiche, rituali* , 70–76; Bellabarba, "Pace pubblica e pace privata," 190–93.

86. Niccoli, *Perdonare. Idee, pratiche, rituali,* 32.

87. Mazzoni-Toselli, *Cenno sull'antica storia*, 74.

88. Cucini, "Législation statutaire," 1:312.

89. Vallerani, *Medieval Public Justice*, 306–47.

90. Cucini, "Législation statutaire," 1:314–18.

91. BCA, Fondo Ottavio Mazzoni-Toselli, Busta I, fasc. 12, fol. 567.

92. The *congregazione criminale* is mentioned for the first time in 1662. Di Zio, "Il tribunale di Torrone," 345–47.

93. Although at first glance this fact seems puzzling, it relates to common provisions concerning occurrences when a victim was buried or an offender was found within Church territory. Frequently the immunity was shortly lifted, demonstrating collaboration among the various authorities present in the city.

94. ASB, Atti e Processi, 7336, fasc. 16, *in fine*.

95. Sbriccoli, *Storia del diritto penale e della giustizia*, 1:5.

96. ASB, Atti e Processi 3790, fols. 305r–374v.

97. Bellabarba, "La représentation des délits."

Chapter Eight

Accusations of Rape in Thirteenth-Century Bologna

Carol Lansing

Rape is notoriously difficult to study, in the Middle Ages as in the contemporary world. In my research in the especially rich criminal court records from late medieval Bologna, I have found a surprisingly large number of rape and attempted rape cases. For this chapter, I have analyzed sixty accusation cases from a three-year period (1286, 1287, and 1289), with discussion of twenty-three contemporary sentences from inquisition trials to provide context. I argue that these Bolognese cases raise questions about current understandings of rape in late medieval Italy. My sample comprises a larger number of rape accusations than current scholarship would lead us to expect, and the penalty for a rape conviction when the accused was contumacious was usually decapitation. Further, a significant proportion of accusations were probably lodged by low-status women. Scholars of medieval rape, myself included, have suggested that women and their families were reluctant to charge rape. In doing so they risked damage to reputation and honor, and unless they sought to settle with a marriage between the alleged rapist and victim, the chances of any benefit or of a conviction were small.[1] Why then did unmarried women from the *contado* and the periphery of the city file rape accusations?

Rape is of course a painful topic, and one in which assumptions about attitudes toward male and female sexuality often come into play. To give an example, the distinguished historian of canon law James Brundage wrote in his magisterial *Law, Sex and Christian Society in the Middle Ages*, that:

> abduction and rape of women, particularly wealthy ones, remained a serious but not common crime; it does not appear nearly so frequently in civic court records as larceny, burglary, theft or even homicide. It is likely, however, that

> then, as now, rape was seriously underreported. Men tended to be skeptical about rape complaints, and defendants often claimed that the woman had invited the attack, but courts rarely found the charge wholly without merit.[2]

Brundage was entirely correct in suggesting that rape cases are relatively rare in civic court records, and surely also that the crime was underreported. However, the assertions that men tended to be skeptical and that defendants often claimed that the woman had invited the attack derive from modern patterns of victim-blaming, and are not borne out by medieval trials, certainly not those from Bologna.[3] The trials hinged not on whether the alleged victim had been enticing or lying, but on her status, since a woman who was *inhonesta* (disreputable) could not be raped.[4] Moreover, the idea that women who were abducted and raped tended to be wealthy targets is not supported by these accusation cases.

A major reason that rape in medieval Europe can be difficult to research is that evidence for social practice is thin. Studies are often largely based on literary accounts, which can tend to depict rape as casual and opportunistic. In French pastourelles, a knight who spots a pretty shepherdess often simply assaults her.[5] Famously, Andreas Capellanus in his *Art of Love*, a seduction manual based on Ovid and written in the 1170s, advised a man attracted to a peasant woman to flatter and then simply force her.[6] As Marjorie Woods has pointed out, many of the standard texts used to teach Latin in grammar schools used stories of rape.[7] The effect was to naturalize sexual violence. For late medieval Italy, central sources include the many discussions of the rape of Lucretia, and also rapes in the *novelle*, notably Boccaccio's *Decameron*.[8] *Novelle* tend to depict rapes in which there is no prior relationship between the victim and the perpetrator, as when a pirate happens to capture a woman. In the *Decameron*, the female victim inevitably enjoys the experience.

The assumption that rape tended to be opportunistic also derives from the scarcity of evidence that provides context. When evidence for the context of a rape charge can be found, generally in testimony in trials by inquisition procedure, it often suggests that the alleged perpetrator and victim knew each other. The assumption that rape was an impulsive attack on a stranger also misses the current understanding of court cases as aspects of broader conflicts.[9] To my knowledge, the most detailed evidence that rape could be a strategy appears in the inquests of the mid-fourteenth-century registers of the Florentine Executor of the Ordinances of Justice, a tribunal created to facilitate denunciations of noble violence.[10] I have argued elsewhere that three cases in which nobles abducted and raped married women reveal a strategy of domination. The women came from communities under the control of the nobles' families. In another series of cases, a Tornaquinci noble was charged with a series of attempts to rape a married woman. She and her husband had inherited a house adjoining the Tornaquinci's urban compound, and the rape attempts may have been efforts to intimidate in a property dispute, efforts which also included theft of their household goods.[11] Some cases from Bologna also indicate a strategy of domination, like the inquisition case discussed below in which an elite male made at least two attempts to rape a woman, or a series of rape charges against Martinus, the son of Pietro Ravignani.[12] However, I have not found evidence from Bologna as convincing as that found in the Florentine records.

Normative materials, including canon law and civic statutes, have been used to trace changing attitudes toward rape, and a number of scholars argue that attitudes toward rape and sexuality more generally became harsher and punishment more severe in the fourteenth and fifteenth centuries.[13] The use of capital penalties in thirteenth-century Bolognese cases potentially qualifies this view. Again, scholars, myself included, have argued that women and their families were reluctant to accuse men of rape in the courts. The charge was hard to prove and could easily damage a woman's reputation. Trevor Dean, following Brundage, argues in a recent study of crime in medieval Europe that "[o]f all the crimes perpetrated against women, rape stands out for the ineffectiveness of the law."[14] Ruth Mazo Karras, a leading historian of medieval sexuality, explains that there are no statistics on the prevalence of rape: "We have some court cases, but we can assume that the crime went unreported even more often than it does today, so the number of cases is not a good indication of the incidence of the offense."[15] A corollary to this view is the idea that rape charges were rare, as I have asserted, because family honor was closely bound up with female sexuality and a sexual assault could affect not only the woman's status and reputation but the honor of her kin and even her community. This view imagines victims as respectable women, with kin groups who were concerned about honor. In Bologna in the 1280s this was not always the case. As I show in this chapter, Bologna had a significant population of women who were too poor to have dowries and marry, and a number of the victims probably came from this group.

Studies of late medieval court records generally suggest that rape charges were rare, as Ruth Karras pointed out. One study of rape in medieval England found that twenty eyre records from 1202–76 included 142 rape cases, compared to 3,492 homicides, with an overall conviction rate for rape of 6 percent.[16] Giovanna Casagrande and Michele Pazzaglia, in a study based on three years of the thirteenth-century Perugian judicial records, found a total of 121 females who appear as victims, and twenty-three of them were cases of carnal violence.[17] Several studies of rape cases in fourteenth-century Italian civic courts found only low numbers of cases. Lynn Laufenberg in her 2000 dissertation sampled records from Florence's criminal court for each decade between 1340 and 1415. Out of roughly 1,500 cases from the podestà's court, she reports that one hundred concerned *raptus* and/or *stu-*

prum, which roughly translate as abduction and rape.[18] Samuel Cohn, also working in the Florentine criminal court records, found five cases of heterosexual rape in 1344–45 and two in 1374–75.[19] Trevor Dean analyzed cases from the Bolognese criminal court for the 1390s and found five cases of rape or attempted rape.[20]

My sample of records from Bologna's criminal court in the 1280s does not neatly fit this pattern. Rape cases are more numerous and penalties could be severe. Surveying the surviving records of accusations to the criminal court over six semesters, 1286, 1287, and 1289, I found sixty cases of rape or attempted rape. Records of sentences in cases tried by inquisition in the same period include another twenty-three rape or attempted rape cases. This figure does not include cases that appear only in inquisition registers. The comparison with Dean's evidence from roughly a century later is striking, even given the sharp decline in the city's population in the interim. This evidence of course is hardly complete. Nevertheless, the contrast between a minimum of roughly twenty-seven cases a year and one case every two years is dramatic. Furthermore, the late thirteenth-century Bolognese records include more bans than current scholarship would predict. I will first discuss the contemporary definition of rape and the Bolognese statutes, then set out what can be known from the rape accusation cases, discussing cases by inquisition for context. Finally, I will step back and attempt to locate the rape cases within the framework of what we know of court practices and the broader patterns of womens' experience in the late thirteenth-century city.

THE LAW, THE COURTS, AND THE RAPE CHARGES

Medieval laws on rape were heavily influenced by Roman law. The legal terms commonly used in Italian civic statutes were *stuprum*, which literally meant to debauch or defile, and *raptus*, a term that in late Roman law had meant abduction and rape, but by the thirteenth century could simply mean abduction.[21] Both terms were potentially ambiguous, since *stuprum* could mean sexual defilement without coitus, and *raptus* abduction without coitus. The Bolognese statute of 1288 addressed *stuprum*, holding that a person guilty of *stuprum* by force of a widow or virgin was to suffer either a fine or a corporal punishment, at the discretion of the podestà, according to the quality of the persons and actions.[22] In practice, as I will discuss below, the podestà sentenced all but one of the men banned for rape in 1286–87 and 1289 to decapitation if captured. We cannot know from the trial records how often those declared contumacious were captured and the sentence carried out. Trevor Dean has argued that the threat of decapitation was a strategy to force a man to settle.[23] Sentences for attempted rape generally consisted of fines of

500 *lire* and the requirement that the culprit make a peace accord with his accuser.

The laws of many early fourteenth-century Italian towns suggest a growing concern that crimes of passion posed a threat to civic order, and Bologna was no exception.[24] The Bolognese statutes of 1335 elaborated on penalties for sexual crimes and limited the discretion of the podestà in crimes evidently considered especially serious. Forcible adultery, incest with a male or a female, and *stuprum* of a virgin nun or woman dedicated to God could not be punished with a fine. Corporal punishment was to be at the podestà's discretion, according to the quality of the persons and actions. The penalty for sex with an unwilling widow was to be decided in the same manner. Sex with a willing widow drew the fines for adultery, 500 *lire* for the man and 200 for the woman.[25]

The imprecise distinction between *raptus* and *stuprum* challenged even the famed contemporary Italian jurist Albertus Gandinus. At the end of a term he served as a judge in Bologna, he reports that the legality of one of his judicial actions was questioned in his syndication (end of term review). Gandinus had ordered a man tortured over a charge of *raptus* of a child. The Bolognese statute of 1288 that listed the crimes for which torture was permitted did include *stuprum*. The alleged perpetrator happened to be the servant of a legal scholar who surely had formulated the complaint against Gandinus, claiming that because the servant was charged with *raptus*, which simply meant abduction, the torture was illegal.[26] Gandinus was exonerated. Rape accusations in practice were usually clear: they followed the formulas set out in procedural manuals, which used the unambiguous phrase "to know carnally (*cognoscere carnaliter*)," specifying carnal knowledge with force against the victim's will.

In late thirteenth-century Bologna, rape charges could be initiated in two general ways. The first was a straightforward accusation, in which either the victim or a representative, usually a kinsman or legal guardian, directly accused the alleged perpetrator or perpetrators. The exact text was important because if the case went to the probatory phase, the entire accusation had to be proven. If not, the charge failed and the accuser was liable for court costs. The second way was through an inquisition. Inquisitions could be *ex officio* or initiated by a notification or denunciation to the court. Parish officials, including urban *ministrales* and rural *massari*, were required to notify the court of crimes within their parishes. Not surprisingly, they did not always do so. Individuals could also notify or denounce a crime to the court, and in this period could do so anonymously. Notifications and denunciations had to include a list of witnesses. Provided they met the criteria, the court was obligated to hold an inquisition. Crucially, conviction was possible even if only a portion of the charge was proven.

As Massimo Vallerani and others have shown, once a case was initiated, the procedures followed by the court were often very similar. However, the distinction between whether a case was initiated through an accusation or a denunciation, notification, or *ex officio* is crucial for this study. An accusation is good evidence that the victim and/or the victim's kin chose to publicly admit to the rape or attempted rape. That could be true of a notification or denunciation, as for example, a case from Florence in which a father included his name when he denounced the attempted rape of his daughter.[27] However, as I will show, third parties could and did notify the court of rapes for their own ends, even if against the wishes of the victim and the victim's kin. For this reason, despite the potential similarities in the way these trials were conducted, accusations are for the most part better evidence for the choices of the victim and/or the victim's kin.

Conviction was often because of the accused's contumacy, and was a slow process. Summoning and banning a suspect took approximately three weeks. The imputed was cited three times, over at least nine days. Then, two *gride* were issued, again several days apart. If the imputed still failed to appear in court, the *bannitor* issued a summons in the communal council, usually with an eight-day deadline and a provisional ban. After that deadline, the ban was issued (*bannum formatum*) and then recorded (*bannum exemplatum*). The person's contumacy was considered a confession of guilt.[28]

The majority of the cases ended in bans. If the sentences from accusation and inquisition trials in this sample are combined, the rape cases led to twelve bans in which the imputed was to suffer decapitation if captured.[29] One exception was a sentence to pay a fine of 1,000 *lire* and to make a peace concord with the victim.[30] Thirty-three attempted rape cases led to bans, twenty-two of them in fines of 500 *lire*, and the rest ranged from 200 to 600 *lire*. In effect, while the 1288 statutes gave the podestà discretion in sentences, the magistrates rarely deviated from standard punishments in rape and attempted rape cases. Again, most capital penalties probably were not carried out because the convicted were never captured. The imputed had eight days to appear in court and provide guarantors and a defense after the issuance of the provisional ban. In at least one case, an accused man was absolved after his ban was issued and recorded, supporting Dean's view that the threat of capital punishment could be a way for a victim to pressure for a settlement.[31]

Bologna's thirteenth-century criminal court records are an extraordinarily rich trove of evidence. They are a superb source for legal procedure and patterns of enforcement, notably what Sarah Blanshei has demonstrated to be the shifting influence of politics on justice, including a turn to summary justice that shortened the slow process of summons and ban. The records of course do not survive systematically, and are not a solid source for crime rates because they only contain the crimes that people brought to the court, as

Ruth Karras has pointed out. Furthermore, the evidence contained in accusations, denunciations, and testimony is hardly a direct representation of events. Any charge to the court was shaped by the motives and maneuverings of participants, although witness testimony could lead to unexpected consequences, as I show in an inquisition trial discussed below. And of course, charges and testimony were shaped by the requirements of the law, especially if a case went to trial and witnesses on both sides testified to precise lists of positions crafted by lawyers. Still, the records do provide evidence for how the residents of Bologna and its *contado* sought to use the courts, including the choice to charge rape or attempted rape. In addition, the texts can provide evidence for social status, family, residence, and even social attitudes.

The six semesters of accusation records from 1286, 1287, and 1289 that form the core of this study are not a scientific sample.[32] I chose them because they are extensive, include rapes and attempted rapes, and also registers of sentences.[33] They are by no means the only semesters of records that include rape. I also have drawn on a broader range of evidence to provide context, including further accusations and also inquisitions. Of course, the distribution of cases is in part the result of the survival of registers. Still, rape or attempted rape cases are fairly evenly spread across the six semesters, with higher numbers in *buste* that include registers of sentences.[34] The sixty accusation cases include forty-three cases of attempted rape and seventeen of rape. Beyond this, there are a number of cases of the abduction and detention of unmarried girls, which imply rape, although the formula for a rape charge (carnal knowledge with force against her will) was not used, quite possibly as part of a strategy to encourage a settlement. Forty-four of the eighty-three cases are clearly rural. Of the sixty accusation cases, the victim was the accuser in forty-three cases, a male kinsman in eleven cases, and a notary or other unrelated male, perhaps a *procuratore*, in seven.

Why is the incidence of rape or attempted rape charges higher for thirteenth-century Bologna than for Florence or Bologna in the fourteenth century? One of the most interesting findings from this sample concerns the status of the alleged victims. Evaluating any individual's status can be imprecise, particularly in a brief accusation case. However, the overall pattern is revealing. In thirty-two cases, the alleged victim was unmarried and did not have a living father, and in only seven of those cases is there mention of male kin.[35] Of course, fathers could die while their children were young, but this datum does suggest that many victims were unmarried adult women. In fifteen cases, the women acted with the consent of a *curator* (guardian or trustee), indicating as Sarah Blanshei pointed out, their vulnerability.[36] Some were probably underage and lacked parents. Others may have been women with few resources who somehow gained the assistance of a trustee. Ten of the women with *curatores* had no mention of a living father, a husband, or other male kin.[37] Not all of these thirty-two women were necessarily poor: three were identified as *domina*, one of whom had the resources to go through a full trial, although it did not result in a conviction.[38] Other cases have clues that suggest domestic service, like residence in a house belonging to an unrelated person identified as a *dominus*.[39] One victim was a shepherdess working for a widow, a case that, as I discuss below, was settled with a marriage.[40] My working hypothesis is that the decision whether or not to make an accusation reflected status differences. Prosperous families had the resources to protect their women, especially unmarried daughters, and strong incentives to do so, although they still might suffer sexual assaults. Prosperous families thus best fit the standard model in current scholarship: they would have been deeply concerned about honor and reputation, and not apt to charge rape. If a woman who was unmarried and lacked a dowry suffered a sexual assault, she might calculate the possible consequences of lodging an accusation differently.

THE SOCIAL EXPERIENCE OF POOR WOMEN

I know of no systematic way to calculate the number of unmarried adult laywomen in Bolognese society. However, it is possible to know the rough proportion of households that were too poor to afford dowries for their daughters. A remarkably complete source for the distribution of wealth exists in Bologna, an *estimo* or tax survey from 1296–97.[41] The *cedule* or individual returns survive for a large proportion of the population. There are 9,635 extant legible returns. The *estimo* has been meticulously studied by Francesca Bocchi, Antonio Ivan Pini, Massimo Giansante, and Rosa Smurra, among others.[42] Residents of the city, the suburbs, and new *borghi* were required to list immovable property, large animals, credits, invested capital, rights, and large quantities of grain and/or wine over 100 *corbe*.[43] The median wealth was 232 *lire*. Roughly 13 percent of the total (1,331 households) declared that they held nothing.[44] Another 2,566 households, roughly 26 percent, held between one and 25 *lire*. How good a measure of poverty is this? As Giansante points out, the 1296–97 *estimo* is a frozen measure of what was in fact a very fluid reality, especially of wealth distribution. It is not a complete picture: the statute excluded movables like household goods, clothing, and linens.[45] Further, some who declared nothing ultimately were assigned assessments by the officials, perhaps because of evidence from a previous return. Nevertheless, it does reveal something of the proportion of very poor households: at least 13 percent did not own their places of residence. Giansante's close analysis by parish is revealing: the wealthiest households lived in the center, the poorest on the periphery, particularly *contadini* and textile workers. Thus, although women who had never married were not required to file a *cedula* and do not appear, the *estimo* does suggest a sizeable population of women never married because they lacked dowries. Some daughters of these households might find opportunities to earn dowries in domestic service, a practice studied by Christiane Klapisch-Zuber in Florentine family memoirs.[46]

There were prosperous unmarried women. Adelina Teutonica, a washerwoman who filed an *estimo* return, has been analyzed by Rosa Smurra.[47] Her *cedula* does not identify her by a father's name or that of a husband, which according to Smurra is unlike every other woman in the *estimo*. She evidently had no husband, and the epithet Teutonica suggests that she had emigrated from Germany. Adelina was successful. She had a house on land that was part of the great breakup of the holdings of the monastery of San Procolo and paid a modest rent for its use, an amount that indicates that she held 130 square meters, including the portico and a space in the back that was probably used to dry laundry.[48] Adelina was prosperous enough to extend credit, an interest-free six-*lire* loan to her neighbor Amadore. A student owed her an unpaid laundry bill of 8 *lire*, which, as Smurra points out, was just under half the assessment for her house. Smurra also found that Adelina's assessment of 18 *lire* remarkably made her the wealthiest foreigner in the 1296–97 *estimo*.

One unsystematic source for unmarried women in Bologna is the common use of the term *amasia*, a word that literally translates as friend but implies sexual relations.[49] Judging from mention of *amasie* in contemporary court records, the word could refer to women who lived in long term co-residential unions that might be termed informal marriages or concubinage, often a union between an unmarried man with property and a woman who surely provided domestic work as well as sex. An *amasia* and her children had no legal claims, and the man might—and demonstrably often did—expel them when he married. The word *amasia* was also used for women who verged on prostitution. Inquests in which women termed *amasie* were accused of prostitution include testimony depicting a range of relationships. Some were depicted as living in brothels and selling sex. An *amasio* in that case might be the woman's pimp. Other *amasie* provided services to one or several men whom they termed their *domini*, notably university students. In exchange, they received "expenses." In all of these scenarios the children were illegitimate; the daughter of an *amasia* would inherit her irregular and insecure status.

The presence of *amasie* was a product of the way the rigid Roman dowry system restricted legal marriage.[50] Reported speech in a few rape cases suggests the frustration of people who were not able to marry. They include the familiar scenario in which a charge of rape and kidnap is suspected to conceal a young woman's choice to run away to marry.[51] There are also a few men charged with rape and kidnap who are quoted as stating that they were taking wives. In February 1287 an unmarried woman identified as Domina

Umelta accused a certain Azo; both were from a rural commune, Varignana, though Azo now lived in the parish of San Tommaso del Mercato in Bologna.[52] According to the charge Azo came to her father's house, where she lived, and "with force and against her will knew her carnally." Then, he "extracted her from the house against her will, leading her through the Bolognese *contado*, saying to her then, I do not have a wife and now I take her as my wife." Azo surely knew her, had not been able to marry, and chose to carry her off. Perhaps he foolishly hoped that her father would recognize a *fait accompli* and pay a dowry. Azo was contumacious and was banned with a penalty of decapitation if ever caught.

In a 1285 rape inquest initiated by a notification from an innkeeper, the imputed, Zannos, testified that he had met Divitia, a *puella* without resources, staying in a man's house in Bologna. Warning her that she was at risk of prostitution, he persuaded her to come with him to his village, then insisted on sex with her at an inn along the way. Divitia testified that it was against her will because he had promised to marry her but had not done so. Zannos described a different commitment: "I do not have a wife, and if you will come with me I will keep you as an *amica* until I have children from you. When I have children from you I will have just cause to ask my father's permission to take you as my wife without a dowry."[53] There is a sharp contrast between Domina Umelta, with a home, a father, and surely a dowry, and Divitia, with no evident kin or resources.

WHY ACCUSE RAPE?

Any explanation of Bologna's relatively large number of accusations of rape or attempted rape requires an understanding of the accessibility of the tribunal. Massimo Vallerani has demonstrated that accusatory trials were widely diffused in late thirteenth-century Bologna. He estimated that 650–700 trials took place during every semester in the decade discussed here, 1286–96, and termed the tribunal "a privileged place for the mediation of conflict, incomparable for its breadth and range of action to almost any other existing method."[54] Why? The initial stage of an accusatory trial required only the consent of the victim and a brief *libellus* stating the accusation, which meant narrating the name of a person and recounting a specific legal fact. A *libellus* used formulas that were spelled out in procedural treatises, formulas that depicted events in standardized ways. In a rape or attempted rape charge, the formula was simple. It states that a man appears and threatens a woman. Then it states that he knew her carnally. For an attempted rape, the formula is "he certainly would have known her carnally, if it were not for the people who were drawn to the ruckus."[55]

Crucially, initiating an accusation was inexpensive. If an accuser stopped the trial after the *libellus* and the accuser's oath to tell the truth, before prosecution, he or she was simply liable for a modest fine, 12 or 20 *soldi*. If a trial did proceed to the probatory phase, it quickly became much more costly and difficult, requiring witnesses and securities. Vallerani points out that some jurists criticized this light penalty, arguing that an accuser who dropped the charge should be obligated to suffer the penalty for the alleged crime, termed the *pena talionis*. Albertus Gandinus defended the 20-*soldi* fine, since "few men could be found who would want to obligate themselves to the *pena talionis*," and many crimes would remain unpunished.[56] In effect, the system was designed to be accessible. Vallerani found that roughly 30 percent of trials in late thirteenth-century Bologna stopped before prosecution. One reason is contumacy, which again means that the accused did not appear in court, a choice that was considered a confession of guilt. Another possibility is that the accuser did not have the resources to prosecute, and therefore could not produce witnesses and guarantors, a process which was expensive and potentially quite difficult.[57]

An accusation was also used as a pressure tactic. As Sarah Blanshei has argued, the strategy often was to file an accusation in order to pressure the accused to settle. Legal historians in recent decades have demonstrated that court proceedings were often one part of efforts to resolve larger conflicts.[58] Occasionally, the conflict that lay behind an accusation can be gleaned from the records of the case itself. One example derives from an inquest of 1298. A woman named Blonda notified the court that Meglior, her neighbor, was a prostitute, pimp, and sorceress who kidnapped virgins to sell sex with them, including Blonda's daughter.[59] Neighborhood witnesses stated that Blonda's son had been banned for an assault on Meglior, and it was well known in the neighborhood that Blonda was pressuring Meglior to lift the ban. Blonda was reported to have said that if Meglior did not, she would lodge notifications that would get Meglior immolated. Blonda's daughter was an *amasia*.

An accusation of rape could be a strategy to press for a private settlement, which might take the form of a peace accord formalized in a notarial document. It also might be presented orally, directly to the judge.[60] Rape cases could be resolved through settlements that included marriages between the accused and the victim. This was a form of resolution that probably derived from Germanic law, and was officially incorporated into canon law at the end of the twelfth century in decretals of Lucius III and Innocent III.[61] The law did require that the woman consent. One accusation case from this sample was settled with a marriage. A woman identified as Bonaiuxina, daughter of the late Perrezoli, accused Fulcherus of attempted rape. Bonaiuxina had been watching over sheep in a field of plowland owned by a widow. Fulcherus grabbed her with force, threw her to the ground, "wanting to know her carnally, corrupt and violate her." He demanded that she consent. When she did not, he punched her on her shoulders and many other parts of her person and said, "It is necessary that I have you and that you consent to me doing my will to you or else I will kill you," holding her by her face and mouth to stop her from crying out.[62] Nevertheless people were drawn by her cries, stopping the rape. Despite the alleged violence, twelve days after the initial accusation the two came before the judge and Fulcherus stated that he accepted her as his legitimate wife. Bonaiuxina said that she accepted him as her man or rather husband by her own free will and that she did not wish to pursue the accusation.

There is little context given in the trial record for this case. Accuser and accused came from two different rural communities, and she at least was evidently a low-status shepherdess, unmarried, with no living father, nor mention of supporting kin. It is possible that Fulcherus contributed some portion of a dowry, as in a Sienese peace settlement analyzed by Glenn Kumhera. However, the Sienese case involved a higher-status woman aided by her brothers, and included a peace accord, a marriage, and the perpetrator's contribution of lands to her dowry, including land provided by a woman who was probably his kin. The settlement was recorded in seven notarial documents.[63]

Another Bolognese case of attempted rape that was settled with notarial instruments including a promise of marriage is known because it sparked an inquisition trial over false testimony. Bonora Nascimbenis from Olgiano had charged a man named Jacobus and nicknamed Ugolus with attempted rape. He was a servant in Castrum Britonum. As a result of the accusation, he had been banned and taken into custody. Bonora made a notarial peace accord, with her father's consent, in the house of a furrier in Strada Maggiore. The notary drew up a second instrument in which Ugolus promised that if he did evade the charge he would marry her. The case ignited a lengthy trial because Bonora falsely stated to the judge that Ugolus was present when the peace was made. In fact, he was in jail and Brunus represented him. Ultimately, she testified that the reason she falsely claimed that Ugolus was present was that she was a "person who has little sense."[64] Sarah Blanshei has analyzed another marriage settlement, which resolved an inquisition trial of 1285. The father of the alleged rape victim was the notifier. He charged rape after his daughter gave birth to a child, and as Blanshei argues was pressuring for an out of court settlement. The trial did end with the marriage of the daughter to her attacker.[65]

Nevertheless, recent scholarship indicates that extant notarial peace pacts that settle rape cases are rare. Shona Kelly Wray examined 122 notarial peace pacts in Bologna from 1337, the year Taddeo Pepoli became *signore* of Bologna. She found no rape settlements for that year, though she noted that two exist from 1348.[66] Glenn Kumhera found fourteen rape cases from Siena's podestarial judge for the *contado* over two semesters in 1343 and 1345.

In twelve of those cases the parties made peace.[67] Katherine Jansen examined 514 peace contracts in Florentine notarial cartularies, 1237–1343, and found one concord between a convicted rapist and the victim's father.[68] Alberto Onori discusses a peace accord in a seduction case that he characterizes as *stupro* in Valdinievole in 1325.[69] However, the rarity of notarial peace pacts settling rape cases does not mean that settlements were rare in practice, since they could be made orally before the judge, as did Bonaiuxina and Fulcherus.

If a woman and her kin did not seek to force a marriage, what was the point of charging rape or attempted rape? What benefits were possible? Bolognese judicial sentences for attempted rape in this period often not only imposed a fine but required the perpetrator to make peace with the victim.[70] The settlement might mean that the victim received a payment. Kumhera, citing Baldus de Ubaldis, points out that in theory paying someone to make peace invalidated the concord. However, peace settlements could address the issue of compensation, including court and even medical costs. Both Kumhera and Wray explore ways in which payments that effectively were bribes could be worked into a peacemaking process.[71] It may also be that accusers or potential accusers hoped for a bribe that was distinct from a legal settlement, particularly when a high-status man was at risk of accusation by a poor woman.

A trial by inquisition of August 1295 from Bologna reveals one example of bribery of an alleged rape victim, in this case a large bribe to forestall an accusation. The case draws together the threads of this chapter: it includes enough context to indicate prior relations between an alleged rapist and victim, their status differences, and also the probable role of community attitudes. The court was notified that Nicolao of the elite Bentivoglio family had entered the house of a woman name Tomasina Lanfredi. Nicolao "grabbed her by force and violently knew her, holding a knife to her throat and saying to her 'unless you do my will I will kill you.'" Tomasina "because of Nicolao's power and her fear" had not dared to accuse him.[72] The notification was anonymous. The notifier listed sixteen witnesses, including eleven from San Egidio, Tomasina's parish.

The first witness in the initial trial, on 13 August, was the alleged victim, Tomasina. She denied the rape, and explained that on a Saturday evening in June she opened her door to her godmother's knock, and Nicolao quickly entered along with that woman. Tomasina told him to leave and cried out for help; he put his hand on her throat but did not harm her and left. The godmother, deposed four days later, agreed, stating that she went to Tomasina's house at Nicolao's request because he wanted to rest and stable his horse there before riding out to his villa. In all, eleven witnesses supported this story, including Bonamico Bonjohanis, nicknamed Micolo. Tomasina was his *amasia*, but he had been out in the *contado* for eight days and had only heard on his return that she had cried out for help.

Then, three local witnesses broke with the given story. One woman stated that it was *publica fama* in the neighborhood that Nicolao had forced Tomasina, placing a knife at her throat, and that she accepted money from him to not speak the truth. She had heard from some that it was 50 gold *soldi*, others said 50 *lire*. When her husband testified, he was more specific. He had not been there, but it was common knowledge in Nicolao's street that he had entered her house against her will and raped her, and many people were drawn to the fracas. He also testified that the priest of her parish, San Egidio, brokered an oral agreement between them, making Nicolao pay her 50 *lire* to keep silent. He had also heard that Nicolao's friends had made "big efforts" to keep him from being inculpated.

Two points are important. First, 50 *lire* was a very large bribe, potentially a substantial dowry. For context, Adelina Teutonica's assessment of 18 *lire* made her the wealthiest foreigner in the *estimo*. Adelina's house was valued at 16 *lire*. Second, the status discrepancy is crucial. Tomasina was an *amasia*; her *amasio* Micolo testified that she had been with him for over eight years, that he had promised to marry her but had not done so. She lived in San Egidio, one of the three poorest parishes in the quarter of Porta Piera, outside the *Circla* walls, which meant on the city's periphery.[73] Micolo's status is unclear, though his long relationship with Tomasina suggests that he was unable to marry. His eight-day stay in the *contado* in July probably means that he was taking part in the harvest, like other witnesses in the trial. Nicolao by contrast was a member of the Bentivoglio, a rising family in Bologna's *popolo* regime. In the 1290s, family members were well placed in two powerful guilds, the butchers and the notaries. In 1294, fourteen Bentivoglio belonged to the butchers' guild, giving them access to civic office. Family members had extensive rural lands, probably used for raising cattle; Nicolao mentioned riding out to his villa in his testimony. The Nicolao imputed in the trial may have been one of the nine sons of Bentivoglio, the family founder, in which case he would have been inscribed in the butchers' guild, though he may instead have been a grandson.[74] Given the family's political prominence, it is not surprising that a witness had heard that Nicolao's friends made "big efforts" to avoid having him inculpated for this rape, especially in 1295, when the regime was struggling because of a desperate war with Azzo VIII d'Este, marchese of Ferrara. Was a peace settlement between a man of his wealth and political status with an *amasia* imaginable, either through a notarial document or a statement before the judge?

On 19 August, Nicolao responded to the court's summons and told a story that was very close to Tomasina's: he had merely wanted to rest and stable his horse before riding out to his villa. When she told him to leave, he did touch her chest, she cried out and he left. The next day, however, he confessed to premeditated rape. It is possible that he was tortured. Rape was on the list of crimes for which torture was permissible, if the court had strong indications that a charge was true, but lacked proof, which required two eyewitnesses or a confession. As a member of the guilds and arms societies, Nicolao was a privileged person who could be tortured only with the permission of the *capitano del Popolo*, in the presence of six *anziani*.[75] The court was most apt to torture privileged *popolani* in cases of fraud, forgery and false testimony. In this case, three witnesses had provided indications of false testimony. Another clue that he was tortured is that he was called to the judge's bench to reaffirm his confession, since a confession made under torture had to be repeated away from the place of torture. After Nicolao's confession, the trial hinged on Tomasina's character. Thirteenth-century jurists held that only a woman who was *honesta* could be the victim of a rape.[76] She produced six witnesses who testified to her good character. All testified that she was considered a good, honest woman. She had stayed with Micolo for eight years at his request, he treated her as an honest woman, the couple had a daughter, she at times wore a ring. Micolo concurred: he lived with his father but had been with Tomasina, often staying with her, for over eight years, He "treated her as a wife in bed and at table and in other necessities."

On 23 August, Nicolao produced four guarantors, all Bentivoglio, and posted a 600-*lire* security. His defense was read: Tomasina was a woman of vile condition and dishonest life, and had been vile and *inhonesta* in the neighborhood for many years. Eight witnesses testified to her sharp tongue, bad character, and promiscuity. That same day someone filed a new notification to the court: two months earlier Petruciolo, described as a wine carrier and notorious thief, had persuaded Tomasina to open her door, and Nicolao rushed in and attempted to rape her, but the crowd of people drawn to her cries prevented it.[77] The charge was against Petruciolo, but the notification suggested that Nicolao had made a prior attack, using the same *modus operandi*. Ultimately, Nicolao was fined 300 *lire*, the standard penalty against a false witness in a civil case.

We can draw some conclusions from this trial. First, although impulsive, opportunistic sexual assaults surely took place, rapes also were often planned and could be strategic. Nicolao planned this assault: he clearly knew who Tomasina's godmother was and somehow persuaded the woman to trick Tomasina and get him in the door, a shocking betrayal of her role as spiritual parent. Nicolao may have made a previous effort to rape Tomasina, using the same *modus operandi*. I know nothing further about relations among Tomasina, Nicolao, and perhaps Micolo, but the attacks may well have been part of a larger conflict.

Second, the case points to some reasons why a poor, unmarried woman might file an accusation of rape, or at least consider one. She would have less concern for honor and reputation than a dowered woman from a prosperous family. The easy and inexpensive availability of the initial stage of the court procedure meant that an accusation was possible, and presented a real potential threat to her assailant. She might hope for a settlement, or in a case with less status discrepancy, perhaps a marriage. She also might hope for a fine, for damages, even for a bribe. Perhaps she even hoped for justice. In a case involving a high-status man and an *amasia*, the risk was to the reputation of the alleged rapist and his family, not to the alleged victim. In Nicolao's case, perhaps there was also fear of damage to a struggling regime, a possibility supported by the statement that Nicolao's friends made "big efforts" to avoid a charge, by the size of the bribe and by Nicolao's evident willingness to give false testimony.

The case allows us to glimpse how community attitudes could play a role in the outcome of a rape case. When the parish priest brokered the deal, he may well have intended to aid Tomasina—who had lived in his parish for at least eight years—and perhaps also to protect her from the threat of harsher efforts to prevent her from accusing Nicolao. Further, members of the community may have been angry about the rape, and reluctant to see Nicolao escape justice. Some of Tomasina's neighbors knew about the sexual assault and the bribe, and had the courage to testify to them. And of course, someone chose to notify the court of the rape.

Finally, why did the rate of rape cases evidently decline between the late thirteenth and late fourteenth centuries? It would be odd to argue that this was somehow a result of a change in the pattern of survival of criminal court registers. It also would be implausible to suggest that the actual rate of rapes declined. Sarah Blanshei has suggested another explanation: a dramatic reduction in the number and accessibility of accusation trials linked to political developments. During the 1296–99 crisis caused by the war with the lord of Ferrara, the regime raised money by denying tax delinquents the ability to file a complaint or defend themselves in court. Most significantly, she argues, the regime in 1310 and 1319 granted privileged status and legal immunities to thousands of members of the guilds and arms societies, including immunity from prosecution for all but capital crimes. The effect was to diminish the number of accusation trials and also "to make accusation procedure a vehicle for inter-class conflict rather than intra-class conflict resolution."[78] The accessibility of accusation procedure, characteristic of the 1280s and the 1290s, soon faded in the following decades and Blanshei finds a continuing decline in accusation trials throughout the fourteenth century. In effect, charges of rape or attempted rape declined with accusation trials and the increasing politicization of justice. This is a strong hypothesis that could be pursued through a comparison of the proportion of rape cases and the status of the victims in accusation and inquisition trials in the 1280s with the proportion and victim status in the second decade of the fourteenth century.

I have suggested in this essay that the evidence of accusation cases from the Bolognese criminal court from 1286, 1287, and 1289 raises questions about current scholarly assumptions concerning charges of rape or attempted rape. There are far more cases than research on other Italian cities or Bologna in the late fourteenth century would suggest. Why? A part of the answer may be the inexpensive accessibility of accusation procedure in its initial stage. Analysis of the often thin evidence for the status of alleged victims shows that a large number of them were poor, unmarried women. They may have been less worried about reputation and honor than higher-status women and their families, and might have charged rape in hopes of a settlement that would benefit them.

NOTES

1. See, for example, Dean, *Crime in Medieval Europe,* 82, and Lansing, "Conflicts over Gender."
2. Brundage, *Law, Sex, and Christian Society*, 469–70.
3. There is an extensive literature on victim-blaming in modern rape cases. A critical early study is Brownmiller, *Against Our Will.*
4. Brundage, "Rape and Seduction," 144–45, discusses the opinions of medieval jurists on female honesty.
5. The knight rapes the shepherdess in 38 of 160 extant pastourelles. See Karras, *Sexuality in Medieval Europe*, 163, based on Barsch, *Romances et Pastourelles françaises*, 2:17; translated in Gravdal, *Ravishing Maidens*, 110–11.
6. Andreas Capellanus, *The Art of Courtly Love*, 150.
7. Woods, "Rape and the Pedagogical Rhetoric." See the discussion in Karras, *From Boys to Men*, 77–78.
8. Jed, *Chaste Thinking*; Russell, "Courtship, Violence and the Formation of Marriage." Boccaccio, *Decameron,* 2,7 and 2,10 for examples.
9. For an overview with extensive bibliography, see Kuehn, "Conflict Resolution."
10. Lansing, "Humiliation and the Exercise of Power."
11. ASF, Capitano del Popolo 103, fols. 7r and 22r; Atti dell'Esecutore degli Ordinamenti di Giustizia 119, fol. 40r; 122, fols. 5r and 14r–15r.
12. ASB, Accusationes, Busta 8a, Register 10, fols. 1rv; Register 11, fol. 16r.
13. Dean, *Crime and Justice*, Ch. 3, and Idem "Fathers and Daughters."
14. Dean, *Crime in Medieval Europe*, 82.
15. Karras, *Sexuality in Medieval Europe,* 146.
16. Kittel, "Rape in Thirteenth-Century England. Also Hanawalt, *'Of Good and Ill Repute,'* 131–32.
17. Casagrande and Pazzaglia, "'Bona mulier in domo.'" The registers derive from 1262–63, 1286, and 1287.
18. Laufenberg, "Women, Crime and Criminal Law," 42–43, 337–39.
19. Cohn, *Women in the Streets*, 30.
20. Dean, *Crime and Justice*, 140.
21. Brundage, "Rape and Seduction," 141–48. On the evolution of understandings of *raptus* in late medieval English law, see Kelly, "Statutes of Rapes."
22. Fasoli and Sella, *Statuti di Bologna dell'anno 1288*, 1:139–40, Bk. IV, Rubric 30, "De pena adulterium et strupum vel incestum committentis tam in masculo quam in feminis."
23. Dean, *Crime and Justice*, 139–40.
24. For contemporary discussions of the threat posed by passionate emotion, see Lansing, *Passion and Order*, chapter 6.

25. Trombetti Budriesi, *Lo Statuto del comune di Bologna dell'anno 1335*, 1:693. Bk. VIII, Rubric 67, "De pena adulterium vel strupum comitentis in feminam vel mascullum. Rubrica."

26. Kantorowicz, *Albertus Gandinus,* 2:398–99, discussed in Blanshei, *Politics and Justice,* 322–23.

27. ASF, Atti dell'Esecutore degli Ordinamenti di Giustizia, 69, fols. 48r–50r.

28. Blanshei, *Politics and Justice*, 485.

29. ASB, Accusationes, Busta 5a, Register 7, fols. 2r, 3r, 4v; Register 8, fol 18r; Register 10, fol. 8v, 11r; Busta 5b, Register 17, fols. 21v, 22v; Busta 5a, Register 1, fols. 17r, 40r; Busta 6b, Register 7, fol. 16v; Busta 8b, Register 10, fol. 7v.

30. ASB, Accusationes, Busta 8a, Register 14, fol 7v.

31. ASB, Accusationes Busta 5a, Register 2, trial of 8 May, 1296 (unclear pagination).

32. ASB, Accusationes, Buste 5a, 5b, 6a, 6b, 8a, 8b.

33. ASB, Accusationes, Busta 5b, Register 16 and Busta 6b, Register 13. For an inventory of condemnation registers see Blanshei, *Politics and Justice*, 335n.

34. I found twenty-six cases or sentences in ASB, Accusationes, Busta 5a, ten in Busta 5b, six in Busta 6a, fifteen in Busta 6b, nine in Busta 8a, and seventeen in Busta 8b.

35. Cases that identify the victim as unmarried, with a dead father and make no mention of other male kin are ASB, Accusationes, Busta 5a, Register 1, fol 23v; Register 2, fols. 11r, 65r, 121r; Register 3, fol. 26r; Register 5, fol. 1v; Register 8, fol. 6r; Register 10, fol. 10v; Busta 5b, Register 18, fol. 17v, Register 19, fol. 8r, Busta 6a, Register 1, fols. 36v, 89v; Register 3, fol. 13v; Busta 6b, Register 10, fols. 52v, 68r; Register 11, fol. 2v; Register 14, fol. 2; Register 15, fol. 4v, 5v, 22r; Busta 8a, Register 1, fol. 79r; Register 8, fol, 20v; Busta 8b, Register 10, fols. 1r, 40r; Register 11, fols. 6v, 14v, 16r; Register 14, fols. 6v, 7v, 38r.

36. E-mail communication of 9 September, 2017.

37. For cases of women with a *curator* who probably lacked parents or resources: ASB, Accusationes, Busta 5a, Register 2, trial of May 8, 1296 (unclear pagination); Busta 5b, Register 17, fol. 22v; Busta 6a, Register 1, fols. 17r; Busta 6b, Register 15, fol. 24r; Busta 8a, Register 12, fol. 20r. For cases of women with a *curator* and no mention of a husband or male kin: ASB, Accusationes, Busta 5a, Register 2, fols. 11r; Busta 6a, Register 1, fols. 36v, 89v; Busta 8a, Register 1, fol. 78v; Register 7, fol. 16v; Register 10, fol. 1r; Register 11, fol. 14v; Register 14, fols. 6r, 7v, 38r.

38. ASB, Accusationes, Busta 6a, Register 1, fol. 36v.

39. ASB, Accusationes, Busta 6a, Register 15, fol. 4v.

40. ASB, Accusationes, Busta 8a, Register 1, fols. 78v.

41. The entire source has been digitized and is available at http://www.centrofasoli.unibo.it/asbo/index.html#.

42. Bocchi, "Le imposte dirette"; Pini, "Gli estimi cittadini"; Giansante, *L'usurario onorato*, Ch. 3; Smurra, *Città, cittadini e imposta diretta*. The latter work provides a valuable study of the *estimo*'s statutory and institutional framework.

43. These had to be listed if they were over 100 *corbe*. A *corba* was 78.64 liters for dry goods and 78.59 for wet. Smurra, *Città, cittadini e imposta diretta*, 204.

44. Giansante, *L'usurario onorato*, Table 13, 191.

45. Smurra, *Città, cittadini, e imposta diretta*, 157.

46. Klapisch-Zuber, "Female Celibacy."

47. Smurra, "Studiare, lavorare a Bologna." She discusses Adelina on 92 and 104.

48. Fanti, "Le lottizzazioni monastiche."

49. See Lansing, "Concubines, Lovers, Prostitutes." On concubinage see Karras, *Unmarriages: Women, Men and Sexual Unions.*

50. Stuard, "Brideprice, Dowry."

51. ASB, Accusationes, Busta 5b, Register 11, fol. 18v may be an example.

52. ASB, Accusationes, Busta 6a, Register 1, fol. 17r.

53. ASB, Inquisitiones, Mazzo 3, fols. 21r–22v. I discuss both these cases in "Concubines, Lovers, Prostitutes," 93–94.

54. Vallerani, *Medieval Public Justice*, 127–28.

55. Vallerani, *Medieval Public Justice*, 129–30.

56. Quoted by Vallerani, *Medieval Public Justice*, 124–25.

57. Vallerani, *Medieval Public Justice*, 158–59.
58. There is a rich literature on dispute resolution. See Dean, *Crime and Justice*, 18–20.
59. ASB, Inquisitiones, Mazzo 46, Register 2, fols. 41r–47v.
60. Vallerani, *Medieval Public Justice*, 192–94.
61. Brundage, *Law, Sex, and Christian Society*, 396–98. See also Brundage, "Rape and Seduction," 141–48, esp. 146 for the discussion of marriages between the accused and the victim.
62. ASB, Accusationes, Busta 8a, Register 3, fol. 79r.
63. Kumhera, *The Benefits of Peace*, 208–10.
64. ASB, Inquisitiones, Mazzo 12, Register 5, fols. 15r–18v, January 9–16, 1288.
65. Blanshei, *Politics and Justice*, 344. She cites ASB, Inquisitiones, Mazzo 4, fols. 50v–52v.
66. Wray, "Instruments of Concord."
67. Kumhera, *The Benefits of Peace*, Appendix B, Table 5, 265.
68. Jansen, "'Pro bono pacis.'" The peace over the rape case is discussed in her *Peace and Penance*, 121-25.
69. Onori, "Pace Privata e regolamentazione della vendetta." The peace is discussed on 222–23.
70. See ASB, Accusationes, Busta 6b, Register 10, fol. 52v and Register 15, fol. 4v.
71. Kumhera, *The Benefits of Peace*, 241; Wray, "Instruments of Concord," 747.
72. ASB, Inquisitiones, Mazzo 35, Register 6, fols. 32r–42r. This account is based on my more extensive discussion of the case in "Conflicts over Gender."
73. Giansante, *L'usurario onorato*, Table 7, 181.
74. Bentivoglio-held offices included *anziano*, consul, and advisor to the guild. Blanshei in *Politics and Justice*, 544, ranked them tenth among families holding twenty or more terms of office in the *consiglio del popolo*. See Antonelli and Poli, *Il Palazzo dei Bentivoglio*, 13–23 for a meticulous reconstruction of the family's guild memberships, civic offices, and properties.
75. Blanshei, *Politics and Justice*, 321, 331.
76. Brundage, "Rape and Seduction," 144–45.
77. ASB, Inquisitiones, Mazzo 35, Register 4, fols. 24r–26v.
78. See the chapter by Sarah Blanshei in this volume.

Chapter Nine

To the Podestà or the Inquisitor?

Adjudicating Violence against God in Bologna, 1250–1450

Melissa Vise

> " . . . it becomes difficult for the secular liberal to understand the passion that informs those for whom, rightly or wrongly, *it is impossible to remain silent when confronted with blasphemy* . . . "
> Talal Asad, *Is Critique Secular?*[1]

During the thirteenth century the medieval communes of northern Italy increasingly enacted a number of so-called "morality" laws. Statutes punishing gambling, prostitution, insult and blasphemy, sumptuary laws, and harsh anti-adultery laws are some of the legal injunctions typically associated with this development.[2] Many historians tie the increase in moral policing to the rise of the *popolo*, often citing the *popolo*'s efforts to achieve self-legitimization by invoking a sacralized "law and order" rhetoric. The laws of the *popolo* were, in the dominant political rhetoric, the laws of peace and order.[3]

The extent of the gap between the rhetoric and practice of these policies has been studied by both historians of rhetoric and social historians.[4] Others have investigated the relation of procedure (accusation vs. inquisition) to the type of crime prosecuted.[5] Yet one crucial aspect of these morality laws—and I would argue, of law and order in the commune generally—has been overlooked: their relation to similar criminalization patterns in ecclesiastical organs of justice. Standard analyses of crime and criminality tend to study the history of crime according to individual jurisdictions—that of the podestà or that of the friar inquisitor.[6] In part, this historiographical tradition stems from a continuing approach to legal history that separates secular from ecclesiastical courts. In this chapter I show that the prosecution of blasphemy in

Bologna demonstrates how this methodological tendency can obscure more than it reveals about justice and violence in communal Italy.

The crucial determinant of jurisdictional crossover in the prosecution of blasphemy was not the authorities' concern for public morality. Or better said, it was not *simply* their concern for public morality that brought cases of blasphemy before both ecclesiastical and secular courts. Rather, blasphemy occupied a semantic space in communal thought that bridged two categories: the immoral *and* the violent. While certainly considered immoral, blasphemy was also—and more importantly—viewed as a violence. This chapter will first assess dominant European and local Italian thought on blasphemy in order to offer a context for the statutory and case history of blasphemy in Bologna. Second, it will investigate court practices, a study made possible by the special wealth of preserved documents in the Bolognese archives. In addition to the records of cases of blasphemy brought before the podestà, two registers of the Dominican inquisition into heresy have survived. Reading both the civic and inquisition records allows us to recognize blasphemy as the prosecutable violence that it represented to the citizens of the commune.

TERMS AND METHOD

Definitions of blasphemy in the Christian West changed with some frequency. As a sin that also became defined as a crime in various jurisdictions, secular and ecclesiastical, blasphemy could often occupy a rather ambiguous cultural and legal place. Augustine has been credited with one of the reigning medieval definitions for blasphemy: "To say evil words against God."[7] But even in the early Church, his was in fact only one of many interpretations.[8] In medieval Italy, pastoral theologians and jurists thus inherited a wealth of definitions for blasphemy, but little in the way of clarity. Therefore they often attempted to differentiate blasphemy of the heart from blasphemy of the mouth, blasphemy of the Holy Spirit from simple blasphemy, blasphemy against God in opposition to blasphemy against God's saints, and even occasionally placed heresy and blasphemy together in some ambiguous definitional territory. Aquinas offered one of the clearest articulations of what has been called the tripartite definition: "According to some, there are three kinds of blasphemy. The first of these is when something unfitting is affirmed of God; the second is when something fitting is denied of Him; and the third, when something proper to God is ascribed to a creature."[9] Later theologians borrowed this definition freely, seemingly without realizing or caring that Aquinas himself had postulated that definition only to dispute it. For Aquinas, blasphemy as a sin existed only in the will of the blasphemer—it could not, by definition, truly cause harm to an impassible God. Instead, blasphemy resided in the will to detest God and thus belonged in the category of unbelief, the most grievous of all possible sins. Its intended object (God) made it more evil than murder categorically, but its effect (none) made its punishment less severe than that for murder in the terrestrial sphere.

Domenico Cavalca (ca. 1270–1342), a Dominican preacher, prolific writer, and translator, active most of his life in Pisa or its territory, acknowledged the many definitions of blasphemy in his *Pungilingua*, or *Prick of the Tongue*. The text was an Italian vernacularization and expansion of the last chapter of William Peraldus's *Summa de virtutibus et vitiis*, a text which had inaugurated an eighth category of deadly sin, the sins of the tongue.[10] After quickly listing some of the many definitions for blasphemy, Domenico chose to focus on "vocal blasphemy, by which man uses his tongue to say words in contempt of God or to curse Him or to reproach Him or—to the shame of Him and his mother—to name or recall those members which God in His charity assumed for us."[11] For Domenico, the blasphemy that mattered most was the verbal kind that aims to affect some kind of harm on the deity. His approach differs from Aquinas, largely because his focus was on pastoral and social concerns, rather than on a strictly theoretical or scholastic goal. Like any good pastoral writer, Domenico sought to inculcate within his readers' hearts the "right hate" or detestation of sin that could save their souls.

Domenico amended Peraldus's text in significant ways, adjusting the text for the lay reader.[12] Not only did he add and embellish existing *exempla*, he also reframed the text to better fit an Italian communal context. Unlike later writers of the fifteenth century, Domenico did not view blasphemy as a source of God's wrath.[13] Rather, for him the problem with blasphemy was its inherently violent nature. It was not atypical for pastoral writers to compare the tongue of the blasphemer to various kinds of weapons, and this trope Domenico certainly borrows from Peraldus. However, in a telling moment, immediately after relating an *exemplum* that compares blasphemy to shooting an arrow into the heart of one's beloved father, he departs from his model text and implores his readers to legislate against blasphemy: "Many rulers use their power to hunt heretics and other malefactors on account of justice: better that they should all the more quickly hunt down these cursed blasphemers because they are much worse [than heretics and other criminals]."[14] The violence of blasphemy, like that of heresy and other crimes, merits capital punishment. Thus, Domenico departs from Aquinas not only in his definition of blasphemy but also in the severity of the punishment he deems it merits.[15]

Blasphemy was no clearer to the jurists than it was to the theologians. They considered it a *crimen mixti fori*—it could be subject to both spiritual and temporal powers. But normally, even after the inauguration of the office of the inquisition into heresy, this meant an offender would be charged either in the bishop's or the podestà's court. The *Decretals* of Gregory IX of 1234 assigned an elaborate penance for the blasphemer before the bishop, but left open the possibility of a *tandem* prosecution by the podestà.[16] The renowned jurist Bartolo da Sassaferrato (1313–57) did not directly treat the question of jurisdiction in his known *consilia*, but he did consult on the issue of distinguishing heresy from blasphemy. According to him, pure blasphemy was distinguished from blasphemy that smacked of heresy by the circumstances and the mind of the blasphemer. In theory, an orthodox person could say something like "may God be cursed" without actually meaning to imply any disbelief in the articles of faith.[17] Nevertheless, he deferred to the Church as the final arbiter on these matters. Blasphemy was thus by no means a straightforward juridical or theological category. What can already be seen in Domenico Cavalca's work, and what the following survey of trial records in Bologna will confirm, is that while blasphemy may share some of the moral opprobrium encoded in the naming of the obscene, it was in fact far more than that to its medieval witnesses. That is, if blasphemy might have been obscene—leaving aside the difficulty of reconstructing that category for an era long past—it was also, and more importantly, a violence.

Although their histories are not generally told together, the courts of the podestà and the inquisitor shared many features: a common procedure, language, counsel-seeking process, use of notaries and heralds, and—as the case of Bologna demonstrates—the deviances they prosecuted. While their jurisdictions sometimes clashed and contemporaries for the most part would have acknowledged their differing competencies, we run the danger of losing sight of the common culture underlying both institutions when we too cleanly isolate the ecclesiastical from the civic courts. This is especially the case for blasphemy, which was a sin (subject to confession), a crime (subject to the podestà), and criminally sinful (precociously, subject to the inquisitor). Reading the two bodies of records together, as is done in this chapter, with an eye to cultural history, furnishes a wide-angle lens with which to view the economy of linguistic deviance in the communes.

While scholars like James Given have begun to excavate the institutional and bureaucratic originality of heresy inquisition courts and their influence on the development of civic courts, cultural and social historians in general—even when explicitly addressing the complexity of the religious-political matrix of the Italian communes—still tend to restrict their attention to one court at a time.[18] Given reads the inquisition as symptomatic of (or perhaps just a bit more successful than) medieval governance generally. He compiles documentation to show that political power in medieval society was a highly negotiated phenomenon, dependent on situational contingencies and the mastery of techniques of discipline (record-keeping, organization, educative punishment, etc.).[19] I develop Given's basic insight of the interdependency of these bureaucratic structures by examining their documentation together and by embedding my interpretation within the matrix of a localized history of blasphemy.

CIVIC COURTS

For insulting God, the Virgin Mary, or the saints by the crime of blasphemy, the earliest surviving Bolognese statutes of 1250 mandated a 40-*soldi* fine or a public whipping—markedly lenient in comparison to later iterations of the same statute. The statute explicitly ties blasphemy to gambling (which is also condemned).[20] Moreover, anyone who witnessed the blasphemy but did not report it was also subject to a penalty.[21] According to the statutes of 1288, however, someone who blasphemed God, the Virgin Mary, or any of the saints would be fined 25 *lire*. If they could not pay the fine, they were to be led, head uncovered, by a chain through the city and stationed in the main piazza, there to suffer insult and have filth launched against them. If they were contumacious, they were to be placed under a ban until the fine was paid. If they were ever captured, their tongues were to be cut out unless they could pay the fine within three days.[22] In the next surviving statutory redaction (1335), the fine was increased to 50 *lire*.[23] The statutes of 1352 and 1357 retain the same penalties as those in 1335, but those from 1389 add an increased financial penalty for the second (100 *lire*) and third (150 *lire*) offenses. The final set of Bolognese statutes, those of 1454, contain exactly the same penalties.[24] Statutes from other communes, for example from Montepulciano in Tuscany, imposed similar penalties and reflect the same trend toward increasing monetary penalties.[25] The Bolognese statutes do not set limitations on the geographical spaces that were prosecutable for blasphemy, nor do they offer much in the way of explanation as to why blasphemy was considered to be a crime.

In certain cases, the extant trial records from Bologna reflect the statutory dictates, but in several telling ways they do not. Very few blasphemy trials survive from the period 1280–1450, even in years that have otherwise fairly complete records. For my sample, I compiled four cases by accusation in the late thirteenth century and seven by inquisition in the Tre and Quattrocento.[26] One might suppose that this means the *bolognesi* refrained from blaspheming their deity, but this seems quite unlikely given the tendency for blasphemy to follow quite closely upon gambling and in light of trials in other courts to be examined below. What is more likely, and what the extant records seem to indicate, is that other concerns governed the likelihood that blasphemers would find themselves charged in court. Citizens were unlikely to denounce and judges unlikely to act *ex officio* to prosecute a blasphemer unless the crime had occurred in certain locations. This tendency, however, did not remain constant over time. The trial records indicate that a gradual expansion took place in the circle of locations protected from blasphemy. They also detail an increasing severity in the fines and punishments imposed by the podestà's judges. Third, they offer some insights as to why blasphemy was considered such a serious criminal act.

The earliest records of blasphemy from the Duecento proceed as accusations and almost every trial ended with the accused party absolved and the accuser condemned to pay a small fine in court fees.[27] The reasons for an acquittal are rarely given and in this handful of cases we cannot be sure why the suits were unsuccessful.[28] Nevertheless, these trials do provide some compelling evidence. In November 1295, a certain Phillipus accused Laurentius, the son of Albertinus, of blaspheming while gambling in a private house. Laurentius was acquitted, but we have very little information about the trial itself. However, in his accusation, Phillipus alleged that Laurentius was "blaspheming God and the saints" by saying "cursed be God and the saints and Saint Mary" and many other "injurious words" (*verba iniuriosa*).[29] "*Verba iniuriosa* against the saints" was not part of the usual *libellus* for blasphemy accusations. Thus, one may assume that for Phillipus, blasphemy was the same kind of crime as *verba iniuriosa*—it just had a celestial target. In legal terms, injurious words were a kind of verbal assault. Indeed, as often as not, when a record of an assault case begins with the phrase "so-and-so assaulted . . . " (Petrus fecit insultum . . .), the case, in fact, turns out to be an allegation of a verbal threat, sometimes, but not always, promising physical assault in the future. Verbal assault was a kind of violence, and for Phillipus it was a violence against divine targets.

For the Trecento, I have found several *inquisitiones* into blasphemers and can begin to trace a trend to a broader circle of protected locations.[30] In 1355, a Milanese man named Ghironus de Tuschis was gambling in the courtyard of the Palazzo Nuovo, in which building—the record is careful to note—resided the *signore* of Bologna, Giovanni Visconti d'Oleggio. On an unlucky toss of the dice, Ghironus lost a small amount of money, at which point he blasphemed God and his mother saying "God can't do this," making the fig with both his fists against God, shouting against heaven and the saints, and then biting his fist.[31] In yet another blasphemy case lodged against him we learn that earlier that day Ghironus had been at the altar of the church of Santa Maria dei Rustigani to swear his indebtedness to Jacobus della Mirandola and to forswear any further litigation over the debt in the presence of the judge Jacobus de Naulis and his staff. During that ceremony, Ghironus had blasphemed God's power, vainly attempting to coerce divine aid in the payment of his debts.[32] Perhaps as he awaited his trial outside the court later that day, he had resorted to gambling his last *soldo* away in the hope of generating the money he owed; in any event, both outbursts involved a poor choice of location. And despite sharing a home city with the current *signore* of Bologna, he found no mercy coming his way. Each charge of blasphemy earned him a 50-*lire* fine or banishment from the city if he failed to pay.

From Ghironus's case we can make three important observations about the prosecution of blasphemy in this period. The two locations in which Ghironus had blasphemed—one, a church, the other, a government building—were highly charged spaces. Major crimes committed in either space could be subject to a double penalty. Later cases, as we will see, would not be limited by this geographical criterion. Second, Ghironus was not charged with gambling even though that was a prosecutable crime. This might seem to imply that in the eyes of the judges, games of hazard were of a different and less serious genre of criminality than the blasphemy that sometimes accompanied them. However, as Gregory Roberts points out in his chapter in this volume, charges of gambling were usually reported to the *ad maleficia* judge by the notary of the *corone ed armi* office, who kept separate records of such charges, so such a conclusion is problematic. Later cases before the inquisitor into heresy would parallel this judicial distinction. Third, the nature of the violence that blasphemy represented—a kind of insult to God—is made clearer by the fact that Ghironus engaged not only in verbal but also gestural assaults. Ghironus made the fig and then bit his fist—a grand provocation to an earthly foe and certainly egregious against a deity.[33]

A case from 1335 indicates that judges could consider physical repudiation of God and God's saints to be worthy of extreme punishment. In May of that year, a citizen of Bologna, Martinus Michaelis, was charged in somewhat ambiguous terms; he was alleged to have thrown a rock at an image of the Virgin Mary, straight in her face. The image was painted on the wall of the new prison below the Palazzo Vecchio. Martinus quickly confessed that he had indeed thrown a rock at the image. Perhaps his confession came under the influence of torture, although, as is often the case, no application of torture was recorded. While the trial notary did not transcribe the sentence, it has survived in the list of condemnations, bans, and absolutions of that year—he was condemned to be burned alive and a marginal note next to the sentence reports that it was carried out.[34] Like all sentences, Martinus's sentence concludes with language claiming that it follows the demands of the statutes of the city, but I have found nothing in the Bolognese statutes that could explain this punishment.[35] The corollary statutes from Montepulciano cited above explicitly define such attacks on images as blasphemy and leave them subject to the normal fines, not to immolation. Nor was Martinus under investigation for any other crime that I could find. The penalty seems patently to exceed the crime, so there may be hidden factors at work in this case. Whatever else stands behind Martinus's extreme sentence, it at least indicates that this judge believed that immolation was within the realm of possibilities for punishing an assault on a sacred image. Even if the theologians insisted that no mere human could truly hurt God, the judge in this case found that violent acts against celestial targets could be treated even more severely than similar acts against humans.

By the late Trecento, locations beyond the spiritual and political centers of the city had gained protection from blasphemy. In 1385, a Florentine named Nannes found himself on trial for having blasphemed the Virgin Mary while he stood under the portico of his own house. Nannes quickly confessed and three days later initiated proceedings before the court to prove that he was a pauper in order to have his fine mitigated. We do not know the outcome of that case.[36] By 1430, in addition to cases now originating from a wider geographical range, financial penalties had increased significantly. That February, Carolus, nicknamed Bandra, was gambling in a tavern and had a spat with a certain Giovanni about the next round. As a result, he began to blaspheme repeatedly against God and the Virgin, culminating with "By the cunt of the Virgin, you will play." For his litany of blasphemies he was banned from the city under the penalty of a 300-*lire* fine or the cutting out of his tongue—a fairly high fine for a citizen of the city, but perhaps he had blasphemed one time too many. Such heavy fines were more representative of the court of the podestà in Florence.

According to the 1322–25 statutes, blasphemy in Florence was roundly condemned and culprits were given a fine of 100 *lire* or a humiliating march through the city, beaten while naked.[37] Other court records show the judges exercising an even heavier hand. In 1353, when Çanobio blasphemed the name of Jesus Christ and the Virgin by saying "A fistula upon God and his holy mother," the judge remanded him to prison (Le Stinche) unless he paid a 800-*lire* fine. If Çanobio could not pay the full amount in fourteen days, he was to be whipped and beaten naked through the city.[38] In 1354, Giovanna did not fare much better when she was condemned for blaspheming Jesus Christ and his mother: "May God and the Virgin Mary get a fistula and in spite of God and the Virgin Mary, they cannot force me to do what I don't want to do." Her fine was 400 *lire* or a whipping and beating through the city.[39] To be caught blaspheming in Florence was to become impoverished or humiliated. But Florence may have been an outlier regarding blasphemy: cases from Lucca more closely follow the Bolognese pattern.[40]

To return to the case of Carolus in Bologna, besides his high fine as discussed above, also of note is the location of his alleged crime: a tavern. If blasphemy were to be expected anywhere, one might expect to hear it in the tavern and especially around a game of dice. Earlier, in the Trecento, blasphemy cases were more likely to be like that of Ghironus, that is, brought against people who had blasphemed in a church or government building. Later, as we see with Carolus and Nannes, the places protected from blasphemous speech had expanded. This trend parallels the contemporary history of *verba iniuriosa* cases in the Duecento and early Trecento, when they were almost exclusively prosecuted only if they infringed on spaces sacred to Church or commune. This may also explain why so few of the Duecento accusations resulted in a condemnation: almost none of them occurred in a sacred space. In contrast, in the later Tre and Quattrocento, *verba iniuriosa* in general, uttered anywhere in the city, found a ready ear and prosecuting hand in the judges of the podestà.[41]

In sum, the evidence from trial records before the podestà demonstrates an understanding of the *what* of blasphemy: namely that it was conceived of as a kind of violence. The civic trial records also indicate a growing severity of punishment against blasphemers, a trend that parallels the increasing severity with which the courts punished other crimes as well. And lastly, if at first blasphemy prosecution might have depended on the location in which the blasphemy was pronounced, eventually that point became moot with all zones of the city protected from violent blasphemous speech.

COURT OF THE INQUISITOR

Clerical authorities also were concerned with the sin of blasphemy, but mostly as a subject for preaching or confession. If Church authorities did prosecute blasphemy in any official capacity, it should have been in the bishop's court.[42] Therefore it is surprising to find an inquisitor into heresy who made blasphemy his special project.[43] Fra Johannes de San Domenico was the Dominican inquisitor in Bologna from 1392 to 1395. His register is the only medieval Bolognese register for heresy inquisition to survive besides another one from the turn of the thirteenth century that has been edited by Lorenzo Paolini and Raniero Orioli.[44] Fra Johannes's register is ninety-four folios long and contains twenty-eight prosecutions and fourteen convictions. The register is unique to this period because Fra Johannes did not try a single case of heresy.[45] Instead, almost all of the men and women who were summoned before him had blasphemed God and/or the saints, most often while gambling. While the later Roman and Spanish Inquisitions would pursue blasphemers with gusto, it was not the general practice of medieval inquisitors to do so—I know of no other inquisitor from the Middle Ages who prosecuted simple blasphemers. As noted earlier, the *Decretals* of Gregory IX assigned an elaborate penance for the blasphemer who appeared before the bishop, but left open the possibility of a *tandem* prosecution by the podestà.[46] They are silent on any role for the inquisitor. Indeed, other Dominican writers like Peraldus and Cavalca had worked at length to differentiate heresy from blasphemy in order to demonstrate how much more evil blasphemy was—at least heretics believed what they said. Fra Johannes looks even more unusual when compared to his confreres Fra Guido da Vicenza and Fra Guido da Parma from the earlier Bolognese heresy inquisition register. They never hunted for blasphemers *per se*, although their notaries did use the verb "blasfemare" to depict insults hurled at the inquisitor and his Dominican brothers.[47] Even Bartolo da Sassaferrato did not suggest that the inquisitor adjudicate cases of heresy that might be blasphemy, but rather that the pope do so.[48] Moreover, it is not clear whether or not the podestà ceased his own prosecutions for blasphemy during Fra Johannes's tenure.[49] So, what then was Fra Johannes's objective? Was he the advance guard of the early modern expansion of the inquisitorial leviathan?

The dangers of heresy and heretical speech had long been noted by clerical writers and civic legislators. As in many other communes, Florentine law provided as part of the punishment of heretics that they be silenced in the commune.[50] The speech of condemned heretics was not to be trusted in any way: it could not be listened to and certainly could not be used in court or in official communal capacities. The speech of heretics, whether about their heresy or any words spoken in an official forum, was fundamentally dangerous to proper civic order. Thus, although in communal juridical practice the distinction between blasphemy and heresy was relatively clear, both were crimes of speech and the sheer danger that each of them posed to both civic and ecclesiastical leaders created considerable potential for elision between their jurisdictions.

A manual for heresy inquisition from Bologna written circa 1321 does not discuss blasphemy *per se* but does leave the interpretive door open to its possible inclusion within the inquisitional mandate. Its author remains anonymous but was almost certainly a Dominican theologian. According to him, even if the accused should claim that they said heretical errors out of levity, anger, a joke, or confusion, the inquisitor must carefully weigh their excuses "because almost all modern heretics excuse themselves in this way."[51] The author does not fully resolve the question, merely citing the opinion of those who say that even if the accused's excuses prove true (that they spoke from anger or levity), they should still be punished because a person saying things for those reasons still "ought not be pronouncing heretical words (*verba heretica*) against the faith and good mores."[52] Heretical words spoken, no matter the reason, must be punished. The danger was one of publicity: erroneous words eddying into the aural space of the faithful posed a clear and present danger. According to this logic, actual belief, although important, was not the sole reason for punishing *verba heretica*.

The Catalonian inquisitor, Nicholas Eymerich, in his *Directorium inquisitorium*, written sometime after 1376, treats the issue more directly. Eymerich distinguishes between simple and heretical blasphemy. The former includes words "which do not forswear the articles of faith, such as ascribing wickedness to God or the Virgin, cursing them, or not exhibiting gratitude to God." These simple blasphemers Nicholas sends to the courts of secular justice.[53] Heretical blasphemers are those:

> who offer words against the articles of faith, such as those who infringe on God's omnipotence by saying God has not the time or cannot do whatsoever deeds, which is against the article of faith to believe in one omnipotent God the Father. Or who cast dirtiness on Blessed Virgin Mary, mother of God by saying that she is a whore or other words equal in their effect, which is against

the article of faith to believe the son of God conceived of the Holy Spirit and born of the Virgin Mary.[54]

Such words were heretical blasphemy and, Nicholas believed, merited the investigations of the inquisitor. The zealous inquisitor could make the case that even simple blasphemies contradicted an article of faith in some way. In any event, Nicholas further qualifies heretical blasphemy by taking into account the context in which it may have been uttered. If the person blasphemes very frequently during and outside of gambling, the inquisitor may not need to prosecute, but should make sure the accused abjures any heresy and should remain vigilant, since such language may be an indication that the accused is indeed a heretic. If a person blasphemes infrequently and only while gambling, the inquisitor need only be mildly suspicious, but should ensure that the accused abjures all heresy nonetheless.[55] Thus, Nicholas maintains a somewhat blurred distinction between the types of blasphemous speech with which the inquisitor should be concerned, leaving the door wide open for inquisitors to expand their jurisdiction. And indeed, that is what would occur a few centuries later in the Spanish Inquisition, which primarily relied on Nicholas's manual for procedure.

There is no evidence to suggest that Fra Johannes read Nicholas's manual. In fact, it seems unlikely that he did since he made no effort to discern whether the blasphemers also believed the heresy their blasphemies suggested. Nicholas's logic was not Fra Johannes's. Fra Johannes's description of the sins he investigated accents the fluidity between the categories of blasphemy and heresy: almost uniformly he or his notaries describe the illicit speech as *verba heretica*.[56] Even the most banal of blasphemies, the ubiquitous "God cannot make [me lose/marry your daughter/etc.] . . . " (*El non porave fare*), is labeled as such. There is only one instance of *blasfemando* in the entire register.[57] All but one of Fra Johannes's fourteen convictions are for what elsewhere would be identified as blasphemous words, half of them taking place in the context of gambling. The single exception is that of the repeat offender, the prostitute Nobile of Verona who not only was accused of saying "Not even God can . . . " [*sic*, left incomplete by the notary] and, more specifically, "God cannot make it that my cunt is not worth more than those of most other women in this land," but was also charged with two related sorcery charges: trying to use a consecrated host as a love charm, and instructing a young woman on how to curse her lover. Yet even Nobile received punishment only for the blasphemous speech to which she confessed. Her penance was a year's worth of weekly visits to Santa Maria in Monte, a chapel about an hour's uphill walk outside the city walls. Because she was able to guess the name of her accuser and his motive, the charges for the other alleged crimes were dismissed.[58]

Nobile's penance reflects the kind of punishment Fra Johannes's blasphemers received for *verba heretica*. For example, Dom Berço confessed to and was absolved for saying "Neither God nor his mother can make it that you will win this toss."[59] He received a penance of fasting every Saturday for a year, making an offering of a candle to the church of San Domenico (the inquisitor's home church), and a fine of 10 gold *ducats* payable to the bishop should he ever again in his mortal life play at dice.[60] In his sentencing, Fra Johannes seems to have been following the sense, if not the letter, of canon law. According to Gregory's *Decretals*, a blasphemer condemned before a bishop had to present himself before the church doors for seven successive Sundays, fast on bread and water for a week before the final Sunday, and perform some act of charity. If the criminal were a poor man, the bishop could also consign him to the temporal powers for further punishment; if rich, the bishop could fine him 40 *soldi*.[61]

Raniero Orioli maintains that Fra Johannes's pattern of assigning penance signifies that the inquisitor was not motivated by a zeal for persecution nor by the prospect of economic gain, but rather by moral concerns. It is this concern, he believes, that differentiates the inquisitor's motives from the interests of civic officials to regulate the economic impact of gambling. In Orioli's eyes, Fra Johannes stepped in to fill the gap left by a complacent secular power and the divisive ecclesiastical politics of the Schism.[62] I agree with Orioli regarding what seems to be Fra Johannes's ethical motivations, but do not think his steps indicate a desire or need to fill any perceived gap on the part of the secular powers. It would be a mistake to think the statute writers and civic judges did not maintain a concern for citizens' morality, as the earliest sets of statutes regarding blasphemy mentioned above indicate otherwise. Moreover, given the penitential nature of his sentencing, the inquisitor was trespassing just as much on the sphere of influence of the parish priest—to whom all parishioners were obliged to confess their sins, including blasphemy—as on that of the podestà.

More importantly, as I have been arguing here, what allows for this semantic jump from prosecuting heresy to prosecuting blasphemy is the understanding that both are forms of verbal violence. The only crimes Fra Johannes condemned were cases of blasphemy. He did not condemn the prostitute Nobile for accusations of love magic; nor did he follow up on accusations against a priest who owned a book of love charms; and he released without charges a parish priest who was interrogated about a love-magic dabbling parishioner.[63] Fra Johannes's efforts were not the work of an officious general moralist but rather a defined response to the violence of words. In fact, what differentiated the inquisitor's prosecution of blasphemy from the podestà's was not the perceived genre of the crime, but rather what kind of juridical response might best combat this kind of violence.

Penances like Dom Berço's were clearly designed not simply to punish, but to rehabilitate the blasphemer. His penance was intended to remove the near occasion of sin (gambling), to disincline the tongue toward repeat error by means of fasting (sins of speech were often perceived to be tied to gluttony), and to bend the heart toward charity rather than violence. Other offenders would be assigned to pray decades of the Pater Noster, further reorienting the habits of the tongue.[64] Perhaps the ameliorative nature of this justice accounts for the relatively strong cooperation of the accused. Witnesses, accusers, and the accused participated in the activity of the court, offering no major resistance; only one person proved contumacious.[65] Confessions occurred rapidly and the penances followed the logic of the confessional, not the civic court. Penitents appearing before Fra Johannes certainly left the courtroom with much lighter sentences than fellow citizens left the courtroom of the podestà.

And perhaps the people of the commune knew that to be tried for blasphemy before the inquisitor was a much better fate than being tried before the podestà. As early as 1299, after an uprising against the inquisitor, it seems that some citizens feared the commune much more than they feared the inquisitor. Giacopo Ser Arardi was overheard saying "Is that inquisitor here? I would gladly cut him with a knife, more happily than I would eat. If I did not fear the commune of Bologna more than God, I would cut him with pleasure."[66] Giacopo may have spoken too freely as the inquisitor fined him 100 *lire*.[67] But he may still have been correct in his presumption. A much later case of blasphemy, from 1450, shows ecclesiastical authorities moderating the proceedings of the podestà through the cardinal legate. On 19 August, Cristoforo Jacobi was charged with blasphemy for saying "in spite of God" and "by the cunt of the Virgin Mary."[68] Things were not looking good for Cristoforo—he had been remanded to prison, usually a sign that a condemnation was forthcoming (the fine for blasphemy at this time could be between 50 to 100 *lire*). But a letter from the cardinal legate asked the podestà to release Cristoforo, who would make penitential amends by climbing barefoot to Santa Maria in Monte and make an offering of 4 *lire*—a penance remarkably similar to those Fra Johannes assigned.[69] Cristoforo, or someone on his behalf, knew where to turn—the podestà acceded to the legate's request. Two months later when Donatus, son of Albertinus, found himself in the same position, he too appeared in court with a similar supplication. In that case, the legate's response to the supplication did not record the substitute penance that Donatus would perform but did mention that he would have faced a 100-*lire* fine from the podestà. In its place, the legate sent the podestà 25 *lire*. It is not clear if this was Donatus's or the legate's money.[70]

Were the civic courts beginning to take a turn toward the penitential or was the cardinal legate simply exerting influence? All we can assert is that taken together, Fra Johannes's register and these fifteenth-century cases illustrate the easy crossover between jurisdictions and between definitions of illicit speech. Even Fra Johannes's one moment of pause in the following case indicates the kind of interaction and crossover in which the various jurisdictions over blasphemy could engage. In July 1397, Fra Johannes began a trial against a certain Antonio—a gambler who not only blasphemed but spit at and threw his unlucky dice at an image of the cross. Antonio's sentence records that Fra Johannes had petitioned *consilia* from several authorities, including his learned Dominican colleagues and the bishop's vicar. He may have been in doubt as to whether Antonio's words could be defined as *verba heretica* or whether the dice-throwing constituted a crime of heresy. The *consilia* are not included in the sentence, but they must have affirmed Fra Johannes's inclination since he proceeded with his typical assignation of penance.[71]

For Fra Johannes and his consultants, blasphemy, or rather *verba heretica*, was a verbal violence with such sufficient protean power that, for the first time in the medieval West that I have encountered, it could suffer easy slippage not only between jurisdictions but also devolve into one of the deadliest of sins, heresy. For Cristoforo, his friends, the cardinal legate, and the podestà, without question blasphemous speech had to be expunged, but exactly how this could be accomplished was an open question that discerning persons could exploit to gain leniency. Blasphemy could be sin and/or crime, but it was never neither. For the *bolognesi*, regulating blasphemy was never about personal rights or about a competition between Church and State—the fluid crossover between their two courts makes that clear. Blasphemy was a violence from which everyone and every place needed to be protected.

Although differentiating sin from crime may be a concern for the modern historian, for the citizens of the communes it was not a high priority. Rather, they lived comfortably with the ambiguous—or, more accurately, multiple—categorizations of illicit speech. For them, the matter of import was that order be rectified and violence compensated, not whether the court of the podestà or the Dominican inquisitor was the more appropriate one to which to denounce their neighbor's blasphemy. The "cities of God" were holy not just because of their vibrant orthodoxy and their church-dotted geography, but because their institutions and people were united by an ethic of speech more comprehensive than either "Church" or "State." And according to that ethic, jurisdictions and definitions could compete and the accused might always prefer (and be legally due) the more lenient of two possible punishments, but the need to protect people and places from the violent power of words remained uncontested.

The study of blasphemy thus requires that we look beyond our current interpretive explanations of juridical prosecution in the communes. Narratives of the tightening grip of ecclesiastical or state persecution, of judicial vengeance, of the political weight of morality laws, or of conflict management in the courts, are not sufficient. Instead, by reading the records of the different jurisdictions over blasphemy in medieval Bologna together, we have derived another narrative, one that is not entirely intuitive for the modern Western historian. While Talal Asad wrote of a different time and place, his fundamental insight into the seemingly incommensurable divide between Eastern and Western experiences of blasphemy is helpful to consider here (see the epigraph at the beginning of this essay). Writing in response to the 2008 conflict over a Danish newspaper's printing of derogatory images of the Prophet Mohammed, Asad provides a philosophical critique of liberal Western notions of blasphemy. In the West, while perhaps not upheld by its actual history,[72] tolerance for blasphemy as protected free speech became a cipher for Western civilizational identity. This understanding was meant to serve in contradistinction to a perceived backwards religious rigorism at the heart of the Islamic response to the cartoons. But the word that Muslim commentators had predominantly used to describe the cartoons was not blasphemy (*tajdīf*), but *isā'ah*, meaning insult, harm, or offense, a disruption of the living relationship between believers and their God.[73] For these commentators, the cartoons were a violent assault to which they responded with passionate outrage; for the publishers, the cartoons were an exercise in blasphemy, an emblem of their enlightened freedom of speech. Asad therefore emphasizes that any attempt to understand "blasphemy" that remains beholden to the narrow expectations of Western perception will always fail. In order to understand blasphemy in medieval Italy, I suggest that we must similarly shed our expectations and reconsider what it is that words could do. This study has attempted just such a reconsideration by means of a new approach to the many types of court records preserved from late medieval Bologna. By reading the records of the court of the inquisitor alongside those of the court of the podestà, we have been able to discern that for late medieval *bolognesi*, blasphemy—whatever else it might have been—was first and foremost a violence. That is why it came to be prosecuted and why it could experience easy elision between jurisdictions. These findings suggest that there may be still more profitable work to be done by reading the records of the multiple late medieval jurisdictions together.

NOTES

1. Asad, "Free Speech, Blasphemy," 46.
2. However, for a critique of reading sumptuary laws as fundamentally about morals, see Stuard, *Gilding the Market*.
3. For the association of the *popolo* with an increase in morality legislation, see Thompson, *Cities of God*, 138–39. Of course, who counted as a member of the *popolo* was and remains a difficult categorization task. Traditionally thought of as the non-noble artisan class, this is the definition of the *popolo* that Thompson seems to assume; also see Jones, *The Italian City-State*, 513–14; Giansante, *Retorica e politica*, 16, 40–49, 110–17; Fasoli and Sella, *Statuti di Bologna*

dell'anno 1288, 1:xxv–xxvi; Blanshei, "Criminal Law and Politics," 13. Blanshei recognizes the coincidence of interest between the *popolo* and the religious reform movements of the thirteenth century. For the "peace and justice" rhetoric of the *popolo*, see Jones, *The Italian City-State*, 510–16; Ascheri, *The Laws of Late Medieval Italy*, 291; Blanshei, "Criminal Justice in Medieval Perugia and Bologna," 265–67.

4. Giansante, *Retorica e politica nel Duecento*, 5, and on the liberation of the serfs in 1256–57 and the rhetoric of *libertas*, 74–75; Cox, "Ciceronian Rhetoric in Late Medieval Italy," 133. Artifoni, "Retorica e organizzazione del linguaggio politico," esp. 158, illustrates how the rhetorical disciplines offered communal rulers a language for governing. He explicitly notes that his study depends on following Brunetto Latini by excluding "la politica 'in fatti'" in favor of "quella 'in detti.'" The gap between the republican and peace-invoking rhetoric of the *popolo* and the political reality of *popolo* rule has provided a great deal of material for the positive and negative traditions interpreting the rise of the *popolo*. For a review of that historiography, see Blanshei, *Politics and Justice*, 1–11. Blanshei offers an interpretive solution via closure theory that transcends the mires of that debate. Also see Waley, *The Italian City-Republics*, 141–43; Jones, *The Italian City-State*, 148–49, 231; and Pullan, *History of Early Renaissance Italy*, 121–24.

5. Dean, *Crime and Justice* , 37–38; Vallerani, *Medieval Public Justice*, 132–38, 244–46.

6. A notable exception to this trend is Helmholz's study of defamation suits in the medieval and early modern ecclesiastical, local, and royal courts of England. Of course, since defamation was not a crime within the mandate of inquisitors into heresy, Helmholz does not consider any inquisition records. Helmholz, *Select Cases on Defamation to 1600*. In her study of blasphemy in medieval France, Corinne Leveleux does pair readings of ecclesiastical and secular proscriptive texts regarding blasphemy. Missing from her history, however, are case studies. Leveleux, *La parole interdite*.

7. Augustine, *De moribus ecclesiae catholicae*, Bk. II.11.20, "mala verba de Deo dicere."

8. See Leveleux for a listing of these authors: *La parole interdite*, 34–58.

9. Aquinas, *The Summa Theologica* 3, pt. II–II.13.1.ob 3.

10. William Peraldus (Guillaume Peyraut) (ca. 1190–1271) was a French Dominican preacher and writer. His *Summa de virtutibus et vitiis* was intended as a guide for confessors. It was widely quoted and survives in many variations, but no modern critical edition yet exists.

11. Cavalca, *Pungilingua*, fol. 7r. I have preserved the spelling from the 1490 incunabulum: "la bestemia vocale per la quale lhuomo con lasua lingua dice parole di contumelia contro Dio o maladicelo o biasimalo o nomina o ricorda in sua vergognia e della sua madre quelle membra le quale Dio per grande charita prese per noi."

12. Most estimates for medieval Italian male literacy are quite high—Jones suggests about 60 percent of men in Florence in 1330 had a form of pragmatic literacy, defined as the ability to read in Latin and/or volgare. Jones, *The Italian City-State*, 157.

13. Dean, *Crime and Justice*, 33, 119.

14. Cavalca, *Pungilingua*, fol. 9r: "molti signori per debito di giustitia caccino delle loro forze glieretici e altri mali factori: ben doverrebono cacciare piu presto questi maladecti bestemiatori peroche sono molto piggiori."

15. Aquinas did not call for any specific punishment; he made reference only to the fact that murder deserves greater punishment than blasphemy. *The Summa Theologica* 3, pt. II–II.13.3.ob 1.

16. Richter and Friedberg, *Corpus juris canonici*, vol. I. Decret. Greg. IX, 5.26.2: "Statuimus, ut, si quis contra Deum, vel aliquem sanctorum suorum, et maxime beatam Virginem, linguam in blasphemiam publice relaxare praesumpserit, per episcopum suum poenae subdatur inferius annotatae, videlicet, ut septem diebus dominicis prae foribus ecclesiae in manifesto, dum aguntur missarum solennia, blasphemus existens, ultimo illorum die dominico pallium et calceamenta non habeat, ligatus corrigia circa collum, septemque praecedentibus sextis feriis in pane ieiunet et aqua, ecclesiam nullatenus ingressurus. Quolibet quoque praedictorum dierum tres, si poterit, alioquin duos reficiat pauperes sive unum. Et, si nec ad hoc eius suppetant facultates, id in ponam aliam commutetur; cui etiam, si renuerit recipere ac pergere poenitentiam supra dictam, ecclesiae interdicatur ingressus, et in obitu ecclesiastica careat sepultura. Per temporalem praeterea potestatem, coactione, si necesse fuerit, episcopi diocesani adhita contra

eum, blasphemus, si dives fuerit, quadraginta solidorum usualis monetae, poena mulctetur, nullam in hoc misericordiam habiturus; quod etiam inter alia communitatum statuta ponatur."

17. Bartolo da Sassoferrato, *Bartoli a Saxoferrato, lucernae iuris*, vol. 10, *Consilia, quaestiones et tractatus*, Bk. II, cons. 31–32.

18. Given, *Inquisition and Medieval Society*; Thompson, in *Cities of God*, directly engages "the religion of the Italian communes" (by which he means orthodox Catholicism) to illustrate the "sacred geography" of the commune itself. It is a sweeping, if rose-colored, study of the communes wherein the civic courts are nevertheless nearly absent. For inquisitional cultures, jurisdictions and courts, see: Elliott, *Proving Woman*; Arnold, *Inquisition and Power*; Lansing, *Power and Purity*; Ames, *Righteous Persecution*; Benedetti, *Inquisitori lombardi*; Kieckhefer, "The Office of Inquisition." For the civic courts, see Blanshei, "Criminal Law and Politics in Medieval Bologna," and especially the chapter by Massimo Vallerani in this volume and his *Medieval Public Justice*, 4–44. Vallerani specifically excludes use of the inquisition records against heretics for understanding civil procedure on the assumption that heresy inquisitors proceeded according to the presumed guilt of the accused.

19. Given, *Inquisition and Medieval Society*, 213, 220.

20. The statute from 1250 reads: "Statuimus quod quicumque blasfemaverit Deum et sanctam Mariam vel alios sanctos ad ludum biscaçarie vel ad aliquem ludum solvant communi bon. nomine bani xl sol. bon. . . . " Thus blasphemy was tied to gambling in the sense that it was gamblers who blasphemed who were to be prosecuted. The statute does not refer to non-gambling blasphemers. By the iteration of 1252–67, gambling became its own prosecutable offense (presumably not having been so before).

21. Frati, *Statuti di Bologna dall'anno 1245 all'anno 1267.* For the year 1250, see vol. I, 301, Bk. II, Rubric 43. In the iterations from 1259 and 1260, the fine increases to 20 *lire*; in 1262–67 it increases again to 25 *lire*.

22. Fasoli and Sella, *Statuti di Bologna dell'anno 1288*, 1:191, Bk. IV, Rubric 23.

23. Trombetti Budriesi, *Lo statuto del comune di Bologna dell'anno 1335*, 2:669–70, Bk. VIII, Rubric 45.

24. ASB, Statuti 44 (formerly XI) (1352), fol. 147r, Bk. 2, Rubric 1; ASB, Statuti 45 (formerly XII) (1357), fol. 137r, Bk. 2, Rubric 1; and ASB, Statuti 47 (formerly XIV) (1389–1453), fol. 309v, Bk. 5, Rubric 38. For the 1454 rubric see Cucini, "Législation statutaire," 2:136–37, Bk. IV, Rubric 37. I thank Sara Cucini for bringing these references to my attention and sharing with me her photos of the 1352–57 and 1389 statutes. Orioli discusses the statutes of 1250, 1288, and 1389 but not those of mid-century or 1454. Orioli, "Inquisizione e turpiloquio," 187–89.

25. Morandi, *Statuto del comune di Montepulciano, 1337*, 169, Bk. III, Rubric 10. "Si quis blasfemaverit Deum vel beatam Virginem matrem eius, aut fileccum fecerit, vel alia turpia dixerit, vel fecerit adversus predictos vel aliquem predictorum vel eorum picturas seu ymagines, puniatur in quinquaginta libris. Si vero adversos alios sanctos vel sanctas Dei aliquid turpe dixerit vel fecerit vel contra eorum ymagines vel picturas condennetur in viginti quinque libris. Et si predicta vel aliquod predictorum commissa fuerint in aliqua ecclesia dicte terre vel eius districtus, puniatur in dupla pena predictarum penarum. Et possint teneatur et debeat potestas ex suo officio, ad penam viginti quinque librarum eidem per sindicum auferendam, de predictis quolibet mense inquirere, et quilibet bone condictionis et fame possit denuntiare et accusare et credatur sibi cum uno teste bone condictionis et fame, qui de veritate deponat et teneatur sibi credentia et habeat quaram partem banni. Et si condannatus ex predictis mallefitiis vel aliquo predictorum non solverit condennationem infra decem dies, fustigetur per totam terram cum uncio in lingua et postea reducatur ad catenam, et ibi stet per totam diem. Et ad predicta mallefitia investiganda et referenda ponantur in qualibet contrata et villa in terra et extra custodes celati per dominos Quinque quorum custodum denuntiationi cum iuramento et cum uno teste, qui de veritate deponat, bone condictionis et fame, fides plenaria habeatur." For the trend to increasingly severe penalties for certain crimes in the fifteenth century, including blasphemy, see Dean, *Crime and Justice in Late Medieval Italy*, 201; and for the thirteenth century, Blanshei, "Criminal Justice in Medieval Perugia and Bologna," 256–58.

26. See Vise, "The Threat of the Tongue," Chapter 3. I surveyed the extremely rich records of the trials before the judges of the podestà in Bologna in both accusation and inquisition

format (if preserved) in an entire year (two semesters), for approximately every five years between 1285 and 1450. If any given fifth year seemed to have suffered record attrition, I selected a nearby year with more surviving records.

27. For the Duecento, I documented four cases of blasphemy, two each in 1289 and 1295, all of them accusations. For the later period, see end note 30.

28. The marginal notation that accompanies two of these cases states that the trials ended with the accuser being condemned, but not with any notation of a renunciation or failure to proceed. Those two cases also include witnesses. The third is simply noted as acquitted.

29. ASB, Accusationes, Busta 16, Register 12, fol. 26v: "blasfemando Deum et santos dicendo maledictus sit Deus et sanctos et sanctam Mariam et multa allia verba iniuriosa contra ipsos santos et sanctas . . . [sic]."

30. ASB, Inquisitiones, Mazzo 140, Register 8, fol. 54 (1335); Mazzo 182, Register 3, fols.184r and 187r (1355); Mazzo 248, Register 1, fol. 40r (1385); Mazzo 330, Register 2, fol. 53r (1430); Mazzo 355, Register 1, fol.110r, and Mazzo 355, Register 2, fol. 214r (1450). The sample size is small, but the pattern follows the geographical trend for *verba iniuriosa*, a genre of crime closely related to blasphemy.

31. ASB, Inquisitiones, Mazzo182, Register 3, fol.187r, "quod Deus non posset facere."

32. ASB, Inquisitiones, Mazzo 182, Register 3, fol. 184r.

33. As with other specified insults perceived to be particularly provocative, some cities provided particular penalties for gestural insults like making the fig, see Dean, *Crime and Justice in Medieval Italy*, 116–17.

34. ASB, Inquisitiones, Mazzo 140, Register 8, fols. 54rv; ASB, Sententiae, Busta 10, Register 5.

35. Although a penalty of immolation is not mentioned, the listing of specific penalties for damage to sacred images begins with the statutes of 1376, in which the penalty for damage to the face of an image representing God or the Virgin is amputation of the hand; if the image is of the Virgin and the damage is other than to the face or if the image represents the saints, the penalty is pecuniary and varies according to the part of the body damaged. ASB, Statuti 45 (formerly XIII) (1376), fols. 237v–38v, Rubric 60 "De pena vulnerantis, seu percutientis vel insultantis aliquem," as cited in Sara Cucini, "Les normes en matière criminelle dans les statuts bolognais." I thank Sara Cucini for bringing this reference and her forthcoming article to my attention.

36. ASB, Inquisitiones, Mazzo 248, Register 1, fols. 40r–43r. On the use of poverty pleas to mitigate penalties, see the chapter by Sarah Blanshei in this volume.

37. Caggese, *Statuti della Repubblica Fiorentina*, vol. II, 172, Bk. 3, Rubric 14.

38. ASF, Podestà, Atti criminali, condepnationes et assolutiones, Busta/Register 900, fol. 221r: "fistola abbia Dio et sancta Maria sua madre."

39. ASF, Podestà, Atti criminali, condepnationes et assolutiones, Busta/Register 921, fol.75v, "fistol venga a Deo enlla virgene Maria adespecto de Deo e della vergene Maria non potrabeno fare cheo non facesse a meo senno de quello cheo vollese."

40. ASL, Curia del Podesta, Libri Inquisitionum et Testium, Busta 4746, fol. 19r (1339) and Busta 4788, fol. 92r (1394).

41. See Vise, "The Threat of the Tongue," 154–64.

42. Richter and Friedberg, *Corpus juris canonici*, vol. I. Decret. Greg. IX, 5.26.2; Helmholz, *The Spirit of Classical Canon Law*, 274.

43. Orioli, "'E nol porave fare Dio. . . . '" As Orioli points out, the cataloguing hand on the manuscript's first folio mistakenly assumes that Fra Johannes de San Domenico is the same as Fra Johannes Sulimanis, the inquisitor associated with the first act of the register. In fact, these were two different men. With the exception of the first act, however, the register is exclusively the preserve of Johannes de San Domenico.

44. BCA, MS. B. 1858; Paolini and Orioli, *Acta S. Officii Bononie*, for the edition of the only other surviving register (BCA, MS. B 1856). The edited register was compiled at the turn of the thirteenth century. It contains no blasphemy cases and focuses on heresy and heretics, especially against Cathars and Dolcinians.

45. Only Raniero Orioli, one of the co-editors of the other surviving Bolognese inquisition register, has utilized the register, first briefly in a popular article, "Inquisizione e turpiloquio,"

48–53, and secondly in an extensive study with an extremely useful appendix detailing the contents of each of the *acta* in the register. My figures from the register are based on Orioli's appendix, but differ from Orioli's tabulation of twenty-seven inquisitions and fifteen convictions. One of the acts I have included and treated as one prosecution is excluded by Orioli; it is a single accusation made against three persons for various crimes. My thanks to Sarah Blanshei and Riccardo Parmeggiani for bringing the second article to my attention.

46. Richter and Friedberg, *Corpus juris canonici*, vol. I. Decret. Greg. IX, 5.26.2.

47. For example, Paolini and Orioli, *Acta S. Officii Bononie*, 163 (I:169).

48. Bartolo da Sassoferrato, *Bartoli a Saxoferrato, lucernai iuris,* vol. 10, *Consilia, quaestiones et tractatus*, Bk. III, cons. 7.

49. Contrary to what Orioli asserts in "Inquisizione e turpiloquio," there is an extant blasphemy trial from the period 1385–1400. See the case against Nannes Ser Umili de Florencie: ASB, Inquisitiones, Mazzo 248, Register 1, fols. 40r–43r. In "'E nol porave fare Dio . . . ,'" 189, Orioli modifies his claim to say that there were no blasphemy prosecutions between 1387–92. However, given the spotty prosecution record of the civic courts on blasphemy throughout the late medieval period, one finds frequently that the court did not hear a case in a five-year interval. It is overhasty to suggest, therefore, as Orioli does, that the inquisitor sought to fill a gap left by the civic courts, especially since no other inquisitor that we know of did so in Bologna or elsewhere on the Italian peninsula.

50. Caggese, *Statuti della Repubblica Fiorentina*, 2:168–69, Bk. 3, Rubric 3: "qui tale labe polluti sunt, postquam fuerint ab Ecclesia denotati, nisi ad mandata Ecclesie redire voluerint, de ipsa heresi sive credentia in sua iustitia non audiantur aliquo modo, nec quisquam eis in aliquo respondere . . . nullus preterea audiatur ad testimonium, vel aliquod officium publicum vel privatum . . . assumatur."

51. Paolini, *Il "De Officio Inquisitionis,"* Bk. II, no. 45: "Si vero dicit quis, quod ex levitate, vel ex ira, ioco et turbatione, et sine deliberatione docuit vel dixit aliquid contra fidem, tunc ipse reus debet probare predicta et perfecte et inquisitor debet predicta diligenter investigare et non debet esse facilis ad recipiendum talem excusationem, quia quasi omnes moderni heretici sic se excusant."

52. Paolini, *Il "De Officio Inquisitionis,"* Bk. 2, no. 45–46: "verba heretica non debet proferre contra fidem et bonos mores."

53. Eymerich, *Directorivm Inqvisitorvm*, Question 41.1. "qui articulis fidei non obiurant quoquomodo, utpote malum Deo vel beate Virgini imprecantes, eisdem maledicentes, vel gratias Deo non exhibentes." Orioli also suggests that Fra Johannes might have taken his motive from Eymerich's work. Orioli ultimately concludes that this would have been unlikely given the short period of time separating Eymerich's work and Fra Johannes's and given that they supported different pontiffs in the Schism. Orioli, "'E nol porave fare Dio . . . ,'" 190–96. Orioli wonders if this expansion of the inquisitorial mandate might have been a subject of conversation at chapter meetings. I do not think we must suppose even such an organized genesis of this inquisitor's actions. The 1321 manual cited above already suggests this course of action and a zealous inquisitor could just as easily come to the conclusion on his own. Given the highly individualistic nature of inquisitorial activity in this era, as discussed by both Edward Peters and Karen Sullivan, I think it more likely that we have a case of multiple points of genesis for broadening the reach of inquisitorial justice. See Peters, *Inquisition*, 69; Sullivan, *The Inner Lives*.

54. Eymerich, *Directorivm Inqvisitorvm*, Question 41.2, "qui contra fidei articulos verba sua proferunt & eos agitant de directo, utpote qui Dei onmipotentiam infringunt dicentes Deum tempus clarum vel huiusmodi factibilia non posse facere; quod est contra primum fidei articulum: qui est, Credere in unum Deum patrem omnipotentem. Vel qui beate Mariae virginis matris Dei pudicitiam tollunt, dicentes, eam meretricem vel verba aequipollentia in effectu: quod est contra articulum fidei: qui est credere filium Dei conceptum de spiritu sancto, natum fore ex Maria virgine."

55. Eymerich, *Directorivm Inqvisitorvm*, Question 41.5–6.

56. BCA, MS. B. 1858, fols. 65r–68v.

57. BCA, MS. B. 1858, fol. 22v.

58. BCA, MS. B. 1858, fols. 24r–27r; 91r–94v, "El nol porave fare" and "El nol porave fare Dio che la mia pota non vaglia piu che quante femine eno in questa terra."

59. BCA, MS. B. 1858, fol. 10v, "Dio ne la madre sui non porave fare che questa posta tu habi vinto."

60. BCA, MS. B. 1858, fol.12v.

61. Richter and Friedberg, *Corpus juris canonici*, vol. I. Decret. Greg. IX, 5.26.2.

62. Orioli, "'E nol porave fare Dio . . . '," 222.

63. BCA, MS. B. 1858, fols. 26v–27r; 57v–58r, 33v.

64. BCA, MS. B. 1858, fols. 68rv. This is part of the sentence against Antonio, mentioned below.

65. The case of Gnudo. BCA, MS. B. 1858, fol.17bis v.

66. Paolini and Orioli, *Acta S. Officii Bononie*, 328 (I: 219). "Est ille inquisitor hic, ego libenter percuterem eum cum uno cultello, libentius quam comederem, et si non timerem plus commune Bononie quam Deum libenter percuterem eum." For the uprising of 1299, see my forthcoming article, "The Women and the Inquisitor."

67. Paolini and Orioli, *Acta S. Officii Bononie*, 345 (I:226–27).

68. ASB, Inquisitiones, Mazzo 355, Register 2, fol. 100r, "adespecto di Dio" and "perlapotta dela vergine Maria."

69. ASB, Inquisitiones, Mazzo 355, Register 2, fol. 100v. Trevor Dean suggests that this case was like several other cases where penance served as the rationale for the governor's intervention in trials. However, this case is rather the exception to all of the other "penance" cases he cites where convicted criminals could pay a sum of money to a current building project. This is an actual penance, not a payment into government coffers. I think its existence and character owe more to actual penances such as those assigned by Fra Johannes than to these "donations." See Dean, *Crime and Justice*, 43.

70. ASB, Inquisitiones, Mazzo 355, Register 3, fols. 214r–15r. The language from the letter reads: "Mandamus domino potestati ut solutis per eum vigintiquinque libris . . . " If it had been definitively Donatus's money, I would expect the letter to say so (as it had indicated for Cristoforo above). For the burgeoning use of *supplica*, see Vallerani, *Medieval Public Justice*, 305.

71. BCA, MS. B. 1858, fols. 65r–68v.

72. As Asad notes, in different times and places in the West, tolerance for blasphemy could depend just as much on who was speaking as on what was said. As such, it depends on contextual structures of power and subjectivity more than it does on a stable conception of free speech. Asad, "Free Speech, Blasphemy," 22–35.

73. Asad, "Free Speech, Blasphemy," 38.

Chapter Ten

Student Violence in Late Medieval and Early Modern Bologna

Christopher Carlsmith

> "The students do not have a Rector, nor any good leader, so that every day they become more licentious and more insolent. They interrupt lessons when they feel like it, and they show great discourtesy to certain professors in disrupting their teaching. They carry around weapons, and wound each other during lessons. They write and draw a thousand lies on the walls and the desks of the university. . . . During academic exercises they avoid neither obscenities, nor irreverence, nor any other type of indecencies, so while the university ought to have a good reputation, it is instead reduced to infamy."
> —Gabriele Paleotti to Giambattista Castagna (30 January 1577)[1]

University towns have frequently been the site of mayhem and violence as students, professors, and townspeople each sought to establish their respective privileges. From the hanging of two Oxford students for murder in 1209, to the insolent and aggressive Bolognese students described by Gabriele Paleotti in 1577, to student unrest at Paris and Berkeley in 1968, and even to recent riots on campus in response to the (un)desired outcome of major sporting events or the presence of provocative speakers, universities have witnessed myriad examples of physical and verbal conflict. While professors, shopkeepers, and university officials have been involved in these debates, students have been the driving force. Student actions could have lasting influence: the early thirteenth-century example from Oxford led to widespread protest, the closure of the university for five years, the first list of student privileges at Oxford, and ultimately a student exodus and the formation of the University of Cambridge by 1226.[2] Similar cases of violence and emigration occurred at Paris in 1192, 1229, 1278, and 1304, and at Bologna in 1215, 1222, and again in 1321, when the entire university decamped to

Imola (and later, Siena) following the execution of a student.[3] Student violence continued to be visible, and problematic, in the sixteenth and seventeenth centuries, but the tenor of such violence changed over time. Whereas medieval students were frequently the beneficiaries of government protection and privileges, early modern students were increasingly the object of discipline by civic, ecclesiastical, and university authorities.

Older historiography on individual universities often includes anecdotes about student riots or walkouts, but rarely places those events in any kind of historical or comparative context.[4] Nearly twenty-five years ago, Peter Denley urged historians to be more attentive to the "myth" of student violence, and to use the tools provided by anthropologists and cultural historians to create a more thoughtful and specific analysis of those rituals. Denley did not deny that students were rebellious or disorderly, but suggested that the traditional narration of student violence should be studied as a cultural construct rather than accepted as unvarnished truth, and that we must beware the tendency to focus upon the most egregious or salacious of student actions as normative.[5] Historians of medieval and early modern Europe have taken student misbehavior as a rich subject of inquiry; a recent volume surveys student revolt(s) across nearly a millennium of university history.[6]

For the Italian peninsula, while significant scholarship exists on violence generally, and especially on the role of honor and of duels, scholars have devoted less attention to the issue of student violence.[7] Nevertheless, Paolo Rosso has examined student misbehavior in fifteenth-century Pavia, Paul Grendler has briefly summarized early modern cases from Padua and Siena, and Jonathan Davies has mined judicial records from the court of the university rector in sixteenth and seventeenth-century Pisa.[8] Peter Denley's essay on "Transgressions and Disorder" focuses primarily on examples from late medieval Italian cities, and is accompanied by a series of excellent images.[9] Gian Paolo Brizzi has written extensively about Italian students, universities, and Jesuits, as well as founding the Center for the Study of Italian Universities (CISUI) and creating a massive database of all university students in Italy between 1500 and 1800 (ASFE).[10] Piero Del Negro has also authored excellent works on students and institutions in Padua, especially the history of colleges there.[11] All of these contributions have enriched our understanding of student life, including student conflict and resistance.

Perhaps the most poignant commentary about student violence in Italy comes from the governor of Padua, Tommaso Contarini, in his *relazione* of 1609: "It is certain that nothing has contributed more to the decline of the University than the misbehavior of the students and the fights that occur between them. The students are the first and worst of all those who behave poorly, because they have little intelligence and less property."[12] In the same report, the governor alleged that a wave of violence had overwhelmed citizens and artisans outside the university, placing the blame squarely upon the students for initiating fights "every day." The governor further alleged that these students felt no sense of responsibility or propriety, since they had little obligation to pay their own bills. Contarini's report makes clear that student violence concerned him deeply, and he urged the Venetian Senate to remain aware of the potential for continued disorder.

Given the primacy of the *Alma Mater* as the oldest continuously operating university in Europe, it is no surprise that historians also have found evidence of student violence in Bologna. For the late Middle Ages, Antonio Pini, Cècile Fabris, and Scott Jenkins have each examined this topic.[13] For the early modern period, Giancarlo Angelozzi and Cesarina Casanova, Gian Paolo Brizzi, and Ilaria Maggiulli have each utilized the criminal records of the *Torrone* archive to analyze student violence.[14] In order to understand what makes student violence unique, I focus initially on the structural and immediate causes of such violence, before turning to examples and case studies from the late medieval and early modern periods. Student violence shared many characteristics with the violence that bedeviled Italian society, but students were also unusual in certain ways, such as their propensity to appear in the courts as victims as well as perpetrators, their frequent reports of stolen books, and their special privileges.

CATALYSTS

The causes of Italian student violence have been examined by several scholars, producing a wide variety of explanations.[15] Some violence committed by students stemmed from causes that were ubiquitous across Italian society: alcohol, gambling, lust, machismo, pride, political instability, or Carnival. Theft, fraud, and debt were also common causes of violence across all sectors of society.[16] Town-gown squabbles (often sparked by jealousy of foreign students who appeared rich, carefree, and exempt from local laws), inadequate or incompetent policing, and linguistic or cultural misunderstandings might also lead to violence by students or by townspeople.

What characteristics, then, might set *student* violence apart? Students often came from elite social classes, where military training, defense of personal honor, and the right to bear arms were common practice. Scions of noble families—whether ecclesiastical or secular—viewed violence as a necessary means of upholding status. Second, this tendency toward violence may have been intensified by the single-sex environment of all universities, for we know that the formation of masculinity was an essential element of socialization in university life, and that violence was often committed against housekeepers, prostitutes, and female siblings of students.[17] A third explanation can be found in the parallel between intellectual contests in the academy and physical contests in the arena, a point already made by Peter Abelard in the twelfth century: "I preferred the weapons of dialectic to all the other teachings of philosophy, and armed with these I chose the conflicts of disputation instead of the trophies of war."[18] William Courtenay has made a similar observation in his study of fourteenth-century England, pointing to the essential practice of *disputatio* within the university as an example of rhetorical combat necessary for both students and professors.[19] The practice of disputations and debates remained an essential element of university pedagogy well into the early modern period, as evidenced by Gabriele Paleotti's complaint of 1577, cited at the outset of this chapter. Unlike soldiers who enjoyed an *esprit de corps* and unconditional support from their fellows, however, medieval and early modern students were nearly always battling each other for a limited number of scholarships, teaching posts, or promotions, thus fostering a hyper-competitive environment.[20]

Despite the strenuous efforts of university administrators and college founders to impose a rigorous schedule upon their daily life after 1500, students regularly found opportunities for unstructured time that could be channeled into misbehavior. As Elisabetta Patrizi has observed in her analysis of Cesare Crispolti's 1604 treatise on the ideal university student, "not a single moment of a student's life should be left to chance, indecision, or improvisation; even in his free time it was necessary to maintain order and a certain behavioral *habitus*."[21] This effort to regulate student life peaked in the second half of the sixteenth century with Tridentine decrees emphasizing obedience and discipline, moralistic treatises by Silvio Antoniano (1584), Bartolomeo Meduna (1588), and Orazio Lombardelli (1594), and the ascendance of strictly orthodox figures like Gian Pietro Carafa, Carlo Borromeo, or Pier Donato Cesi (the latter two serving as papal legate and vice-legate in Bologna).[22]

The student colleges that proliferated in Bologna (and in other university towns) in the sixteenth and seventeenth centuries play an important role in consideration of student violence. Bologna had about fifteen lay student colleges in the early modern period, housing a total of perhaps 400 students. These colleges—each with their own statutes, buildings, academic costume, and specific admission requirements—ranged from the tiny Collegio Vives for two to four Spanish students to the powerful Collegio Montalto with eighty to ninety Italian students. Colleges existed for Bolognese boys (Collegio Poeti, Collegio Panolini, Collegio Dosi), for Italian boys from other cities or regions (Collegio Ancarano, Collegio Ferrero, Collegio Sinibaldi), and for boys from other countries (Collegio di Spagna, Collegio Ungaro-Illirico, Collegio Jacobs).[23] All of these residential colleges inspired a strong sense of communal identity for their students, which frequently resulted in altercations with rival colleges or local officials, ranging from verbal squabbles to pitched battles. The irony, of course, is that student colleges were first instituted in late medieval Oxford and Paris specifically to *combat* student violence and horseplay; the goal was to have collegiate residences closely supervised by the masters rather than the laissez-faire student inns or hostels that had predominated earlier. Similar concerns about student violence were one of the major factors in the upsurge of collegiate foundations in the mid-fourteenth century and again in the mid-to-late sixteenth century.

Bologna's first student college was founded in 1257 by the Bishop of Avignon, Zoen Tencarari, for students from his home diocese. The most successful student college in Bologna—and one that appears regularly in accounts of student violence—was the Collegio di Spagna (also known as the Collegio di San Clemente), founded in 1364 by Cardinal Gil Alvarez Carrillo de Albornoz for students from Iberia. The Collegio di Spagna served as a hub for Spanish students, travelers, and other co-nationals, just as other Bolognese colleges did for Hungarians, Belgians, or Neapolitans. In some ways these colleges (whether national or regional) served a function similar to that of the *natio* (nation), the regional corporations of students that proliferated across medieval Europe and that served to protect the interests and privileges of students who usually shared a common language and cultural background. As we shall see, the *natio*, too, was frequently a catalyst of student violence.

Swords and daggers were ubiquitous at universities, and the right to bear arms was a fundamental aspect of aristocratic culture, as explained at length in Annibale Roero's 1604 treatise *Lo scolare* (The Student). Both Jonathan Davies and Paul Grendler have examined this treatise, written by Roero just two years after completing his law degree at Pavia.[24] Grendler further discusses the increasing presence of firearms within the university, citing both homicide statistics and the concerns of university administrators such as the governor of Padua, Angelo Correr, that "long harquebuses, short harquebuses, and pistols have been carried by students publicly in the schools and in the piazzas of the city."[25] In Bologna, too, weapons were brandished (and hidden) in student colleges and classrooms. In 1563–64, a group of students from the Collegio di Spagna defied the prohibition of weapons, claiming that their collegiate privileges exempted them from such a ban.[26] In the Collegio Montalto, the student Francesco Ferri was wounded "once in the chest above his right breast, again in the stomach, and finally in the left arm" by fellow student Lorenzo Cacciaconti in November 1620; about a decade later another student, Pietro Simonetti, was wounded in his room at 2:00 a.m. by a fellow student wielding an harquebus.[27] Both students died as a result of their wounds. Despite the frequent efforts to limit arms only to priors or rectors, Ilaria Maggiulli's investigation of the *Torrone* archives for the early 1560s confirms the proliferation of weapons in Bologna among all students.[28] In 1666, the Collegio Comelli prohibited the possession of offensive or defensive weapons inside the college on pain of a one-month suspension.[29]

The issue of precedence (*precedenza, praecedentia*) lay at the heart of many conflicts within the university. The essential issue was one of hierarchy: who marched first in a parade, who sat at the front of the dais, who should step aside to allow another to pass? This issue was certainly not limited to academe; guilds, confraternities, ecclesiastical chapters, military units, and other institutions also vigorously debated issues of hierarchy and social standing. Nevertheless, it came into stark relief in the university and in related civic events where one's status was evident to a broader audience. For example, between 1467 and 1487 the university rector and the archdeacon of the cathedral in Bologna disagreed over who should march first in an Easter procession; after years of debate Pope Innocent VIII ordered the civic and university officials in Bologna to resolve the matter.[30] In 1491 a similar dispute arose between the rector of the German nation in Bologna (Austrian nobleman George de Newdeck) and the legate of the duke of Milan (Francesco Tancredini). Although the papal legate initially convinced the rector to absent himself from the city, the students rioted and soon the rector returned with an escort of 300 horsemen, whereupon he held a series of parties in the street to celebrate the power of the students.[31] In Ferrara in 1507, the rectors of the law students and the arts students jointly appealed to Bologna to decide which had been founded first and thus deserved precedence.[32]

For students, the issue of *precedenza* most commonly arose when two (or more) groups of students met on a street or in a piazza, and then disagreed on who should have the right-of-way. Responding to a spate of brawls in the second half of the seventeenth century, a committee of cardinals in Rome had decreed on 13 June 1682 that members of Bolognese colleges "must hug the wall to their right."[33] The sub-text here was clearly about demonstrating superiority vis-à-vis other students or institutions, whereby the inferior group would be forced to give way (i.e., to cede the wall) to others. The debate about precedence seems to have intensified in the later sixteenth and seventeenth centuries as international and institutional rivalries became more pronounced, as students sought to defend their privileges more vigorously, and as colleges became more numerous.

A final cause of university violence can be found in student nationalism, a sentiment often reinforced by the camaraderie and resources of the student colleges and the nations. Jacques de Vitry famously (and viciously) described the different nations in late medieval Paris, calling the French "proud and effeminate," the Germans "furious and obscene," and the Lombards "avaricious and cowardly."[34] Bitter rivalries between the nations resulted in frequent bloody clashes in the late thirteenth and fourteenth centuries in Oxford, Paris, and Bologna. In the mid-thirteenth century, Bologna had three citramontane nations from the Italian peninsula (Lombard, Tuscan, and Roman), and fourteen ultramontane nations for students beyond the Alps; by the mid-sixteenth century the number of nations had grown to more than fifty and the student population returned to nearly 2,000.[35] The German nation, widely viewed as the most powerful of the student nations, was often viewed as the primary instigator of riots, brawls, and duels, particularly in Bologna, Pavia, and Siena.[36] The Hungarian students in Bologna were regularly involved in scuffles in the seventeenth and eighteenth centuries, including a pair of fights in 1672–73 and another one nearly a century later in 1762. During the latter, they marched through the streets of Bologna arm-in-arm, chanting "We Are Hungarian!" and displaying national flags.[37]

The Collegio di Spagna of Bologna provides repeated examples of student nationalism, and of student violence. Despite (or perhaps because of) its distinguished pedigree, ample economic resources, and academic privileges, the college seems to have been a flash point for assaults and brawls over the centuries.[38] In October 1493 the rector of the Collegio di Spagna was murdered in his bed by his own pupil, who had been resident inside the college. With a reward of 100 *ducats*, the offender was captured and decapitated the following spring.[39] In 1553–54 several members of the college (known as *bolònios*) were investigated and ultimately forced to abjure publicly after "offering wicked opinions and arguing in a malicious and slanderous way."[40] In 1564 the rector of the Collegio di Spagna (Diego Gasque) was at the heart of a clamorous dispute with the university rector (Cesare Rivera) about precedence, but with clearly nationalist overtones, which led to one of several student secessions in that decade.[41] In 1591 the *bolònios* squabbled with the Collegio Montalto over the question of precedence, with the *montaltisti* claiming that "the chief cause from which all of this unpleasantness was born [. . .] was the desire of the Collegio di Spagna that we must concede precedence to them."[42] In 1632, after a verbal altercation between the Spanish students and a local nobleman named Paris Maria de Grassi, an anonymous Spaniard's body was found outside the gates of the college by a Bolognese resident named Alessandro Rossi. The subsequent investigation fills nearly 400 folio pages, and resulted in the conviction of two brothers named Landini.[43] In 1672–73 the bad blood between the Collegio di Spagna and the Collegio Montalto boiled over again; the Bolognese chronicler Antonio Francesco Ghiselli wrote on New Year's Day 1673 that "this disagreement was born because of [an argument about] the wall, and from it I know that he who possesses the wall must keep [close to] it, while still observing the precept to not bump into others."[44]

These examples should not be construed to place blame primarily upon non-Italians; students from Bologna, Parma, Milan, and elsewhere were regularly involved in melees too.[45] In sum, there were multiple reasons for students to brawl, and they frequently did so—with each other, with the police (*sbirri*), and with townspeople.

EXAMPLES OF STUDENT VIOLENCE: THIRTEENTH TO FIFTEENTH CENTURIES

From the thirteenth to the fifteenth century, students in Bologna exercised direct authority within the university through their representatives, as well as indirect authority in the community by virtue of their numbers and economic impact.[46] Like scholars everywhere, students in Bologna benefited from Emperor Frederick I Barbarossa's *Authenica Habita* of 1158, granting freedom of travel, exemption from the law of reprisals, and immunity from the jurisdiction of local civil magistrates.[47] Additional privileges were enshrined in the Bolognese civic statutes of 1288 and 1454, including the right of students to bring an accusation without giving evidence or surety, and a special penalty of permanent banishment for those who injured or killed a student and were contumacious.[48] However, the commune (usually in the person of the podestà) reserved the right to prosecute criminal behavior of students, and this is where we often find records of student violence.

Antonio Ivan Pini has described student life in late medieval Bologna in considerable detail, from the number of students and their geographic origin, to travel and housing, to lessons and exams.[49] He has also summarized examples of their philosophy of *gaudeamus igitur* [So Let Us Rejoice], including drinking, feasting, whoring, and singing.[50] Most relevant for our purposes is his analysis of student violence, from which he concludes that students in thirteenth-century Bologna were more likely to be involved in judicial proceedings than the average townsman.[51] In support of this argument, Pini drew upon a collection (*Maestri e Scolari*) of notarial acts extracted in the late nineteenth century from the *Carte di Corredo fondo* of the podestà for the period 1280–1350, comprising elements from 618 criminal cases involving students. Half of the crimes are not specified; Pini divided those that are identified into four categories: crimes against a person (e.g., insults, injuries, homicides), crimes against property (e.g., theft of books, clothes, or money), crimes against morality (kidnapping and rape, sodomy), and miscellaneous crimes (e.g., gambling, home invasion).[52] The first two categories are far more numerous, with nearly 95 percent of the known crimes (297/318) being committed against another person or property. Beyond individual student crimes, Pini also addressed collective student action, including scuffles between German and French students (1289), between Germans and Poles (1301, 1310) and between Germans and Hungarians (1310).[53] Nor were fights between the Italian nations absent; in 1302 the Tuscan and Roman nations attacked Lombard and Ligurian students in the classroom of professor Orlandino da Pisa in the middle of a lesson.[54]

Additional analysis of late medieval judicial records is offered by Cècile Fabris, who examined the notarial acts from 400 cases involving students or professors during the period 1281–1317 from the same *Carte di Corredo fondo* of the podestà that Pini analyzed, as well as another 1,300 trials in the *Accusationes* and *Inquisitiones fondi* of the podestà from the year 1298.[55] In contrast to the conclusions of Pini and Zaccagnini, Fabris notes that only 4 percent (50/1,300) of the cases from 1298 involved students, a statistic at odds with the traditional impression of students regularly in and out of court.[56] She also challenges the conclusion that students were more violent than townspeople, noting that each group had virtually identical proportions of assaults, homicides, and riots.[57]

Fabris does, however, also note several areas in which the student profile was decidedly different from that of local citizens. One was the students' dominant role as plaintiff rather than victim, with nearly two-thirds of students bringing a complaint rather than receiving it.[58] This anomaly is likely a vestige of the 1158 imperial decree of Frederick I that permitted students to bring forward a case without evidence; it may also reflect the financial security of many students who could afford the cost of legal representation and court fees. Another notable aspect of student criminality in late medieval Bologna was the high number of book and manuscript thefts, totaling nearly 15 percent of all cases, reflecting the critical importance of textual materials for students, and the high price that such items could command on the black market.[59] A third finding of Fabris is that spring was the most litigious time of year for students; perhaps the students grew tired of each other, and of their neighbors and professors, after a year in close quarters (both academically and residentially).[60] Fabris also found that cases of student criminality were dispersed across the city; there was no "student quarter" that suffered unusually high rates of violence or theft.

Secession was an occasional tactic of medieval students, such as that of 1215 when the Tuscan nation left for Arezzo, that of 1222 with the migration to Padua, or (most famously) in 1321 when the students left for Imola and then Siena, in protest of the decapitation of Spanish student Giovanni di Valenza by civic authorities after his alleged kidnapping of Giovanna, the daughter of a local notary and niece of the noted jurist Giovanni d'Andrea. In the latter case, the city fathers quickly sent professor d'Andrea to woo the students back and promised the construction of a chapel in via San Mamolo dedicated to Santa Maria della Pace as a conciliatory gesture.[61] The student colleges were not a significant factor in inciting academic violence in the thirteenth and fourteenth centuries, as their presence was very small. With the exception of the Collegio di Spagna, which was always on firm financial and administrative footing, most of the other Bolognese colleges merged or disappeared without too much notice by 1500. As noted above, however, many new ones were founded in the sixteenth and early seventeenth centuries.

Scott Jenkins has argued that the stereotype of medieval students as a "drunken, violent minority who, as a result of clerical privileges bestowed upon [them], did not fear temporal justice," is misguided.[62] Instead he seeks other explanations for student violence in Bologna (and Oxford), pointing to three broad categorizations: town vs. gown, rivalry between nations, and interpersonal rivalry between individuals. His analysis broadly agrees with that of Pini, and with my prior explanation of catalysts, although Jenkins tries to give more agency to the students, viewing them as individuals who made conscious choices rather than pawns of larger structural systems that pushed them toward confrontation.[63]

SIXTEENTH CENTURY

Student authority underwent a precipitous decline in sixteenth-century Bologna as both Church and civic officials strove to expand their respective control over students and townspeople.[64] The increased authority of the papal legate, the creation of the *Assunteria dello Studio*, the construction of the Archiginnasio, the dissemination of Tridentine orthodoxy—each of these events limited student (and university) freedoms in Bologna.[65] The role of university rector, which had been so important in medieval Bologna, gradually withered away, with only seven students holding the annual post between 1560 and 1604. In 1564 the papacy attempted to reduce or even eliminate the number of student rectors.[66] Despite (or perhaps because of) efforts to limit student power, student brawls and riots continued to occur regularly. Nevertheless, one can see several turning points—in the 1520s, 1560s, and 1604—when student authority was reined in by the city and/or the pope.

Toward the beginning of the sixteenth century students still held sway in many ways. The chronicler Antonio Francesco Ghiselli recounts that in 1515 a local governor had prohibited the bearing of arms by everyone within the city, whereupon the defiant students armed themselves with weapons, flags, and drums for a march to the city center and then to the monastery of San Domenico, where they barricaded themselves inside. The vice-legate ordered cavalry and artillery to be brought round, but cooler heads prevailed in the Senate, and the students were permitted to return to the city. Ghiselli, however, expressed his frustration with the misbehaving students, noting that they "wore the clothing of soldiers, not of scholars, and they were very dishonest, and had no fear at all."[67] In that same year (1515), a student from Parma murdered another student and promptly sought refuge in his residence at the Collegio Ancarano. Ten days later, when his companions moved him from the college to a house owned by the Pepoli family, the accompanying students waved their swords and shouted insults at a house owned by the Marescotti. The result was a furious fracas that eventually resulted in multiple deaths and a long-running vendetta between two of Bologna's powerful families.[68] Three years later (23 May 1518) students killed a guard at the Palazzo

Pubblico. In retaliation, the vice-legate called out his guards and arrested three students; the student body promptly kidnapped three additional guards and threatened to treat them identically to their captured compatriots. Once again the vice-legate backed down, demonstrating that students still held the upper hand.[69]

In 1519, however, Pope Leo X announced severe penalties for all students bearing arms. As expected, the students revolted and the rector of the arts students, Mantovano, "used harsh language and violent words, then mounted his horse and left the city."[70] But this time the vice-legate did not waver: Mantovano was arrested and sent to Rome, and the prohibition on arms remained in place. This incident would seem to indicate an initial turning of the tide against the traditional pattern of negotiation and forgiveness that usually characterized town-gown relations in Bologna.[71]

A second turning point may be evident in the 1560s, when the students' once-reliable threat of mass exodus began to weaken. At least three distinct secession efforts occurred between 1561 and 1564; the first two may be viewed as either a draw or a victory for students, while the third was clearly a loss for them. The initial incident occurred in March 1560 when a student of the German nation, Otto von Hoym, was arrested (and quickly released) by the police for a minor curfew violation. On the following day the police broke into von Hoym's house, ostensibly to search for prohibited weapons, and left his personal belongings strewn across the floor. The students protested to the *gonfaloniere di giustizia*, who refused to intervene, and the police dragged von Hoym into prison. Four hundred of his companions, *omnes armati variis armis*, arrived at the Governor's office demanding justice. When the students exited the building to organize a meeting at the church of San Domenico, they wounded one policeman in the piazza. In response, other policemen ran inside the Governor's palace to grab their harquebuses, and within a few minutes two students were killed: a Neapolitan student was struck down by an harquebus, and a Flemish student was mortally wounded by a large stone hurled from a second-story window. Enraged, the students organized a large funeral parade through the university quarter, and the next day they began to march to Ferrara. Within two days the city fathers had publicly whipped the police captain and executed the stone-throwing policeman (Vittorio Paci) by dropping him from a high window, concessions that ultimately persuaded the students to return.[72]

A second secession—which was significantly more protracted and ultimately more successful for the students—began in 1562, when a group of German students were publicly subjected to corporal punishment with a whip. In response, many members of the German nation transferred to Padua and remained there for more than a decade. (One of the reasons for such an extended stay was that Protestant students were not required to sign a Tridentine profession of faith as a condition of graduation.) In 1573, the Bolognese

Senate invited the students to return with expanded privileges, including the right for the leaders of the German nation to bear arms.[73]

The third secession occurred in November 1564 when the Spanish and Italian students disagreed about the order of precedence between the university rector (Cesare Rivera) and the Collegio di Spagna rector (Diego Gasque). Hundreds of students brawled in the street and in the classrooms of the Archiginnasio; one eyewitness estimated "three hundred youth wearing breastplates, thirty holding large shields, and everyone wearing helmets and holding long lances."[74] The papal vice-legate, Pier Donato Cesi, criticized Rivera and indicated support for the Spanish position. About eighty students followed Rivera to Ferrara, but a lack of promised support from Alfonso II d'Este there led them to soon return to Bologna.[75] Cesi's firm position against the *universitates* was certainly noticed by the students, one of whom observed that the vice-legate "does not close his eyes [to student misbehavior] as the other has done."[76] Cesi's tough stance is indicative of the Church's desire to more closely regulate not only students, but also professors, townspeople, and even the movement of books during the Tridentine period. (Arch)bishop Gabriele Paleotti, who served in Bologna from 1567–89, shared similar sentiments about reining in student misbehavior.[77]

A third turning point would be the election of Giovanni Domenico Spinola as the last student rector on 5 January 1604. Indeed, Spinola served as rector for just four months, resigning from his post in April 1604 after deeming his rectorate incompatible with his new clerical office in the Apostolic Camera.[78] He was the first student rector elected since 1579–80, a gap of nearly twenty-five years. Students were reluctant to take up the post of rector in the second half of the sixteenth century for a number of reasons, including the necessary expenses, the onerous responsibility, the limited pool of candidates, and the larger number of transfer students.[79] The increasing power of the papal legate, and of Bolognese bishops, also played an important role here, as the legate gradually absorbed many of the responsibilities formerly expected of the student rector. If the student body no longer had a recognized leader, then its ability to engage in mass collective action was greatly diminished.

SEVENTEENTH CENTURY

It is perhaps not surprising, then, that in the seventeenth century we see examples of student violence and misbehavior increasingly centered in the student colleges. Within these residential colleges the students *did* have some elected leaders, and a stronger sense of communal identity reinforced by distinctive dress, traditions, and (sometimes) language. The colleges were never truly independent, nor truly student-run; the statutes of the founders made clear that a Cardinal Protector or other senior figure(s) would always be in charge of collegiate admission, finances, and administration. And the same forces that sought to promote orthodoxy and instill social discipline in other sectors of society were also present in the student colleges of Bologna. Nevertheless, it is striking to see how the colleges become the loci of student violence in the second half of the Settecento.

From 1640 to 1702, more than half a dozen major altercations took place between Bolognese student colleges. Repeat offenders were common: the Collegio Ancarano, the Collegio Montalto, the Collegio Ungaro-Ilirico, and the Collegio di Spagna were frequently involved, while the smaller colleges (Dosi, Sinibaldi, Jacobs, et al.) seem to have stayed on the sidelines. Often these conflicts were rooted in the same causes that had fueled previous disagreements: *precedenza*, nationalism, personal honor, militaristic culture, prevalence of weapons, heightened masculinity, and so forth. Some of this student violence bubbled along for years, or even decades; later conflicts often point back to earlier incidents, indicating that the memory of prior slights was not easily forgotten.

One example is that between the Collegio Ancarano and the Collegio Montalto, two of the larger and more well-funded colleges in seventeenth-century Bologna. A severe crisis began for the Montalto in 1641, as Pope Urban VIII slashed the size of the college by 40 percent, confiscated much of its property, and sparked a heated rivalry between two cardinal protectors.[80] The Ancarano, founded in 1414 by jurist Pietro Ancarano exclusively for the study of civil and canon law and subsequently under the control of the Farnese family, began to challenge the Montalto in 1641 over questions of precedence.[81] More conflict ensued in April 1650 when the Ancarano students insisted on carrying weapons to the classroom for self-defense. In 1662 the Cardinal Protector Giovanni Battista Pallotta wrote to the legate in Bologna, Cardinal Girolamo Farnese, that "the residents of the Montalto college were wounded after being shot at by the harquebuses of the Ancarano students . . . and in self-defense the Montaltisti injured some of the Ancarani with their own weapons." Pallotta insisted that the Ancarano students had displayed "little respect and great disobedience" with their "imperious and arrogant" behavior and thus deserved an "exemplary punishment."[82]

In the late 1650s a conflict erupted between the Ancarano students and the clerics of the Seminary.[83] On a Tuesday afternoon, three students of the Collegio Ancarano (Marioni, Passionei, Morandi) were walking in the street of Santo Stefano in order to watch a procession or a horse race. Upon encountering the seminarians, the Ancarani stepped into the street; a few moments later when the two groups met again, the Ancarano leader "grabbing them (i.e., seminarians) by the hand together with his companions, pulled them into the street, and thus succeeded in preserving the rights of the [Ancarano] college and not allowing themselves to be discredited."[84] Two days later the Ancarano students were once again in the same street, and this time it was the seminarians who doffed their hats and agreed to walk in the street. But as the rector of the seminarians (Severo Masetti) passed by the Ancarano students, he "pulled out a white club and holding it in his hand he walloped Sig. Marioni." Marioni responded by stabbing the priest in the left shoulder, whereupon a general melee broke out until the police arrived. Forty years later (February 1703), another scuffle broke out between the same two groups. Archbishop Giacomo Boncompagni had foreseen this difficulty, writing to the duke of Parma in December 1702 that "these students of the Collegio Ancarano have for some time been pestering the clerics of my seminary about the precedence which they claim [to possess], and they [the Ancarani] refuse to stop shoving these clerics or to allow them to pass freely." The 1703 incident was largely limited to verbal violence and the exchange of angry letters and treatises in which each side enumerated the many reasons for their own superiority.

In 1672 the Collegio Montalto became involved in a heated pair of conflicts against the Collegio di Spagna.[85] Just before New Year's Eve 1672, the vice-rector of the Montalto and his companions were walking home from the Franciscan church on via Barberia when their way was blocked by some *bolònios* en route to their own church of San Barbaziano. Each side claimed to have doffed their hat and courteously asked the others to move, but after "disharmonious words" were exchanged, the Spanish student hurled the vice-rector to the other side of the street and commanded his servant to "beat these boys who wish to take the wall away from us." Tense negotiations ensued between the cardinal protector, the archbishop, and the legate; representatives from each college wrote letters defending their position and emphasizing their privileges and seniority. Although a compromise was reached, two months later another fight broke out between the two sides over who might sit where during the Lenten sermons at the Carmelite church of Santa Maria delle Grazie, resulting in fisticuffs and drawn swords. This particular squabble between the Montalto and the Spanish colleges was further intensified by the murder of the legate's chief security officer, Innocenzo Mancini, on Easter Sunday 1673; the suspected assailant lived next door to the Collegio di Spagna, and when the legate ordered his arrest, multiple shots rang out and the students barricaded themselves inside the college.

In 1675 the Collegio Montalto was once again involved in a public fight, this time with the members of the Collegio Ungaro-Illirico.[86] In fact, there were two separate incidents on 6 January 1675: the first occurred about three o'clock in the afternoon in the piazza outside the church of Santa Maria dei Servi in Strada Maggiore, and the second two hours later outside the Augustinian convent of San Giacomo near via Zamboni (then via San Donato). In the first incident, a dozen or so Hungarian students wielding clubs surrounded a trio of Montalto students bearing short swords or knives. Each group insulted the other's linguistic skills and denigrated its opponent's status; a few moments later all three of the Montalto students fled inside the church and out the back door. Later in the afternoon, two different Montalto students made a point of standing their ground when they encountered the same group of Hungarians. The Hungarians declared loudly that "If you are claiming the right [of the wall] from us . . . since you have no right to claim it, we have no intention to yield it to you." The Montalto students drew their swords and inflicted a serious wound upon the hand of a Hungarian, whereupon the Montalto students fled down an adjacent street.

In virtually all of the collegiate cases cited above, we have competing narratives from each side, as well as more neutral eyewitness accounts, judicial investigations, senatorial summaries, and chroniclers' accounts. The variety of sources make it possible to compare and contrast the rhetorical and strategic tactics of each side as they utilized physical and verbal attacks upon each other. It is clear that many of these seventeenth-century students were spoiling for a fight. Unlike their late medieval predecessors, however, the early modern students relied heavily upon their residential colleges to provide support and camaraderie. The early modern students also faced a more restrictive environment in Bologna, one where traditional student privileges were challenged by the new emphasis upon social discipline and religious orthodoxy.

CONCLUSION

Student violence in Bologna occurred frequently, and for a wide variety of reasons. Sometimes that misbehavior rose to the level of criminal activity and was prosecuted as such; at other times it was more akin to pranks or protest. Student violence could be individual or collective, and could as easily be directed against each other as against townspeople or civic officials. *Sbirri* (policemen) were a favorite target of students for the spiteful and arbitrary way in which they often persecuted students, especially foreigners. Throughout the history of the university, students have found themselves in either a precarious or a prestigious position; whether they felt comfortable or at risk, they often looked to violence as a solution.

This chapter has provided an overview of student violence in late medieval and early modern Bologna as well as some consideration of its proximate and immediate causes. By and large such violence was consistent with the broader violence found in Italian society, and often occurred for similar reasons. Nevertheless, university students (and to a lesser degree, professors) represent a special category in the history of violence and crime. The threat to secede from one city to another, the high number of book thefts, or the ability to lodge an accusation without presenting evidence or surety: all were unique aspects of student violence. Moreover, the nature of student violence did change between the thirteenth and seventeenth centuries, with significantly more brawls occurring between defined student groups, probably due, *inter alia*, to the proliferation of student colleges in the later period. Student privileges were a key aspect of this history, ranging from the imperial decree of 1158 and the Bolognese statutes of 1288 through the additions granted (or deleted) in the sixteenth and seventeenth centuries. Such privileges provided legal protection for students while simultaneously breeding resentment from townspeople, and regularly resulted in town-gown violence. Prior scholarship has demonstrated the abundant primary sources available to document academic violence. From the picaresque but acritical excerpts of Zaccagnini a century ago to the more recent nuanced and rigorous studies of medievalists like Pini and Fabris and early modernists like Brizzi and Maggiulli, it is clear that the Bolognese archives offer rich opportunities to further analyze student violence and crime and craft microhistories with vivid drama and colorful characters.

NOTES

1. "Li scolari non hanno Rettore, nè capo buono, onde ogni dì diventano più licentiosi et insolenti. Impediscono quando vogliono ogni lettione et usano a particolari dottori alle volte grandi scortesia, nel turbarli a posta il leggere. Mettono mani all'armi, e si feriscono nell scole. Scrivono et dipingono mille dishonestà nelli muri et banchi delle scole. Ad ogni piccolo rumore fanno setta et vanno in fretta et causano sedizioni. Il modo che tengono li scolari Bolognesi in sostentare conclusioni, è poco conveniente et indegno dell'honore dello studio. Nelli circoli non perdonanno nè a obscenità, nè a irreverenza, nè a indegnità alcuna, talchè quel consesso che dovrìa essere di tanta riputatione è ridotto come infame." Archbishop Gabriele Paleotti (1522–97) sent these comments to Archbishop of Rossano Giambattista Castagna (later Urban VII) on 30 January 1577 to outline the problems that he saw at the University of Bologna. Quoted in Lines, "Reorganizing the Curriculum," 37.
2. Rashdall, *The Universities of Europe*, 3:33–34 for the 1209 Oxford incident.
3. Denley, "Trasgressioni e disordini," 83–88.
4. Zaccagnini, *Storia dello Studio di Bologna*; Idem, *La vita dei maestri*, 42–48; Sorbelli and Simeoni, *Storia dell'Università di Bologna* (Sorbelli authored vol. 1 on the eleventh to fifteenth centuries, while Simeoni authored vol. 2 on the period 1500–1888); Gherardi, "Uno scandalo nell'Università Pisana"; Sottili, "Le contestate elezioni rettorali"; Seneca, "Antonio Rosato, bidello generale." See also Davies, "Violence and Universities," 507n11.
5. Denley, "Trasgressioni e disordini," esp. 83–84, 98–99. Denley points out that the most serious allegations against students (or anyone) were the most likely to make it to court, and thus to our notice today, but that provides a skewed interpretation of the entirety of student behavior.
6. Davies, "Preface," 4n2, includes relevant bibliography for England, France, Spain, and Germany. Dhondt and Boran, *Student Revolt, City, and Society* includes twenty-five chapters ranging from the late Middle Ages to the 1970s.
7. Davies, "Preface," 3n1, for bibliography on violence generally; on violence by Italian youth specifically, see also Schindler, "I tutori del disordine"; Niccoli, *Il seme della violenza*; Eisenbichler, *The Premodern Teenager*, esp. essays by Carol Lansing, Christopher Carlsmith, and Ottavia Niccoli.

8. Rosso, "Vicende studentesche pavesi"; Grendler, *The Universities of the Italian Renaissance*, 501–5; Davies, *Culture and Power*, 157–78; Idem, "Violence and Universities"; Idem, *Aspects of Violence in Renaissance Europe*; Idem, *Violence in Early Modern Italy.*

9. Denley, "Trasgressioni e disordini."

10. For Brizzi's publications from 1969–2009, see https://www.unibo.it/sitoweb/gianpaolo.brizzi/pubblicazioni?tab=altre; for CISUI, see http://www.cisui.unibo.it/; for ASFE, see http://asfe.unibo.it/it (weblinks accessed 21 April 2017).

11. For Del Negro's publications from 1967–2013, see Baldini and Brizzi, *Amicitiae Pignus,* 467–508.

12. As quoted in Grendler, *The Universities of the Italian Renaissance*, 500–501 (his translation).

13. Pini, "'Discere turba volens'"; Fabris, "Dallo studio all'esperienza del diritto"; Jenkins, "Medieval Student Violence: Oxford and Bologna."

14. Angelozzi and Casanova, *La giustizia criminale in una città di antico regime*, especially 321–72; Idem, *La nobiltà disciplinata*; Brizzi, "Town and Gown?"; more generally, Idem, "Modi e forme della presenza studentesca"; Maggiulli, "'Tu ne menti per la gola.'" Also useful is Niccoli, *Storie di ogni giorno.*

15. Carlsmith, "Quarrels Under the Portico"; Maggiulli, "Tu ne menti per la gola,'" 34; Davies, "Violence and Universities," 509–12; Idem, *Culture and Power*, 157–78; Grendler, *The Universities of the Italian Renaissance*, 501–5.

16. Maggiulli, "Tu ne menti per la gola,'" 37–39, offers more than a dozen examples from 1563–64 of these so-called "minor transgressions" committed by students in Bologna; Davies, "Violence and Universities," 509–12, also offers citations to archival and published examples of these many different categories.

17. Karras, *From Boys to Men,* 67–69. Davies, "Violence and Universities," 509–11.

18. *The Letters of Abelard and Heloise*, 3, as quoted in Davies, "Violence and Universities," 510.

19. Courtenay, *Schools and Scholars,* 29–30.

20. Denley, "Transgressions and Disorder," 89.

21. Patrizi, *La trattatistica,* 89–90 (my translation).

22. Lines, "Papal Power and University Control"; Idem, "Gabriele Paleotti and the University of Bologna"; see also Grendler, "The University of Bologna, the City, and the Papacy."

23. Carlsmith, "Student Colleges in Early Modern Bologna"; Brizzi, "I collegi per borsisti."

24. Davies, "The Ideal Student."

25. Grendler, *The Universities of the Italian Renaissance,* 503–5.

26. Maggiulli, "Tu ne menti per la gola,'" 40–1, quoting the rector: "I understand that the law declares that one cannot carry arms after the sounding of the bell, but we who are in the [Spanish] college are privileged and we can carry our swords with us" (my translation).

27. Carlsmith, "*Mens Sana in Corpore Sano*," 308.

28. Maggiulli, "Tu ne menti per la gola,'" 37.

29. Dall'Olio, *Il Collegio Comelli*, 78.

30. Zaccagnini, *Storia dello Studio di Bologna*, 76, which includes the text of Innocent's decreee of 6 November 1487; see also De Benedictis, "La fine dell'autonomia studentesca," 197.

31. Zaccagnini, *Storia dello Studio di Bologna*, 77–78; see also Cortese, "L'Università di Bologna," 221. In the 1491 case, Innocent VIII again had to issue a papal brief clarifying the order of precedence: the papal legate, the diocesan bishop, and the *gonfaloniere di giustizia*, followed by the university rector and then other civic officials.

32. Denley, "Trasgressioni e disordini," 98.

33. ASB, Archivio Demaniale, Collegio Montalto, 13/7234, int. 1, fasc. 2, "Decreto Provisionale" (13 June 1682).

34. De Vitry, *Historia occidentalis*, Book II, Chap. VII, trans. in *Translations and Reprints* II/3: 19–20.

35. The number of students is difficult to estimate, as many of the matriculation lists have been lost, and those that survive usually do not count significant categories of students (e.g., the clergy, local Bolognese, students living in colleges). Scholars generally agree on a gradual

decline in the size of the university in the fourteenth and fifteenth centuries, but are divided on the size and speed of any resurgence after that. Pini, "'Discere Turba Volens,'" 62–69, and Fasoli, "Bologna nell'età medievale," 142, calculated 2,000–2,200 students annually in the late thirteenth century; Grendler, *The Universities of the Italian Renaissance*, 19, estimated 1,000 students per year in the early fifteenth century, 1,500 in the late fifteenth century, 2,000 by the mid-sixteenth century, and a decline to 1,500 by century's end; Mario Fanti maintains that the sixteenth-century student population was more than 1,000 (Fanti, "Bologna nell'età moderna," 228).The estimate of Zaccagnini (*Storia dello Studio di Bologna*, 189) of 15,000 students ca. 1550 is clearly a discredited outlier. The most thoughtful estimates of student populations, and how to calculate them for the sixteenth and seventeenth centuries, are by Gian Paolo Brizzi, including "Matricole ed Effettivi"; Idem, "La presenza studentesca"; Idem, "Lo Studio di Bologna." Brizzi estimates perhaps 1,500 students in the sixteenth century.

36. Davies, "Violence and Universities," 511; Maggiulli, "Tu ne menti per la gola,'" 39, recounts two specific fights between German and Polish students in Fall 1564.

37. Carlsmith, "*Siam Ungari*."

38. It is also true that the Collegio di Spagna has been more carefully studied because of its long history and excellent archive, and thus we know more about misbehavior there.

39. Zaccagnini, *Storia dello Studio di Bologna,* 74, citing ASB, Libri Partitorum, n. 389, Register 11 (1490–1500), fols. 80, 97v.

40. This was really heresy more than violence; see Prosperi, "Un gruppo ereticale."

41. See notes 74–76 below for more details.

42. ASB, Demaniale, 73/7293, "Libro delle lettere, 1589–1626," fol. 5r (13 Nov. 1591), as explained in Carlsmith, "Collegiate Conflict," 52–53.

43. This case was generously brought to my attention by Colin Rose, whose chapter appears in this volume; I have not yet had time to investigate the case more fully.

44. BUB, Ms. 770, Antonio Francesco Ghiselli, *Memorie antiche manuscritte di Bologna raccolte et accresciute sino a' tempi presenti*, XXXVI:242, as in Carlsmith, "Collegiate Conflict," 53.

45. Maggiulli, "Tu ne menti per la gola,'" 43–44, offers citations to other scuffles in 1563–64 between Italian students from different regions; for a case study of conflict between students from Milan and Parma on 31 December 1564, see Eadem, "'Li scholari."

46. Prior to the thirteenth century, student associations selected and paid the professors, but between 1280 and 1350 the commune of Bologna gradually assumed this responsibility for professorial salaries. Grendler, *The Universities of the Italian Renaissance,* 6–7, 157–58.

47. Kibre, *Scholarly Privileges*, 10. The decree is also known as the *Privilegium scholasticum.* The right of reprisals permitted student property to be seized for debts incurred by their countrymen. Under Frederick's decree, students could have their case heard by either their own professor or by the bishop; in Bologna student rectors sometimes heard cases too.

48. Fasoli and Sella, *Statuti di Bologna dell'anno 1288*, 2:101–03, Bk. VIII, Rubric 9, "De privillegio scolarium patientium furta vel rapinus vel iniurias," and Bk. VIII, Rubric 12, "De bannitis prooffensione alicuius scolaris de banno non extrahendis." Edward Dettman Loss (e-mail of Edward Dettman Loss to Sarah Rubin Blanshei, 12 June 2017) has identified identical privileges in the 1454 statutes, ASB, Statuti 50 (formerly XVII) fols. 486–88, Bk. V, Rubric 86, "De privilegiis scholarium pacientium furta seu iniiurias vel rapinas," and Bk. V, Rubric 87, "De bannito pro ofensa alicuius scolaris et de banno non extrahendis"). Fabris "Dallo studio all'esperienza del diritto," 14–18, traces the details of student juridical privileges in Bologna between 1281–1317. My thanks to Sarah Blanshei for sharing all of the above information with me in June 2017.

49. Pini, "'Discere turba volens,'" 62–108.

50. Pini, "'Discere turba volens,'" 109–16.

51. This is the judgment of Denley, "Trasgressioni e disordini," 98; cf. the conclusions of Fabris below.

52. Pini, "'Discere turba volens,'" 121.

53. Pini, "'Discere turba volens,'" 128–32.

54. Pini, "'Discere turba volens,'" 128–29.

55. Fabris, "Dallo studio all'esperienza del diritto"; Fabris selected the year 1298 because that was the year for which the *Carte di Corredo* series held the largest number of elements from trials involving students (sometimes as accusers or accused, but in other instances as witnesses, etc.)

56. Fabris, "Dallo studio all'esperienza del diritto," 23.

57. Fabris, "Dallo studio all'esperienza del diritto," 25.

58. Fabris, "Dallo studio all'esperienza del diritto," 31.

59. Fabris, "Dallo studio all'esperienza del diritto," 27.

60. Fabris, "Dallo studio all'esperienza del diritto," 33–34.

61. Pini, "'Discere turba volens,'" 131–32; see also Filippini, "L'esodo degli studenti" and Wray, *Comunities and Crisis*, 80–83.

62. Jenkins, "Medieval Student Violence"; for examples from Oxford only, see Idem, "Violence between Student Nations."

63. Jenkins, "Medieval Student Violence: Oxford and Bologna"; the full dissertation has not been made available to me, including chap. 5, 67–181, and chap. 6, 210–38, which appear to focus on the way conflicts would develop and be resolved in medieval towns like Oxford and Bologna.

64. De Benedictis, "La fine dell'autonomia"; Lines, "Papal Power."

65. The *Assunteria dello Studio* was one of about fifteen magistracies created by civic authorities to oversee specific responsibilities. In this case, the *Assunteria* worked closely with the *Riformatori dello Studio* (another civic body) and the aristocratic Senate, as well as with the papal legate, to supervise the *studium*. The Archiginnasio was the first purpose-built academic building in Bologna, constructed in 1561–63 to consolidate classroom teaching in one place and to provide greater supervision of both faculty and students.

66. Lines, "Papal Power," 677n62.

67. BUB, Ms. 770, Antonio Francesco Ghiselli, *Memorie antiche manuscritte di Bologna raccolte et accresciute sino a' tempi presenti*, XII:584, as cited in Zaccagnini, *Storia dello Studio di Bologna,* 187.

68. BUB, Ms. 770, Antonio Francesco Ghiselli, *Memorie antiche manuscritte di Bologna raccolte et accresciute sino a' tempi presenti*, XII:556, as cited in Zaccagnini, *Storia dello Studio di Bologna,* 188.

69. BUB, Ms. 770, Antonio Francesco Ghiselli, *Memorie antiche manuscritte di Bologna raccolte et accresciute sino a' tempi presenti*, XIII:193, as cited in Zaccagnini, *Storia dello Studio di Bologna,* 190.

70. BUB, Ms. 770, Antonio Francesco Ghiselli, *Memorie antiche manuscritte di Bologna raccolte et accresciute sino a' tempi presenti*, XIII:196, as cited in Zaccagnini, *Storia dello Studio di Bologna,*, 190.

71. Brizzi, "Town and Gown?," 88, has observed that while Bolognese patricians and civic authorities were often tolerant with students because they recognized the students' vital economic contributions, the Bolognese lower classes and the Catholic Church were much less sympathetic toward students.

72. The best account is Brizzi, "Town and Gown?" which analyzes multiple perspectives of the event; briefer treatment is found in Maggiulli, "Tu ne menti per la gola,'" 41–42; Zaccagnini, *Storia dello Studio di Bologna*, 188–89.

73. Maggiulli, "Tu ne menti per la gola,'" 42.

74. Quoted in Brizzi, "Town and Gown?" 89n7; the primary source is not specified.

75. Cortese, "L'Università di Bologna," 219–23 .

76. Quoted in Maggiulli, "Tu ne menti per la gola,'" 42: "è venuto a Bologna un nuovo legato che non chiuderà gli occhi come l'altro."

77. See notes 1 and 22 above.

78. De Benedictis, "La fine dell'autonomia studentesca," 196–99.

79. De Benedictis, "La fine dell'autonomia studentesca," 203.

80. Cagni, "Il Pontificio Collegio," 67–81 describes the "extensive bitterness" (*infinite amarezze*) that ensued until the 1670s.

81. ASB, Demaniale 13/7234, int. 2, fasc. 5: "Coll. Montalto con il Coll. Ancarano: Differenza sopra precedenza del muro nell'anni 1641–1650–1662–1672."

82. ASB, Demaniale 72/7234, int. 2, fasc. 1, f. 3 (8 Apr. 1662): "li Collegiali di Montalto furono feriti e tirategli delle archibugiate dalli Ancarani . . . e che per necessaria difesa ferirono alcuni delli Ancarani con le stesse loro armi che gli levarono;" "e con tutto l'affetto la supplico non solo di procedere, che la contumacia, poco rispetto e disubbidienza delli Ancarani non tenga istretti per più lungo tempo, ma che delitto così imperioso, e soverechieria così insegna non resti senza castigo essemplare." Many more documents are to be found in this fascicle, entitled "Fatti, Informazioni, Istanze riguardanti l'affare da precedenza con il Collegio Ancarano."

83. Carlsmith, "*Cacciò fuori un grande bastone bianco*."

84. This account comes from an anonymous source, but was likely Camillo Paleotti, governor of the Collegio Ancarano.

85. Carlsmith, "Collegiate Conflict," for the information in this paragraph.

86. Carlsmith, "*Siam Ungari*," for the information in this paragraph.

Bibliography

PRIMARY SOURCES

Aegidiane constitutiones cum additionibus carpensibus . . . Cum glossis non minus doctis quam utilibus Gaspari Caballini de Cingulo, Venice: 1571.

Alberti, Leandro. *Historie di Bologna: 1479–1543*, edited by Armando Antonelli and Maria Rosaria Musti. 3 vols. Bologna: Costa Editore, 2006.

Alighieri. Dante. *La Commedia secondo l'antica vulgata*, edited by Giorgio Petrocchi. Florence: Le Lettere, 1994.

———. *The Inferno of Dante: A New Verse Translation*. Translated by Robert Pinsky. New York: Farrar, Straus and Giroux, 1996.

Andreas Capellanus, *The Art of Courtly Love*, trans. John J. Parry. New York: Norton, 1941.

Aquinas, Thomas. *The Summa Theologica of St. Thomas Aquinas*, trans. Fathers of the English Dominican Province. 5 vols. 1st ed. New York: Benzinger Brothers, 1948. Revised edition Notre Dame, IN: Christian Classics, 1981.

Augustine. *De moribus ecclesiae catholicae et de moribus Manichaeorum libri duo*, edited by Johannes B. Bauer. Vienna: Hoelder-Pichler-Tempsky, 1992.

Barbo, Pietro, *Criminalium consiliorum atque responsorum tam ex veteribus quam iunioribus celeberrimis iurisconsultis collectorum*. 2 vols. Venice: 1562.

Barsch, Karl, ed. *Romances et Pastourelles françaises des XIIe et XIIe siècles*. Darmstadt: Wissenschaftliche Buchgesellschaft, 1870, reprint 1967.

Bartolo da Sassoferrato. *Bartoli a Saxoferrato, lucernae iuris, omnia quae extant opera.* 11 vols. Venice: Giunta, 1590.

Benatti, Corrado. *Gli statuti del contado di Imola, 1341–1347*. Imola: La Mandragora, 2005.

Boccaccio, Giovanni. *Decameron,* edited by Vittore Branca. Milan: Mondadori, 1985.

Braidi, Valeria, ed. *Gli Statuti del Comune di Bologna degli anni 1352, 1357; 1376, 1389. Libri I – III*. 2 vols. Bologna: Deputazione di Storia Patria per le Province di Romagna, 2002.

Bruni, Francesco, Guido da Suzzara, and Baldus de Ubaldis. *Tractatus de indiciis et tortura D. Francisci Bruni de S. Severino . . . D. Guidonis de Suzaria . . . et D. Baldi de Periglis . . . cum additionibus D. Ludovici Bolognini.* Venice: F. Bindoni and M. Pasini, 1549.

Caggese, Romolo ed. *Statuti della Repubblica Fiorentina*, edited by Giuliano Pinto, Francesco Salvestrini, and Andrea Zorzi. 2 vols. Florence: Leo S. Olschki, 1999.

Caporali, Giulio, ed. *Gli statuti di Montepulciano, 1337*. Montepulciano: Banca di Credito Cooperativo di Montepulciano, 1996.

Capra, Benedetto, and Ludovico Bolognini. C*onsilia domini Benedicti Caprae et Ludovici de Bologninis.* Lyon, 1556.

Casoni, Francesco. "Tractatus maleficii praemeditati." In *Tractatus universi iuris*, vol. 11, pt. 1. Venice: Societas Aquilae se renovantis, 1584.

Cavalca, Domenico. *Pungilingua*. Florence: Lorenzo di Mathio, 1490.

Chartularium Studii Bononienis, Documenti per la storia dell'università di Bologna, vol. 1. Bologna: Commissione per la Storia della Università di Bologna, 1909, reprint 1982.

Chronicon Parmense: ab anno MXXXVIII usque ad annum MCCCXXXVIII, edited by Giuliano Bonazzi. Rerum Italicarum Scriptorum 2, vol. 9. Città di Castello: Lapi, 1902.

Cicero, "Pour Cluentius," in Cicero, *Discours*, vol. 8, Paris: Les Belles Lettres, 1953.

Cipolla, Bartolomeo. *Consilia criminalia celeberrimi ac prestantissimi utriusque juris illuminatoris domini Bartholomei Cepole Veronensis.* N.p., 1531.

———. *Consilia criminalia celeberrimi ac praestantissimi Iur. vtr. Interpretis Domini Bartholomaei Caepollae Veronensis*, Venice: Bartholomaeum Rubinum, 1575.

"Continuazione della 'Cronaca' di Bologna detta Varignana (Cronaca B) dal 1471 al 1500." In *Corpus chronicorum Bononiensium*, edited by Albano Sorbelli, Rerum Italicarum Scriptores 2, vol. 18 no. 4, 421–566. Città di Castello: Lapi, 1940.

Cronica gestorum ac factorum memorabilium civitatis Bononie edita a fratre Hyeronimo de Bursellis con la continuazione di Vincenzo Spargiati, edited by Albano Sorbelli, Rerum Italicarum Scriptores 2, vol. 23 no. 2. Città di Castello: Lapi, 1911–29.

"Cronaca Rampona." In *Corpus chronicorum Bononiensium*, edited by Albano Sorbelli. Rerum Italicarum Scriptores 2, vol. 18 nos. 1–4. Città di Castello: Lapi, 1903–40.

"Cronaca Varignana." In *Corpus chronicorum Bononiensium*, edited by Albano Sorbelli. Rerum Italicarum Scriptores 2, vol. 18 nos. 1–4. Città di Castello: Lapi, 1903–40.

Dalla Tuata, Fileno. *Istoria di Bologna: Origini – 1521*, edited by Bruno Fortunato. 3 vols. Bologna: Costa Editore, 2005.

D'Anagni, Giovanni. *Consilia.* Lyon, 1534.

De' Cerchi, Raffaele Pietro. *Libellus qui vulgari sermone nuncupatur el Birracino compositus per Raphaelem Petri de Cerchiis notarium peritissimum Florentinum.* Siena: N. de Aristotelibus, 1530.

Deciani, Tiberio, *Tractatus criminalis d. Tiberii Deciani Vtinensis, comitis, equitisque, ac celeberrimi iuris vtriusque consultis*. 2 vols. Turin: Eredi Nicola Bevilacqua, 1593.

Doeberl, Michael, ed. *Monumenta Germaniae selecta ab anno 768 usque ad annum 1250.* Munich: J. Lindauersche buchhandlung, 1889.

Eymerich, Nicolas. *Directorivm Inqvisitorvm R. P. F. Nicolai Eymerici, Ord. Præd. S. Theol. Mag. Inquisitoris hæreticæ prauitatis in Regnis Regis Aragonum, Denvo Ex Collatione Plvrivm, exemplarium emendatum, et accessione multarum literarum, Apostolicarum, officio Sanctæ Inquisitionis deseruientium, locupletatum, Cvm Scholiis Sev Annotationibvs eruditissimis D. Francisci Pegnæ Hispani, S. Theologiæ et Iuris Vtriusque Doctoris. Accessit rerum et verborum multiplex et copiosissimus Index. Cum Priulegio, et Superiorum approbatione.* Rome: In Aedibus Pop Rom, 1578.

Fasoli, Gina, and Pietro Sella, eds. *Statuti di Bologna dell'anno 1288*. 2 vols. Vatican City: Biblioteca Apostolica Vaticana, 1937–39.

Frati, Luigi, ed. *Statuti di Bologna dall'anno 1245 all'anno 1267.* 3 vols. Bologna: Regia Tipografia, 1869–77.

Gambiglioni, Angelo, *Angeli de Aretio legum doctoris tractatus de criminibus seu maleficiis.* Paris, 1476.

Ghirardacci, Cherubino. *Della historia di Bologna: Parte Terza, 1426–1509*, edited by Albano Sorbelli, Rerum Italicarum Scriptores 2, vol. 33, no. 2. Città di Castello: Lapi, 1912–32.

Gigli, Giacomo. *Cronica: 1494–1513*, edited by Bruno Fortunato. Bologna: Costa Editore, 2008.

Grammatico, Tommaso. *Clarissimi iuriscons. Thomae Grammatici Neapolitani, Regii Consiliarii Decisiones, quas ex causis potissimum per eum in sacro Regio Neapolitano Consilio relatis selegit: ac consilia duo in materia foriudicationis, quaestionesque aliquot notabiles & quotidianae: nunc denuo per auctorem ipsum diligenter recognitae, ac plurimis in locis ampliatae*. Venice: Iunta, 1551.

Henderson, Ernest F., ed. *Select Historical Documents of the Middle Ages*. London: George Bell & Sons, 1892.

Hulot, Henri, Jean-François Berthelot, Pascal Alexandre Tissot, and Alphonse Berenger, eds. *Les cinquante livres du Digeste ou des Pandectes de l'empereur Justinien*. Metz: Behmert et Lamort, 1803Imperiale di Sant' Angelo, Cesare, ed. *Codice diplomatico della repubblica di Genova*. 3 vols. Rome: Tipografia del Senato, 1936.

Krüger, Paul, and Theodor Mommsen, eds. *Corpus Juris Civilis*. 3 vols. Berlin: Weidman, 1877–95.

The Letters of Abelard and Heloise, trans. Betty Radice. Harmondsworth: Penguin, 2003.

The Liber Augustalis; Or, Constitutions of Melfi, Promulgated by the Emperor Frederick II for the Kingdom of Sicily in 1231, trans. James M. Powell. Syracuse: Syracuse University Press, 1971.

Machiavelli, Niccolò. *Istorie Fiorentine*, edited by Alessandro Montevecchi and Carlo Varotti. Niccolò Machiavelli: Edizione Nazionale delle Opere; Opere Storiche, vol. 2, no. 2. Rome: Salerno Editore, 2010.

Magnificae ciuitatis Fauentie Ordinamenta nouissime recognita & reformata ac in lucem edita. Regnante sanctissimo in christo patre & domino nostro. d. Clemente papa septimo. Faenza, 1527.

Marescotti De' Calvi, Galeazzo. *Cronica come Anniballe Bentivoglij fu preso et menato de presone et poi morto et vendicato per misser Galeazzo Marscotto di Calvi*, edited by Francesco Giudicini. Bologna: Società Tipografica Già Compositori, 1883.

Morandi, Ubaldo, ed. *Statuto del comune di Montepulciano, 1337*. Florence: Le Monnier, 1966.

Paolini, Lorenzo, ed. *Il "De Officio Inquisitionis": La Procedura inquisitoriale a Bologna e a Ferrara nel trecento*. Bologna: Bononia University Press, 1976.

Paolini, Lorenzo, and Raniero Orioli, eds. *Acta S. Officii Bononie: ab anno 1291 usque ad annum 1310*. Fonti per la storia d'Italia 106. Rome: Istituto storico italiano per il Medio Evo, 1982.

Peraldus, William. *Summa de virtutibus et vitiis*. Lyon, 1668.

Piccolo, Paolo, ed. *Liber Augustalis di Federico II di Hohenstaufen: le costituzioni di Melfi, 1231*. Naples: Luciano, 2001.

Richter, Aemilius Ludwig, and Emil Friedberg, eds. *Corpus juris canonici*. Graz: Akademische druck u. Verlagsanstalt, 1959.

Rinaldi, Evelina. *Statuto di Forlì dell'anno 1359 con le modificazioni del 1373*. Rome: Loescher & C., 1913.

Sella, Pietro, ed. *Costituzioni egidiane dell'anno MCCCLVII*, Corpus statutorum italicorum, 1. Rome: Loescher, 1912.

Statuta ciuitatis Caesenae cum additionibus, ac reformationibus, pro tempore factis, ex ordine M. ill. Consilii, et DD. Conseruatorum eiusdem ciuitatis ad perpetuam rei memoriam nouiter impressa. Cesena: Bartholomaeus Rauerius, 1590.

Statuta magnificæ ciuitatis Parmae, Parma: Ex officina Erasmi Viothi, 1590.

Statuta Mirandulae, 1386. Modena: Vincenzi e nipoti, 1887.

Statuta populi et communis Florentiae publica auctoritate, collecta, castigata et præposita anno salutis MCCCCXV. Freiburg: Kuch; Florence: Stamperia Bonducciana, 1778–83.

Statuta terræ Centi, nuper reformata anno Domini 1607. Ferrara: Victorius Baldinus, typographus cameralis, 1609.

Statuta urbis Ferrariae reformata anno Domini 1567 nouissime excussa quibus accessere quae sequens pagina indicabit. Ferrara: Typographia Camerali, 1690.

Translations and Reprints from the Original Sources of European History. 6 vols. Philadelphia: University of Pennsylvania Press, 1897–1912.

Trombetti Budriesi, Anna Laura, ed. *Lo Statuto del Comune di Bologna dell'anno 1335*. 2 vols. Rome: Istituto Storico Italiano per il Medioevo, 2008.

Ubaldis, Angelus de. *Consilia*. Pavia: Bernardinus et Ambrosius de Rovellis, 1499.

Ubaldis, Baldus de. *Consilia*. Lyon: Claude Servain, 1559.

SECONDARY SOURCES

Ady, Cecilia M. *The Bentivoglio of Bologna: A Study in Despotism*. London: Oxford University Press, 1937.

Albertani, Germana. "Al cospetto dei giudici: Percorsi processuali e casistica dei reati." In *Laboratorio sulle fonti d'archivio: Ricerche su società e istituzioni a Bologna nel tardo Trecento*, edited by Antonella Campanini and Rossella Rinaldi, 55–101. Bologna: CLUEB, 2005.

Algazi, Gadi. "Pruning Peasants: Private War and Maintaining the Lords' Peace in Late Medieval Germany." In *Medieval Transformations: Texts, Power, and Gifts in Context*, edited by Esther Cohen and Mayke De Jong, 245–74. Leiden: Brill, 2001.

———. "The Social Use of Private War: Some Late Medieval Views Reviewed." *Tel Aviver Jahrbuch Für Deutsche Geschichte* 22 (1993): 253–73.

Ames, Christine Caldwell. *Righteous Persecution: Inquisition, Dominicans, and Christianity in the Middle Ages*. Philadelphia: University of Pennsylvania Press, 2009.

Angelozzi, Giancarlo, and Cesarina Casanova. *Donne criminali: Il genere nella storia della giustizia*. Bologna: Pàtron, 2014.

———. *La giustizia criminale a Bologna nel XVIII secolo e le riforme di Benedetto XIV*. Bologna: CLUEB, 2010.

———. *La giustizia criminale in una città di antico regime: Il tribunale del Torrone di Bologna, secc. XVI–XVII*. Bologna: CLUEB, 2008.

———. *La nobiltà disciplinata: Violenza nobiliare, procedure di giustizia e scienza cavalleresca a Bologna nel XVII secolo*. Bologna: CLUEB, 2003.

Antonelli, Armando, and Marco Poli. *Il Palazzo dei Bentivoglio nelle fonti del tempo.* Venice: Marsilio, 2006.

Antonioli, Guido. *Conservator pacis et iustitie: La signoria di Taddeo Pepoli a Bologna (1337 – 1347)*. Bologna: Il Mulino, 2004.

Arnold, John H. *Inquisition and Power: Catharism and the Confessing Subject in Medieval Languedoc*. Philadelphia: University of Pennsylvania Press, 2001.

Artifoni, Enrico. "Corporazioni e società di 'popolo': un problema della politica comunale nel secolo XIII." *Quaderni storici* 74 (1990): 387–404.

———. "Retorica e organizzazione del linguaggio politico nel Duecento italiano." In *Le forme della propaganda politica nel Due e nel Trecento. Relazioni tenute al convegno internazionale organizzato dal Comitato di studi storici di Trieste, dall'École Française de Rome e dal Dipartimento di storia dell'Università degli studi di Trieste (Trieste, 2–5 marzo 1993)*, 157–82. Rome: Ecole Française de Rome, 1994.

Asad, Talal. "Free Speech, Blasphemy, and Secular Criticism." In *Is Critique Secular? Blasphemy, Injury, and Free Speech*, edited by Talal Asad, Wendy Brown, Judith Butler, and Saba Mahmood, 20–63. Berkeley: Townsend Center for the Humanities, University of California Press, 2009.

Ascheri, Mario. "I *consilia* dei giuristi: una fonte per il tardo Medioevo." *Bullettino dell'Istituto storico italiano per il Medioevo* 105 (2003): 305–34.

———. "Le fonti e la flessibilità del diritto comune: il paradosso del *consilium sapientis*." In *Legal Consulting in the Civil Law Tradition*, edited by di Mario Ascheri, Ingrid Baumgärtner, and Julius Kirshner, 11–53. Berkeley: Robbins Collection, 1999.

———. *The Laws of Late Medieval Italy (1000–1500): Foundations for a European Legal System*. Leiden: Brill, 2013.

Astarita, Tommaso. *Village Justice: Community, Family, and Popular Culture in Early Modern Italy*. Baltimore, MD: Johns Hopkins University Press, 1999.

Azzara, Claudio. "Pene 'infamanti' nelle leggi dei Longobardi," in *Historiae: scritti per Gherardo Ortalli*, edited by Claudio Azzara, Ermanno Orlando, Marco Pozza, and Alessandra Rizzi, 11–22. Venice: Edizioni Ca' Foscari, 2013.

Bacchelli, Franco. "La legazione bolognese del cardinal Bessarione (1450–1455)." In *Bessarione e l'Umanesimo*, edited by Gianfranco Fiaccadori, 137–47. Naples: Vivarium, 1994.

Baldini, Ugo, and Gian Paolo Brizzi, eds. *Amicitiae Pignus: Studi storici per Piero Del Negro*. Milan: Edizioni Unicopli, 2013.

Barbero, Alessandro. "Gruppi e rapporti sociali." In *Il basso Medioevo e la prima età moderna, (1280–1536)*, vol. 2 of *Storia di Torino,* edited by Rinaldo Comba, 161–210. Turin: Einaudi, 1997.

Barthélemy, Dominique, François Bougard, and Régine Le Jan, eds. *La vengeance, 400–1200.* Rome: École Française de Rome, 2006.

Basile, Bruno, ed. *Bentivolorum Magnificentia: Principe e Cultura a Bologna nel Rinascimento.* Rome: Bulzoni Editore, 1984.

Bellabarba, Marco. "Pace pubblica e pace privata: linguaggi e istituzioni processuali nell'Italia moderna." In *Criminalità e giustizia in Germania e in Italia: Pratiche giudiziarie e linguaggi giuridici tra tardo Medioevo ed età moderna,* edited by Marco Bellabarba, Gerd Schwerhoff, and Andrea Zorzi, 189–213. Bologna: Il Mulino, 2001.

———. "La représentation des délits en droit public et droit privé. L'infrajustice dans les criminalistes italiens de l'époque moderne (XVe–XVIIe siècle)." In Garnot and Fry, *L'infrajudiciaire du Moyen Age à l'époque moderne*, 55–68.

Bellomo, Manlio. Quaestiones in iure civili disputatae*: didattica e prassi colta nel sistema del diritto comune fra Duecento e Trecento.* Rome: Istituto storico italiano per il Medioevo, 2008.

———. *I fatti e il diritto: Tra le certezze dei giuristi medievali (secoli XIII–XIV).* Rome: Il Cigno, 2000.

Belloni, Annalisa. *Le questioni civilistiche del secolo XII: Da Bulgaro a a Pillio da Medicina e Azzone*. Frankfurt: Klostermann, 1989.

Belvederi, Raffaele. "I Bentivoglio e i Malvezzi di Bologna negli anni 1463–1506." *Annali della Facoltà di Magistero. Università degli Studi di Bari* 6 (1967): 33–78.

Benedetti, Marina. *Inquisitori lombardi del Duecento.* Rome: Edizioni di storia e letteratura, 2008.

Bettoni, Antonella. "Fama, shame punishment and metamorphoses in criminal justice: Fourteenth–Seventeenth centuries." *Forum Historiae Iuris* (2010). http://www.forhistiur.de/2010-03-bettoni/.

Black, Jane. *Absolutism in Renaissance Milan: Plentitude of Power under the Visconti and the Sforza 1329–1535.* Oxford: Oxford University Press, 2009.

Blanshei, Sarah Rubin. "Aristocratization of Late Medieval-Early Modern Bolognese Government and Society." In *The Far-Seeing Gaze of Capital Cities. Essays in Honour of Francesca Bocchi,* edited by Rosa Smurra, Hubert Houben, and Manuela Ghizzoni, 231–48. Rome: Viella, 2014.

———. "Cambiamenti e continuità nella procedura penale a Bologna, secolo XII–XVII. Parte 1. Le procedure del processo penale in età comunale e signorile." *Documenta* 1, no. 1 (2018, forthcoming).

———. "Crime and Law Enforcement in Medieval Bologna." *Journal of Social History* 16 (1982): 121–38.

———. "Criminal Justice in Medieval Perugia and Bologna." *Law and History Review* 1 (1983): 251–75.

———. "Criminal Law and Politics in Medieval Bologna." *Criminal Justice History. An International Review* 2 (1981): 1–30.

———. "Foreword to the English Edition." In Vallerani, *Medieval Public Justice*, ix–xii.

———. "Gruesome Penalties and Merciful Pardons: Bologna 1250–1454," paper presented at the 130th Annual Meeting of the American Historical Association, Atlanta, GA, January 8, 2016.

———. "Homicide in a Culture of Hatred: Bologna 1352–1420." In *Murder in Renaissance Italy*, edited by Trevor Dean and K. J. P. Lowe, 106–22. Cambridge: Cambridge University Press, 2017.

———. *Politics and Justice in Late Medieval Bologna.* Leiden: Brill, 2010.

———. "Postfazione," paper presented in the Cappella Farnese of the Palazzo d'Accursio, Bologna, May 5, 2017.

Blanshei, Sarah Rubin, and Sara Cucini. "Criminal Justice and Conflict Resolution." In *A Companion to Medieval and Renaissance Bologna*, edited by Sarah Rubin Blanshei, 335–60. Leiden: Brill, 2018.

Blastenbrei, Peter. "Violence, Arms and Criminal Justice in Papal Rome, 1560–1600." *Renaissance Studies* 20 (2006): 68–87.
Bocchi, Francesca. "Le imposte dirette a Bologna nei secoli XII e XIII," *Nuova rivista storica,* 57 (1973): 273–312.
Boehm, Christopher. "The Natural History of Blood Revenge." In *Feud in Medieval and Early Modern Europe*, edited by Jeppe Büchert Netterstrøm and Bjørn Poulsen, 189–203. Aarhus: Aarhus University Press, 2007.
Bonfiglio Dosio, Giorgetta. "Criminalità ed emarginazione a Brescia nel primo Quattrocento." *Archivio Storico Italiano* 136 (1978): 113–64.
Bossy, John, ed. *Disputes and Settlements: Law and Human Relations in the West*. New York: Cambridge University Press, 1983.
Bowsky, William M. "The Medieval Commune and Internal Violence: Police Power and Public Safety in Siena, 1287–1355." *The American Historical Review* 73, no. 1 (1967): 1–17.
Brainerd, C. J. "Murder Must Memorise." *Memory* 21 (2013): 547–55.
Brackett, John K. *Criminal Justice and Crime in Late Renaissance Florence, 1537–1609*. Cambridge: Cambridge University Press, 1992.
Brizzi, Gian Paolo. "I collegi per borsisti e lo Studio bolognese. Caratteri ed evoluzione di un'istituzione educativo-assistenziale fra XIII e XVIII secolo." *Studi e Memorie per la storia dell'Universita di Bologna,* n.s. 4 (1984): 11–186.
———. "Matricole ed Effettivi: Aspetti della presenza studentesca a Bologna fra Cinque e Seicento." In *Amicitiae Pignus: Studi storici per Piero Del Negro*, edited by Ugo Baldini and Gian Paolo Brizzi, 227–59. Milan: Edizioni Unicopli, 2013.
———. "Modi e forme della presenza studentesca a Bologna in età moderna." In *L'università a Bologna. Maestri, studenti e luoghi dal XVI al XX secolo*, edited by Gian Paolo Brizzi, Lino Marini, and Paolo Pombeni, 59–74. Bologna: Cassa Risparmio di Bologna, 1988.
———. "La presenza studentesca nelle università italiane nell prima età moderna. Analisi delle fonti e problemi di metodo," In *L'università in Italia fra età moderna e contemporanea*, edited by Gian Paolo Brizzi and Angelo Varni, 85–101. Bologna: CLUEB, 1991.
———. "Lo Studio di Bologna tra *orbis academicus* e mondo cittadino." In *Cultura, istituzioni culturali, Chiesa e vita religiosa.* Bk. 2 of *Bologna nell'Età Moderna*, edited by Adriano Prosperi, 5–113. Storia di Bologna, vol. 3. Bologna: Bononia University Press, 2008.
———. "Town and Gown? Bologna 1560: la città di fronte a una rivolta degli studenti." In *Amicitiae Pignus: Studi storici per Piero Del Negro*, edited by Ugo Baldini and Gian Paolo Brizzi, 87–104. Milan: Edizioni Unicopli, 2013.
Brogi, Mario. "Il fondo 'Giusdicenti dell'antico Stato senese' dell'Archivio di Stato di Siena (fine secolo XIV–1808)." In Giorgi, Moscadelli, and Zarrilli, *La documentazione degli organi giudiziari*. 275–314.
Broomhall, Susan and Sarah Finn, eds. *Violence and Emotions in Early Modern Europe*. Abingdon, Oxfordshire: Routledge, 2016.
Brown, Warren C. *Violence in Medieval Europe*. New York: Longman, 2011.
Brown, Warren, and Piotr Górecki, eds. *Conflict in Medieval Europe: Changing Perspectives on Society and Culture*. Burlington, Vt.: Ashgate, 2003.
Brownmiller, Susan. *Against Our Will: Men, Women and Rape*. Harmondsworth: Penguin, 1975.
Brundage, James A. *Law, Sex, and Christian Society in Medieval Europe*. Chicago: The University of Chicago Press, 1987.
———. "Rape and Seduction in the Medieval Canon Law." In *Sexual Practices and the Medieval Church*, edited by Vern L. Bullough and James A. Brundage, 141–48, 262–66. Buffalo, NY: Prometheus Books, 1982.
Bubeniceck, Michelle. "Dénoncer son maître, dénoncer ses comparses: L'homme de main, le judge, la foule et l'aveu 'spontané' (Comté de Bourgogne, fin du XIVe siècle)." In *Dénoncer le crime du Moyen Age au XIXe siécle*, edited by Martine Charageat and Mathieu Soula, 143–58. Pessac: Maison des sciences de l'homme d'Aquitaine, 2014.
Burckhardt, Jacob. *The Civilization of the Renaissance in Italy*. Translated by S. G. C. Middlemore. 1878. Reprint, New York: Modern Library, 2002.

Buyck, Margaux. "Crimes de poison dans la Bologne médiévale et moderne (XIVe–XVIIe siècle)." Doctoral diss. University Paris Nanterre la Défense and University of Verona. 2016.

Cagali, Ardea, "La criminalità a Bologna alla fine del XIII secolo." Tesi di laurea. Alma Mater Studiorum—University of Bologna, 1967–68.

Cagni, Giuseppe. "Il Pontificio Collegio 'Montalto' in Bologna (1585–1797*)*." *Barnabiti Studi*, 5 (1988), 1–194.

Cantelmi, Simona. *Bologna fra Trecento e Quattrocento: La testimonianza di Pietro di Mattiolo* Bologna: CLUEB, 2011).

Carbonnières, Louis de. "Le pouvoir royal face aux mécanismes de la guerre privée à la fin du Moyen Âge. L'exemple du Parlement de Paris." *Droits. Revue française de théorie, de philosophie et de cultures juridiques*, no. 46 (2007): 3–18.

Carlsmith, Christopher. "*Cacciò fuori un grande bastone bianco:* Conflict between the Collegio Ancarano and the Seminarians in Early Modern Bologna." In *The Culture of Violence in Late Medieval and Early Modern Italy*, edited by Fabrizio Ricciardelli, 191–216. Florence: Le Lettere, 2012.

———. "Collegiate Conflict: Two Brawls in Bologna between the Collegio di Spagna and the Collegio Montalto, 1672–73." *Annali di Storia delle università italiane* 20, no. 1 (June 2016): 47–63.

———. "*Mens Sana in Corpore Sano:* Health in the Montalto College of Bologna, 1585–1700." *Annali di Storia delle università italiane* 13 (2009): 305–16.

———. "Quarrels Under the Portico: Student Violence in Early Modern Italian Universities." In *Student Revolt, City, and Society*. Dhondt and Boran, 39-53.

———. "*Siam Ungari*: Nationalism, Students, and Misbehavior at the University of Bologna in the Late Seventeenth Century" *History of Universities* 26/2 (2012): 113–49.

———. "Student Colleges in Early Modern Bologna." In *Bologna—Cultural Crossroads from the Medieval to the Baroque: Recent Anglo-American Scholarship*, edited by Gian Mario Anselmi, Angela De Benedictis and Nicholas Terpstra, 71–81. Bologna: Bononia University Press, 2012.

Carmichael, Ann G. "Epidemics and State Medicine in Fifteenth-Century Milan." In *Medicine from the Black Death to the French Disease*, edited by Roger French, Jon Arrizabalaga, Andrew Cunningham, and Luis Garcia-Ballester, 220–47. Aldershot: Ashgate, 1998.

Carroll, Stuart, ed. *Cultures of Violence: Interpersonal Violence in Historical Perspective*. Basingstoke, UK: Palgrave Macmillan, 2007.

———. "Stuart Carroll on Homicide and the Civilizing Process." Filmed 21 February, 2013. Youtube video, 4:21. Posted by Berkley Center for Religion, Peace, and World Affairs—Georgetown University, 13 March, 2013. https://www.youtube.com/watch?v=6Z+1xSMGYWQ.

Carter Wood, J. "Conceptualizing Cultures of Violence and Cultural Change." In *Cultures of Violence: Interpersonal Violence in Historical Perspective*, edited by Stuart Carroll, 79–96. Basingstoke, UK: Palgrave Macmillan, 2007.

———. "The Limits of Culture? Society, Evolutionary Psychology and the History of Violence." *Cultural and Social History* 4 (2007): 545–52.

Casagrande, Giovanna, and Michele Pazzaglia. "'Bona mulier in domo.' Donne nel Giudiziario del Comune di Perugia nel Duecento." *Annali della Facoltà di Lettere e Filosofia dell'Università degli Studi di Perugia. 2. Studi-storici-antropologici* 22 (1998–99): 127–66.

Cavina, Marco. "I luoghi della giustizia." In *Istituzioni, forme del potere, economia e società.* Bk. 1 of *Bologna nell'Età Moderna*, edited by Adriano Prosperi, 367–411 Storia di Bologna, vol. 3. Bologna: Bononia Univesity Press, 2008.

Cecchini, Giovanni. "L'assassinio del padre del Poliziano." *Bullettino senese di storia patria* 60 (1953): 202–41.

Celli, Roberto. *Studi sui sistemi normativi delle democrazie comunali: secoli XII–XV*. Florence: G. C. Sansoni, 1976.

Cherubini, Paolo. "Una fonte poco nota per la storia di Roma: I processi della curia del Campidoglio (sec. XV)." In *Roma: Memoria e oblio*, edited by Fabio Troncarelli, 157–82. Rome: Tiellemedia, 2001.

Cohen, Esther. "Inquiring Once More After the Inquisitorial Process." in *Die Entstehung des öffentlichen Strafrechts: Bestand aufnahme eines europäischen Forschungsproblems*, edited by Dietmar Willoweit, 41–59. Cologne: Böhlau, 1999.

———. *The Modulated Scream: Pain in Late Medieval Culture*. Chicago: The University of Chicago Press, 2010.

Cohn, Samuel. K. Jr. "Criminality and the State in Renaissance Florence, 1344–1466." *Journal of Social History* 14 (1980): 211–33.

———. "Repression of Popular Revolt in Late Medieval and Early Renaissance Italy." In *The Culture of Violence in Renaissance Italy*, edited by Samuel Kline Cohn Jr. and Fabrizio Ricciardelli, 99–120. Florence: Le Lettere, 2012.

———. *Women in the Streets: Essays on Sex and Power in Renaissance Italy.* Baltimore, MD: Johns Hopkins University Press, 1996.

Collard, Franck. *Le crime de poison au Moyen Age*. Paris: Presses Universitaires de France, 2003.

———. "*Horrendum scelus*. Recherches sur le statut juridique du crime de poison au Moyen Âge." *Revue Historique* 300 (1998): 737–64.

———. *Pouvoir et poison. Histoire d'un crime politique de l'Antiquité à nos jours*. Paris: Seuil, 2007.

———. "Quand l'épidémie sert d'alibi au crime: Dysenterie et empoisonnement au Moyen Age." In *Air, miasmes et contagion: Les épidémies dans l'Antiquité et au Moyen* Age, edited by Sylvie Bazin-Tacchella, Danielle Quéruel, and Évelyne Samama, 189–97. Langres: Dominique Guéniot, 2001.

———. "Les risques d'un métier ou quand l'apothicairerie devient débit de poisons (France, XIIIe–XVIe s.)." In *Pharmacopoles, et apothicaires. Les "pharmaciens" de l'Antiquité au Grand Siècle*, edited by Franck Collard and Evelyne Samama, 135–50. Paris: L'Harmattan, 2006,

———. "*Veneficiis vel maleficiis*. Réflexion sur les relations entre le crime de poison et la sorcellerie dans l'Occident medieval," *Le Moyen Age* 109.1 (2003): 9–57.

Colliva, Paolo. "Bologna dal XIV al XVIII secolo, 'Governo misto' o signoria senatoria?" In *Storia dell'Emilia Romagna*, edited by Aldo Berselli, 2:13–44. 3 vols. Bologna: University Press, 1977.

———. *Il Cardinale Albornoz, lo Stato della Chiesa, le Costituzioni Egidiane (1353–1357) con in appendice Il testo volgare delle Constituzioni di Fano dal ms. Vat. Lat. 3939*. Studia Albornotiana XXXII. Bologna: Colegio de España, 1977.

Constant, Monique. "La justice dans une châtellenie savoyarde au Moyen Age: Allinges-Thonon." *Revue historique de droit français* 50 (1972): 374–97.

Cooney, Mark. *Warriors and Peacemakers: How Third Parties Shape Violence*. New York: New York University Press, 1998.

Cortese, Ennio. *Il basso medioevo*. Bk. 2 of *Il diritto nella storia medievale*. Rome: Il Cigno editore, 1995.

———. *Il rinascimento giuridico medievale.* Rome: Bulzoni, 1992.

———. "L'Università di Bologna e il Collegio di Spagna nel Cinquecento: Uno scontro tra i rettori Cesare Riva e Diego Gasque." In *Studi in memoria di Giuliana D'Amelio,* 2:219–72. 2 vols. Milan: Giuffré, 1978.

Coss, Peter, "Introduction." In *The Moral World of the Law*, edited by Peter Coss, 1–16. Cambridge: Cambridge University Press, 2000.

Courtenay, William. *Schools and Scholars in Fourteenth-Century England.* Princeton, NJ: Princeton University Press, 1987.

Covini, Maria Nadia. *L'esercito del Duca: Organizzazione militare e istituzioni al tempo degli Sforza, 1450–1480.* Rome: Istituto storico italiano per il Medioevo, 1998.

———. "Milano e Bologna dopo il 1455: Scambi militari, condotte e diplomazia." In *Condottieri e Uomini d'arme nell'Italia del Rinascimento*, edited by Mario Del Treppo, 165–214. Naples: Liguori Editore, 2001.

Cox, Virginia. "Ciceronian Rhetoric in Late Medieval Italy." In *The Rhetoric of Cicero in Its Medieval and Early Renaissance Commentary Tradition*, edited by Virginia Cox and John O. Ward, 109–43. Leiden: Brill, 2006.

Crouzet-Pavan, Elisabeth. "Potere politico e spazio sociale: il controllo della notte a Venezia nei secoli XIII–XV." In *La notte. Ordine, sicurezza e disciplinamento in età moderna*, edited by Mario Sbriccoli, 46–66. Laboratorio di storia 3. Florence: Ponte alle grazie, 1991.
Crouzet-Pavan, Elisabeth, and Jacques Verger, eds. *La dérision au Moyen Age. De la pratique sociale au rituel politique*, Paris, Presses de l'Université Paris-Sorbonne, 2007.
Cucini, Sara. "Législation statutaire et gouvernement pontifical en Italie centrale: Le cas de l'administration de la justice criminelle à Bologne, deuxième moitié du XVe siècle." Doctoral diss. University Paul-Valéry—Montpellier 3 and Alma Mater Studiorum—University of Bologna. 2 vols. 2014.
———. "Les normes en matière criminelle dans les statuts bolognais des XIIIe–XVe siècles: Un exemple d'évolution structurelle du statut," in *Les statuts vus de l'intérieur: La structure, le plan et les thèmes. Actes du colloque de Nimes, 14–15 January 2016*, edited by Didier Lett. Paris: Publications de La Sorbonne, forthcoming.
———. "Violenza 'femminile' e violenza 'maschile': Alcuni esempi tardoquattrocenteschi dai *Libri Maleficiorum*." In *Les registres de la justice pénale (*Libri Maleficiorum*) et les sociétés de l'Italie communale (XIIe–XVe siècles). Actes du colloque, Rome, Ecole Française de Rome, 6–8 juin 2017*, edited by Didier Lett. Rome: Ecole Française de Rome, forthcoming.
Cummins, Stephen, and Laura Kounine. "Introduction: Confronting Conflict in Early Modern Europe." In *Cultures of Conflict Resolution in Early Modern Europe*, edited by Stephen Cummins and Laura Kounine, 1–14. Burlington, VT: Ashgate, 2016.
Dall'Olio, Alberto. *Il Collegio Comelli in Bologna*. Bologna: Zanichelli, 1932.
Davies, Jonathan, ed. *Aspects of Violence in Renaissance Europe*. Farnham: Ashgate, 2013.
———. *Culture and Power: Tuscany and Its Universities, 1537–1609,* 157–78. Leiden: Brill, 2009.
———. "The Ideal Student: Manuals of Student Behavior in Early Modern Italy." *Scholarly Self-Fashioning and Community in the Early Modern University*, edited by Richard Kirwan, 297–305. Farnham: Ashgate, 2013,
———. "Preface." in *Annali di Storia delle università italiane* (June 2016) 20:1–6.
———. "Violence and Universities in the Italian Renaissance." *Renaissance Studies* 27/4 (2013): 504–16.
———. *Violence in Early Modern Italy: The Academic Environment* (forthcoming).
Davies, Wendy, and Paul Fouracre, eds. *The Settlement of Disputes in Early Medieval Europe*. Cambridge: Cambridge University Press, 1986.
Davis, Robert C. *The War of the Fists: Popular Culture and Public Violence in Late Renaissance Venice*. Oxford: Oxford University Press, 1994.
Dean, Trevor. *Crime and Justice in Late Medieval Italy*. Cambridge: Cambridge University Press, 2007.
———. *Crime in Medieval Europe 1200–1550*. London: Longman, 2001.
———. "Criminal justice in mid-fifteenth-century Bologna." In Dean and Lowe, *Crime, Society and the Law,* 16–39.
———. "Domestic violence in late-medieval Bologna." *Renaissance Studies* 18 (2004): 527–43.
———. "Eight Varieties of Homicide: Bologna in the 1340s and 1440s." In *Murder in Renaissance Italy*, edited by Trevor Dean and K. J. P. Lowe, 83–105. Cambridge: Cambridge University Press, 2017.
———. "Fathers and daughters: Marriage laws and marriage disputes in Bologna and Italy, 1200–1500." In *Marriage in Italy 1300–1650*, edited by Trevor Dean and K. J. P. Lowe, 85–106. Cambridge: Cambridge University Press, 1998.
———. "Fornicating with nuns in fifteenth–century Bologna." *Journal of Medieval History* 34 (2008): 374–543.
———. "Gender and insult in an Italian city: Bologna in the later Middle Ages." *Social History* 29 (2004): 217–31.
———. "Marriage and Mutilation: Vendetta in Late Medieval Italy." *Past and Present* 157 (1997): 3–36.
———. "Plague and Crime: Bologna, 1348–51." *Continuity and Change* 30 (2015): 367–93.
———. "Sodomy in Renaissance Bologna." *Renaissance Studies* 31 (2016): 426–43.

———. "Theft and Gender in Late Medieval Bologna." *Gender History* 20 (2008): 399–415.
———. "Violence, Vendetta, and Peacemaking in Late Medieval Bologna." *Criminal Justice History. An International Review* 17 (2002): 1–17.
Dean, Trevor and K. J. P. Lowe, eds. *Crime, Society and the Law in Renaissance Italy*. Cambridge: Cambridge University Press, 1994.
———. "Introducing Renaissance Killers." In *Murder in Renaissance Italy*, edited by Trevor Dean and K. J. P. Lowe, 1–11. Cambridge: Cambridge University Press, 2017.
De Benedictis, Angela. "Da confalonieri del popolo a tribuni della plebe: onore, insigne e visibilità di una magistratura popolare (Bologna, XIV–XVI secolo)." *Ricerche Storiche* 32 (2002): 223–45.
———. "La fine dell'autonomia studentesca tra autorità e disciplinamento." In *Studenti e università degli studenti dal XII al XIX secolo*, edited by Gian Paolo Brizzi and Antionio Ivan Pini, 193–224. Bologna: Istituto per la storia dell'Università, 1988.
———. "Il governo misto." In *Cultura, istituzioni culturali, Chiesa e vita religiosa.* Bk. 2 of *Bologna nell'Età Moderna*, edited by Adriano Prosperi, 201–69. Storia di Bologna, vol. 3. Bologna: Bononia Univesity Press, 2008.
———. *Una guerra d'Italia, una resistenza di popolo: Bologna 1506*. Bologna: Il Mulino, 2004.
———. "Quale 'corte' per quale 'signoria'? A proposito di organizzazione e immagine di potere durante la preminenza di Giovanni II Bentivoglio." In Basile, *Bentivolorum Magnificentia.* 13–33.
———. *Repubblica per contratto: Bologna; Una città europea nello Stato della Chiesa*. Bologna: Il Mulino, 1995.
———. " . . . 'Sendo la parte de' Bentivogli et confirmata et unita': Per una storia del costituirsi dei rapporti di potere in una realtà della prima età moderna." In *"Familia" del Principe e Famiglia Aristocratica*, edited by Cesare Mozzarelli, 2:437–469. 2 vols. Rome: Bulzoni editore, 1988.
———. "Lo 'stato popolare di libertà': pratica di governo e cultura di governo." in *Bologna nel Medioevo*, edited by Ovidio Capitani, 899–950. *Storia di Bologna*, vol. 2. Bologna: Bononia University Press, 2007.
Demuro, Gianpaolo. *Il Dolo. Svolgimento storico del concetto*. Milan: Giuffré Editore, 2007.
Denley, Peter. "Trasgressioni e disordini studenteschi." In *Le università dell'Europa: Gli uomini e i luoghi, sec. XII–XVIII.* edited by Gian Paolo Brizzi and Jacques Verger, 83–103. Milan: Silvana Editoriale, 1993.
Dhondt, Pieter, and Elizabethanne Boran, eds. *Student Revolt, City, and Society: From the Middle Ages to the Present*, International Commission of the History of Universities. London: Routledge.
Dinges, Martin. "Usi della giustizia come elemento di controllo sociale nella prima età moderna." In *Criminalità e giustizia in Germania e i Italia. Pratiche giudiziarie e linguaggi giuridici tra tardo medioevo ed età moderna*, edited by Marco Bellabarba, Gerd Schwerhoff, and Andrea Zorzi, 285–326. Bologna: Il Mulino, 2001.
Ditchburn, David. "'Saints at the Door don't make Miracles?' The Contrasting Fortunes of Scottish Pilgrimage, c. 1450–1550." In *Sixteenth-century Scotland: Essays in Honour of Michael Lynch*, edited by Julian Goodare and Alasdair A. MacDonald, 69–98. Leiden: Brill, 2008.
Di Zio, Tiziana. "Il tribunale criminale di Bologna nel se. XVI." *Archivi per la storia. Rivista dell'Associazione nazionale archivistica italiana* 1–2 (1991): 125–35.
———. "Il tribunale del Torrone," *Atti e Memorie della Deputazione di Storia Patria per le Province di Romagna* 43 (1992): 333–48.
Dondarini, Rolando. "The Bentivoglio and Agreements with the Church (1401–1466)." In *Atlante storico delle città italiane. Emilia-Romagna. Bologna*, vol. 3. *Da una crisi all'altra (secoli XIV–XVII)*, edited by Rolando Dondarini and Carlo De Angelis, 130–34. Bologna: Grafis, 1997.
———. *Bologna medievale nella storia delle città*. Bologna: Pàtron, 2000.
———. "Il declino della pseudosignoria bentivolesca e Alessandro VI." In *Alessandro VI e lo Stato della Chiesa: Atti del Convegno; Perugia 13–15 Marzo 2000*, edited by Carla Frova

and Maria Grazia Nico Ottaviani, 174–202. Rome: Istituto storico italiano per il Medioevo, 2003.

Dorini, Umberto. "La vendetta privata al tempo di Dante." *Giornale dantesco* 29 (1926): 56–68.

Dubber, Markus. *The Police Power: Patriarchy and the Foundations of American Government.* New York: Columbia University Press, 2005.

Duby, Georges. *Dames du XIIe siècle*. 3 vols. Paris: Gallimard, 1995–96.

Duranti, Tommaso. "Un compromesso per il privilegio: Il rapporto tra Giovanni Bentivoglio ed i Sedici Riformatori dello Stato di Libertà di Bologna; In margine all'edizione di un carteggio diplomatico." *Nuova Rivista Storica* 92, no. 3 (2008): 713–42.

———. *Diplomazia e autogoverno a Bologna: Fonti per la storia delle istituzioni.* Bologna: CLUEB, 2009.

———. "*Libertas*, Oligarchy, Papacy: Government in the Quattrocento." In *A Companion to Medieval and Renaissance Bologna*, edited by Sarah Rubin Blanshei, 260–88. Leiden: Brill, 2018.

Eisenbichler, Konrad, ed. *The Premodern Teenager: Youth in Society, 1150–1650.* Toronto: Center for Reformation and Renaissance Studies, 2002.

Eisner, Manuel. "Long-Term Historical Trends in Violent Crime." *Crime and Justice. A Review of Research* 30 (2003): 83–142.

Elias, Norbert. *The Civilizing Process: Sociogenetic and Psychogenetic Investigations*. Rev. ed., trans. Edmund Jephcott. Oxford: Blackwell, 2000.

Elliott, Dyan. *Proving Woman: Female Spirituality and Inquisitional Culture in the Later Middle Ages*. Princeton, N.J: Princeton University Press, 2004.

Enders, Jody. *The Medieval Theater of Cruelty: Rhetoric, Memory, Violence*. Ithaca, NY: Cornell University Press, 1999.

Enriques, Anna Maria. "La vendetta nella vita e nella legislazione fiorentina." *Archivio storico italiano* 19 (1933): 85–146, 181–224.

Epstein, Steven. *Genoa and the Genoese, 958–1528*. Chapel Hill: University of North Carolina Press, 1996.

Esmark, Kim, Lars Hermanson, Hans Jacob Orning, and Helle Vogt, eds. *Disputing Strategies in Medieval Scandinavia*. volume 16. Leiden: Brill, 2013.

Fabris, Cècile. "Dallo studio all'esperienza del diritto: gli studenti davanti alla giustizia a Bologna (fine XIII–inizio XIV sec.)." In *Medioevo a Bologna*, edited by Roberto Sernicola, special issue, *I quaderni del M.Ae.S.* 8 (2005): 9–38.

Fanti, Mario. "Bologna nell'età moderna." In *Storia di Bologna*, edited by Antonio Ferri and Giancarlo Roversi, 197–282. Bologna: ALFA, 1978.

———. "Le lottizzazioni monastiche e lo sviluppo urbano di Bologna nel Duecento," *Atti e Memorie della Deputazione di Storia Patria per le Province di Romagna,* n. s., 27 (1976): 120–44.

Fasoli, Gina. "Bologna nell'età medievale." in *Storia di Bologna* edited by Antonio Ferri and Giancarlo Roversi, 129–96. Bologna: ALFA, 1978.

———. "Le compagnie delle armi a Bologna." *L'Archiginnasio* 28 (1933): 158–83, 323–40.

Felson, Marcus. *Crime and Everyday Life.* 2nd ed. Thousand Oaks: Sage, 1998.

Filippini, Francesco. "L'esodo degli studenti da Bologna nel 1321 e il 'Polifemo' dantesco." *Studi e Memorie dell'Università di Bologna* 6 (1921): 105–85.

Firnhaber-Baker, Justine. "Seigneurial War and Royal Power in Later Medieval Southern France." *Past & Present*, no. 208 (2010): 37–76.

———. *Violence and the State in Languedoc, 1250–1400*. Cambridge: Cambridge University Press, 2014.

Fosi, Irene. *Papal Justice, Subjects and Courts in the Papal State, 1500–1750*, trans. Thomas V. Cohen. Washington, DC: The Catholic University of America Press, 2011.

Fowler Magerl, Linda.Ordines iudiciarii *and* Libelli de ordine iudiciorum*: from the middle of the twelfth to the end of the fifteenth century*. Turnhout: Brepols, 1994.

———. *"Ordo iudiciorum vel ordo iudiciarius": Begriff und Literaturgattung*, Frankfurt, 1981.

Fraher, Richard. "The Theoretical Justification for the New Criminal Law of the High Middle Ages: 'Rei Publice Interest Ne Crimina Remaneant Impunita.'" *The University of Illinois Law Review* (1984): 577–95.

———. "Tancred's 'Summula de Criminibus': A New Text and a Key to the *Ordo Iudiciarius*." *Bulletin of the medieval canon law* 9 (1979): 23–36.

Fransen, Gerard. "Les questions disputées dans les facultés de droit." In *Les questions disputées et les questions quodlibétiques dans les facultés de théologie, de droit et de médicine*, edited by Bernardo C. Bazan, 225–77. Turnhout: Brepols, 1985.

Frati, Lodovico. *La vita privata di Bologna dal secolo XIII al XVII con appendice di documenti inediti e sedici tavole illustrative*. Bologna: Nicola Zanichelli, 1900.

Freund, Julien. *Sociologie du conflit*. Paris: Presses universitaires de France, 1983.

Galatolo, Renata, and Paul Drew. "Narrative Expansions as Defensive Practices in Courtroom Testimony." *Text & Talk*, 26 (2006): 661–98.

Gamberini, Andrea, and Isabella Lazzarini, eds. *The Italian Renaissance State*. Cambridge: Cambridge University Press, 2012.

Gardi, Andrea. "The Making of an Oligarchy: The Ruling Classes of Bologna." In *A Companion to Medieval and Renaissance Bologna*, edited by Sarah Rubin Blanshei, 310–34. Leiden: Brill, 2018.

Garnier, Claudia. *Amicus amicis, inimicus inimicis: politische Freundschaft und fürstliche Netzwerke im 13. Jahrhundert*. Stuttgart: Hiersemann, 2000.

Garnot, Benoît, and Rosine Fry, eds. *L'infrajudiciaire du Moyen Age à l'époque contemporaine. Actes du colloque de Dijon, 5–6 octobre 1995*. Dijon: Editions Universitaires de Dijon, 1996.

Gauvard, Claude. *"De grace especial": Crime, état et société en France à la fin du Moyen Age*. Paris: Publications de la Sorbonne, 1991.

———. ed. *L'enquête au Moyen Age*. Rome: École Française de Rome, 2008.

———. "Grâce et exécution capitale: les deux visages de la justice royale française à la fin du Moyen Âge." *Bibliothèque de l'école des chartes* 153.2 (1995): 275–90.

———. "La violence commanditée: La criminalisation des "tueurs à gage" aux derniers siècles du Moyen Age." *Annales: Histoire, Sciences Sociales* 62 (2007): 1005–29.

Gazzini, Marina. "I Disciplinati, la milizia dei frati Gaudenti, il comune di Bologna e la pace cittadina: statuti a confronto (1261–1265)." *Bollettino della Deputazione di Storia Patria per l'Umbria* 101 (2004): 419–37.

Geary, Patrick. "Extra-Judicial Means of Conflict Resolution." In *La Giustizia Nell'alto Medioevo, Secoli V–VIII: 7–13 Aprile 1994*. Spoleto: Centro italiano di studi sull'alto Medioevo, 1995.

Geltner, G. *Flogging Others: Corporal Punishment and Cultural Identity from Antiquity to the Present*. Amsterdam: Amsterdam University Press, 2014.

Gherardi, Alessandro. "Uno scandalo nell'Università Pisana, l'anno 1474." *Archivio Storico Italiano,* s. 4, 7 (1881): 114–19.

Giansante, Massimo. *Retorica e politica nel Duecento: i notai bolognesi e l'ideologia comunale*. Rome: Istituto storico italiano per il Medio Evo, 1998.

———. *L'usurario onorato: Credito e potere a Bologna in età comunale.* Bologna: Il Mulino, 2008.

Ginatempo, Maria, and Lucia Sandri. *L'Italia delle città: il popolamento urbano tra Medioevo e Rinascimento (secoli XIII–XVI)*. Florence: Le Lettere, 1990.

Giorgi, Andrea, Stefano Moscadelli, and Carla Zarilli, eds. *La documentazione degli organi giudiziari nell'Italia tardo-medievale e moderna. Atti del convegno di studi Siena, Archivio di Stato 15–17 settembre 2008*. Rome: Direzione generale per gli archivi, 2012.

Giuffrida, Antonino. "Giustizia e società." In *Storia della Sicilia*, edited by Rosario Romeo, 3:545–73. 10 vols. Naples: Società Editrice Storia di Napoli e della Sicilia, 1977–81.

Giusberti, Fabio, and Francesca Roversi Monaco. "Economy and Demography." In *A Companion to Medieval and Renaissance Bologna*, edited by Sarah Rubin Blanshei, 154–84. Leiden: Brill, 2018.

Given, James Buchanan. *Inquisition and Medieval Society: Power, Discipline, and Resistance in Languedoc*. Ithaca, NY: Cornell University Press, 1997.

Gluckman, Max. "The Peace in the Feud." *Past and Present*, no. 8 (1955): 1–14.

Gonthier, Nicole. *Le châtiment du crime au Moyen Age: XIIe–XVIe siècles*. Rennes: Presses universitaires de Rennes, 1998.

Gould, Roger V. *Collision of Wills: How Ambiguity about Social Rank Breeds Conflict.* Chicago: The University of Chicago Press, 2003.

Gouron, André. "L'enseignement du droit civil au XIIe siècle." In *Juristes et droits savants:Bologne et la France médiévale.* Aldershot: Ashgate, Variorum Collection Studies, 2000.

Gravdal, Kathryn. *Ravishing Maidens: Writing Rape in Medieval French Literature and Law.* Philadelphia: University of Pennsylvania Press, 1991.

Graziotti, Tamara. *Giustizia penale a San Gimignano (1300–1350)*. Florence: Leo S.Olschki, 2015.

Grendi, Edoardo. "Micro-analisi e storia sociale." *Quaderni storici* 35 (1977): 506–20.

Grendler, Paul F. "The University of Bologna, the City, and the Papacy." *Renaissance Studies* 13, no. 4 (Dec. 1999): 475–85.

———. *The Universities of the Italian Renaissance.* Baltimore and London: Johns Hopkins University Press, 2002.

Grundman, John P. *The Popolo at Perugia, 1139–1309.* Perugia: Deputazione di storia patria per l'Umbria, 1992.

Guarisco, Gabriele. "Il 'popolo' e le pratiche della vendetta a Parma." In Zorzi, *Conflitti, paci e vendetta*. 131–54.

Gundersheimer, Werner L. "Crime and Punishment in Ferrara, 1440–1500." In *Violence and Civil Disorder in Italian Cities, 1200–1500*, edited by Lauro Martines, 103–28. Berkeley: University of California Press, 1972.

Gurr, Ted R. "Historical Trends in Violent Crime: A Critical Review of the Evidence." *Crime and Justice: An Annual Review of Research* 3 (1981): 295–353.

Hanawalt, Barbara A. *'Of Good and Ill Repute': Gender and Social Control in Medieval England.* Oxford: Oxford University Press, 1998.

Hanlon, Gregory, "In Praise of Refeudalization: Princes and Feudataries in North-Central Italy from the Sixteenth to the Eighteenth Century." In *Sociability and Its Discontents: Civil Society, Social Capital, and Their Alternatives in Late Medieval and Early Modern Europe*, edited by Nicholas Eckstein and Nicholas Terpstra, 213–25; Turnhout: Brepols, 2009.

Heers, Jacques. *Family Clans in the Middle Ages: A Study of Political and Social Structures in Urban Areas*. Amsterdam: North-Holland, 1977.

Heffer, Chris. "Narrative Navigation: Narrative Practices in Forensic Discourse." *Narrative Inquiry* 32 (2012): 267–86.

Helmholz, Richard, ed. *Select Cases on Defamation to 1600.* London: The Selden Society, 1985.

———. *The Spirit of Classical Canon Law*. Athens, GA, University of Georgia Press, 2010.

Hughes, Steven. "Fear and Loathing in Bologna and Rome: The Papal Police in Perspective." *Journal of Social History* 21 (1987): 97–116.

Huizinga, Johan. *The Waning of the Middle Ages*, trans. Fritz Hopman. Hammondsworth: Penguin, 1924.

Hyams, Paul R. "Neither Unnatural Nor Wholly Negative: The Future of Medieval Vengeance." In *Vengeance in the Middle Ages: Emotion, Religion and Feud*, edited by Susanna A. Throop and Paul R. Hyams, 203–20. Burlington, VT: Ashgate, 2010.

Isenmann, Moritz. "From Rule of Law to Emergency Rule in Renaissance Florence." In *The Politics of Law in Late Medieval and Renaissance Italy*, edited by Lawrin Armstrong and Julius Kirshner, 55–76. Toronto: University of Toronto Press, 2011.

Jansen, Katherine Ludwig. *Peace and Penance in Late Medieval Italy*. Princeton, NJ: Princeton University Press, 2018.

———. "'Pro Bono Pacis': Crime, Conflict, and Dispute Resolution. The Evidence of Notarial Peace Contracts in Late Medieval Florence." *Speculum* 88 (2013): 427–56.

Jed, Stephanie. *Chaste Thinking: The Rape of Lucretia and the Birth of Humanism*. Bloomington: Indiana University Press, 1989.

Jenkins, Scott. "Medieval Student Violence." available at http://www.medievalists.net/2011/11/medieval-student-violence/, published 22 Nov. 2011.

———. "Medieval Student Violence: Oxford and Bologna, c. 1250–1400." Doctoral diss. Swansea University, 2014.

———. "Violence between Student Nations in Medieval Oxford." in *Annali di Storia delle università italiane* 20, no. 1 (June 2016): 7–26.

Johnson, Eric A., and Eric H. Monkkonen, eds. *The Civilization of Crime: Violence in Town and Country since the Middle Ages*. Urbana: University of Illinois Press, 1996.

Jones, Philip. "Communes and Despots: The City State in Late–Medieval Italy." *Transactions of the Royal Historical Society*, 5th series. 71–96. Cambridge: Cambridge University Press, 1965. Reprinted in *Communes and Despots in Medieval and Renaissance Italy*, edited by John E. Law and Bernadette Paton, 3–24. Farmham, Surrey: Ashgate, 2010.

———. *The Italian City-State: From Commune to Signoria*. Oxford, UK: Clarendon Press, 1997.

Jordan, John. "Rethinking Disputes and Settlements: How Historians Can Use Legal Anthopology." In *Cultures of Conflict Resolution in Early Modern Europe*, edited by Stephen Cummins and Laura Kounine, 17–50. Burlington, VT: Ashgate, 2016.

Kantorowicz, Hermann. *Albertus Gandinus und das Strafrecht der Scholastik*. 2 vols. Berlin: J. Guttentag, 1907 and Leipzig: Walter De Gruyter & Co., 1926.

———. "The *quaestiones disputatae* of the Glossators," in Hermann Kantorowicz, *Rechtshistorische Schriften*, edited by Helmut Coing and Gerhat Immel, 137–84. Karlsruhe: Müller 1970.

Kaeuper, Richard W. *War, Justice, and Public Order: England and France in the Later Middle Ages*. Oxford: Clarendon Press, 1988.

Kaminsky, Howard. "The Noble Feud in the Later Middle Ages." *Past & Present*, no. 177 (2002): 55–83.

Karras, Ruth Mazo. *From Boys to Men: Formation of Masculinity in Late Medieval Europe*. Philadelphia: University pf Pennsylvania Press, 2002.

———. *Sexuality in Medieval Europe: Doing unto Others*. 2nd ed. Abington, Oxfordshire: Routledge, 2012.

———. *Unmarriages: Women, Men and Sexual Unions in the Middle Ages*. Philadelphia: University of Pennsylvania Press, 2012.

Kelly, Henry Ansgar. "Statutes of Rapes and Alleged Ravishers of Wives: A Context for the Charges Against Thomas Malory, Knight." *Viator* 28 (1997): 361–419.

Kéry, Lotte. "'*Inquisitio-denunciatio-exceptio*: Möglichkeiten der Verfahrenseinleitung im Dekretalenrecht." *Zeitschrift der Savigny-Stiftung für Rechtsgeschichte, Kanonistische Abteilung* 87 (2001): 226–68.

Kibre, Pearl. *Scholarly Privileges in the Middle Ages*. Cambridge, MA: Mediaeval Academy of America, 1962.

Kieckhefer, Richard. "The Office of Inquisition and Medieval Heresy: The Transition from Personal to Institutional Jurisdiction." *Journal of Ecclesiastical History* 46 (1995): 36–61.

Kirshner, Julius. "*Consilia* as Authority in Late Medieval Italy: the Case of Florence." In *Legal Consulting in the Civil Law Tradition*, edited by Mario Ascheri, Ingrid Baumgärtner, and Julius Kirshner, 107–40. Berkeley: Robbins Collection, 1999.

Kittel, Ruth. "Rape in Thirteenth-Century England: A Study of the Common-Law Courts Courts." In *Women and the Law: The Social Historical Perspective,* edited by D. Kelly Weisberg, 2:101–15. 2 vols. Cambridge, MA: Schenkman, 1982.

Klapisch-Zuber, Christiane. "Female Celibacy and Service in Renaissance Florence." In *Women, Family and Ritual in Renaissance Florence*, trans. Lydia Cochrane, 165–77. Chicago: The University of Chicago Press, 1985.

Kohler, Josef. *Das Strafrecht der Italienschen Statuten vom 12.–16. Jahrhundert*. Mannheim: J. Beusheimer, 1895.

Kuehn, Thomas. "Conflict Resolution and Legal Systems." In *A Companion to the Medieval World*, edited by Carol Lansing and Edward D. English, 335–53. Oxford: Blackwell, 2013.

———. "*Fama* as legal status in Renaissance Florence." In Fama: *The Politics of Talk & Reputation in Medieval Europe*, edited by Thelma Fenster and Daniel Lord Smail, 27–41. Ithaca, NY: Cornell University Press, 2003.

———. *Law, Family & Women: Toward a Legal Anthropology of Renaissance Italy*. Chicago: The University of Chicago Press, 1991.

Kumhera, Glenn. *The Benefits of Peace: Private Peacemaking in Late Medieval Italy*. Leiden: Brill, 2017.

Kuttner, Stephen. "The Revival of Jurisprudence." In *Renaissance and Renewal in the Twelfth Century*, edited by Robert L. Benson and Giles Constable, with Carol D. Lanham, 299–323. Oxford: Clarendon Press, 1982.

LaFree, Gary. *Losing Legitimacy: Street Crime and the Decline of Social Institutions in America*. Boulder, CO: Westview Press,1998.

Lansing, Carol. "Concubines, Lovers, Prostitutes: Infamy and Female Identity in Medieval Bologna." In *Beyond Florence: The Contours of Medieval and Early Modern Italy*, edited by Paula Findlen, Michelle M. Fontaine, and Duane J. Osheim, 85–100. Stanford, CA: Stanford University Press, 2003.

———. "Conflicts over Gender in Civic Courts." In *The Oxford Handbook of Women and Gender in Medieval Europe*, edited by Judith M. Bennett and Ruth Mazo Karras, 118–32. Oxford; Oxford University Press, 2013.

———. "Donna con Donna? A 1295 Inquest into Female Sodomy." In *Studies in Medieval and Renaissance History: Sexuality and Culture in Medieval and Renaissance Europe*, edited by Philip M. Soergel, 109–22. New York: AMS Press, 2005.

———. "Humiliation and the Exercise of Power in the Florentine *Contado* in the Mid-Fourteenth Century," in *Emotions, Passion and Power in Renaissance Italy*, edited by Fabrizio Ricciardelli and Andrea Zorzi, 77–91. Amsterdam: Amsterdam University Press, 2015.

———. *Passion and Order: Restraint of Grief in the Medieval Italian Communes*. Ithaca, NY: Cornell University Press, 2008.

———. "Poisoned Relations: Marital Conflict in Medieval Bologna." In *Bologna. Cultural Crossroads from the Medieval to the Baroque: Recent Anglo-American Scholarship*, edited by Gian Mario Anselmi, Angela De Benedictis, and Nicholas Terpstra, 129–41. Bologna: Bononia University Press, 2013.

———. *Power and Purity: Cathar Heresy in Medieval Italy*. Oxford, Eng.: Oxford University Press, 2001.

Lantschner, Patrick. "Justice Contested and Affirmed: Jurisdiction and Conflict in Late Medieval Italian Cities." In *Legalism: Community and Justice*, edited by Fermanda Pirie and Judith Scheele, 77–96. Oxford: Oxford University Press, 2014.

———. *The Logic of Political Conflict in Medieval Cities: Italy & the Southern Low Countries, 1370–1440*. Oxford: Oxford University Press, 2015.

———. "'The Nourisher of Seditions': The Negotiation of Coalitions and the Pluralistic Order of Politics." In *The Culture of Violence in Renaissance Italy*, edited by Samuel Kline Cohn Jr. and Fabrizio Ricciardelli, 167–90. Florence: Le Lettere, 2012.

———. "Revolts and the Political Order of Cities in the Late Middle Ages," *Past and Present*, no. 225 (2014): 3–46.

Laufenberg, Lynn Marie. "Women, Crime and Criminal Law in Fourteenth Century Florence." Doctoral diss. Cornell University, 2000.

Lazzarini, Isabella, and François Menant. "Les podestats." In *I comuni di Jean-Claude Maire Vigueur: Percorsi storiografici*, edited by Maria Teresa Caciorgna, Sandro Carocci, and Andrea Zorzi, 177–200. Rome: Viella, 2014.

Leo, Richard A. "False Confessions: Causes, Consequences and Implications." *Journal of the American Academy of Psychiatry and the Law* 37 (2009): 332–43.

Leo, Richard A., and Richard J. Ofshe. "The Consequences of False Confessions: Deprivations of Liberty and Miscarriages of Justice in the Age of Psychological Interrogation." *Journal of Criminal Law and Criminology* 88 (1998): 429–96.

Leveleux, Corinne. *La parole interdite: Le blasphème dans la France médiévale (XIIIe–XVIe Siècles): Du péché au crime*. Paris: De Boccard, 2001.

Levy, Renè, and Xavier Rousseaux. "Stato, giustizia penale e storia: bilancio e prospettive." *Ricerche storiche* 26 (1996): 127–60.

Lines, David A. "Gabriele Paleotti and the University of Bologna: Documents from the Archivio Arcivescovile." In *Bologna—Cultural Crossroads from the Medieval to the Baroque: Recent Anglo-American Scholarship*, edited by Gian Mario Anselmi, Angela De Benedictis, and Nicholas Terpstra, 58–69. Bologna: Bononia University Press, 2012.

———. "Papal Power and University Control in Early Modern Italy: Bologna and Gregory XIII." *Sixteenth Century Journal* 44, no. 3 (2013): 663–82.

———. "Reorganizing the Curriculum: Teaching and Learning in the University of Bologna, c. 1560–1590." *History of Universities* 26, no. 2 (2012): 1–59.

Lucchesi, Marzia. Si quis occidit occidetur. *L'omicidio doloso nelle fonti consiliari (secoli XIV–XVI)*. Pavia: CEDAM, 1999.

Maggiulli, Ilaria. "'Li scholari per il più vivono, et vestono a guisa di soldati, con grande licenza . . . :' 1564, un episodio di violenza studentesca a Bologna." *Annali di Storia delle università italiane* 18 (2014): 313–26.

———. "'Tu ne menti per la gola': Scontri tra scolari dello Studio bolognese nella seconda metà del XVI secolo." *Annali di Storia delle università italiane* 20, no. 1 (June 2016): 27–46.

Magnússon, Sigurdur Gylfi and István M. Szijártó. *What is Microhistory? Theory and Practice*. London: Routledge, 2013.

Maire Vigueur, Jean-Claude. *Cavaliers et citoyens. Guerre, conflits et société dans l'Italie communale, XIIe–XIIIe siècles*. Paris: Ecole des hautes études en sciences sociales, 2003.

———. "Progetti di trasformazione della società nei regimi di Popolo." In *La ricerca del benessere individuale e sociale: ingredienti materiali e immateriali (città italiane, XII–XV secolo): 22o Convegno internazionale di studi, Pistoia, 15–18 maggio 2009*, edited by Centro italiano di studi di storia e d'arte (Pistoia, Italy), 281–316. Rome: Viella, 2011.

———. "L'ufficiale forestiero." In *Ceti, modelli, comportamenti nella società medievale (secoli XIII–metà XIV) (Pistoia, 14–17 maggio 1999)*, 75–97. Pistoia: Centro italiano di studi di storia e d'arte, 2001.

Manikowska, Halina. "Il controllo sulle città. Le istituzioni dell'ordine pubblico nelle città italiane dei secoli XIV e XV." In *Città e servizi sociali nell'Italia dei secoli XII–XV: 12 ° Convegno di studi: Pistoia, 9–12 ottobre 1987*, edited by Emilio Cristiani and Enrica Salvatori, 481–511. Pistoia: Centro italiano di studi di storia e d'arte, 1990.

———. "Polizia e servizi d'ordine a Firenze nella seconda metà del XIV secolo." *Ricerche storiche* 16 (1986): 17–38.

Martin, John Jeffries. "Francesco Casoni and the Rhetorical Forensics of the Body." *Journal of Medieval and Early Modern Studies* 45 (2015): 103–30.

Martines, Lauro. *Violence and Civil Disorder in Italian Cities, 1200–1500*. Berkeley: University of California Press, 1972.

Martone, Luciano. *Arbiter-arbitrator: forme di giustizia privata nell'età del diritto comune*. Naples: Jovene, 1984.

Maugain, Gabriel. *Mœurs italiennes de la renaissance. La vengeance*. Paris: Les Belles lettres, 1935.

Mazzoni-Toselli, Ottavio. *Cenno sull'antica storia del foro criminale bolognese*. Bologna: Tipografia del Genio, 1835.

———. *Racconti storici estratti dall'Archivio criminale di Bologna ad illustrazione della storia patria*. 3 vols. Bologna: A. Chierici, 1866–70.

McCormick, John P. *Machiavellian Democracy*. Cambridge: Cambridge University Press, 2011.

Menzinger, Sara. "*Consilium sapientum*. Lawmen and the Italian Popular Commune." In *Politics of Law in Late Mediveal Italy. Essays in Honour of Lauro Martines*, edited by Lawrin Armstrong and Julius Kirshner, 40–54. Toronto: University of Toronto Press, 2011.

———. *Giuristi e politica nei comuni di Popolo. Siena, Perugia e Bologna: tre governi a confronto*. Rome: Viella, 2006.

Menzinger Sara, and Massimo Vallerani. "Giuristi e città: fiscalità, giustizia e cultura giuridica tra XII e XIII secolo. Ipotesi di ricerca." In *I comuni di Jean Claude Maire Vigueur*.

Percorsi storiografici, edited by Maria Teresa Caciorgna, Sandro Carocci and Andrea Zorzi, 201–34. Rome, Viella 2014.

Miglio, Gianfranco, Moreno Morani, Pier Paolo Portinaro, and Alessandro Vitale, eds. *Amicus (inimicus) hostis: le radici concettuali della conflittualità "privata" e della conflittualità "politica."* Milan: Giuffrè, 1992.

Migliorino, Francesco. *Fama e Infamia: Problemi della società medievale nel pensiero giuridico del XII e XIII secolo*. Catania: Editrice Giannotta, 1985.

Milani, Giuliano. "Banditi, *malesardi* e ribelli. L'evoluzione del nemico pubblico nell'Italia comunale (secoli XII–XIV)." *Quaderni fiorentini per la storia del pensiero giuridico moderno* 38 (2009): 109–40.

———. *L'esclusione dal comune: Conflitti e bandi politici a Bologna e in altre cittá italiane tra XII e XIV secolo*. Rome: Istituto storico Italiano per il Medio Evo, 2003.

———. "Prime note su disciplina e pratica del bando a Bologna." *Mélanges de l'Ecole Française de Rome—Moyen Age* 109 (1997): 501–23.

Miller, William Ian. *Bloodtaking and Peacemaking: Feud, Law, and Society in Saga Iceland*. Chicago: The University of Chicago Press, 1990.

Monson, Craig A. *Habitual Offenders: A True Tale of Nuns, Prostitutes, and Murderers in 17th-Century Italy*. Chicago: The University of Chicago Press, 2016.

Montorsi, William, ed. *La Giustizia del Capitano del Popolo di Bologna, 1275–1511: Inventario*. Revision, introduction, and index by Lorena Scaccabarozzi. Modena: Aedes Muratoriana, 2011.

———. "Involuzione del capitanato del popolo in Bologna: L'esecutore e il conservatore di giustizia." *Bullettino dell'Instituto storico Italiano per il medioevo* 73 (1972): 165–217.

Moore, Sally Falk. *Law as Process; An Anthropological Approach*. London: Routledge, 1978.

Muchembled, Robert. *A History of Violence: From the End of the Middle Ages to the Present*, trans. Jean Birrell. Cambridge, UK: Polity Press, 2012.

———. *La violence au village: sociabilité et comportements populaires en Artois du XVe au XVIIe siècles*. Turnhout: Brepols, 1989.

Muir, Edward. *Mad Blood Stirring: Vendetta & Factions in Friuli during the Renaissance*. Baltimore: Johns Hopkins University Press, 1993.

Muir, Edward, and Guido Ruggiero, eds. *Microhistory & the Lost Peoples of Europe*, trans. Erin Branch. Baltimore, MD: The Johns Hopkins University Press, 1991.

Nasalli Rocca di Corneliano, Emilio. "Il card. Bessarione legato pontificio in Bologna (1450–1455)." *Atti e Memorie della Regia Deputazione di Storia Patria per le Provincie di Romagna*, s. 4, 20 (1929–30): 17–80.

Nash, David. "Blasphemy and the Anti-Civilizing Process." In *Assaulting the Past: Violence and Civilization in Historical Context*, edited by Katherine D. Watson, 58–76. Newcastle, UK: Cambridge Scholars, 2007.

Netterstrøm, Jeppe Büchert. "The Study of Feud in Medieval and Early Modern History." In *Feud in Medieval and Early Modern Europe*, edited by Jeppe Büchert Netterstrøm and Bjørn Poulsen, 9–67. Aarhus: Aarhus University Press, 2007.

Niccolai, Franco. *I consorzi nobiliari ed il comune nell'alta e media Italia*. Bologna: N. Zanichelli, 1940.

Niccoli, Ottavia. *Perdonare. Idee, pratiche, rituali in Italia tra Cinque e Seicento*. Rome: Laterza, 2007.

———. *Il seme della violenza: Putti, fanciulli e mammoli nell'Italia tra Cinque e Seicento*. Rome: Laterza, 2007.

———. *Storie di ogni giorno in una città del Seicento*. Rome: Laterza, 2000.

North, Douglass C. *Institutions, Institutional Change, and Economic Performance*. New York: Cambridge University Press, 1990.

North, Douglass C., John Joseph Wallis, and Barry R. Weingast. *Violence and Social Orders: A Conceptual Framework for Interpreting Recorded Human History*. New York: Cambridge University Press, 2009.

Onori, Alberto. "Pace Privata e regolamentazione della vendetta in Valdinievole," in *Conflitte, paci e vendetta nell'Italia comunale*, edited by Andrea Zorzi, 219–36. Florence: Firenze University Press, 2009.

Orioli, Raniero. "Inquisizione e turpiloquio. Bestemmie e gioco d'azzardo nel medioevo." *Abstracta* 1, no. 4 (1986): 48–53.

———. "'E nol porave fare Dio . . . ' Documenti dell'Inquisizione bolognese alla fine del Trecento," *Rendiconti dell'Accademia Nazionale dei Lincei. Classe di Scienze morali, storiche e filologiche* s. 8, 43 (1988): 173–234.

Orlandelli, Gianfranco. "Appunti sulla scuola bolognese di notariato nel secolo XIII. Per un'edizione della *Ars notariae* di Salatiele." In Gianfranco Orlandelli. *Scritti di paleografia e diplomatica*, edited by Roberto Ferrara and Giovanni Feo, 347–98. Bologna: Istituto per la storia dell'università di Bologna, 1994.

———. *La supplica a Taddeo Pepoli*. Bologna: Pàtron, 1962.

Ortalli, Gherardo. "*. . . Pingitur in Palatio." La pittura infamante nei secoli XIII–XIV*. Rome: Jouvence, 1979.

Oxburgh, Gavin E., Trond Myklebust, and Tim Grant. "The Question of Question Types in Police Interviews: A Review of the Literature from a Psychological and Linguistic Perspective." *Journal of Speech, Language and the Law* 17 (2010): 45–66.

Padoa-Schioppa, Antonio. "Delitto e pace privata nel pensiero dei legisti bolognesi. Brevi note." *Studia Gratiana* 20 (1976): 269–87.

———. "La giustizia milanese nella prima età viscontea (1277–1300)." In Antonio Padoa-Schioppa, *Giustizia medievale italiana dal* Regnum *ai comuni*, 299–344. Spoleto: Centro italiano di studi sull'alto medioevo, 2015.

———. "Profili del processo civile nella summa *artis notariae* di Rolandino." In *Rolandino e l'Ars notaria da Bologna all'Europa*, edited by Giorgio Tamba, 586–609. Milan: Giuffrè, 2002.

Palmer, James A. "Piety and Social Distinction in Late Medieval Roman Peacemaking." *Speculum* 89 (2014): 974–1004.

Pastore, Alessandro. "Poison and Poisoning in Renaissance Italy." In *Murder in Renaissance Italy*, edited by Trevor Dean and K. J. P. Lowe, 228–46. Cambridge: Cambridge University Press, 2017.

———. *Veleno. Credenze, crimini, saperi nell'Italia moderna*. Bologna: Il Mulino, 2010.

Patrizi, Elisabetta. *La trattatistica educativa tra rinascimento e controriforma: L'"idea dello scolare" di Cesare Crispolti*. Pisa: Istituti editoriali e poligrafici internazionali, 2005.

Pellegrini, Marco. *Congiure di Romagna: Lorenzo de' Medici e il duplice tirannicidio a Forlì e Faenza*. Florence: Leo S. Olschki, 1999.

Pene Vidari, Gian Savino. "Sulla criminalità e sui banni del commune di Ivrea nei primi anni della dominazione sabauda (1313–1347)." *Bollettino storico-bibliografico subalpino* 68 (1970): 157–211.

Perrot, Ernest. *Les cas royaux: origine et développement de la théorie aux 13e et 14e siècles*. Paris: Arthur Rousseau, 1910.

Pertile, Antonio. *Storia del diritto italiano dalla caduta dell'Impero Romano alla codificazione*. 6 vols. 2nd ed. Turin: Unione tipografica, 1892–1902.

Peters, Edward. *Inquisition*. Berkeley: University of California Press, 1989.

Pini, Antonio Ivan. "'Discere turba volens': Studenti e vita studentesca a Bologna dalle origini dello Studio alla metà del Trecento." In *Studenti e università degli studenti dal XII al XIX secolo*, edited by Gian Paolo Brizzi and Antonio Ivan Pini, 45–136. Bologna: Istituto per la storia dell'Università, 1988.

———. "Gli estimi cittadini di Bologna dal 1296 al 1329," *Studi medievali* 18, no. 1 (1977): 111–59.

———. "Manovre di regime in una città-partito. Il falso teodosiano, Rolandino Passaggeri, la Società della Croce e il 'barisello' nella Bologna di fine Duecento." *Atti e memorie della Deputazione di storia patria per le province di Romagna* n.s. 49 (1998): 281–318.

Pini, Raffaella. *Le giustizie dipinte*. Bologna: Minerva, 2011.

Pinker, Steven. *The Better Angels of Our Nature: Why Violence Has Declined*. New York: Viking, 2011.

Poloni, Alma. "Disciplinare la società. Un esperimento di potere nei maggiori Comuni di Popolo tra Due e Trecento." *Scienza e politica* 37 (2007): 33–62.

Prosperi, Adriano. "Un gruppo ereticale italo-spagnolo: la setta di Giorgio Siculo." *Critica storica* XIX (1982): 335–51.

Prosperi, Ilaria. "Il quadro politico-istituzionale: Note preliminari." In *Laboratorio sulle fonti d'archivio: Ricerche su società e istituzioni a Bologna nel tardo Trecento*, edited by Antonella Campanini and Rossella Rinaldi, 27–53. Bologna: CLUEB, 2005.

Provero, Luigi. "Dai testimoni al documento: La società rurale di fronte alle inchieste giudiziarie (Italia del nord, secoli XII–XIII)." In Gauvard, *L'enquête au Moyen Age*. 75–88.

Pullan, Brian. *History of Early Renaissance Italy: From Mid-thirteenth to the Mid-fifteenth Century*. London: Allen Lane, 1973.

———. "'A Ship with Two Rudders': 'Righetto marrano' and the Inquisition in Venice." *Historical Journal* 20 (1977): 25–58.

Quadrini, Flavia. "Primi sondaggi sulla criminalità a Bologna nel 1500." Tesi di laurea. Alma Mater Studiorum—University of Bologna, 1975–76.

Quaquarelli, Leonardo, ed. *Censimento delle Cronache bolognesi del Medioevo e del Rinascimento*. Vol. 1 of *Memoria Urbis*. With introduction by Fulvio Pezzarossa. Bologna: Il Nove, 1993.

Rashdall, Hastings. *The Universities of Europe in the Middle Ages*, edited by F. M. Powicke and A. B. Emden. 3 vols. Oxford: Oxford University Press, 1936. Reprint, Oxford: Clarendon Press, 1987.

Redon, Odile. *Les langues de l'Italie médiévale: textes d'histoire et de* littérature Xe–XIVe siècle. Turnhout: Brepols, 2002.

Le règlement des conflits au Moyen Âge. Actes des congrès de la Société des historiens médiévistes de l'enseignement supérieur public, 31e congrès, Angers, 2000. Paris: Publications de la Sorbonne, 2001.

Reyerson, Kathryn L. "Le témoignage des femmes d'après quelques enquêtes montpelliéraines du XIV siècle." In Gauvard, *L'enquête au Moyen Age*, 153–68.

Riches, David. "The Phenomenon of Violence." In *The Anthropology of Violence*, edited by David Riches, 1–27. Oxford, UK: Blackwell, 1986.

Rivers, James B. "Magic, Religion, and the Law: The Case of the *Lex Cornelia de sicariis et veneficis*." In *Religion and Law in Classic and Christian Rome*, edited by Clifford Ando and Jörg Rüpke, 47–67. Stuttgard: Franz Steiner Verlag, 2006.

Roberts, Gregory G. "Policing and Public Power in Communal Italy." Doctoral diss., Yale University, 2013.

Roberts, Simon. *Order and Dispute: An Introduction to Legal Anthropology*. New York: Penguin, 1979.

Robertson, Ian, *Tyranny under the Mantle of St Peter: Pope Paul II and Bologna*. Turnhout: Brepols, 2002.

Rose, Colin S. "Homicide in North Italy: Bologna, 1600–1700." Doctoral diss. University of Toronto, 2016.

———. "Justice in the *Contado*: Rural Vendetta and Urban Authority in Bologna, 1600." *Krypton: Identità Potere, Rappresentazioni* 5–6 (2015): 17–24.

Rosenwein, Barbara H., ed. *Anger's Past: The Social Uses of an Emotion in the Middle Ages*. Ithaca, NY: Cornell University Press, 1998.

Rossi, Giovanni. Consilium sapientis iudiciale. *Studi e ricerche per la storia del processo romano*-canonico, Milan, Giuffrè, 1958.

Rosso, Paolo. "Vicende studentesche pavesi nella seconda metà del Quattrocento." *Bollettino della Società Pavese di Storia Patria* 45 (1993): 37–66.

Roth, Randolph. *American Homicide*. Cambridge, MA: Harvard University Press, 2009.

———. "Biology and the Deep History of Homicide." *British Journal of Criminology* 51 (2011): 535–55.

Roversi Monaco, Francesca. *Conflitti oligarchici nella Bologna di Annibale I: La Cronica di Galeazzo Marescotti de' Calvi*. Bologna: CLUEB, 2012.

Rubinstein, Nicolai. *Politics, Diplomacy and the Constitution in Florence and Italy*, vol. 2 of *Studies in Italian History in the Middle Ages and the Renaissance*, edited by Giovanni Ciappelli. Rome: Edizioni di storia e letteratura, 2004.

Ruff, Julius R. *Violence in Early Modern Europe 1500–1800*. Cambridge: Cambridge University Press, 2001.

Ruggiero, Guido. *Violence in Early Renaissance Venice*. New Brunswick, NJ: Rutgers University Press, 1980.

Russell, Sara Elizabeth Christina. "Courtship, Violence and the Formation of Marriage in the Early Modern Italian Novella Tradition." Doctoral diss. University of California, Berkeley, 2010.

Sabapathy, John. "A Medieval Officer and a Modern Mentality? Podestà and the Quality of Accountability." *The Mediaeval Journal* 1, no. 2 (2011): 43–80.

Salfati, C. Gabrielle. "The Nature of Expressiveness and Instrumentality in Homicide." *Homicide Studies* 4 (2000): 265–93.

Salvemini, Gaetano. *Magnati e popolani in Firenze dal 1280 al 1295*. Florence: Carnesecchi, 1899.

Sbriccoli, Mario. *Crimen Laesae Maiestatis: Il problema del reato politico alle soglie della scienza penalistica moderna.* Milan: Giuffré, 1974.

———. "Giustizia negoziata, giustizia egemonica. Riflessioni su una nuova fase degli studi di storia della giustizia criminale." In *Criminalità e giustizia in Germania e in Italia: Pratiche giudiziarie e linguaggi giuridici tra tardo Medioevo ed età moderna. Atti del convegno tenuto a Trento nei giorni 21–23 ottobre 1999*, edited by Marco Bellabarba, Gerd Schwerhoff, and Andrea Zorzi, 345–64. Bologna; Berlin: Il Mulino, Duncker & Humblot, 2001.

———. "Legislation, Justice and Political Power in Italian Cities, 1200–1400." In *Legislation and Justice: The Origins of the Modern State in Europe, 13th to 18th Centuries,* edited by Antonio Padoa-Schioppa, 37–55. Oxford, UK: Oxford University Press, 1997.

———. "Polizia (Diritto Intermedio)." *Enciclopedia Del Diritto*. Milan: Giuffrè, 1985.

———. *Storia del diritto penale e della giustizia: scritti editi e inediti (1972–2007)*. 2 vols. Milan: Giuffrè, 2009.

———. "'Vidi communiter observari': L'emersione di un ordine penale pubblico nelle città italiane del secolo XIII." *Quaderni fiorentini* 27 (1998): 231–68.

Schindler, Norbert. "I tutori del disordine: rituali della cultura giovanile agli inizi dell'età moderna." In *Dall'antichità all'età moderna.* Bk. 1 of *Storia dei Giovani*, edited by Giovanni Levi and Jean-Claude Schmitt, 303–74. Rome: Laterza, 2000.

Scott, Tom. *The City-State in Europe, 1000–1600*. Oxford, UK: Oxford University Press, 2012.

Seneca, Federico. "Antonio Rosato, bidello generale dello Studio Patavino, e i 'disordini' del 1559." *Quaderni per la storia dell'Università di Padova* 16 (1983): 109–17.

Sensi, Mario. "Per una inchiesta sulle 'paci private' alla fine del Medio Evo." In *Santuari, pellegrini, eremiti nell'Italia centrale*, 3:1455–92. Uomini e mondi medievali 6. Spoleto: Fondazione centro italiano di studi sull'alto Medioevo, 2003.

Shaw, Christine. "Honour, Faction and Private Wars." In *Barons and Castellans: The Military Nobility of Renaissance Italy*, 67–99. Leiden: Brill, 2015.

———. *The Politics of Exile in Renaissance Italy.* Cambridge: Cambridge University Press, 2000.

Sherwin, Richard K. "Law Frames: Historical Truth and Narrative Necessity in a Criminal Case." *Stanford Law Review* 47 (1994): 39–84.

Shuy, Roger W. *The Language of Confession, Interrogation and Deception.* Thousand Oaks: Sage, 1998.

Signorotto, Gianvittorio, and Maria Antonietta Visceglia, eds. *Court and Politics in Papal Rome, 1492–1700*. Cambridge: Cambridge University Press, 2002.

Skoda, Hannah. *Medieval Violence: Physical Brutality in Northern France, 1270–1330*. Oxford, UK: Oxford University Press, 2013.

Smail, Daniel Lord. "Aspects of Procedural Documentation in Marseille (14th–15th centuries)." In *Als die Welt in die Akten kam. Prozeßschriftgut im europuaischen Mittelater*, edited by Susanne Lepsius and Thomas Wetzstein, 138–63. Frankfurt am Main: Vittorio Klostermann, 2008.

———. *The Consumption of Justice: Emotions, Publicity, and Legal Culture in Marseille, 1264–1423*. Ithaca, NY: Cornell University Press, 2003.

———. "Hatred as a Social Institution in Late-Medieval Society." *Speculum* 76, no. 1 (2001): 90–126.

———. *On Deep History and the Brain*. Oakland: The Regents of the University of California, 2008.

———. "Telling Tales in Angevin Courts." *French Historical Studies* 20 (1997): 183–215.

———. "Violence and Predation in Late Medieval Mediterranean Europe." *Comparative Studies in Society and History* 54 (2012): 1–28.

Smurra, Rosa. *Città, cittadini e imposta diretta a Bologna alla fine del Duecento: Ricerche preliminari.* Bologna: CLUEB, 2007.

———. "Fiscal Sources: The *Estimi*." In *A Companion to Medieval and Renaissance Bologna*, edited by Sarah Rubin Blanshei, 42–55. Leiden: Brill, 2018.

———. "Studiare, lavorare a Bologna nel Medioevo: forestieri/stranieri in città." *Ricerche di pedagogia e didattica—Journal of Theories and Research in Education* 7, no. 2 (2012): 79–110.

Somaini, Francesco. "The collapse of the city-states and the role of the urban centres in the new political geography of Renaissance Italy." In Gamberini and Lazzarini, *The Italian Renaissance State*, 239–60.

Sorbelli, Albano, and Luigi Simeoni. *Storia dell'Università di Bologna,* 2 vols. Bologna: Zanichelli, 1944–47.

Sottili, Agostino. "Le contestate elezioni rettorali di Paul van Baenst e Hohannes von Dalbert all'Università di Pavia." *Humanistica Lovaniensa* 31 (1982): 29–75; 114–19.

Spierenburg, Pieter. *A History of Murder: Personal Violence in Europe from the Middle Ages to the Present.* Malden, MA: Polity Press, 2008.

Stern, Laura Ikins. "Public Fame in the Fifteenth Century." *American Journal of Legal History* 45 (2000): 198–222.

Stollberg-Rilinger, Barbara. "The Impact of Communication Theory on the Analysis of the Early Modern Statebuilding Processes." In *Empowering Interactions: Political Cultures and the Emergence of the State in Europe 1300–1900*, edited by Wim Blockmans, André Holenstein, and Jon Matthieu in collaboration with Daniel Schläppi, 313–18. Burlington, VT: Ashgate, 2009.

Stuard, Susan Mosher. "Brideprice, Dowry and Other Marital Assigns." In *The Oxford Handbook of Women and Gender in Medieval Europe*, edited by Judith M. Bennett and Ruth Mazo Karras, 148–62. Oxford, UK: Oxford University Press, 2013.

———. *Gilding the Market: Luxury and Fashion in Fourteenth-Century Italy*. Philadelphia: University of Pennsylvania Press, 2006.

Sullivan, Karen. *The Inner Lives of Medieval Inquisitors*. Chicago: The University of Chicago Press, 2011.

Tamba, Giorgio. "I XVI Riformatori dello stato di libertà nella loro prima esperienza." In *L'eredità culturale di Gina Fasoli: Atti del Convegno di Studi per il centenario della nascita (1905–2005); Bologna-Bassano del Grappa, 24–26 novembre 2005*, edited by Francesca Bocchi and Gian Maria Varanini, 401–60. Rome: Istituto storico italiano per il Medioevo, 2008.

———. "Civic Institutions. 12th–early 15th Centuries." In *A Companion to Medieval and Renaissance Bologna*, edited by Sarah Rubin Blanshei, 211–38. Leiden; Brill, 2018.

———. *Il regime del popolo e delle arti verso il tramonto: Innovazioni e modifiche istituzionali del comune bolognese nell'ultimo decennio del secolo XIV*. Bologna: Arnaldo Forni, 2009.

Tamba, Giorgio, and Isabella Zanni Rosiello, eds. "Archivio di Stato di Bologna." In *Guida generale degli archivi di Stato italiani*, 1:549–645. Rome: Ministero per i beni culturali e ambientali, 1981.

Terpstra, Nicholas. "Apprenticeship in Social Welfare: From Confraternal Charity to Municipal Poor Relief in Early Modern Italy." *Sixteenth Century Journal* 23, no. 1 (1994): 101–20.

———. "Body Politics: The Criminal Body between Public and Private." *Journal of Medieval and Early Modern Studies* 45 (2015): 7–52.

———. "Competing Visions of the State and Social Welfare: The Medici Dukes, the Bigallo Magistrates, and Local Hospitals in Sixteenth-Century Tuscany." *Renaissance Quarterly* 54 (2001): 1319–55.

———. "Confraternities and Civil Religion." In *A Companion to Medieval and Renaissance Bologna*, edited by Sarah Rubin Blanshei, 386–410. Leiden: Brill, 2018.

———. "Theory into Practice: Executions, Comforting, and Comforters in Renaissance Italy." In *The Art of Executing Well: Rituals of Execution in Renaissance Italy*, edited by Nicholas Terpstra, 118–79. Kirksville, MO: Truman State University Press, 2008.

Théry, Julien. "*Atrocitas/Enormitas*. Esquisse pour une histoire de la catégorie d'énormité ou 'crime énorme' du Moyen Age à l'époque modern." *Clio@Themis: Revue électronique d'histoire du droit,* 4 (2011), available at http://www.cliothemis.com/Atrocitas-enormitas-Esquisse-pour

———. "*Fama*: L'opinion publique comme preuve judiciaire; Aperçu sur la révolution médiévale de l'inquisitoire (XIIe–XIVe siècle)." In *La preuve en justice de l'antiquité à nos jours*, edited by Bruno Lemesle, 119–47. Rennes: Presses Universitaires de Rennes, 2003.

Thompson, Augustine. *Cities of God: The Religion of the Italian Communes, 1125–1325*. University Park, PA: Pennsylvania State University Press, 2005.

Throop, Susanna A., and Paul R. Hyams, eds. *Vengeance in the Middle Ages: Emotion, Religion and Feud*. Burlington, VT: Ashgate, 2010.

Todeschini, Giacomo. *Visibilmente crudeli. Malviventi, persone sospette e gente qualunque dal medioevo all'età moderna.* Bologna: il Mulino 2007.

Torre, Angelo "Feuding, Factions, and Parties: The Redefinition of Politics in the Imperial Fiefs of Langhe in the Seventeenth and Eighteenth Centuries." In *History from Crime: Selections from* Quaderni Storici, edited by Edward Muir and Guido Ruggiero, 135–70. Baltimore, MD: Johns Hopkins University Press, 1994.

Toulet, Michel. "L'Incrimination de port d'armes au bas moyen-âge." *Mémoires de la société pour l'histoire du droit et des institutions des anciens pays bourguignons, comtois, et romands* 45 (1988): 435–48.

Tracy, Larissa. *Torture and Brutality in Medieval Literature: Negotiations of National Identity*. Cambridge: D. S. Brewer, 2012.

Trombetti Budriesi, Anna Laura. "Alessandro VI e i Bentivoglio: Bologna, una conquista in differita." In *La Norma e la Memoria: Studi per Augusto Vasina*, edited by Tiziana Lazzari, Leardo Mascanzoni and Rossella Rinaldi, 661–90. Rome, Istituto storico italiano per il Medio Evo, 2004.

Trusen, Winfried. "Der Inquisitionprozess: Seine historische Grundlagen und frühen formen." *Zeitschrift für Rechtsgeschichte* 118, Kanonistische Abteilung 105 (1988): 163–230.

Tuten, Belle S., and Tracey L. Billado, eds. *Feud, Violence and Practice: Essays in Medieval Studies in Honor of Stephen D. White*. Burlington, VT: Ashgate, 2010.

Vallerani, Massimo. "L'arbitrio negli statuti cittadini del Trecento." In *Tecniche di potere nel tardo medioevo: Regimi comunali e signorie in Italia*, edited by Massimo Vallerani, 117–47. Rome: Viella, 2010.

———. "Conflitti e modelli procedurali nel sistema giudiziario comunale: I regesti di processi di Perugia nella seconda metà del XIII secolo." *Società e storia* 48 (1990): 267–99.

———. "*Consilia iudicialia*. Sapienza giuridica e processo nelle città italiane." *Mélanges d'école francaise de Rome—Moyen Age* 123 (2011): 129–39.

———. "Il diritto in questione. Forme del dubbio e produzione del diritto nella seconda metà del duecento." *Studi medievali* 48 (2007): 1–41.

———. "La fama nel processo tra costruzioni giuridiche e modelli sociali nel tardo Medioevo." In *La fiducia secondo i linguaggi del potere*, edited by Paolo Prodi, 93–111. Bologna: Il Mulino, 2007.

———. "The generation of the *moderni* at Work. Jurists between School and Politics in Medieval Bologna (1270–1305)." In *Europa und seine Regionen*: *2000 jahre Rechtsgeschichte*, edited by Andreas Bauer and Karl L. Welker, 139–56. Vienna: Böhlau, 2007.

———. "Giochi di posizione tra definizioni legali e pratiche sociali nelle fonti giudiziarie bolognesi del XIII secolo." In *Gioco e giustizia nell'Italia di comune*, edited by Gherardo Ortalli, 13–34. Rome: Viella, 1993.

———. "Il giudice e le sue fonti: Note su *inquisitio* e fama nel *Tractatus de maleficiis* di Alberto da Gandino." *Rechtsgeschichte* 14 (2009): 50–54

———. "Giustizia e documentazione a Bologna in età comunale (secoli XIII–XIV)." In Giorgi, Moscadelli, and Zarilli. *La documentazione degli organi giudiziari.*

———. "Justice publique et compétences des personnes dans les villes italiennes du bas Moyen Age. Une esquisse problématique." In *Valeurs et justice: Écarts et proximités entre société et monde judiciaire du Moyen Age au XVIIIe siècle*, edited by Bruno Lemesle and Michel Nassiet, 37–49. Rennes: Presses universitaires de Rennes, 2011.

———. *Medieval Public Justice*, trans. Sarah Rubin Blanshei. Washington, DC: The Catholic University of America Press, 2012.

———. "Pace e processo nel sistema giudiziario del comune di Perugia." *Quaderni storici* 101 (1999): 315–54.

———. *Il sistema giudiziario del comune di Perugia: conflitti, reati e processi nella seconda metà del XIII secolo*. Perugia: Deputazione di storia patria per l'Umbria, 1991.

Venticelli, Maria. "Metodologie elettroniche per l'edizione di fonti: Lo statuto del comune di Bologna dell'anno 1376." Doctoral diss. Alma Mater Studiorum—University of Bologna, 1999.

———. "Normative medievali bolognese: gli statuti criminali." *Il Carrobbio* 26 (2000): 31–48.

Verdon, Laure. *La voix des dominés: Communautés et seigneurie en Provence au bas Moyen Age*. Rennes: Presses Universitaires de Rennes, 2012.

Verga, Ettore. "Le sentenze criminali dei podestà milanesi, 1385–1429." *Archivio Storico Lombardo*, 5th ser. 16 (1901): 96–142.

Vestrucci, Valentina. "Un confronto tra gli statuti criminali di Bologna nel tardo medioevo." *Il Carrobbio* 30 (2004): 33–60.

Vise, Melissa. "The Threat of the Tongue: Illicit Speech in Late Medieval Italy, 1250–1450." Doctoral diss., Northwestern University, 2015.

———. "The Women and the Inquisitor: Bologna, 1299." *Speculum* (forthcoming, April 2018).

Vitale, Vito. *Il dominio della parte guelfa in Bologna (1280–1327)*. Bologna: A. Forni, 1901.

Vitiello, Joanna Carraway. *Public Justice and the Criminal Trial in Late Medieval Italy: Reggio Emilia in the Visconti Age*. Leiden: Brill, 2016.

———. "Trial Procedure, Dispute Settlement, and the Criminal Judge in Fourteenth-Century Italy." Paper presented at the 86th Annual Meeting of the Medieval Academy of America. Scottsdale: Arizona, April 14–16, 2011.

———. "Vengeance, Vendetta, and Justice in Late Medieval Italy." In *A Global History of Crime and Punishment in the Renaissance*, edited by Clive Emsley and Sara McDougall, vol. 3 of *Renaissance*, edited by Laura Stokes. New York: Bloomsbury Press, forthcoming.

Waley, Daniel. *The Italian City-Republics*. 3rd ed. Harlow, Eng.: Longman, 1988.

Waquet, Jean-Claude. *Corruption: Ethics and Power in Florence, 1600–1770*. University Park, PA: Pennsylvania State University Press, 1992.

Watson, Katherine, ed. *Assaulting the Past: Violence and Civilization in Historical Context*. Newcastle, UK: Cambridge Scholars, 2007.

White, Stephen D., ed. *Feuding and Peace-Making in Eleventh-Century France*. Burlington, VT: Ashgate, 2005.

Wickham, Chris. *Courts and Conflict in Twelfth-Century Tuscany*. Oxford, UK: Oxford University Press, 2003.

———. *Legge, pratiche e conflitti: Tribunali e risoluzione delle dispute nella Toscana del XII secolo*. Rome: Viella, 2000.

Woods, Marjorie Curry. "Rape and the Pedagogical Rhetoric of Sexual Violence." In *Criticism and Dissent in the Middle Ages*, edited by Rita Copeland, 56–86. Cambridge: Cambridge University Press, 1996.

Wray, Shona Kelly. *Comunities and Crisis: Bologna during the Black Death*. Leiden: Brill, 2009.

———. "Instruments of Concord: Making Peace and Settling Disputes Through a Notary in the City and Contado of Late Medieval Bologna." *Journal of Social History* 42, no. 3 (2009): 733–60.

Zaccagnini, Guido. *Storia dello Studio di Bologna durante il Rinascimento*. Geneva: Leo S. Olschki, 1930.

———. *La vita dei maestri e degli scolari italiani nello Studio di Bologna nei secc. XIII e XIV* Geneva: Leo S. Olschki, 1926.

Zorzi, Andrea. *L'amministrazione della giustizia penale nella repubblica fiorentina: aspetti e problemi*. Florence: Leo S. Olschki, 1988.

———. "Conflits et pratiques infrajudiciaires dans les formations politiques italiennes du XIIIe au XVe siècle." In Garnot and Fry, *L'infrajudiciaire du Moyen Age à l'époque contemporaine*. 19–36.

———, ed. *Conflitti, paci e vendette nell'Italia comunale*. Florence: Firenze University Press, 2009.

———. "Consigliare alla vendetta, consigliare alla giustizia. Pratiche e culture politiche nell'Italia comunale." *Archivio storico italiano* 170, no. 2 (2012): 263–84.

———. "Contrôle social, ordre public et répression judiciaire à Florence à l'époque communale : éléments et problèmes." *Annales. Économies, Sociétés, Civilisations* 45, no. 5 (1990): 1169–88.

———. "La cultura della vendetta nel conflitto politico in età comunale." In *Le memorie e la storia: In onore di Arnold Esch*, edited by Roberto delle Donne and Andrea Zorzi, 135–70. Florence: Firenze University Press, 2002.

———. "Dérisions des corps et corps souffrants dans les executions." In Crouzet-Pavan and Verger, *La dérision au Moyen Age*. 225–240.

———. "L'egemonia del penale in Mario Sbriccoli." In *Penale giustizia potere: metodi, ricerche, storiografie: per ricordare Mario Sbriccoli*, edited by Luigi Lacchè, Carlotta Latini, Paolo Marchetti, and Massimo Meccarelli, 155–78. Macerata: EUM, 2007.

———. "'Fracta est civitas magna in tres partes.' Conflitto e costituzione nell'Italia comunale." *Scienza & Politica. Per una storia delle dottrine* 39 (2008): 61–87. Available at https://scienzaepolitica.unibo.it/article/view/2749/2146.

———. "'Ius erat in armis.' Faide e conflitti tra pratiche sociali e pratiche di governo." In *Origini dello stato: processi di formazione statale in Italia fra medioevo ed età moderna*, edited by Giorgio Chittolini, Anthony Molho, and Pierangelo Schiera, 609–29. Bologna: Il Mulino, 1994.

———. "Justice." In Gamberini and Lazzarini, *The Italian Renaissance State*. 490–514.

———. "Legitimation and Legal Sanction of Vendetta in Italian Cities from the Twelfth to the Fourteenth Centuries." In *The Culture of Violence in Renaissance Italy: Proceedings of the International Conference (Georgetown University at Villa Le Balze, 3–4 May, 2010)*, edited by Samuel Kline Cohn, Jr. and Fabrizio Ricciardelli, 27–54. Florence: Le Lettere, 2012.

———. "Pace e conflitti nelle città comunali italiane." In *Idees de pau a l'edat mitjana: reunió científica. XIII Curs d'Estiu Comtat d'Urgell celebrat a Balaguer els dies 2, 3 i 4 de juliol de 2008*, edited by Flocel Sabaté and Maite Pedrol, 265–302. Lleida: Pagès, 2010.

———. *Le signorie cittadine in Italia (secoli XIII–XV)*. Milan-Turin: Mondadori, 2010.

———. *La trasformazione di un quadro politico*. Florence: Firenze University Press, 2008.

Index

About the Contributors

Sarah Rubin Blanshei is professor of history emerita and dean of the college emerita, Agnes Scott College. She is the author of two monographs: *Perugia, 1260–1340: Conflict and Change in a Medieval Italian Urban Society* (1976), which was awarded the American Catholic Historical Association's Howard R. Marraro Prize, and *Politics and Justice in Late Medieval Bologna* (2010). She is the translator of Massimo Vallerani, *Medieval Public Justice* (2012); editor of *A Companion to Medieval and Renaisance Bologna* (2018); and has published twelve articles and essays on the society, economy, and legal culture of late medieval Bologna and Perugia.

Margaux Buyck teaches early modern history at the Université Toulouse 2 Jean Jaurès. She completed her doctorate in 2016 at the Université Paris Nanterre. Her dissertation, "Crimes de poison dans la Bologne médiévale et moderne (XIVe-XVIIe siècle)," was directed by Frank Collard (Université Paris Nanterre) and Alessandro Pastore (Università degli Studi di Verona) and will be published by the Presses Universitaires de Rennes (2018–19). She has presented papers about criminality and medicine at conferences in Paris, Lille, Poitiers, Verona, and Toulouse.

Christopher Carlsmith is professor of history at the University of Massachusetts, Lowell. He was a Fulbright scholar to Italy in 1996–97 and a Fellow at Villa I Tatti, the Harvard University Center for the Study of the Italian Renaissance, in 2009–10. He has published a monograph, *A Renaissance Education: Schooling in Bergamo and the Venetian Republic, 1500–1650* (2010), and several articles on student violence at the University of Bologna in the early modern era. He also edited volume 20 of the *Annali di storia delle università italiane* (2016). He is currently writing a chapter on education in Renaissance Rome, to be published in Brill's *A Companion to Early Modern Rome*.

Sara Cucini is an assistant editor at Weigl Publishers. She completed her doctorate *summa cum laude* at the Universitè Paul Valéry Montpellier 3 in 2014. Her dissertation, "Législation Statutaire et gouvernement pontifical en Italie centrale. Le cas de l'administration de la justice criminelle à Bologne, deuxième moitié du XVe siècle," was directed by Patrick Gilli (Universitè Paul Valéry) and Angela De Benedictis (Alma Mater Studiorum – Università di Bologna). She has presented papers at conferences in Prague, Montpellier, Perpignan, and Bologna and co-authored several archaelogical articles in various anthologies and an essay on criminal justice for *A Companion to Medieval and Renaissance Bologna* (2018).

Trevor Dean is professor of medieval history at the University of Roehampton. He has published three monographs: *Land and Power in Late Medieval Ferrara: The Rule of the Este 1350–1450* (1987); *Crime in Medieval Europe* (2001); and *Crime and Justice in Late-Medieval Italy* (2007). He also has co-authored *Clean Hands and Rough Justice: An Investigating Magistrate in Renaissance Italy* (1997) and edited or co-edited six other volumes and published more than twenty-five articles in journals and anthologies.

Carol Lansing is professor of history at the University of California, Santa Barbara and was Robert Lehman Visiting Professor at Villa I Tatti, the Harvard University Center for Italian Renaissance Studies, in 2008. She is the author of *The Florentine Magnates: Lineage and Faction in a Medieval Commune* (1991), *Power and Purity: Cathar Heresy in Medieval Italy* (1998), and *Passion and Order: Restraint of Grief in the Medieval Italian Communes* (2008). She also is co-editor of *A Companion to the Medieval World* (2007).

Gregory G. Roberts is foreign affairs officer, U.S. State Department, and was historian, U.S. Army Center of Military History, Fort McNair, from 2014 to 2016. He received his PhD from Yale University in 2013 with a dissertation, "Policing and Public Power in the Italian Communes," directed by Anders Winroth. He has presented papers at meetings of the Medieval Academy of America (2013), the International Congress on Medieval Studies, Kalamazoo, MI (2013), the International Congress of Medieval Canon Law (2012), the New College Conference on Medieval and Renaissance Studies, Sarasota, FL (2012), and the Centro studi sulla civiltà del tardo medioevo, San Minato (2011). The views expressed are the author's own and not necessarily those of the U.S. government.

Colin S. Rose is assistant professor of European and digital history at Brock University. He received his PhD from the University of Toronto in 2016. His dissertation, "Homicide in North Italy: Bologna, 1600–1700," was awarded the Michael Finlayson Gold Medal for Best Dissertation in the Department of History. He has published articles on the persistence of vendetta in Bologna and on petitions to the criminal court of Parma and presented papers at the New College Conference on Medieval and Renaissance Studies, Sarasota, FL (2014, 2016), the Renaissance Society of America (2014, 2015, 2016), and the American Historical Association (2018) among others. He also is co-editor of *Mapping Space, Sense, and Movement in Florence: Historical GIS and the Early Modern City* (2016).

Massimo Vallerani is professor of history at the Università di Torino. His scholarly focus is on medieval criminal justice, to which he has dedicated two monographs and numerous articles relative to the development of trials and the cultural formation of procedure: *Sistema giudiziario del comune di Perugia: Conflitti, reati e processi nella seconda metà del XIII secolo* (Perugia: Deputazione di storia patria per l'Umbria, 1991) and *Medieval Public Justice* (2012). Most recently he has initiated research in a series of articles on systems of inclusion and definition of critera for belonging to the city, based on the study of supplications, fiscal systems as a qualification of citizenship, and the legal opinions and interventions by jurists in the criminal courts.

Melissa Vise is Solmsen Fellow at the Institute for Research in the Humanities at the University of Wisconsin, Madison. During 2015–2017 she was visiting assistant professor of Italian studies at New York University. She completed her doctorate in 2015 at Northwestern University with a dissertation, "The Threat of the Tongue: Illicit Speech in Late Medieval Italy, 1250–1450," under the direction of Dyan Elliott. She has an article on the Bolognese inquisition forthcoming in *Speculum* (April 2018), and has presented papers at the Medieval Intellectual History Seminar, Newberry Library, Chicago (2010), the International Congress of Medieval Studies, Kalamazoo, MI (2011, 2017), the Notre Dame Medieval Studies Interdisciplinary Working Group (2014), the Cambridge Graduate Conference in Political Thought and Intellectual History, Cambridge, UK (2015), the Renaissance Society of America (2016), and the Ecole Français de Rome (2017).

www.ingramcontent.com/pod-product-compliance
Ingram Content Group UK Ltd.
Pitfield, Milton Keynes, MK11 3LW, UK
UKHW041126071026
15587UKWH00009B/255

9 781498 546331